A PRACTICAL GUIDE TO GREENER THEATRE

INTRODUCE SUSTAINABILITY INTO YOUR PRODUCTIONS

STAGE DOOR

Sean Gladwell/Shutterstock.

A PRACTICAL GUIDE TO GREENER THEATRE

INTRODUCE SUSTAINABILITY INTO YOUR PRODUCTIONS

BY ELLEN E. JONES
with Jessica Pribble
Additional Contributions by
Paul Brunner and Maja E. White

NEW YORK AND LONDON

First published 2014
by Focal Press
70 Blanchard Road, Suite 402, Burlington, MA 01803

and by Focal Press
2 Park Square, Milton Park, Abingdon, Oxon OX14 4RN

Focal Press is an imprint of the Taylor & Francis Group, an informa business

Library of Congress Cataloging in Publication Data
Jones, Ellen E., 1959-
A practical guide to greener theatre: introduce sustainability into your productions / by Ellen E. Jones; with Jessica Pribble; additional contributions by Paul Brunner and Maja E. White.
pages cm
ISBN 978-0-415-66324-3 (pbk.)
1. Theater–Production and direction–Environmental aspects. 2. Sustainability. 3. Theater management. I. Pribble, Jessica. II. Brunner, Paul, 1976- III. White, Maja E. IV. Title.
PN2053.J66 2013
792.02–dc23

ISBN: 978-0-415-66324-3 (pbk)
ISBN: 978-0-203-55599-6 (ebk)

Printed and bound in China by C&C Offset Printing Co., Ltd.

Protecting the environment should be a priority of every theatrical production, but it can be challenging to mount an environmentally friendly show with limited time, resources, and information. *A Practical Guide to Greener Theatre: Introduce Sustainability Into Your Productions* not only gives you the information you need to make greener decisions, but provides you with practical, workable solutions. You will learn how to assess and improve every production area—from costuming and painting, lighting and technical direction, to administrative offices and the rehearsal process. Checklists, examples of successful strategies, and step-by-step instructions will show you how to identify areas where manageable, sustainable changes can make your productions greener, and advice from working professionals, with experience greening their own productions, will leave you confident that your processes are environmentally sound. Even non-technical people who find themselves responsible for supervising productions will find green solutions that can be instituted with a staff of volunteers or students. Remember: Every step toward sustainability is a step forward.

- Discover small fixes that will make your theatre productions greener.
- Examine ways to introduce greener practices in the design, execution, and strike process.
- Explore how introducing sustainability into your theatre productions can save your company time and money.
- Learn how sustainability and safety intersect to help protect your workers and volunteers.

Ellen E. Jones holds USA Local 829 credentials as a lighting designer, scenic designer, and scenic artist. She has held numerous academic posts as well as working for theatrical vendors. Her 20-plus year career in the industry has included designing and painting scores of productions for various theatre companies and shops in the United States. She particularly enjoys working with students as emerging artists and joined the faculty of the Department of Theatre and Dance at Youngstown State University in the fall of 2013, where she serves as the scenic and lighting designer.

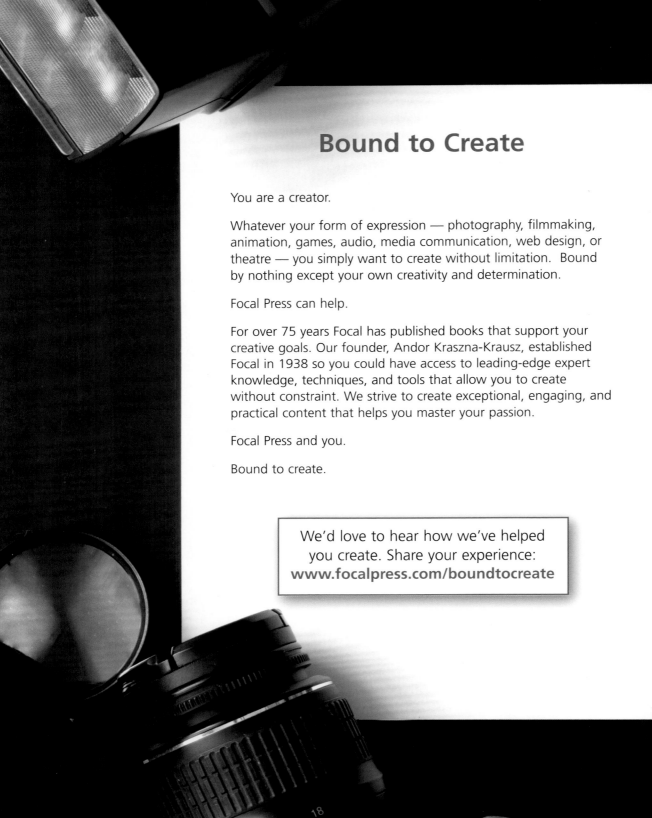

Contents

Foreword

The entertainment industry's best known amphibian once sang, *"It's not that easy being green."* Though I am reluctant to disagree with the famous frog's sentiment, *A Practical Guide to Greener Theatre: Introduce Sustainability Into Your Productions* will make it easier—if not easy—for every person working in theatre to be greener. By bringing together a small cast of knowledgeable and experienced contributors, Ellen E. Jones has produced a valuable resource for making theatre practices more environmentally responsible at every level of production.

Theatre people have largely resisted putting greener practices into place, whether from ignorance or concern about somehow lessening the aesthetic impact of our work. This book provides incontrovertible evidence that we can indeed make art while helping to preserve the environment. Many ideas offered in these pages can easily be put into practice without additional cost. Other proposals will serve the added benefit of protecting our health while preserving the environment. Some suggestions may require rethinking techniques we have used uncritically for generations. Still other plans will demand a major commitment to the ideal of environmental sustainability over the long term.

Change will come to our practices inevitably. It is in our best interest to determine how those changes will happen. Some of us may remember when we lauded the fire-safety benefits of papier-mâché props made from asbestos pulp. Others will recall when new regulations forced manufacturers to stop using mercury-based fungicides in scenic paint. While those just entering the profession may be horrified to think anyone ever thought of such practices as sound, we now acknowledge that our understanding of environmental issues is constantly evolving. Sustainability and environmental concerns are not passing fads; these issues will fundamentally affect how we do our work in the future. This book, the first of its kind, challenges us to think about how that future should look.

A Practical Guide to Greener Theatre provides suggestions we can and should embrace the moment we finish reading them, as well as complex solutions requiring serious planning and resources to accomplish. Ellen E. Jones' volume pushes the issue downstage center for our consideration. After all, as theatre production people, we pride ourselves on our ability to solve problems creatively, despite limitations of time, money, or labor. Can we ask any less of ourselves when considering the potential global consequences of our actions?

This book will motivate readers to take serious steps toward creating greener theatre today; it will promote conversations that will lead to better and bigger ideas for achieving sustainability within our industry; and it will remind each of us about the importance of the choices we make—big and small—along this journey. Using the tools, ideas, plans, and resources provided in these pages, we may soon find ourselves singing with new enthusiasm and conviction the final line with Kermit, *"I'm green, and it'll do fine; it's beautiful, and I think it's what I want to be."*

Andi Lyons
Lighting Designer/Professor of Theatre
University at Albany, SUNY

Preface

This book is not a lighting design, scene design, or costume design book. Nor does it pretend to be a stagecraft textbook, a safety manual, or an introduction to industrial hygiene or arts management. All of these topics are linked to greening production and where needed there is a rudimentary explanation of technical information or production practices. Professionals in those specific disciplines will undoubtedly find some of that information a review, but it is included to provide a basic foundation for those who have been assigned responsibilities outside their own area of expertise. Readers looking for more comprehensive information can use the included bibliography as a list of suggested further reading.

The greening process takes time. The competing goals of remaining financially sustainable, working within available resources, filling the audience seats, and adopting a greener production process must receive equal focus and respect. There is no one-size-fits-all solution because the circumstances of each company and staff are so different.

The ideas presented in this book are meant to be educational and motivate readers to consider if there is a greener choice before approaching any task "*the way we have always done it.*" Hopefully the included strategies, experience based tips and specific information will spark your imagination and offer guidance or inspiration that allows your company to move toward a more sustainable production model.

It can be difficult to focus on the issues of environmental stewardship when mounting every show is a challenge. For small producers who create theatre as an avocation or for the individual for whom production is a tiny sliver of her job responsibilities, the staff and financial reserves may be so small that finishing the show is the primary focus. This book recognizes those dilemmas and is based on the notion that all theatre companies and academic institutions can find manageable common ground between greener theatre and mounting a show with the production values they desire.

If you have thoughts and ideas that you want to share please contact me through my web page: http://ellenejones.com. All of us can make a difference as we move forward in this new world of environmentally conscious production and design.

This book is dedicated to all of my past, present, and future colleagues, students, friends, associates, and employers in the industry. Thanks for making my exciting and challenging professional life possible.

Special Thanks and Acknowledgments

Thank you to Hillary Stevens whose support (and willingness to edit material) was vital to finishing this project. Steve Shelley also deserves special thanks for all his advice and good humor throughout the writing of this book.

The contributors, Jessica Pribble, Paul Brunner, and Maja White, also have my sincere appreciation as well as Stacey Walker and Meagan White of Focal Press who have shepherded me through this process. To Michael Mehler, the technical reader, thank you for taking on this project and providing such insightful comments and suggestions. I also want to acknowledge those who allowed their work to be reproduced: Amanda Nelson, the artist who created *Kinkade*; Bob Smith of Image Photography; David Rodger of Broadway Press; and Terry Gips of Sustainability Associates.

For those who were willing to read copy and make comments—Claire Dana, Chris Fretts, Andi Lyons, Timothy Spencer, Wayne Pribble, and Rob Gerlach—thank you!

To the many individuals who agreed to formal interviews or provided face time on the 2013 USITT show floor (and these are in no particular order): Peter Borchetta, Joe Fahey, Kal Poole, Stephen Rueff, Monona Rossol, Bob Usdin, John Saari, Kim Bent, Madison O'Brien, Justin Miller, Ian Garrett, James McKernan, Michael Mahler, Rachel Keebler, Alan Kibbe, Seema Sueko, Sholeh Johnston, Alison Tickell, Garvin Eddy, Lea Asbell-Swanger, Damon Runnels, Lea Dutton, Erika Baily-Johnson, Rebecca Burgess, Jerry Dougherty, Renae Skoog, and Matthew Armenariz-Kerr: Thank you.

Thanks go as well to those who provided information in more casual conversations and emails, again in no particular order: David Rodger, Robert Zuckerman, James Bedell, Richard Cadena, Brenda K. Brown, William Beautyman, Kathleen Keenan, Kim Bent, Patrick Hudson, Lisa Lazar, Donald Fox, and everyone involved in the MN Sustainability in Theatre Task Force.

Many companies and organizations were generous in providing images of their products or their organizational logos and emblems for use in this book. All are credited within the text, but each deserves a special thank you for allowing that reuse.

If I have missed including anyone, the fault is in my memory, not in the value of your help. Thank you again to one and all.

– Ellen E. Jones

I would like to reiterate Ellen's thanks and add a very special thanks to my colleagues at Central Washington University both for supporting my work as a designer and giving generously of their time in support of this project. Especially to M. Catherine McMillen who understands the costume shop to be a laboratory where we experiment, challenge, and grow together with our students. And finally a thank you to my husband, Timothy, a true artist and my dearest friend.

– Jessica Pribble

Tips for Using the Book

Several icons are used throughout the book to draw attention to specific ideas.

Icon 1 The leafy footprint icon denotes a larger concept of philosophical idea. art4all/Shutterstock.

Icon 2 The handprint icon is associated with ideas to develop strategies or action plans. miha19750405/Shutterstock.

Icon 3 This fuzzy friend connotes experience based tips. Albert Ziganshin/Shutterstock.

Icon 4 The green idea pencil is linked with checklists. thaikrit/Shutterstock.

Additional Important Information

Writing a book occurs months before publication. Any websites indicated within the text were active at the time of writing. Because of the value of the material included on those sites I chose to include them knowing there was a possibility they might no longer be active at a future date.

Throughout the book you will see references to Material Safety Data Sheets (MSDS) followed by Safety Data Sheets (SDS). In 2003 the United Nations adopted the Globally Harmonized System of Classification and Labeling of Chemicals (GHS) as the criteria for the classification of health, physical, and environmental hazards. The GHS also specifies what information should be included on labels of hazardous chemicals as well as safety data sheets. In 2009 OSHA proposed aligning its Hazard Communication Standard to meet those requirements. In March 2012 Secretary of Labor Hilda L. Solis announced that this change would indeed take place. Manufacturers and distributors do not have to be in full compliance with the changes until December 2015. (http://www.osha.gov/as/opa/quicktakes/qtGHS03212012.html#10).

The transition is in progress at the time of writing. Some readers may have MSDS, some may have the newer SDS, and some may have a mix of the documents. Use whichever version of the documents you have and keep checking with manufacturers and distributors for the newest version.

Frequently Used Abbreviations

There are several organizational and agency abbreviations that are used through the text. The names are written out completely the first time they are used, but anyone reading chapters out of order may miss the full names.

- AHJ—Authority Having Jurisdiction: The governmental agency or law enforcement entity having authority in a given area.
- ANSI—American National Standards Institute: An organization that oversees the development and assessment of norms and guidelines across industries.
- EPA—Environmental Protection Agency: US governmental agency charged with protecting the public by protecting the environment.
- LEED—Leadership in Energy and Environmental Design: A voluntary program that provides certification for green buildings.
- NFPA—National Fire Protection Association: An international not-for-profit agency that originates many standards for public safety. Established in 1896.

- OSHA—Occupational Safety and Health Administration
- USA Local 829—United Scenic Artists: The labor union and a professional association for designers, artists, and craftspersons working in theatre, film, television, opera, ballet and other dance, exhibits, commercials, and industrials.
- USITT—United States Institute for Theatre Technology: US Association of professionals, educators, and students involved in design and technical production in the entertainment industry.

The Disclaimers

Nothing in the book should be taken as a substitute for advice from a licensed or otherwise certified, qualified, and/or trained professional with expertise in the area addressed. It is the responsibility of the reader to understand and obey any local, regional, state, federal statute or standard associated with the topic.

Any equipment or materials suggested or pictured in the book are products that we, the collective contributors, are familiar with or have seen in use by others. We may use that product exclusively or we may use a range of similar products. It is not meant to be an advertisement or endorsement for any manufacturer or vendor nor is the failure to mention any manufacturer, business, or product intended as an evaluation of quality of their products, expertise in the industry, or meant to have any negative connotation.

The Authors and Contributors

I was fortunate to meet and talk with **Jessica Pribble**, an experienced costumer who was also interested in greening her production and design processes. She is the primary author of the costume chapters and has brought a delightful and unique vision to the material overall.

Paul Brunner, Assistant Professor of Technical Direction at my graduate school alma mater, Indiana University, Bloomington, and I met at an LDI Green Day Session. Since then we have worked on several presentations and published a juried article together for *TD&T, Green at the University: Teaching Green by Being Green*. I wanted to add his expertise to the book and he is a major contributor to the scene shop chapter, particularly the segments on commonly used materials and best construction techniques.

Maja White, Assistant Professor at University of Richmond, and I became acquainted through various professional organizations including USITT and ATHE. When I learned she had completed a research project lighting the same production with both conventional and LED fixtures that was not just about energy savings, but also the impact for performers and the audience in response to the art of the lighting design, I wanted to include her story about the project.

Biographies

Ellen E. Jones holds USA Local 829 credentials as a lighting designer, scenic designer, and scenic artist and her professional credits include work in Chicago, the Midwest, and the eastern United States. She has served USITT as both a Lighting Vice-Commissioner and Commissioner and as Co-Chair of the Caucus on Human Issues.

Ms. Jones' professional career has been intertwined with academic posts around the country. She has focused on introducing safety and sustainability in theatre design and production to interested schools and theatre companies and has presented on the topic at LDI, USITT, ATHE, and the inaugural 2012 *Sustainability in Theatre Conference* in Minneapolis. As of fall semester 2013 she has been a faculty member in the Department of Theatre and Dance at Youngstown State University in Youngstown, OH.

Jessica Pribble is a professional costume designer and educator currently based in Washington State. She received her MFA in Theatre from Purdue University. Before and during graduate school, Jessica was a freelance designer for the Chicago area.

She has worked for several regional Shakespeare Festivals as a designer (Fairbanks Shakespeare Festival, Kentucky Shakespeare Festival), Craft Artisan (Idaho Shakespeare Festival), and First Hand (Lake Tahoe Shakespeare Festival). She currently teaches costume design and technology at Central Washington University. Her professional work also includes designing for Cirque Shanghai's production of *Cirque Shanghai: Bai Xi* at Chicago's Navy Pier, and KAT Company's production of *The Wizard of Oz* for which she won a New Hampshire Theatre Award for Best Costume Design.

Paul Brunner is faculty Technical Director and Head of the Theatre Technology program for the Indiana University Department of Theatre and Drama. He teaches courses in technical management, structural design for the stage, electronics for theatre, mechanical design for scenery, and theatrical drafting. He has presented numerous workshops on greener theatre at two high school theatre festivals, USITT, SETC, and LDI.

He has worked professionally as a technical director or designing mechanical effects for Notre Dame Shakespeare Festival, Southern Ohio Light Opera, and Indiana University's Opera and Ballet Theater.

An active member of USITT, he currently serves on the Board of Directors and is a Commissioner for the Technical Production Commission. Regionally, he is a Director at Large on the board of the USITT-Midwest Regional Section and serves as editor of *Design and Production Review* (DPR), the Midwest Regional newsletter. He is also a member of the Broadway Green Alliance and is co-chair of their Education Committee.

Maja E. White (Lighting Designer) has designed lighting for Opera, Theatre, and Dance. Recently, her work has allowed her to light works choreographed by Francesca Harper, Sean Curran, Dana Tai Soon Burgess, Jessica Lang, and Kanji Segawa, among others. Maja is a member of the United Scenic Artists 829 and IALD. She is an Assistant Professor at the University of Richmond and her current research is on the impact and effects on environmentally friendly lighting on live performance.

Book Front and Back Cover Artwork Credits

Painting on Rustic Boards: kenny1/Shutterstock
Sewing Fabric: Africa Studio/Shutterstock
The Drape: pan_kung/Shutterstock
Tape Measure: Vladimir Badaev/Shutterstock
Recycle symbol: barbaliss/Shutterstock

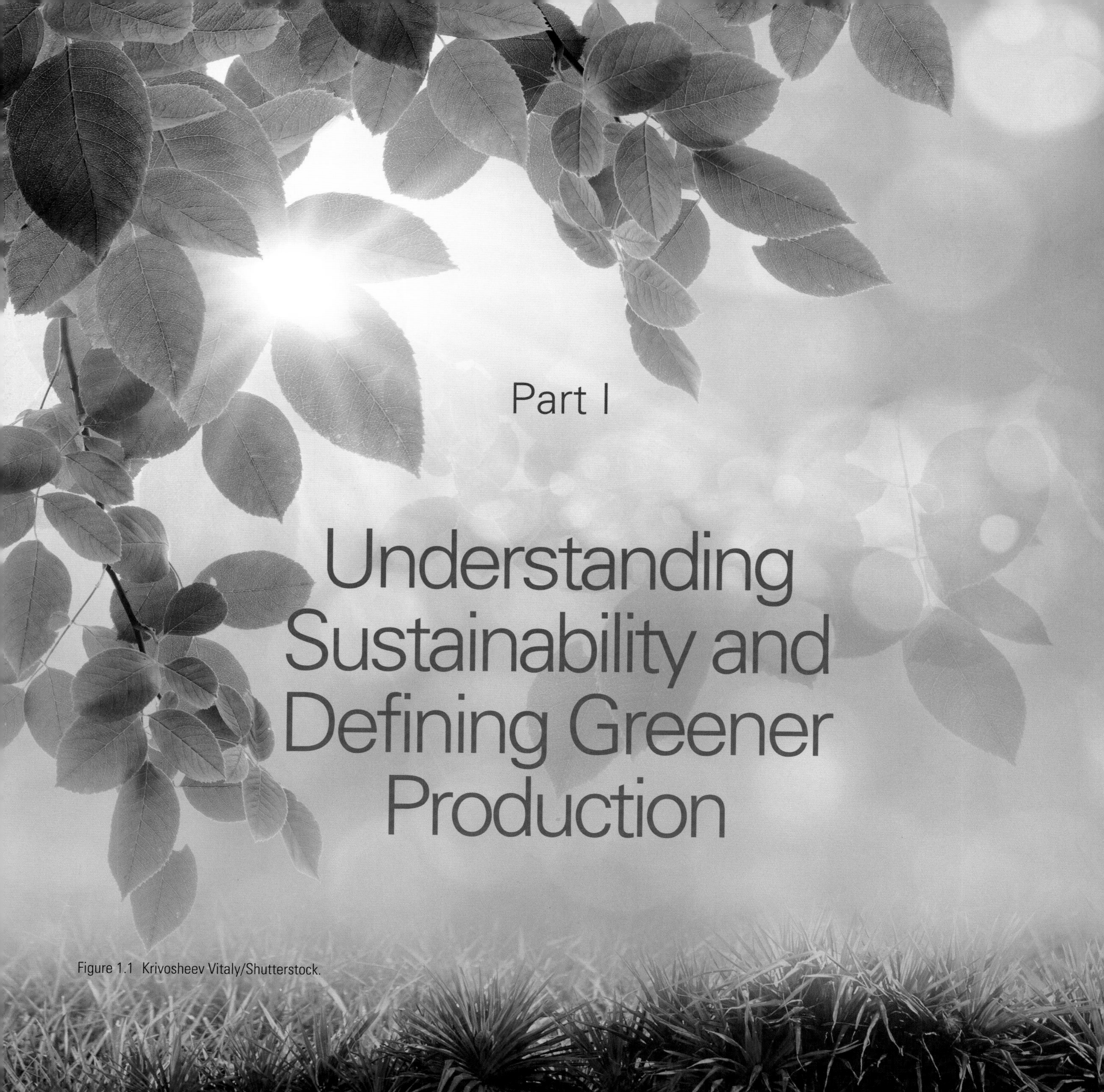

Part I

Understanding Sustainability and Defining Greener Production

Figure 1.1 Krivosheev Vitaly/Shutterstock.

Time to Make a Change

What happens to the scenery, props, and costumes after the run of the show? What about scrap pieces of the virgin construction materials that were used in the creation of visual elements? Theatre productions can generate an enormous amount of waste both during the construction process and at the end of the run.

Early in my career I worked as a freelance scenic artist and designer for urban special events companies as well as theatre companies. While some elements could be stored and reused, every swanky birthday party, wedding, or product launch generated mountains of garbage ranging from handcrafted personalized decorative elements to live plants that died within hours because they were painted the party theme colors with an airless sprayer. When scenic pieces from these live industrial productions were struck at the end of the evening, the dumpsters were filled to overflowing with material that was not salvaged.

The artisans who created the props and scenery would sadly comment, "*There are visual artists who collect trash and create art. We buy art supplies and create garbage*."

We are only beginning to understand the real impact of producing waste. It is time to embrace a change.

Chapter 1

Setting the Stage for Greener Production

I grew up in upper east Tennessee where for many people, including some of my older relatives, *Reduce, Reuse, and Recycle* was a way of life because there was no other choice. My grandmother had no idea she was ahead of the cultural curve growing her own vegetables or recycling leftover fabric from her sewing job into garments. Nor did my great-uncle consider making his own wine a way to be closer to the earth. (To be honest, his stories about the life he and his ten brothers led as young men suggested that making adult beverages at home was simply a long-standing family tradition.)

The self-proclaimed local sophisticates who had managed to go to college or get jobs somewhere other than the farm, the railroad, a factory, or the military viewed those practices as backward country ways or only for the very poor. At this time a focus on ecology for its own sake was viewed as the domain of those disconnected from day-to-day reality. What a difference a few decades make?

Before global warming and greenwashing entered the lexicon, I was interested in environmental issues. By the time I left college, I was the one driving everyone else crazy turning the lights off in empty rooms and collecting everything possible for recycling. I even had a worm composting bin in a fourth floor walk-up apartment in Chicago.

In spite of these choices in my personal life, I managed to achieve a complete disconnect from the same concepts in my work environment. My career includes time as a freelance lighting and scenic designer and scenic artist for professional companies, commercial shops, special event companies, and live industrial producers. I also design for a number of smaller theatre companies that are strongly linked to a specific cultural or geographical community. Most have tremendous artistic heart but few resources. I have spent many years mentoring students in academic settings. I also worked for theatrical vendors who were generous enough to allow me to spend as much time educating customers as selling them products.

I and my colleagues might comment on the amount of garbage produced by a show or event, but we never tried to do much about it. It was only when I became more aware of health and safety in the workplace that I started to think about the environmental impact of my work. To me the intersection of safety and sustainability became obvious and compelling.

When I joined the theatre faculty at Bemidji State University in northern Minnesota, I was able to experiment with production and facility maintenance strategies to green the technical theatre and design process. Director of Theatre, Dr. Patrick Carriere, and Interim Dean of the College of Arts and Sciences, Dr. Elizabeth Dunn, supported those efforts and encouraged the development of a sustainability initiative.

The theatre students and employees were engaged and independently developed ideas for the project. Their enthusiasm for greener theatre production was invigorating and inspiring. Sadly, Minnesota state budget issues led to the total elimination of the Theatre Department there, but what I learned has moved forward with me.

An Introduction to Sustainability

Numerous books about sustainability have been published, but only *Readings in Performance and Ecology*, edited by Wendy Arons and Theresa J. May focuses specifically on theatre. Trade publications have documented green solutions adopted by some theatre companies, but many of the case studies focus as much, or more, on construction based venue changes than operational changes.

At the more manageable, but possibly less effective, end of the solution spectrum are the books of lists—*101 Things to Do to be Green.* These assume a universality of circumstances and most are specific to consumer products and domestic settings rather than entertainment venues. While some of these techniques are applicable to theatre, following a list of instructions does not provide a thoughtful strategy to greening your theatre. A broader foundation is required to make the long-term commitment that a sustainability initiative requires.

Earth Day celebrations and blue recycling bins have been with us for nearly four decades, yet our environmental impact seems to have grown more significant over time instead of decreasing. Are those committed to ecological concerns just a small but vocal slice of the population?

A February 2013 Reuters news article reported that a survey by the international group Globe Scan found that political and financial concerns overshadowed environmental concerns for the polled population. The survey was conducted in July–September 2012 and participants were asked to rate the seriousness of six concerns: air pollution, water pollution, species loss, automobile emissions, fresh water shortages, and climate change. 58% rated the potential lack of fresh water as a significant concern while only around 50% found global warming and the loss of biodiversity a significant worry. The survey contacted almost 23,000 citizens in 22 countries (Reuters: Nina Chestney London | Thu Feb 28, 2013).

Has the general public really lost interest in environmental stewardship? Or is it simply easy to ignore the ramifications of environmental degradation when asked broad, general questions by someone you don't know? Perhaps actions can speak louder than statistics compiled from surveys.

Many theatres and related organizations have begun the conversation about how to make productions, essentially short-term installations, greener to reduce environmental impact. Blogs, feature stories in trade publications, and web pages on green theatre are popping up with regularity. Some regional theatre organizations and public interest groups are committed to disseminating information and creating consortiums to discuss how to reduce the environmental impact of theatre production. This movement includes artists creating theatre at the local level as well as national and international organizations and corporations. It is the result of concern, not regulatory legislation. This evidence of widespread efforts to preserve rather than squander natural resources is exciting and suggests it is time for all of us to explore ways to support this perspective. Engaging your colleagues and patrons in these conversations is one way to reinforce the connection between individual actions and global problems.

In some circles disregarding environmental impact has become a social taboo. Even multinational corporations with poor environmental track records hire publicists to mitigate a potential negative image. The public concerned about adopting a greener lifestyle may choose to vote with their wallets. Consider the rash of advertisements after news coverage of business practices or accidents that impacted the ecosystem.

Zern Liew/Shutterstock

Figure 1.2 We at Fill-in-the-Blank Industries, known as FIB in the trade, are really sorry we dumped something bad in the ocean or leveled those mountains or poured awful things into the groundwater and air. Just turn your head away from those pictures while we distract you with our new greenwashed products. Look! There is less packaging to throw away, because the container is now only twice as big as the product. And we have placed an artistic representation of a green tree on the plastic bottle. See, we are all really swell folks. FIB is just misunderstood as an environmental leader.

Not-for-profits and huge corporations may seem to have little in common. However, explanations for lapses in environmental stewardship, whether by theatres or businesses, seem to fall into the same categories:

- It is too expensive to change the way we do business. In this economy our customers value low prices more than environmental concerns.
- It takes too much time or is too much trouble to use green manufacturing and business practices.
- We cannot produce the same quality products if green practices are instituted or environmental protection acts are enforced.
- Sustainability involves so many details involved in the unique production and sales process of our industry; we cannot determine what steps to take to really make a difference.

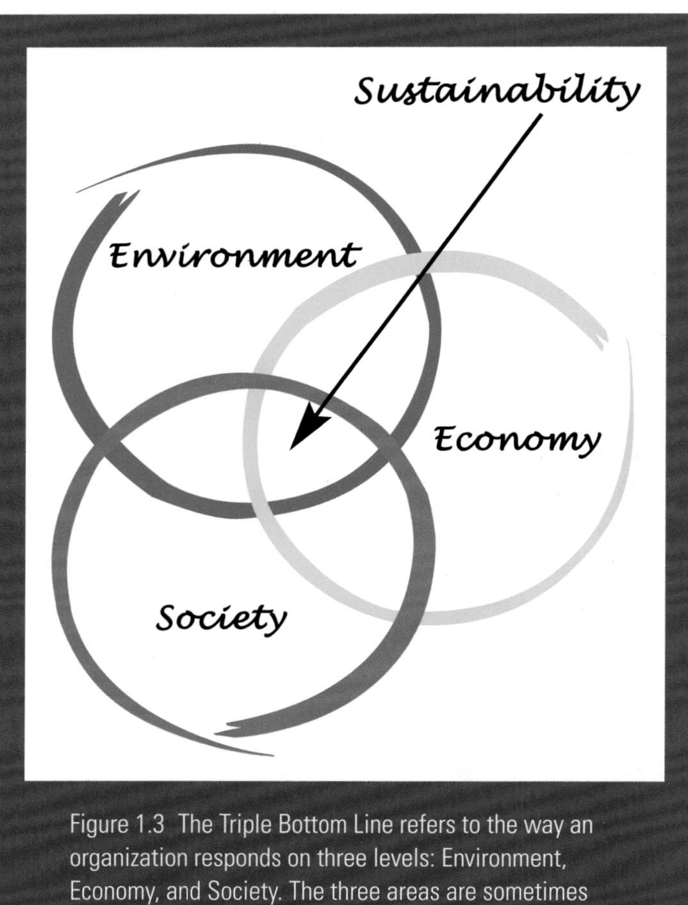

Figure 1.3 The Triple Bottom Line refers to the way an organization responds on three levels: Environment, Economy, and Society. The three areas are sometimes referred to as People, Profit, and Planet. The philosophical foundation of assessing the three areas is that sustainability of the environment, the company, and the people the organization impacts only happens when the interests of all three are considered and intersect. Arka38/Shutterstock.

The Triple Bottom Line

For some time, there has been a movement in business to assess successful operation on more than profit creation. This analysis is called the Triple Bottom Line. Origin of the term in 1994 is attributed to John Elkington, author of *Cannibals with Forks: The Triple Bottom Line of 21st Century Business* and founder of British consulting group, Sustainability. While financial success is important, this philosophy also demands that a corporation's impact on the earth's ecosystem and people be examined as well to determine success.

One goal of this book is to outline Triple Bottom Line concerns for those engaged in theatre production. Whether your company is a small community theatre with a volunteer staff or a large program associated with a state university, you can maintain the quality and artistry of your productions and reduce the environmental impact of your organization by using your available resources with sustainability in mind. Additional strategies may require a financial investment and you must determine if the ROI, or return on investment justifies the expense. More sustainable theatre production is not only good for the environment; it can save labor, material, and resource expenses over time when integrated into your production plan.

Figure 1.4 Did most of the materials from your last show end up in a place like this? Every company can make a difference by embracing environmental concerns and greening production practices. Huguette Roe/Shutterstock.

For most companies, the finished visual elements for a specific production have a predetermined lifespan in a specific configuration, the length of the run. Tours, repertory companies that repeat productions, rental companies or shows with an open-ended run are the exceptions where an entire set or complete complement of costumes and props may be placed in storage for reuse. Even placing individual items into storage for remounts or rentals, or placing them in stock for piecemeal use in the future, helps mitigate the waste. The visual elements of a show might be totally broken apart and pieces recycled if possible or the entire set or show's costumes loaned or given to another company. However, in many cases, resources are used for the short term and quickly become waste products. It increases overall operating costs when resources cannot be reclaimed for future projects. It impacts the ecosystem when reusable materials end up in a landfill.

The enormous scope of activities involved in producing theatre can make it overwhelming to decide on an approach to the problem. Even the most ardent convert to sustainability can be paralyzed by the range of endeavors that must be evaluated and the number of potential changes.

Where do you start? How can you be sure you are investing your time and energy in a way that will offer tangible results? Note that the title of this book is *A Practical Guide to Greener Theatre*. The qualifier underscores the fact that there is probably no way to create a totally green production process that meets all of the other parameters required in every given situation. However, developing a green initiative that outlines the best possible sustainable practices for a specific company is possible.

What is an Environmental Sustainability Initiative?

An environmental sustainability initiative begins with a vision or goal, whether it is for a corporation or a theatre company. You don't have to adopt or even agree with the vision or objective for another organization's environmental sustainability

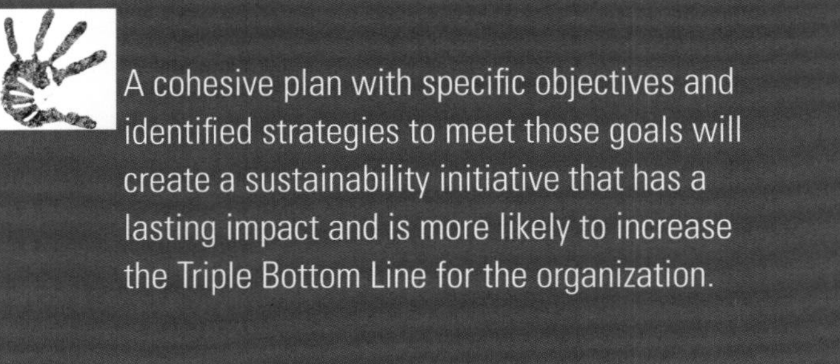

initiative. Your organizational vision will be determined by the scope of your particular operations and may focus on a narrow band of concerns or it may encompass a range of production areas. For example, Texas A&M Technical Director Justin Miller's vision was very specific; to have a zero landfill scene shop. My vision at Bemidji State University was more general. I wanted to reduce the overall carbon footprint of production operations and use greener practices to improve worker and student health and safety.

A cohesive plan with specific objectives and identified strategies to meet those goals will create a sustainability initiative that has a lasting impact and is more likely to increase the Triple Bottom Line for the organization.

Whether your vision is narrowly focused or a broad ranging goal, specific objectives must be articulated to achieve this vision. In turn, these objectives will determine what steps or strategies should be taken as part of the plan. However, until you have an accurate picture of the company's environmental impact, it is difficult to determine whether your overall vision is sound and what strategies will have the greatest impact on greening production.

Why do a Baseline Audit?

The audit process described in the next chapter is required to determine what changes or strategies enable achieving the goals of your green vision. Until you determine the baseline environmental impact of the numerous aspects of the current operation, it is impossible to know where the greatest opportunities for improvement exist. This baseline audit may

The Goal: A Zero Landfill Scene Shop

Justin Miller, Instructional Assistant Professor and Technical Director with the Texas A&M Department of Performance Studies, started his professional career with the notion of sustainability in mind. His initial goal was to create a Zero Landfill Scene Shop by reducing, reusing, and recycling.

Miller says:

> *"Some things have been easier because our local lumber recycler will take items with glue, nails or staples. They won't take painted wood and we are not FR treating everything so that is not an issue. However, there are some things I can't find a way to recycle, like gaffers tape and nitrile gloves. Overall we have been fairly successful at reducing solid waste that goes to the landfill."*

Miller began working on sustainable scenic design while still in graduate school. He has an article in the anthology *Readings in Performance and Ecology* that describes his scenic design for *Love's Labour's Lost* at Michigan State University. Among his experiments were balustrade spindles made out of paper. When asked about safety, Miller says "*Every fourth spindle was wood—someone vaulted over the railing.*" He adds, "*The trade-off was the considerable number of shop hours used in making of the spindles from glue and strips around armature versus lathing them of wood.*" This opportunity to green a design prepared him to introduce the idea at his new job in Texas. He credits the department with embracing his ideas about greening theatre.

Miller's first actions were low cost/no cost choices. Since the university has a small nontraditional venue, one of the first places he suggested change was in the initial designs. Instead of using a lot of vertical elements, designs have evolved toward more use of levels, furniture, and definition of space through lighting design.

Other changes included introducing a "Triscuit" system for platforms that eliminates the need for bolts and only uses traditional legs made of 2x4. (See Chapter 7 for more details on how to build these.) Metal recycling is another element of his initiative and he is recycling more than tubular steel. The shop never reuses drywall screws so those are recycled once or twice a year in pound increments.

He also encourages designing around stock scenery when possible. He describes that experience:

> *"It can be a bigger design challenge and it has had some success. We end up using things over and over, but add elements and detail to create a new and unique look. Given the size of the space and layout of audience, it becomes about designing only what we need."*

Miller has connected with the Texas A&M Sustainability Office. One coup was a grant for creating a rainwater collection system to wash brushes. His idea is to have the collection site on the roof and bring the water into the shop with faucets for filling mop buckets and washing paintbrushes. He admits introducing sustainability has included a lot of reading about what other people have done as well as a lot of trial and error. Justin Miller's success is an example of the green journey requiring that first step.

validate your vision or goal but indicate that different objectives are needed to achieve the vision.

For example, at Bemidji State University, I assumed that reducing carbon footprint for electricity use was linked to replacing older, high wattage stage fixtures. This certainly was a component that needed attention. However, when I did a baseline assessment of all the lighting elements in the theatre area, I realized a great deal more energy was consumed by the house and lobby lights than the stage lights. Over 100 architectural fixtures and task lights used 120 watt incandescent lamps.

They were all turned on together and burned many more hours than the stage lighting rig except during tech weeks.

The data I collected during the baseline audit quickly brought the bigger issue into sharp perspective. I prioritized replacing these lamps before the stage lighting units. The baseline data collected also provided necessary research for a grant application to fund this change.

Your sustainability initiative should include a timeline for completing the baseline audit and establishing future goals and strategies. It should also include projected completion dates for each strategy. In this particular case, the end date of my timeline was established by the granting entity's timetable for completion of the project. Because I wanted to be certain I was choosing the correct dimmable LED direct replacement lamps, completion of two beta tests were included in my timeline. The first test replaced a limited number of lamps in the house lights. I ran those for several weeks. After this test was successful, my next strategy was to replace more of the house lights and a portion of the lobby lights for another test period. After both successful tests, I was able to meet my objective of changing over all of the incandescent lamps to LED replacements by the spring semester. The information from the baseline audit supported my original vision. It also showed me that I needed to use different tactics than those I had originally planned to effectively achieve my goal.

The executives at FIB have decided to adopt a more environmentally friendly stance, but have decided a baseline audit is a waste of time. The company did not do any initial audits to determine its environmental impact. FIB Industries' goal for its sustainability initiative is to make Fill-in-the-Blank Industries known as a green company.

A baseline study would have measured the impact of the FIB manufacturing plant's practice of dumping contaminated water directly into the river. It might have shown that water quality and the surrounding ecosystem were compromised by this practice. It would also reveal that FIB's strategy of converting to the use of 100% post-consumer waste recycled paper products in all corporate printers does not address that environmental impact. The corporation has elected to adopt a greener practice in the offices, but sidestepped the tougher production issue. Whether FIB skipped baseline audits intentionally to avoid substantially changing current operational practices or simply made a bad choice is immaterial. The objectives embraced are superficial and do not address the real points of environmental impact. In fact, they can't until the overall vision of sustainability is based on actual operating practices. Don't make the same mistake that FIB did.

Taking any individual steps that make the organization greener is an improvement. Having a plan is even better because it inculcates a green culture and provides a destination for the journey. The use of audits to identify the biggest opportunities to make a difference is stressed throughout the book.

Defining Sustainability

An action plan is vital, but adopting an analytical mindset is equally important. The first step is agreeing on a vision of sustainability for the organization. Increased mainstream media coverage about sustainable practices in all fields has been triggered by a number of events ranging from the 1997 Kyoto Protocol developed at the United Nations' Framework Convention on Climate Change, to the establishment of the Green Building Council in 1998, to the release of Al Gore's *An Inconvenient Truth* in 2006, and the highly politicized, international debate about the scientific validity of global warming.

Concerns about the impact of development on the environment are not new. In the early 1980s the United Nations established a committee to examine the problem. Formally known as World Commission on Environment and Development, the group became the Brundtland Commission. Its first report suggested a new perspective including a focus on the human element as part of the equation when assessing the benefits of development. This idea veered from the status quo. The core concepts from the Brundtland Commission report in 1987 still influence our current understanding of "sustainable development,"a phrase

Historical Roots of Sustainability

In every deliberation, we must consider the impact of our decision on the next seven generations.

Great Law of the Hau de no sau nee (Iroquois Nation)

The frog does not drink up the pond in which it lives.

Native American proverb

The sun also rises, and the sun goes down, and hastens to the place where it arose. The wind goes toward the south and turns about to the north, it whirls about continuously and the wind returns again according to its circuits. All the rivers run into the sea, yet the sea is not full. Unto the place where the rivers come, they return again. The thing that has been; it is what shall be; And that which is done is that which shall be done.

Ecclesiastes 1:5–9

The world is beautiful and verdant, and verily Allah has made you His stewards in it, and He sees how you acquit yourselves.

Prophet Muhammad, *Hadith*

According to Jewish teachings by those who wrote the Talmud, God showed Adam the Garden of Eden and then warned: Take heed not to corrupt and destroy My world. For if you corrupt it, there will be no one to set it right after you.

Ecclesiastes Rabba 7.13

As a bee gathering nectar does not harm or disturb the color and fragrance of the flower; so do the wise move through the world.

Lord Buddha, *Dhammapada: Flowers, verse 49*

Do not disturb the sky and do not pollute the atmosphere.

Hindu *Yajur Veda, 5:43*

Definitions of Sustainability

To achieve sustainability, a system must be ecologically sound, economically viable, socially just, and humane (embodying our highest values—how we treat animals, people and the Earth).

Alliance for Sustainability, *Manna*, 1984 and www.afors.org

Sustainable development meets the needs of the present without compromising the ability of future generations to meet their needs.

U.N. World Commission on Environment & Development, *Our Common Future*, 1987

Triple Bottom Line, focusing on "economic prosperity, environmental quality and social justice."

John Elkington, *Cannibals with Forks: The Triple Bottom line of 21st Century Business*, 1998

[Also referred to as: economic, social, and environmental; the 3 Ps (People, Planet, and Profits) or 3 Es (Equity, Ecology, and Economy).]

A thing is right when it tends to preserve the integrity, stability and beauty of the biotic community. It is wrong if it tends otherwise.

Aldo Leopold, *Sand County Almanac*, 1949

A sustainable agriculture is one that depletes neither the people nor the land.

Wendell Berry, 1984

Natural Step Framework: In a sustainable society, nature won't be subject to systematically increasing:

1. concentrations of substances extracted from the earth's crust;
2. concentrations of substances produced by society;
3. degradation by physical means; and,
4. people are not subject to conditions that systematically undermine their capacity to meet their needs.

The Natural Step, www.naturalstep.org

coined by the group. In more blunt language it means not allowing progress to deplete the natural resources, contaminate the air and water, and destroy the way of life of the current population in a given area when it is developed. The committee's report called for economic, technological, and industrial development to meet the needs of the present without compromising the ability to meet the needs of the future.

Terry Gips, founder of Sustainability Associates, is a well-known environmentalist based in Minneapolis, Minnesota. He has spent his entire career educating a range of groups about sustainable practices. He offers workshops and tip sheets for businesses, government entities, and not-for-profit associations. Much of his sustainability work is based on the Natural Step Framework (NSF), a sustainability model that originated in Sweden. His look at the culturally diverse ways the core of sustainable living has been described may be helpful as you start to think about your mission statement and strategic plan (page 11).

A less colorful description is found in the Merriam-Webster Dictionary. The first definition of sustainability—whether related to ecology, agriculture, or funding—is simply *capable of being sustained*. However circular that definition seems, almost everyone has seen evidence of the validity. When a theatre is undercapitalized or understaffed it cannot continue to mount quality shows unless more resources are found. Some might argue that capital is not an easily renewable resource, but undeniably its availability impacts staffing.

Greening theatre production focuses on Merriam-Webster's second definition of sustainability: a: "*of, relating to, or being a method of harvesting or using a resource so that the resource is not depleted or permanently damaged*" and b: "*of or relating to a lifestyle involving the use of sustainable methods.*"

Although famed professor Robert Gutman was speaking about architecture when he made the often quoted comment: "*Every profession bears the responsibility to understand the circumstances that enable its existence*," the idea should speak to theatre artisans as well.

Greener theatre production is the action of making choices that meet artistic and financial goals, while having the least environmental impact by eliminating waste, limiting the use of natural resources and man-made artificial products, and avoiding the introduction of hazardous materials and chemicals into the workplace or the environment.

Figure 1.5 The most familiar mantra of sustainability is probably Reduce, Reuse, and Recycle. These practices can diminish environmental impact while supporting artistic and financial goals. Alex Millos/Shutterstock.

The Three Rs: Reduce, Reuse, and Recycle

While the three Rs should be a foundation of your sustainability plan, be sensitive to the possible reservations of colleagues and collaborators. Anyone who has seen a show mounted using the cheapest or most easily found materials and solutions instead of selections designed and crafted to serve the production concept can understand this concern. In truth these practices can be more about expediency or cost than sustainability. When creativity and collaboration are given the same consideration as green practices there is no compromise to production values. Emphasizing the relationship of reducing new construction, reusing stock, and resourcing existing items through resale and consignment with a thoughtful design process that focuses on the core of the production concept may help mitigate concerns.

People are one third of the Triple Bottom Line. Development of a green initiative requires everyone to actively embrace the commitment to produce sustainable theatre and to adopt a mindset that balances green choices, safe and healthy work practices, and artistic expression. While a single individual can make some sustainable choices, it is imperative for the entire group to support the philosophy of creating greener theatre.

The essence of performance is the company's communication with the audience. Focusing design and production to support this goal instead of creating spectacle for the sake of spectacle is actually at the core of producing compelling and thoughtful theatre. Think back to the productions that moved you or made you say, "*This is why I wanted to be in theatre; to tell powerful stories and connect with the audience.*" Was it the flash and complexity of the visual elements that moved you or the connection of the visual elements to the story being told?

Throughout the book there are tips on how to make the most out of what the company already owns, and how to dispose of items in a way that protects the environment. New construction or purchases are inevitable, unless one of the production concepts for a show revolves around eliminating the use of any new resources. Reduce, Reuse, and Recycle when you can. When that is not possible use the guidelines suggested for purchasing and using new resources with as little environmental impact as possible.

There are important caveats to the recycle or reduce by reusing model. Any material that is used for weight-bearing scenery, structural elements, or anything hanging overhead should be of uncompromised quality and strength. You should also know the composition of any material you expose performers, crew, and audience to in the production process. If you don't have this information, you cannot be sure of the potential risk to the health and safety of performers, crew, and/or audience in reuse. Using salvaged, loaned, or looted (if you take cool architectural elements from an abandoned building without permission, you are technically a looter) materials without any idea of condition, quality, strength, or origin is not necessarily acceptable recycling or reuse. If you are not sure of the safety factor, err on the side of caution and protect your company from potential hazards and risks.

Artistic and human resource concerns should be considered as well. Turning an inappropriate object into a marginal version of what is needed is probably not responsible resource management. While it is a terrific accomplishment to turn a sow's ear into a silk purse, think about whether you are spending more natural resources and labor time in the conversion than you would by simply creating the silk purse. Will the revitalized sow's ear meet the visual goals of the silk purse and will the performer feel comfortable using it? Balance integration of the final creation into the production's visual picture with the desire for the greener option. If the prop, costume, or scenery has to be replaced after a few rehearsals because it really does not fit the show, it does not support the goal of moving toward a more sustainable production model.

Garnering Support for a Green Initiative

In spite of the generally accepted standard that theatre is a collaborative art form, participants sometimes think of their artistic contributions as unique creative work that will be diminished by any compromise, even making concessions to meet sustainable goals.

> Implementing a sustainability initiative requires development of an organized approach from the moment plays are selected for the season until the end of strike after the last performance. Achieving your goals will be a long-term commitment. One way to keep all company members invested in the project is commitment to offer respect for every person involved in the process and listen to anyone's concerns about the impact on his or her contributions.

Promote the Plan

Establishing a Green Team

Determine what you can control and which colleagues are likely to be invested in this idea of greener theatre. Forming a Green Team is an easy first step in promoting your sustainability initiative. Green Teams are formed by stakeholders with an interest in sustainable practices and environmental stewardship. Organizations ranging from corporations to cities to grade schools to governmental agencies have formed Green Teams. Interest in green practices is the usual criteria for membership and participants may perform any function within the organization or be at any level in the overall hierarchy of the group. For any Green Team to be effective time must be carved out from the members' normal responsibilities to allow the group to meet and implement any agendas.

Some Green Teams have specific, articulated responsibilities that involve educational programming, formal evaluations, and periodic reporting. Other groups are less formal and function as social networks that pragmatically encourage the adoption of green practices within the organization. The goals and the organizational culture of your company should help determine the level of structure and responsibilities for the Green Team.

The specific mission statement and goals of the Green Team can be created and presented to the potential membership or the Green Team can tackle these two projects once it is formed. A well-defined mission statement that establishes the Green Team's ability to change operational procedures, experiment with new strategies, or implement new sustainability campaigns, will allow the group to have a greater impact on the greening process. Creation of a Green Team will require determining its overall role in company administration and operations. Unless the Green Team is given carte blanche, a member of management or administration must be the designated contact to approve, implement, and/or finance any plans or projects formulated by the group. One typical function of a Green Team is to help publicize sustainability efforts outside the organization as well as within the company.

You can form a regional committee as well. This larger Green Team can also be a formal task force or a more casual association: If you live in an area with a number of theatres and artists, invite others to join the group and remember to include everyone in that invitation. In Minneapolis, a group of artists from several theatre companies came together to form an association: the Sustainability in Theatre Task Force. Any interested individual is invited to participate and every aspect of theatre from front of house operations to onstage to backstage is represented.

In May 2012 the group joined with the Minnesota Theatre Alliance and the Center for Sustainable Practice in the Arts to create a hybrid conference exploring Sustainability in Theatre. By introducing virtual participation as well as onsite attendance, interested parties from across the globe were able to join the conversation. Imagine the possibilities in your region.

Share any plans to initiate a greener theatre program with your audience, sponsors, and local community. Supporters interested in sustainability may come forward to offer monetary support or advice. Environmentalists may express a willingness to serve on your Board of Directors or Green Team. Theatres have successfully used the model of inviting individuals with specific expertise to serve on the Board of Directors to meet many goals. The publicity tells your audience that the company's concern about becoming good global citizens has been translated into action and may bring in invested parties that would not have normally connected with an arts organization.

Corporations are experts at this sort of self-promotion and it can work equally well for a not-for-profit organization. Let's take another look at our friends at FIB Industries. The company decided to pursue credentials from the Institute for Green Business Certification. This first step garnered information about a business model that allowed reduction of pollution in ten key areas. FIB started to work on that list of changes and wanted to publicize their efforts because many assessments have shown that companies who announce green efforts are rewarded with green dollars from new customers.

FIB Industries became part of the Global Reporting Initiative (GRI) Triple Bottom Line self-reporting process. The GRI is a self-selected way to report on sustainable performance in the economic, environmental, and financial areas. Reporting sustainability as part of a public record in something like the Global Reporting Initiative does not necessarily mean the sustainability initiatives are all encompassing. It merely means that the corporation is willing to make some statement about its initiatives and show how they impact that three-prong model, people, profit, and the environment. Companies that have used the GRI option include British Petroleum, ConAgra, and Dow Chemical. The leadership at FIB Industries cares about the environment, but it also cares deeply about the positive publicity. Touting sustainability efforts is not greenwashing if actions match the words.

Your stakeholders include the Board of Directors, staff, company members, sponsors, patrons, and community members. As the greening process takes place include program notes and issue press releases about changes and evaluation. It will not only create general good will toward your group, the publicity may lead to new resources and opportunities. Other ways to publicize your move to a greener model may be to sponsor an e-waste drive and recycle the "contributions" if the local community does not already engage in these activities. Recent statistics from the Earth Day Network, an international environmental group, state that Americans produce 50 million tons of e-waste every year. Almost 75% of that waste is buried or incinerated allowing toxins like mercury and cadmium to enter the soil or air. Not only do you get the word out, you take a step toward responsible disposal of potentially harmful items.

The Big Picture or the Forest View

You can start to see possible avenues for reducing environmental impact before you begin the audit process. Chart how your company allocates its resources. Every company has a style that becomes visible over time. Those choices may develop out of venue configuration, the kinds of shows selected for the season, or even the artistic interests of directors or the areas of expertise of resident designers.

If you always rent spaces and use the lighting inventory offered, investing in LED lighting technology is not going to make much difference. A decision to schedule rehearsals and performances to allow the use of public transportation is more likely to reduce your carbon footprint. If your home venue is a shallow converted vaudeville theatre that requires you to use painted drops instead of dimensional weight-bearing scenery, looking for sustainably harvested wood is not a step that will reap the most benefits. Devising ways to reuse the drops and avoid waste paint will reduce your waste stream. If your company exclusively produces dance in your venue, do not invest energy in researching sustainable scenic construction methods. Look at ways to upgrade your lighting inventory to more efficient fixtures or focus on establishing reciprocal costume -loaning relationships with other dance companies.

Thinking about the big picture can help the company Green Team decide which production areas need in-depth audits. This assessment, whether scientifically accurate or holistically approached, requires a long-term commitment. You can define your sustainability vision before or after the initial audit. The vision may have to be more generic until you have the baseline information. That is an easy way to start the process. Once you have specific information about the organization's waste production, utility use, and material choices, you can refine that larger vision to fit the existing circumstances.

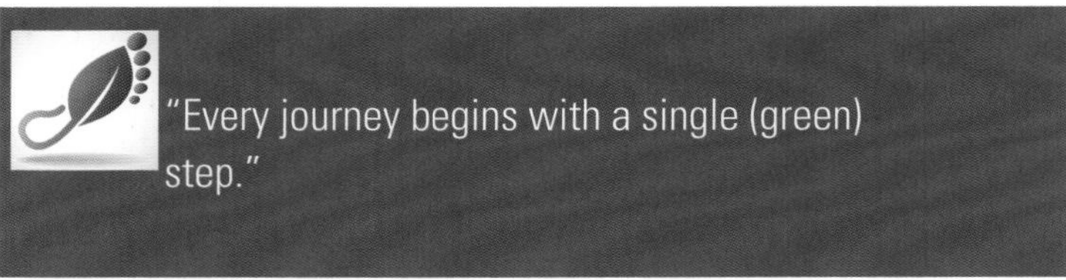
"Every journey begins with a single (green) step."

Chapter 2

Understanding the Assessment Process

Assessing Environmental Impact

Now that your organization has selected an initial vision for its environmental sustainability initiative, it is time to start refining the idea by developing objectives and strategies. It might be easier to take actions listed in *Coco's Guide to Being Green* and assume you have improved operational practices. However, to be able to quantify the difference in environmental impact once strategies are in place, that initial assessment or baseline audit is needed. This initial assessment identifies current practices and depending on the style of audit chosen may provide actual weights, measures, and costs.

Audits require an overview of operational areas because many aspects of sustainable practice are affected by a number of departments. For example, the work in every shop and office can increase the volume of solid waste, influence air quality, or increase the overall carbon footprint. There should also be a focused examination of each individual area to find workable strategies to move forward the green initiative. You have to be able to see both the forest and the trees for a complete picture. I distinguish between the broad based audits that may be based on observation and more focused audits of work process and material use by area by labeling the former a Forest View Audit and the latter a Tree View Audit.

The Forest View Audit that looks at all departmental operations in a broad way without taking actual measurements can alert you to areas where a more in-depth or Tree View analysis is needed. At the end of a broadly based assessment you can determine which production or management processes generate the most solid and hazardous waste, and use the most resources. It may also focus attention on practices that had not been previously considered. For example, you may have been worried about recycling cans and bottles and at the end of this initial examination discover that you are also throwing away pounds of paper every week instead of recycling it.

Health and safety issues areas that require immediate action without any delay to protect company or audience members may also be discovered during the Forest View Audit. If a walk-through reveals that the paper that is not being recycled is placed in garbage cans that block emergency exits, this requires an immediate response. You cannot wait until you find recycling bins to remedy the safety issue.

One final benefit of the Forest View Audit is that the results can help you determine if a green consultant should be engaged or if outside funding must be secured to move forward past the audit stage. These options can be investigated while you finish the more time-consuming Tree View Audits of specific production areas.

Note: These focused assessments should be repeated after greening strategies have been in place for several months. That second set of audits will evaluate the effectiveness of the changes you made and determine if strategies need to be tweaked or even replaced.

The Green Initiative

One goal of embracing a green initiative is to build a green culture within the organization. The staff may have an underlying fear that any evidence of damaging environmental practices will be construed as evidence of poor work performance or a lack of expertise. Always present the audits and discoveries as a positive step forward, so no one views it as a "gotcha" that is embarrassing.

In my opinion, green initiatives that include strategies focused on changing behavior instead of simply meeting numeric goals are more effective. Suppose your green initiative is to limit the use of natural resources. One version of a strategy might be stated as "*Our goal is to reduce use of new material in scene construction by 10%.*" The other version of the same idea may be articulated as "*Our goal is to reuse as much existing material as possible.*"

In version one, it is possible to reach the goal by fudging numbers if workers feel pressured to achieve a successful outcome. The goal has a finite cap that does not directly address work practices and making choices to meet the goal of the green initiative falls on a very small group. Version two engages all the workers by asking them to alter their behavior to support the goal. A behavioral change encompasses all facets from design to construction to strike. Company members take greater ownership of the initiative when they are actively involved in creating multiple strategies that achieve a positive outcome.

The numeric information is still vital for evaluation of the initiative and to determine if greater changes should be made. It should be a tool used in a green initiative, not the only ultimate goal.

Any green initiative takes time to establish. Keeping stakeholders committed to the concept and engaged in the process is part of the work involved. Before beginning the actual audit process determine the planned scope of the project. Keep company members informed of the process and any changes. Focus their efforts on behavioral changes instead of meeting numeric goals.

The Role of a Green Team

Once the Green Team is established, it can be instrumental in conducting baseline audits, assessing the data collected, and developing strategies to make the company's vision a reality. The Green Team should not be disbanded once the strategies are in place. It should continue to monitor and evaluate the sustainability strategies over time and refine strategies.

Include end users in the technical area, administration, and performance to create a Green Team with the broadest perspective. If your company depends on volunteers with great artistic vision, but little real experience or training in technical theatre, find someone with expertise in the production arena to be part of the group. If the organization has a small number of full-time staff members, include volunteers or freelancers to make sure every production area is represented on the team. It may even require hiring an outside consultant with the appropriate expertise in technical theatre and design.

People are one third of the Planet, People, Profit equation that equals sustainability. Make sure that the efforts to make your theatre greener don't have a negative impact on the people. This is advisable whether the assessment involves an outside sustainability consultant or is an in-house project.

Keeping Everyone Engaged

Link the zeal for environmental stewardship with a desire for collaboration from all participants. Recognize the fact that even if the theatre leadership supports a green initiative, some organization members may be reluctant to embrace new green guidelines or participate in the initial or subsequent audits.

This may be a defense mechanism based on having worked with organizations where mission goals change so often that new initiatives quickly fall by the wayside. Their reluctance may be based on the belief that their artistic vision will be limited or an unwillingness to let go of techniques learned long ago when environmental considerations were not part of the process.

Designers or technicians in under-supported production areas may feel that taking time to learn a new technique or adopting any practice that potentially increases the workload will compromise the quality of their work.

There are suggestions in this book on everything from catering to cleaning supplies to building scenery and costumes and selecting lighting fixtures. The personnel who work in each of these discrete areas must commit to the sustainability mission statement and strategic plan in order to facilitate change in those areas and maintain the more sustainable practices. Whether you use group discussions or individual conversations, or ask people to submit concerns anonymously in a wooden box, try to uncover the underlying motivation for any reluctance to participate. You cannot assuage anyone's fears unless you understand them.

Getting Started

This evaluation may be an in-house endeavor, a response from outside experts and consultants, or a combination of the two techniques. Potential outside partners include members of a green theatre consortium, state or municipal funding agencies that support environmental stewardship, and not-for-profit foundations committed to global environmental concerns.

If your theatre is part of a larger organization, for example a university or municipal school system, there may be a person designated as the Environmental Health and Safety Officer. While the actual title varies, these individuals usually have the same job assignment: to limit potential hazards in the workplace and to control contamination by potential toxins and disposal of potentially hazardous materials.

This person is charged with safety, not greening the process. However, he can spot the areas where introducing higher standards of industrial hygiene can have the happy byproduct of greener production. A walk through the shops with this individual will help you identify the intersection of health and safety issues with sustainable practices during the assessment process.

If you are part of an educational system or a corporate entity, there may also be a system-wide Green Team or Sustainability Office already in place. Contact this resource for ideas and support during your initial assessment process.

Even if your company is not part of an academic institution, you may still be able to tap into the resources of an educational campus. A college or university in your town may be interested in an internship opportunity or an individual division or department may find that a partnership with local businesses going green offers a research opportunity for students and faculty. The school may be willing to allow you access to their recycling program and facilities or share storage facilities and theatre stock in the name of sustainability.

The Process

At the most sophisticated level the baseline assessment may include recording scientifically measured information. If you have qualified staff, one possibility is to use monitoring equipment to measure the actual use of electricity and water. Some institutions have saved the garbage and recycling bin contents for several weeks and compared the measurement of pounds of garbage created versus the pounds of materials recycled in some fashion.

Another baseline assessment that is common in industrial settings looks at utility consumption using monthly bills. Consultant Stephen Rueff spearheaded such a study of five theatres in the Twin Cities during the winter of 2013. Water, gas, and electric bills show the actual meter readings that measure use. This consumption can be charted over a period of time that includes both the coldest and warmest months to see a variation in consumption. Examining the same months in two different years is an even better sampling. A consultant can use this data to do statistical analyses that factor in subtleties including the differentials created by seasonal weather changes or utility cost changes based on season or volume of use. Access to this kind of precise calculation may improve chances for outside funding for larger projects.

Even if a consultant is not involved, this same information can be put into a simple graph and your utility use compared with comparable venues' and companies' use over the same calendar period. The process is useful even if there is no comparison. Chart when utility use spikes and determine if it is a consequence of production or rental activities. The patterns may indicate that certain activities do not offer benefits that warrant the increase in environmental and financial costs. This analysis can also reveal any specific activities that need to be scrutinized to determine why they create an unusual increase in use of water, gas, and/or electricity. Facilities that are not metered separately from the rest of a multiuse building may find it possible to have sub-meters installed to secure accurate figures. This requires expertise either from the utility providers or a consultant. If you are billed for utilities by a landlord or building owner without being metered, ask how your share of the bill is formulated. Unless you are paying a flat fee every month, someone is determining your share of the load. The system to split the utility bills among the building tenants may be wildly inaccurate, but if it is, you want to know that as well.

Assessment Through Onsite Observation

Sometimes it is not possible to complete an assessment based on scientifically accurate weight and measures or it is necessary to mix metered data with on-site observations. Common sense can help determine where you need to make some changes.

Take this scenario. Your cast and audience are always complaining that the theatre is too hot or too cold. This is a clue, based on observation only, that the theatre may be wasting energy with the heating and/or cooling system. An examination of the efficiency of the air handling system is in order from both an environmental and financial point of view. The problem may stem from continuing renovations or repurposing of space in the building without making changes in the heating or cooling system. Money may be required to address this problem. HVAC upgrades and repairs are recognized as usually having a fast ROI (return on investment), but before the first cent is allocated, look at the no cost/low cost possibilities.

Is the thermostat behind the stage drapes on the upstage side of the proscenium opening where it cannot accurately measure the temperature? Will adding a programmable thermostat to the system solve the problem? Are people propping exterior doors open to carry in props or concessions and forgetting to close the door? While sensory observation is initially low cost and easy to perform, for it to be effective you have to continue relying on sensory observation to exhaust all of the potential options to the problem.

An Example of an Assessment Process

There is no single correct way to do an initial audit of your baseline environmental impact. The steps outlined here are an example based on a project I completed. My sustainability assessment quickly became an evaluation of health and safety, economic sustainability, and human resource allocation as well.

I used the initial audit to examine work processes and measure waste discarded from two shows. I also examined and inventoried the existing stock of scenery, soft goods, props, and costumes. My technique focused on record keeping of on-site observations. Actual utility consumption was not addressed because the shops and performance venue were in a larger multiuse building and did not have separate water or electric meters.

Reducing Your Carbon Footprint

The goal of reducing carbon footprint is an often cited goal for corporations, individuals, and not-for-profit organizations. It is a commonly heard phrase and people usually associate it with reducing power consumption. In fact, carbon footprint

Some of the things I looked for were:

- Missed recycling opportunities.
- Use of aerosols in the paint and costume shop.
- Volume of materials that could not be reclaimed at strike due to construction choices.
- Use and disposal of chemicals and solvents in the shops including cleaning products.
- Availability of information about the chemical products in use.
- Wattage of lamps used in lighting fixtures and task lighting.
- Whether the use of lower wattage lamps was an option in each location.
- The amount of existing scenery and costume inventory that was not reusable when closely examined and why it was not reusable.
- Inventory of tools, lighting equipment, and stock scenic elements.
- Storage and access to scrap and virgin raw materials and existing stock items.
- Poor general housekeeping practices that blocked emergency exits and areas of refuge in an emergency.
- Quantity of programs and posters that were left over after each production.
- The kinds of scenic units that seemed to be needed for most productions.

The organization and the steps taken to conduct the baseline audit may vary. If at all possible the following areas should be audited either by individual department or broader companywide statistics:

1. Overall energy and water usage including appliance and equipment energy efficiency.
2. Recycling and solid waste.
3. Storage facilities.
4. Transportation including shopping, local and touring company travel, shipment of supplies and materials, and audience commuting.
5. Paper product consumption.
6. Environmental impact of supplies and materials used.
7. Food and beverage areas.
8. Standard operating procedures and how to Reduce, Reuse, and Recycle.

The First Step

Professor Michael Mehler, Associate Professor of Theater Design at Allegheny College in Meadville, PA and former Vice-President of Programming for USITT decided to develop a green plan for the production process at Allegheny. He describes his plans for an initial assessment to move toward a greener production model: "*The Environmental Studies Department has electrical load meters to monitor electricity use so we can get accurate data on electricity use of the stage lighting.*" He goes on to say, "*In the fall semester, students will be assigned hands-on projects where they track use of materials used for scenery. Once we see what is used, what can be kept, and what is thrown away, we can start formulating a plan.*"

This is an example of an initial long-term audit. It took some time to create the problem; it will take some time to find complete solutions.

encompasses far more than simple use of electricity, gasoline, or coal. Carbon footprint is generally defined as the amount of greenhouse gases, including CO_2, produced by an individual or organization over a given period of time. This carbon footprint is created by all kinds of waste streams and consumption, not simply direct use of fuel or energy. All consumption of manufactured items and food has consequences for the environment. The impact of power consumption, travel, environmental controls, and most other activities are converted into a total carbon footprint—usually described in metric tons. Reducing consumption of goods and energy is one way to reduce greenhouse gases.

Purchasing offsets—in other words paying a fee to credit yourself with someone else's conservation measures—is also possible. This idea of purchasing offsets was originally designed for nations and corporations, but now is a possibility for individuals and small organizations as well. For example, Clark Transfer, one of the biggest show movers in the United States, offers this option to customers when they book transportation for moving scenery and equipment. Many airlines offer the option to customers as well.

Purchasing offsets should be part of a larger initiative with strategies in place to reduce waste and consumption. Simply choosing to pay a penalty and continuing to do business as usual does not ultimately address the problem. It simply offers a bandage that may salve the conscience.

Carbon Calculators

Carbon footprint calculators abound on the web, and are offered up by organizations that range from British Petroleum (BP) to the United States Environmental Protection Agency (EPA). Although most are designed to assess the carbon footprint of a domestic household and use general questions for the calculation, you can take the same test plugging in the information for your organization. Make sure you understand the goals of the organization that created the assessment tool when you use a carbon footprint calculator. Remember, too, that only a few of the available free calculators have been evaluated by independent parties for accuracy.

One interesting calculator was distributed by the London Theatre Trust in 2008 as part of the Mayor of London's *Green Theatre Programme*. It was created for the Greater London Authority by the international environmental consultancy firm, AEA. The link to download the carbon calculator is still active. This project has been taken over and further refined by the organization Julie's Bicycle (see sidebar) but the questions on this initial carbon calculator outline the scope of areas that should be assessed to ultimately determine your carbon footprint. Included questions range from how many scripts will be produced for casting and how they will be transported to the actors to whether sound equipment is digital or analog. It offers an interesting window into how many of our everyday activities must be evaluated to determine environmental impact (http://www.theatrestrust.org.uk/news/show/322).

Julie's Bicycle Industry Green Tools

A more refined and production specific carbon calculator is now available online under the name IG Tools. The IG or Industry Green Tools are a suite of free web-based carbon calculators specifically for the creative industry developed by Julie's Bicycle. The suite contains five different calculators geared to venues and cultural buildings, festivals and outdoor events, offices, tours, and productions. Alison Tickell, Chief Executive of Julie's Bicycle describes the carbon calculator project:

> *"The IG Tools carbon calculators were developed to enable creative professionals across the board to measure, understand and reduce their environmental impacts. We purposefully designed them to be internationally applicable, using international conversion factors, so that anyone, anywhere in the world could benefit."*

Julie's Bicycle: Bringing Sustainability to the Arts

Julie's Bicycle is a not-for-profit organization making sustainability intrinsic to the business, art, and ethics of the creative industries. Founded by the music industry, with expertise from the arts and sustainability, Julie's Bicycle bridges the gap between the creative industries and sustainability. Executive Officer Alison Tickell describes the organization's work:

> *"Based on a foundation of peer-reviewed research, we sustain creativity, enabling the arts to create change. Founded in science, with experts spanning sustainability, the creative industries and academia, it is Julie's Bicycle's pragmatic yet creative approach which has earned us the pioneer label from industry experts."*

Julie's Bicycle was set up in 2007 by music industry figureheads who wanted to galvanize a response to climate change that went beyond awareness-raising concerts, and empowered the industry to reduce its own environmental impacts. Ms Tickell goes on to articulate the organization's mission as an effort to "*make environmental sustainability intrinsic to the business, art and ethics of the creative industries, and we're now working across a broader range of sectors including theatre, dance, visual arts, museums, outdoor arts and events, and literature in addition to music.*"

Julie's Bicycle works with over 1000 international groups of varying size and scope; small companies receive the same respect as large organizations. To find out how Julie's Bicycle can work with your organization contact: info@juliesbicycle.com. Partnerships are far reaching. Ms. Tickell describes the efforts:

> *"No community on the planet is untouched by climate change or culture. So naturally, to achieve our mission, Julie's Bicycle must be international as well. The creative industries are by nature international, and as environmental sustainability has increasingly gained awareness and urgency as an issue Julie's Bicycle has been invited to speak at various conferences, gatherings and symposium which have raised our profile considerably over the last couple of years. Our resources, being internationally applicable, have also travelled far and wide via our website and newsletter, which are visited frequently by people in at least 50 countries around the world. We have also built strategic partnerships and kept in touch with organisations abroad who are doing fantastic work in this field, such as the Broadway Green Alliance and The Centre for Sustainable Practice in the Arts in the USA, On The Move and Transartists in Europe, and others, from whom we have learned a great deal and been able to share our resources and research to our mutual benefit."*

Julie's Bicycle is one of the most respected groups associated with sustainability in the creative arts because of the focused intersection on science and industry practices, according to Ms. Tickell:

> *"What gives our work credibility is both our grounding in science – all of our work is informed by research into the environmental impacts of the creative industries, conducted in partnership with Oxford University – and our collaborative work with creative organisations. Our team is made up of both environmental experts and cultural professionals, and all of our projects and programmes are created in consultation with cultural organisations. The science gives us an understanding of how the greenhouse gas emissions of different creative sectors break down, allowing us to prioritise action, and our strategic collaborations with the creative sector enables us to create tools and resources that allow artists and cultural organisations to act with confidence on the issues that matter most, and take workable solutions to scale fast."*

The Julie's Bicycle web site hosts an incredible data repository of practical guidance, and offers thoughtful leadership and advice to creative organizations looking to limit their environmental impact, all for free.

The goal is to make all information accessible for artists. Julie's Bicycle's web page describes the organization's goals:

> *"Research is translated into easy-to-use tools and resources for creative practitioners that want to know where to channel their focus in making the biggest environmental difference. In addition to the IG Tools we have already developed a range of Green Guides for music, orchestras, theatre, visual arts, and festivals and outdoor arts; Practical Guides on everything from sustainable procurement and merchandising, to communicating with your staff and audiences; Fact Sheets on issues such as biofuels, offsetting and freight; and case studies of organisations pioneering environmental best practice. Our latest resources include a Sustainable Production Guide, developed from pilot projects, research and case study findings from across the performing arts."*

These tools measure greenhouse gas emissions generated by energy use, waste production, water use, business travel, audience travel, production freight, accommodations for company members, and production materials. The tool was developed in the UK and information about costs is calculated in British pounds sterling. Future plans include further development of the tools to include options for calculations in US dollars and European Union euros, although a specific date for that addition has not yet been established. Some information about embodied energy in products is also based on region specific information. The IG Tools are internationally applicable. However there is an additional statement that if the user is outside the United Kingdom, "*there might be some discrepancy in the final results as it is likely that conversion factors for electricity and transport might vary slightly from one world region to the next.*" The figures are likely to be very close if not exactly correct.

Go to http://www.juliesbicycle.com/resources/ig-tools/faqs to learn more about the tools or to http://www.ig-tools.com to begin using them. They can be used as planning tools or use information from a specific production to analyze and identify areas for potential reductions.

Services from Julie's Bicycle go beyond the free IG Tools and include custom consultancy packages on all aspects of greening an organization. The organization also has a process for Industry Green Certification, the leading mark of recognition for environmental achievement in the creative industries. The system uses a three-star rating system. Information on the web page explains the process of certification and the criteria for the one star, two star, and three star designations (http://www.juliesbicycle.com/industry-green). Julie's Bicycle is highly regarded as one of the most important voices in greening the entertainment industry. Spend some time examining the resources available on the organization's web site.

Working with a Local Green Consultant

Working with a local green consultant can be helpful. It allows your theatre to take advantage of the insights developed by working with green commercial entities and governmental agencies. Some indication that the consultant has a background in theatre or a strong interest in the performing arts makes her more likely to understand some of unique aspects of producing theatre.

At present the green consulting industry is unregulated although a range of credentialing options exists. If your company decides to hire an outside consultant, determine the real level of expertise offered and the value of any presented credentials. Like any other credentials, some indicate better qualifications than others. Expertise gained through practical experience, education in environmental stewardship and sustainable business management or some combination of those fields may be more valuable than a credential from an online course that requires no hands-on experience.

Any consultant should be able to provide references for your company to contact and provide examples of the results of completed projects. Like most other business operations, a theatre company involves a range of activities. If the consultant's projects seem to all revolve around one or two areas of change will that be adequate? For example, someone with expertise in waste water management may not be able to help you select greener materials for production or make recommendations for reducing energy usage, recycling, or composting waste material. The consultant who can also educate the theatre administration about financial incentives or funding options including examples of other clients who have successfully accessed those resources is another legitimate criterion to use in the selection process.

Depending on your needs and the availability of experts in the region, you may end up working with several different consultants who specialize in different areas of sustainability. Engaging multiple consultants is similar to hiring multiple contractors to work on your house. It is to your advantage to hire and designate one individual as the head of the operation; the general contractor, to continue that analogy. She may bring in colleagues with additional expertise or at the very least make sure there is not duplication of efforts.

Any consultants should be willing to talk with your Board of Directors or the sponsors funding the transition to greener production as well as members of the company. Suggested solutions should be based on the scope of your operation and resources; changes that cost more than your company can ever afford are of no value. The consultant should be able to address the ROI of any changes that require significant funding. Ask if you will simply get a list of things to do or if the consultation includes training. Checklists are a terrific starting point, but an understanding of the underlying principles of an action will allow you to create a strategic plan that continues to serve the company in the future. If you simply follow the laundry list of things to do without adopting some sort of mission statement and action plan about environmental stewardship, you accomplish little more than finishing the list.

Preparing for Consultation

The designated liaison with any consultants has to be clear about needs and priorities of your company. This liaison should be prepared to share your entire production process. This may take the form of a pictorial flow chart or a written report.

Some typical questions include:

- Are remote facilities used for storage or construction?
- Are standard construction materials, for example, lumber, paint, and fabric, obtained locally?
- Are theatre-specific products obtained locally or do they have to ship from a remote vendor?
- If the company does not own the building, can changes be made in larger systems like air handling or lighting without prior approval of the owner? Are changes to someone else's property fiscally prudent?
- Are facilities in the venue rented out for conferences, meetings, or to other producers? What percentage of building use is allocated for each of these kinds of usage?
- Is catering or food service a normal part of the operation?
- What hours are various areas of operation in use?
- When are rehearsals held and do they always involve the entire cast?

- What is your current load in and strike process?
- Is the company considering using the facility for various kinds of special events to raise revenue as well as traditional productions? These events operate very differently from theatrical productions and may have a profound impact on utility use.

Before any initial consultation complete a Forest View Audit and have that information available for the consultant. Prepare a list of the areas the company wants to address, but be ready to adjust those priorities if the consultation reveals greater areas of concern. A certain amount of financial information should also be prepared. Know what, if any, funding is available for systemic upgrades and identify any time constraints that must be addressed in completing the return on the investment so the company can evaluate the feasibility of any ideas presented. Any operational or equipment changes will not occur in a vacuum. Know any other financial or scheduling issues that must be addressed or acknowledged in developing plans for improving sustainability.

Working with a Green Consultant

Stephen Rueff, owner of The Clean Campaign and member of the Twin Cities Sustainability in Theatre group, works with a variety of businesses. His clients include small, mid-size, and municipal performing arts organizations as well as a range of other types of businesses. Mr. Rueff is a volunteer member of the Twin Cities Sustainability in Theatre (SIT) Task Force as well. In early 2013 he and Alicia Wold, Guthrie Costume Rental General Manager, spearheaded a baseline study on utility use by five theatre companies that will eventually result in a white paper on the topic. Study goals included both the initial assessment and an investigation of whether receiving the information from the baseline study motivated each theatre to establish a sustainability initiative.

When engaging a green consultant, Reuff suggests that theatres look for subject matter expertise, familiarity in operation and experience in organizational development and change management:

> *"The consultant should be able to offer specifics about the environmental and financial impact of changes. This information is particularly important if any upgrades must ultimately pay for themselves in savings. It also allows the company administrators and artists to determine if greening the theatre will impact allocation of financial resources or is even possible without additional fund raising."*

Rueff emphasizes that solutions should focus on behavioral changes as well equipment changes and the consultant should help plan that transition. He describes his own consulting work as "*trying to solve the problem of doing the right thing while keeping the doors open and meeting the mission of the organization.*" He adds that an outside consultant has the advantage of being buffered from internal or financial politics as an independent and objective outsider.

He describes the greening process:

> *"Being able to make sustainable choices is not hard; it is just as hard as anything else. People who create and manage theatres complete complex organizational tasks every day. Be at peace with the evolution of it all and keep the big picture in mind."*

Reduce, Reuse, and Recycle

Figure 2.1 Reduce, Reuse, Recycle to limit solid waste. chingyunsong/ Shutterstock.

Solid waste stream assessment is a logical place to start baseline evaluations. A Forest View Audit can reveal that garbage cans are always filled to overflowing while the recycling bins remain empty. Establishing a recycling culture is an effective strategy and an easy place to start the greening process. Suggestions on how to determine what to keep and what to throw away are included throughout the book.

The Solid Waste Audit

The results of a waste stream study will allow a comparison of the overall volume of waste compared to the volume of recycled items and information about what kinds of items are becoming municipal solid waste, the government's name for trash. You may be shocked to discover how many everyday items like paper, glass, metal, cardboard, ink cartridges, batteries, light bulbs, and plastic bottles go into the garbage instead of recycling bins.

A waste stream audit is just what it sounds like—comparing the garbage can's and the recycling bin's contents. This can be a hands-on process that allows you to note exactly what materials that could potentially be reused or recycled are currently part of the waste stream and going to the incinerator or landfill. It is important to try to determine where the garbage originated in the production process and in the building. This information may suggest changes starting at the design level or in work procedures.

For greater accuracy any baseline evaluation of solid waste should include waste audits at regular intervals over time. Notes should indicate whether the measurement results are from weeks of construction, rehearsal, tech, performance, strike, or some combination of those activities. The length of time for this study depends on the number of shows in the season. The more shows included, the more precise results will be. However, if your company is a casual producer without a regular season, even a complete audit of the waste from one production from the first week of planning through strike will provide valuable information. Familiarizing yourself with the local recycling opportunities may reveal new options for recycling materials that are currently entering the solid waste stream.

One hands-on option, sometimes referred to as dumpster diving, is to actually weigh the garbage being added to the waste stream and then weigh the subset of items in the garbage that could be recycled. A hands-on process is common when assessing office waste where the types of items in the trash are limited, but it can be used to audit any type of waste stream.

You may hire salvage professionals or waste stream audit consultants or use company members for the project. If your audit is an in-house project, you become responsible for making sure any auditors are kept safe throughout the process. The range of construction materials and food products that end up in theatre garbage can make separating garbage messy and potentially hazardous. The auditors could be poked, scratched, or cut by any number of things in the trash. Food products may have attracted stinging and biting insects as well as serving as cultures for bacteria. If the garbage has been outside, living scavengers may be visiting at the exact time the sorting process occurs. No company can afford the potential liability or bad karma of intentionally placing workers or volunteers in a potentially hazardous and certainly unpleasant position.

If you cannot in good conscience take that responsibility, I recommend that you hire participants who have training and expertise in salvage or waste stream management and worker health and safety training for the task. Even protective clothing, goggles, dust masks, and heavy gloves may not keep people safe if there is a possibility of hazardous materials or potentially dangerous items in the waste stream.

The most material is usually thrown away during strike at the end of a show. If it is at all possible, avoid a late night strike when everyone is exhausted by the run of the show and the excitement of closing night. Unless another production needs to be in the space the next day, wait and hold the strike after everyone has had a night of rest and natural light can help illuminate at least some of the work areas.

You can also do a visual survey of what is being thrown away that is descriptive rather than a scientifically accurate weight and measure. Remember it is as important to determine where the items enter the waste stream as it is to catalog the actual items. Identifying the source of the waste product is the only way to determine if procedural changes will keep the item out of the landfill.

Assign several people as dumpster monitors and have them log what items are going in the dumpster—digital pictures can be a huge help if the monitors are not familiar with theatre terminology. The monitors can ask why specific items are being put in the dumpster if they appear to be a recyclable material or

There are techniques that help limit the hazards and the ick factor:

- Weigh the waste and recyclable material before it goes into the dumpster or garbage cans. Keep logs of the discarded items.
- Never have anyone climb in the dumpster. Keep all solid waste in cans and put it in the dumpster after it is weighed.
- If solid waste is already in the can, place a drop cloth on the floor and pour the garbage out so the contents are visible instead of reaching into the can.
- Dump out any recycling bins where broken glass, sharp metal, or food items may have been placed.
- Alert the strike crew that any item going into the trash cans must be cleaned of nails, staples, etc.
- Put up signs reminding everyone when the audit will occur and that food and liquids should be placed in labeled, segregated garbage cans.
- Keep the garbage cans indoors until the audit is complete. No one should be handling garbage that may have been visited by rodents, scavengers, or insects.

in good condition and record the answer. The other option is to simply take the log and pictures to the Technical Director or responsible person in charge of the strike and ask if these items should have been thrown out. A communication problem has been discovered if the items were intended for storage or recycling. If he or she truly intended those pieces to be dumpster-bound, it is time to explore why those items entered the waste stream. Let's assume that items that are easily recycled—paper, cardboard, cans, and bottles—are already removed from the waste stream. Make a comprehensive list of what has been thrown away. Ask the following questions:

- Is this too large to store and impossible to break into smaller pieces?
- Did the strike technique damage it so it cannot be reused?
- Did the selection of low strength base materials mean the item cannot hold up to use in another show?
- Did the strike crew choose to throw it away because removing the hardware and fasteners would take too much time and energy?

This information will be valuable when strategies are developed.

If storage is the issue that leads to items being trashed instead of saved, it may be possible to give the materials away. For example, in the Twin Cities, an online theatre web page, www.playlist.com, includes strike announcements that indicate what items will be available for salvage in the classified advertisement section under the title "free stuff."

Deciding what to Keep

Recycling is not limited to discarding items for reclamation at a recycling center. In theatre, recycling may include reclaiming the original materials used in construction to reuse on a future project. Reusing refers to keeping an item and reusing or repurposing it in its original form instead of breaking the object down into its component materials. Breaking an element down into its component materials is usually categorized as deconstruction. In every case, there will have to be a judgment made about the likelihood of reusing something. Experience will tell you when something is too small or too damaged to reuse. Later in the book there are tips to help you determine what can be valuable stock inventory instead of dead weight. Unfortunately, it is always a gamble when you decide what no longer has long-term value unless your seasons are scheduled extraordinarily far in advance or you only produce one or two kinds of shows.

Your company's mission statement usually determines the kinds of scripts most often produced. Even theatres without a specific mission statement or articulated artistic goal tend to produce the same kinds of shows either because they sell well or it is the genre of theatre that interests the membership most. For example, if the company is committed to producing American Classics the shows will probably require realistic settings—flats, platforms, and door units. The company focused on workshops for script development or an improvisational company may find that a neutral unit set or even a few stools on a bare stage will serve the entire season and choose to focus initial greening strategies on lighting and props. A children's dance company that primarily uses flat backdrops may discover it is more sustainable financially and environmentally to rent already painted drops instead of creating new ones for each production. Use the baseline assessment to determine the best allocation of resources for greener production.

Over the course of several shows, make a spreadsheet or graph of the kinds of elements that are used repeatedly for productions. Note how many items are new construction using virgin materials and how many are taken from inventory, rented, or borrowed. This information will help you determine how to prioritize the value of items in the inventory. Unless storage space is unlimited, choices about what to keep and what to let go are going to have to be made at some point.

Where to Put it All—Dealing with Storage Space

Safety standards prohibit storing anything where it will block emergency egress routes, fire suppression equipment, or electrical service panels. You may need to determine how much real storage area is available before it is possible to decide exactly how much material can be effectively reused in the future. Look for dead space: empty areas that might be hard to access but would work well for storing tertiary items that are only used on occasion but are expensive to purchase again and again.

Make sure you are not filling up areas with items that should remain clear for safety reasons. For example, in multi-story buildings, the stairwells may seem enormous. That empty floor space and the open areas under the stairs may look like a terrific storage option. However, those spaces between the fire doors are often considered safety zones where people can be moved in an emergency like fire or tornado. An organizational safety officer or the local Fire Marshal will be able to identify any areas of refuge. A good rule of thumb is that any concrete or cinderblock area around a stairwell or emergency egress path or any room with a sign designating it as some kind of emergency shelter is off limits for storage. Those spaces must remain clear to accommodate people. Like everything else in this world, if it looks too, good to be true, it probably is. Remember too, that any sprinkler heads require a specified clearance, usually 18", in order to function properly during a fire. Do not stack items up to the sprinkler heads.

Some companies make use of grid or catwalk areas where there are no lines sets or moving pieces. This traditionally dead space may be ideal for items that do not require temperature control and are not used frequently. Reflect on whether that choice is actually safe. Don't add trip and fall hazards to those out of the way places or create the potential for life-threatening accidents when something falls out of the sky. Battens that can easily move out of audience sightlines in a fly house may be a better storage option.

Storage is as significant an ongoing problem for companies that rent a venue as those working out of a single home space. Finances alone will determine whether or not you can rent dedicated storage space instead of spreading stock all over town in company members' garages.

Whether the available storage space is in a dedicated theatre or scattered offsite storage, determine the best use of the space. Rooms that are climate and temperature controlled should be designated for costumes, props, and scenery that are subject to mold and mildew. Climate control includes heating, cooling, and humidity control. Painted, stacked scenery and molding is particularly susceptible to sticking together in hot, humid weather, although children's pool noodles or ethafaom rod between the pieces of scenery can help mitigate this problem. Potentially dead space that is hard to access may be perfect for expensive items like hardware that are only used occasionally.

Any evaluation must also include the costs associated with using the storage space. If you are a nomadic company, would you save money and gas by renting a climate controlled, 24-hour access storage unit instead of using multiple sites that are rent free but far apart? It is more difficult to create an initial stock inventory with multiple storage spaces. The inventory has to include not only quantity counts, but information about where each item is located. The crew must then be sure to return it to the original storage area after strike.

In communities where big box stores have turned the downtown area into a ghost town, there are empty storefronts. Is it possible to forge an alliance with a building owner to use one of those empty buildings for little or no money? A business may be able to take some sort of tax allowance. It may be possible to apply for a grant to create a space that becomes a multiuser storage facility and creates a consortium for recycling of stock scenery and costumes. This requires an enormous commitment of time and energy, but the potential for reusing stock increases exponentially. For example, recently publicity indicates the LA Stage Alliance is planning to offer cooperative storage for member organizations in its new facility. The Minnesota Sustainability in Theatre Task Force is exploring options to provide some storage. Discuss all financial and liability ramifications with your legal and insurance advisors if you move forward on this option.

Any storage or sharing option that will ultimately allow for collective use of stock is a win-win situation. It may be possible to create a coalition where everyone stores stock individually and shares the inventory digitally to meet sustainable goals across a broad spectrum of companies.

Consider the people involved as well. Depending on the region, it may be easier and the staff may be more comfortable accessing a storage facility in the middle of the night instead of visiting an empty storefront surrounded by empty buildings. The climate control, security, and lighting can be part of the rental package for a commercially managed storage unit. Taking over an empty structure will ultimately require the company to cover insurance and utility costs.

Housekeeping and storage organization is an easy starting point for assessment, especially when attempting to reduce waste and purchase of raw materials through reuse.

- If you can't find it, you can't reuse it.
- If you can't store it without damaging it, you can't reuse it.
- If it is stored in a way that allows vermin to house in it, you don't want to reuse it.

Creative Reuse, or One Person's Trash Can Be Your Treasure

A number of products that can be recycled or reused are thrown away at theatres. This choice may come from a shortage of storage spaces or time management issues that do not allow ample opportunity for separating recyclables or reclaiming the base materials. In some communities there are no public recycling or reuse options in place and creative reuse options become the company's responsibility.

Throughout the United States there are organizations and consortiums that were created to keep items out of landfills. Some are geared toward domestic use like the nationwide organization, Freecycle, that consists of numerous smaller chapters. By going to Freecycle.org you can select the group closest to your geographic location. This nationwide system started out of a single group in Arizona. Individuals sign up to join a Freecycle group and can either look for specific items or offer free items for pickup by others that can use them. Most groups are moderated and membership is subject to the moderator's approval.

All groups have specific rules for use of the service. For example, some Freecycle groups require the first post to be an offer of an item and many do not allow postings for pets. All refuse any post that is a sales pitch. Like any other online situation, each participant is responsible for his or her own safety and should take common-sense precautions when picking up or offering items to strangers. Freecycle groups used to be hosted on Yahoo.com but now most can be found online through the main web site, Freecycle.org.

Another group of organizations go under the umbrella title of Creative Reuse Centers. Some specialize in arts materials, other offer a broad range of items. http://www.lancastercreativereuse.org/directory-creative-reuse-centers.html, includes a national list of creative reuse centers. For anyone considering creating a similar group a print resource is available: *The Social Entrepreneur's Guide to Starting a Creative Reuse Center*, released in October 2012 by the group at SCRAP Portland. At the time of writing, SCRAP Portland also offers a Reuse Workshop as a blog at http://reuseworkshop.blogspot.com.

There are other kinds of regional centers for creative reuse. Some feature decorative architectural elements from building demolition while other focus on art and craft supplies. Others are the well-known theatre designer haunts like

Goodwill, the Salvation Army Store, and the thrift shops run by charitable or civic organizations. The Habitat for Humanity Reuse Stores offer tremendous options and any purchase there also serves a worthy cause. Items available include building materials, furniture, and appliances. Since some items are cast-offs not needed at the conclusion of a project, it is possible to find everything from laminate counter tops to carpeting that might not be large enough for a dwelling, but are perfectly sized for a set. The stores can be great sources for both pickup and drop off items if you lack storage.

Some commercial scene shops have adopted the policy of accepting the return of any scenery the shop constructed and offering it for reuse to other companies. Showman

Reviewing the Audit Plan

1. List the areas that will be audited either by department or broader operations and functions.
2. Create a prioritized action plan for the audit that includes a timetable for testing, data gathering and completion of each step in the process.
3. Analyze the results of the audit to identify areas where changes should be made.
4. Establish a plan for targeted research to determine how to address the identified problems. This plan should include a budget of available resources.
5. Identify any "low hanging fruit"; implement the low-cost or no-cost changes that can be made immediately. At the same time identify any changes that may be health and safety or code related that must be addressed immediately.
6. Create a strategic plan with a time-table for implementing changes. Include any long-term goals that may require additional fundraising to be addressed.
7. Implement the plan. It may be a good idea to appoint one individual or group as the party responsible for keeping track of changes and making sure the project stays on its timetable.
8. As each change is implemented, monitor the results to determine if the choice met the original goal.
9. Rinse, lather, repeat.
10. Finalize your long-term green initiative goals. This is the mission that your stakeholders will continue to consider with each production process or organizational purchase.
11. Revisit your green initiative periodically as well as doing periodic assessments if other changes should be implemented. This will include research on new options for greener choices that may suggest additional steps that the company can take for more sustainable productions.
12. Accept that greening theatre production is a long-term process and a long-term goal.

Fabricators in the New York City area is one of the most well-known of these creative reuse pioneers.

Consortiums have formed throughout the country in an attempt to support direct reuse of scenic elements. Another group of industry professionals has created ReadySetRecycle, a web page that lists scenery and costumes for sale (http://www.readysetrecycle.com/). Web pages like the one being created in the Twin Cities by the Sustainability in Theatre group may include strike calendars. Others include listings and pictures of individual items or entire sets with rental or sale prices indicated. Whistling in the Dark, a theatre company in Ohio, briefly set up a space called the Green Room that offered a centralized storage location and sharing of visual elements.

The concentration of theatre in a geographical region impacts the success of these reuse models. If participating companies are widely dispersed, the financial and environmental costs of transportation may outweigh the benefits. In many cases the ability of volunteers to carve out enough time to administer the program has impacted the success as well. The Ohio Theatre Alliance spent more than a year creating a web page for this purpose, but had to put the project on hold for this reason. It can be difficult to keep such a project up and running unless a consortium agrees to share costs or grant or donor money can be secured to underwrite operations and staffing. The ideas are worth examining and emulating.

There may also be a need to assess potential liability when giving away structural items. Completely designed items that will be used for the same show may require that royalties be paid to the designer for reuse. Right to intellectual property should be considered and honored. It is possible that a board member has the expertise to shepherd such a project to completion while limiting any potential liability issues for the participants. If not, it is probably wise to consult a legal expert before starting this kind of project.

Later evaluations should examine efficacy of your greener process and evaluate the impact these changes on the production quality of shows. Look for changes in allocation of resources, both capital and human, as part of the analysis. Hardly anyone hits a home run out of the park the first time she comes up to bat. The subsequent audits allow tweaking of the green initiative.

An audit is not a negative process. You should use the assessments to identify your best practices as well. You may be able to identify greener choices already in place. Those ideas may be adaptable for other production areas or you may want to share the information with other similar organizations. Chapter 3 offers some ideas for conducting these early Tree View Audits of individual production areas.

Chapter 3

Beginning the Journey

In the last chapter we looked at the concept of baseline audits and broad operational concepts for becoming more sustainable. It is time to put these ideas into practice and begin the audit process in earnest. For one of the Live Design International Green Day sessions in 2011, I developed a checklist that suggested areas to analyze for an initial assessment. I also created three checklists to track completion of changes toward greener production. Those original documents are posted on the Center for Sustainable Practice in the Arts web page and several other places online. I have adapted these same checklists for use by readers of this book. They are in Appendix A.

Some users find it helpful to scan these checklists and adapt them by adding a space for notes and the date under each bullet point to make it possible to keep track of the development of the green initiative. Others use them as they are. You are welcome to adapt or copy and share either version of the checklists. I only ask that the footer of any version remain intact or the appropriate attribution be included.

These checklists are tools to be used in conjunction with your sustainability mission objectives. They are the beginning of the process, not the end of it. The information will help prioritize your action plan to meet that mission of greener production and design.

The first use of these checklists focuses on understanding your current environmental impact. The checklists can be used again later to track successes in implementing your initiative.

The Performance Spaces

Walk through your performance spaces and take a careful look at the environment. If there was a recent performance check the audience seating area. Any garbage left on the floor will indicate items that should be considered when assessing the solid waste stream.

Document the types of lighting used for audience safety and comfort, including the small pocket lights along the steps. If these units use incandescent lamps, energy savings can be realized by finding direct replacement LED lamps or, if you have the funds, replacing the actual fixtures. It is worth doing a visual test to make sure the existing fixtures actually meet your needs for audience illumination. If they do not, make sure any plans address that problem as well.

This is also an opportunity to look at emergency lighting in the facility. Emergency exit signs must always be visible both during performance and when there is not a show in progress. It is now possible to replace older emergency exit signs with LED units for better energy management. In some cases illuminated signs can be replaced with phosphorescent signage that requires no electricity. Ecoglo (www.us.ecogloo.com) is one supplier of those products.

Turn on the rehearsal lighting. When the stage lighting rig is used for rehearsals both energy and money are being wasted. Explore possibilities that include higher efficiency lower wattage lamps for rehearsal—these may include LED units or dimmable fluorescent units.

If the house or rehearsal lights run through the main lighting console, another option exists. With computer lighting consoles it is usually possible to assign specific rows of house lights and stage lights to channels and park those channels. Parking a channel means setting it at a constant specific level of intensity, usually below 100%. Parking a channel prevents the computer console from recording those channel levels as part of any cue. This eliminates the frustration of accidentally adding house lights to internal show cues without plunging the house into darkness for the entire tech process. At a future time, those channels can be unparked and integrated into cues. During the rehearsal and work process, it limits the amount of electricity being used because the instruments will not come to full intensity and only the lights needed for visibility will be turned on. If you are not familiar with this practice, check the console manual for instructions on the actual key strokes involved. Make sure the manual you are using is for the generation of software operating your console. Sometimes console software is upgraded and no one remembers to print out a new manual.

Walk through every access point in the performance space. Determine what kinds of lamps are in use for the backstage

Figure 3.1 Left to right, an incandescent, a compact fluorescent, and an LED lamp, all with medium screw base. Vladimir Gjorgiev/Shutterstock.

crossover, the trap room, and for props tables. Can the switched task lights be upgraded from incandescent bulbs to some sort of LED lamp? This may seem like a small amount of electricity, but as you increase the number of lamps changed, the energy savings increase. In hard to reach places like the grid and loading rail, it reduces the frequency of changing burnouts because of the long lamp life. If backstage run lights are in place, look at the options available. Can incandescent lamps smothered in blue gel and duct tape be replaced with low wattage blue LED rope lights?

Drop in any battens currently without a load. If the pipes are covered with dirt and dust, you can limit some of the particulate matter floating in the air by using the shop vacuum to dust them occasionally. That dust ends up eventually settling on everything from the stage lights to the stage floor. The impact of free floating dirt can range from requiring more frequent mopping of the stage floor to stage light lenses so dirty that the amount of light coming from the fixture is compromised to marring the finish of just painted scenery that requires touch-up.

While you are doing this walk-through to assess lighting, you can also make note of potential storage areas that can be repurposed for more effective use or that are currently empty. Also note the level of use of the garbage collection centers. If the garbage cans are full of empty water bottles, soda cans, and paper this may be an ideal location for recycling bins.

Think About the Larger Impact

The checklists and audit process focuses on individual choices at the local level to make your operation greener. Keep in mind that all of those small decisions at each theatre have a cumulative effect and ultimately create a much larger impact on the environment as a whole. Every step your company takes toward a more sustainable model moves the goal of environmental stewardship forward and helps protect the larger ecosystem.

Protecting the Water Table

It is easy to forget that any liquids we pour down the sink may have an impact on the overall quality of the available water supply. If you are part of a larger organization there is probably already a liquid waste disposal plan in place. On a corporate or educational campus the Facilities Management Department or the Safety Office can probably provide accurate information about those guidelines.

If no policy currently exists there will be legal standards for the area that set the parameters for appropriate practices. Contact the local governing body's main office to obtain contact information for the Authority Having Jurisdiction (AHJ). This generic designation appears in many regulatory codes. It is a way of stating that the office or individual assessing adherence to various codes may have various titles depending on the location. The local governing body should be able to tell you which person and which office answers these questions for

Figure 3.2 Improper disposal of any liquid contaminants can impact water quality. Toa55/Shutterstock.

your area. It may take several phone calls, but having accurate information is important.

Some hold the philosophy that contacting a regulatory office for information will result in the same problems that folklore describes will happen if you invite a vampire into your home: Nothing but heartache will follow and you have no way to make the interloper leave the premises. I can only address that belief by stating that this has never been my personal experience and that you have an obligation to understand and follow the regulatory guidelines that relate to your company or business. If there is an issue with regulatory violations it may be possible to get a variance that addresses the situation and allows for unique circumstances. If there is a problem, it is better to find out the specifics and correct the oversight instead of being unexpectedly fined or closed down after tickets to a performance have already been sold.

Understand the specifics of water protection regulations and prepare to be surprised by the list of things you are not supposed to pour down the sink. The usual areas of concern in a theatre operation are paint and dye disposal from the paint and costume shop. There may be other liquid products that are left over from mounting a show ranging from fog fluid and flame retardant products to the dirty water from mopping the stage floor that may fall under specific guidelines. Paint disposal is specifically discussed later in Chapter 8.

Your baseline assessment should include a list of all products used in any process that results in waste liquid being dumped down the sink. List every brand and kind of paint or dye, any solvents used to clean brushes or dye equipment, and every cleaning agent. You can then research each item using Material Safety Data Sheets (MSDS) or the new Safety Data Sheets (SDS) to determine if the product contains potential contaminants that require specialized disposal. Note: There is a change in how manufacturers and distributors are required to provide this information. At the time of writing the transition of MSDS to SDS has just started in the United States. You may have only MSDS, both types of documents depending on the product, or only SDS available by the time this book publishes. One of the easiest changes, called reengineering, is to switch to a product that does the same thing but can be disposed of more easily. Every shop should have a clearly labeled and easily accessible book that includes the MSDS or SDS for every product in use.

Also note exactly how leftover items are disposed of when the show is finished. The technicians using these products can

Figure 3.3 Collect the sheets in a notebook. Organize by product type or manufacturer. Photo by EEJ.

estimate the amount of product that enters the waste stream. If there are a lot of leftover liquids going down the drain, this is one area where it will be easy to make the immediate change of mixing smaller batches. It is an issue that should be addressed as soon as possible.

Take a Deep Breath

If you can smell chemicals, paint, and cleaners or start sneezing from the dust in the air, theatre operations may be impacting indoor air quality. Unless you can hire an industrial hygienist or air quality professional, it will be difficult to make an accurate quantitative assessment of the air quality. However, you can be certain that anything that impacts your breathing also impacts the environment. This is an area where you are probably going to have to make an assessment through observation instead of actually measuring contaminant level.

In the scene shop and costume shop look for sawdust or fabric dust on the surfaces of equipment or even floating in the air during work shifts. The particulate matter from napped fabrics is so pervasive that some stage drapery manufacturers have separate air handling systems for the cutting/sewing room.

If you can visually see dust build up, check to see if appropriate dust collection units are attached to all major saws and equipment. If not, that problem should be addressed immediately. Sewing machines do not come with dust collectors, but you can ask the stitchers to determine which fabric products create this problem and ask designers to avoid them.

Aerosol products—spray paint, spray adhesives, and hair spray for color or holding a hairdo—introduce particulate matter into the air. I worked at one theatre where hair spray continually set off the smoke detectors because of the particulate matter in the spray. Create a list of every product in a spray can that is in use in any production area including the make-up rooms. This is particularly important if the make-up room is actually a converted space never intended for use by performers. In a converted space the air handling system was probably not designed to filter the air or perhaps even to move it for appropriate ventilation.

If any of the products you use require special care to avoid contamination of the air in the work area, you have a responsibility to meet those standards. If you cannot, quit using those products. There is an environmental impact as well as an obligation to protect the health and safety of all company members. This is another area where immediate change should be initiated as quickly as possible.

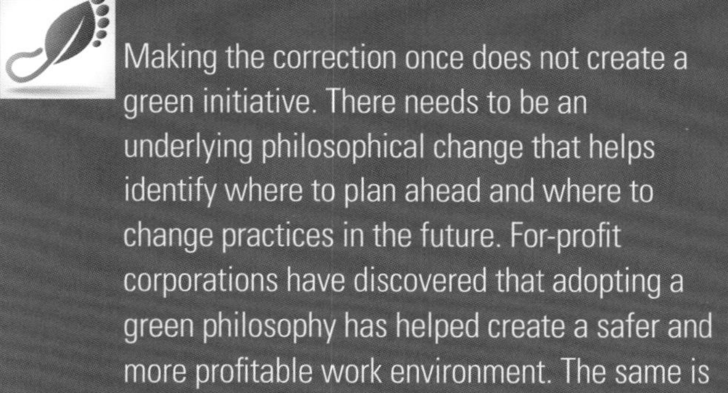

Making the correction once does not create a green initiative. There needs to be an underlying philosophical change that helps identify where to plan ahead and where to change practices in the future. For-profit corporations have discovered that adopting a green philosophy has helped create a safer and more profitable work environment. The same is true for not-for-profit theatre companies.

Taking Stock—Creating an Inventory

Creating an inventory of stock can help with your initial assessment and will become a vital part of your strategic action plan. The creation of a spreadsheet will assist in this process. In some cases a collection of digital photographs may also be helpful, but only if additional empirical information is included with the photos. It does not help to have a photograph of every upholstered unit if you cannot tell if the image is a loveseat or a sofa and have no idea where it is stored or its actual dimensions. Once you have an accurate inventory, it is possible to consider how to reduce use of virgin materials through reuse. This lowers the solid waste stream as well. This inventory will also prove useful later when you start considering sustainability in the design process.

This section focuses on inventory of scenery and lighting. Suggestions for creating and cataloging a costume inventory are in the later costuming chapters.

Scenic Elements and Drapes

Measure flats, step units, platforms, and reusable legs. Your record should include the exact size and base material for each item, as well as the type of covering for each unit if there is a finished surface. Drops and soft goods should be measured and the type of material recorded. Most commercially made drops and masking will include a tag in one corner that indicates the exact material, the size of the piece, the manufacturer, and if the soft good is inherently flame retardant (IFR) or has been treated with flame retardant (FR). If you plan to loan or borrow soft goods, have photocopies of the FR certification available in case proof is required by the borrower. Many corporations that offer FR treatment or manufacture stage drapes send that certification to the office that pays the invoice. If FR certificates are not in the theatre office, check with the accounts payable office or procurement office to see if any are available there. If you have specific data on the service or purchase, the vendor will probably be able to send copies.

You have to remove every piece of scenery from storage in order to measure it for the inventory, so this exercise also offers the first opportunity to cull your stock. Only the useful items should be kept in the theatre's stock inventory. The problem for any company is determining what may actually be useful in the future; that determination is a gamble for every company. These tips are some of the criteria I use when culling scenic stock.

This information should only be used to evaluate what kinds of pieces make good stock inventory. A qualified person on site must determine whether the units are safely constructed and the materials adequate for safe use in the theatre. These suggestions are not a safety evaluation and should not be used to select stock elements without a separate safety assessment of each piece of scenery.

These examples are not a definitive list. Look at the thought process behind these examples to create criteria that supports your theatre's production style. For the greatest success in making the best choices when culling your stock, look back at your assessment of resource allocation and commonly reused types of scenic elements.

Tips for Evaluating Scenic Inventory

- Keep flats and platforms that are a related modular size. Usually these are flats constructed in 1′, 2′, or 4′ widths of a uniform height. That height may be 8′, 10′, 12′ or a mix of these stock heights. Check all flats to make sure they are square—otherwise the units will not join in a smooth line. The diagonal measurements should be equal on square flats or a framing square can be used to check for right angles.

- Muslin-covered flat frames may be salvageable, even if the covering is ripped or coated with layers of paint. Use your best judgment. Anyone of a certain age may remember the days when muslin-covered flats could be washed to remove old paint. Contemporary binders do not normally usually allow for that option unless you are using a power sprayer. If you try this, remember you have to safely dispose of the contaminated waste water.
- Platforms that are regular polygons—squares, rectangles, or triangles—are usually worth keeping. Typically platforms are not constructed any longer than 8′ because that is the size of sheet wood products. Platforms 2′ or 4′ wide are the most useful for a modular scenery stock. Oddly shaped platforms are usually not worth keeping for a long period of time, unless an entire shape can be created—for example four units that can be bolted together to create a half circle. Check the framing to make sure it is not Swiss cheesed from attaching legs in multiple shows. If you find multiple holes in the framing, consider creating a jig, a durable template or pattern that keeps the same action consistent as it is repeated from unit to unit, for legging platforms. The jig allows uniform leg placement from platform to platform and eliminates all extra holes in the platform framing.
- Soft goods that are dry rotted should be removed from inventory. They cannot be reused and will rip to pieces. Don't worry if you are not sure what dry rot looks like; you will know it when you find it.
- While measuring soft goods, track their flame retardant status. There are very specific rules about what criteria theatre drapery must meet for life safety codes. Contact the local AHJ for specific information. Usually the specifics of standards are related to the number of seats in the house and the available fire suppression equipment in the facility.
- Based on these examples, look for units that are well constructed of appropriate materials and in good condition. The units should go together with similar elements to create tight seams and defined angles. These items will become the backbone of your inventory.
- If you have the storage space to spare, do not throw out odd sized units that are in good condition. Keep them to be repurposed into specialty items that must be an odd size for a specific reason or will be treated in a way that would render them useless for future use. For example, if you need a wall textured with scenic dope (latex paint thickened with caulk or some other product) and sawdust, the flats treated in this way will probably not be easily stored after the production. In other words, some waste is going to happen. Work toward using the items that are difficult to reuse instead of pristine elements that can be reused over and over again.

Categorizing and culling inventory is really about recycling and reusing items. There are other areas where we need to make evaluations that focus on energy usage, the impact of production on air quality, and waste water management. In later chapters devoted to the costume shop and the scene shop more specific guidelines for assessing inventory are included as well as tips for storing elements so they are actually reusable in the future.

Lighting and Power Consumption

In Chapter 9 evaluation of energy usage related specifically to stage lighting is more fully treated. However, there are some steps that should be taken to assess energy consumption in the initial assessment process.

This is another area where a baseline evaluation is needed to determine not only how much power you are using but, if possible, what you are using it to do. Ideally an accurate measure of electricity use would be obtained through meter readings over the course of several months. This is impossible if the performance and rehearsal spaces are not metered separately. The lack of submeters makes it impossible to actually measure how much energy the company is using for performances and rehearsals alone.

Look at the options that do not require scientific measurements in this situation. Do a baseline utility assessment like the one described in Chapter 2 where utility bills are monitored over a period of time. The usage is tracked on bills. Talk with the staff of the theatre and get a sense of what is happening when utility usage is the highest. Determining if higher charges correlate to performances, tech week, or rental contracts can help the company know which activities are power hogs.

Work lights and architectural task lighting require as much scrutiny as the stage fixtures. Log which fixtures are used for rehearsals, building maintenance, and general activity. Record how many units there are, the wattages, and try to accurately determine how long they are turned on for specific tasks. Usually these fixtures consume the bulk of the electricity because they are always turned on to full power from a switch and may run any time the building is occupied. The information may be easier to understand if it is placed in a spreadsheet format, but you can use simple math and a sheet of scrap paper.

While this method would not pass muster in the world of scientific research, it does provide a method for reasonably determining energy usage without metering. You can use the same system to determine potential energy savings by swapping out existing stage fixtures for more efficient units. Since metering power use is not involved and stage lights rarely are all on together or running at 100%, you are only assessing potential power use. The carbon calculators described in Chapter 2 also rely on estimated energy use when calculating the carbon footprint of stage lighting so the process is not without precedent. Providing exact information would require you to keep detailed information about the number of fixtures in use, their level in each lighting cue as well as the length of time each cue was up.

Selecting Task and Architectural Lighting

It can be a shock to calculate how many watts house lights consume when they are turned on for rehearsal or work calls. On the other hand, no one wants to participate in a rehearsal when the room is lit like a submarine. Try to determine if lower wattage lamps in work light units would be more effective or if use of a non-lensed luminaire that gives a more even spread of light is a better choice. Closer examination of the situation may reveal that the real problem is a lack of front light for rehearsals. The apparent darkness is enough to cause the cast and director to turn on every light they can in an effort to see from the house. Would the addition of some sort of front light unit that washes the rehearsal area provide more illumination and lead to the use of fewer units?

Computing Your Current Energy Use

- Count the number of house lights including any in aisles or wells that turn on with the main units. All should be the same wattage. In my theatre, I had 60 main lamps and 12 additional units in the entry halls, all lamped at 120 watts. I had six 1000 watt work lights that were used in conjunction with the house lights for all activities other than performance. They all ran at full during work calls and any rehearsals. Total watts involved—14,640.
- The shop was open 24 hours a week for 32 weeks an academic year. Total hours for work regular calls—768 hours.
- Each of the two fully mounted main stage shows rehearsed 20 hours a week for five weeks—an additional 100 hours of use. Once special events and preshow, intermission, and post-show use of the house lights were tallied this number increased to 164 additional hours of use.
- I parked the house lights during tech week to limit the house light use. The work lights were not on during tech rehearsal.
- On average, we were using 14,640 watts for 1,032 hours per academic year before ever turning on the stage lights. When I switched out the 1000 watt lamps in the work lights for 500 watt lamps, that energy usage was cut in half. When I swapped out the 120 watt house light lamps for 24 watt LED direct replacement lamps, I cut the house light system energy use by 6,912 watts.The hours of use did not change, but suddenly the load went from 14,460 watts to 4,728 watts, a considerable reduction in the electrical use.
- A second epiphany occurred when I realized there was as many 120 watt lamps in the lobby as there were in the house. Those were also converted to 24 watt LED lamps.

One option to reduce power consumption in the house and ancillary task lighting is, of course, to switch over to some sort of fluorescent or LED lamp. A direct replacement or retrofit lamp is one designed to go into the existing lamp housing with little or no replacement of any other part of the lighting system. This is the lowest cost upgrade possible. If this is an option, switch over lamps as the incandescent burns out instead of a total transition at one time. A lot of lamps will be involved and a wholesale switchover will leave you with a lot of used lamps with an undetermined life span that will not be used elsewhere.

The more lamps you buy, the more likely it is there will be a few with defects. Ask the distributor if they will replace any lamps that are bad out of the box. Get samples of the lamps to test color temperature, illumination, and light quality. It is also a good idea to make sure the new lamps can be easily installed. I anticipated many different problems in changing over house lights from incandescent to LEDs. The only one we had was the one I never considered. Because of the raked house floor, the lamps at the bottom of the rake had to be installed in the dropped can housing using a pole with a suction cup. The heat sink around the outside of the LED lamp kept it from sitting in the suction cup properly and the increased weight of the lamp made it difficult to direct at the end of the pole. Getting those LED lamps into the housings without losing them from the suction cup required balance, artistry, and terrific coordination.

Lamp efficiency and operation will be discussed in greater detail in the stage lighting chapter, but some basic information will help you make decisions about your task and architectural lighting. The common incandescent lamps that we are accustomed to using have a short life span and convert more electricity to wasted heat energy than visible light. They produce light by heating the lamp filament until it glows or incandesces. This inefficiency has led to the ban of production of many incandescent lamps both in the United States and Europe.

Eventually you may have to find a replacement because the old lamp is no longer being manufactured. The phase out in manufacturing was planned to occur in stages from 2012 to 2014. The commonly used A19 lamp in 100 watt, 75 watt, 60 watt, and 40 watt sizes and PAR 38 lamp in 90 watt, 60 watt, and 45 watt sizes are among the medium screw base lamps (the socket commonly found in your home lamps and fixtures) being phased out. Not every incandescent lamp is being phased out and this is not an exhaustive list of the ones which will become unavailable.

Fluorescent lamps fall into the category of gas discharge lamps that create light in a way that uses less electricity and allow for longer lamp life. Part of that efficiency comes from producing light in a more limited range of wavelengths than the incandescent. The human eye is more responsive to those wavelengths, creating more visible light for the amount of power consumed. This limited range of wavelengths means that these more efficient lamps may not render color as accurately as an incandescent lamp can. In other words, colors may be visually altered in an undesirable way by the lighting. If construction and painting take place in the venue, I would be reluctant to switch everything over to fluorescents for color rendering reasons unless there

Practical Considerations

- Look for direct replacement lamps that dim and fit directly into your housing.
- Ask the vendor if there are any limitations related to housing types that must be addressed. For example, recessed can fixtures may cause the new lamp to build up too much heat, impacting solid state electronics or overall lamp life.
- Look for lamps that include the option of a warm white color. Your audience is accustomed to seeing that color of light. It will allow the new LED lamps to be easily integrated into the house light system while some of the incandescent lamps are still in use.
- Look for LED lamps that offer a range of beam spreads, especially if the house is raked. The further the lamps are from the seats, the less you want the available light to spread out.
- Look at reviews for information about the durability of the product.

is still an incandescent work light option available. Another drawback to fluorescents is the presence of mercury, a recognized hazardous material in both tube and compact fluorescent lamps.

LEDs, short for light emitting diode, operate on a third principle. Light is produced by the activity of electrons in a solid state semiconductor. The LED converts most of the electricity consumed into visible light and has a lamp life that greatly exceeds either of the above products. New LED options enter the marketplace on a continuing basis, so if a direct replacement lamp is not readily available for purchase now, it may be soon. Task lighting will probably use white LEDs which usually show fairly true color.

Some LEDs can be dimmed, perhaps of greatest concern in a house lighting system. When I replaced house and lobby lights it took some time and testing to find an LED product that met my performance needs. The LED lamps I eventually selected were distributed by EarthLED (http://www.earthled.com/). They dimmed on the existing venue dimmers without any equipment modifications. The lamps were available in both a warm and cool white color temperature as well as several different beam angles.

There are few LED lamps manufactured in the United States. Almost all are imported. In situations where purchasing requirements specify domestic products only, there is usually an option that allows import items if a comparable domestic product is not available.

There are many vendors and more products entering the marketplace every month. Expect to spend some time investigating the possibilities and running beta tests with lamps in your venue. LED lamps are expensive, but realize that performance and the quality of the light are as important as the final price per lamp.

If you cannot replace all the lamps in house and work lights there are some other possibilities. One low-cost/no-cost solution is to remove some of the lamps from the fixtures so fewer units turn on when the switch is engaged. You can also install more switches to segregate lighting and allow discrete zones to be turned on individually. If the work lights are conventional stage fixtures operated by the stage dimmers, simply replacing lamps with lower wattage stage lamps will create an energy saving.

Don't ignore the lights that are harder to see during your audit. Take a trip to the grid, fly rail, storage, catwalks, and the booths to count and log the lamps as part of this inventory process.

Assuming every area in the facility must use the same kind of lamp limits your options. Passages and some storage areas can certainly change over to direct replacement LED lamps or fluorescents since visibility, not color rendering, is the primary concern in these areas. There may be work lights on the grid, catwalks, fly rail, and crossover that can be changed from an incandescent source to an equivalent fluorescent or LED unit that can only switch instead of dimming. Maintain adequate intensity for work in each area. You don't want to make a change that impacts the safety of crew or performers by making the area too dark.

Every theatre without a light switch at every entrance should have some kind of ghost light. These should be turned on anytime the space is not in use. They are designed to keep anyone entering from walking off the front of the stage if it is elevated or from tripping over scenery and props that cannot be seen in the dark. Theatre lore says that a ghost light provides lights for all the theatre ghosts in the building and brings the theatre company good luck because the stage is always lit.

While some opt to make a homemade ghost light, a commercially manufactured unit may offer a greater guarantee of safe operation over extended periods of time. For the ghost light to be effective it must be turned on whenever the stage is dark and that can be weeks at a time depending on the production and rehearsal schedule. If you purchase the ESTA Foundation's Behind the Scenes Ghostlight you also support the Behind the Scenes charity. Behind the Scenes, advertised with the tag line, *"Don't Leave Your Colleagues in the Dark,"*

Figure 3.4 The Behind the Scenes Foundation offers a traditional ghost light option. An LED lamp can be used in this model. Image courtesy of Lori Rubenstein, ESTA.

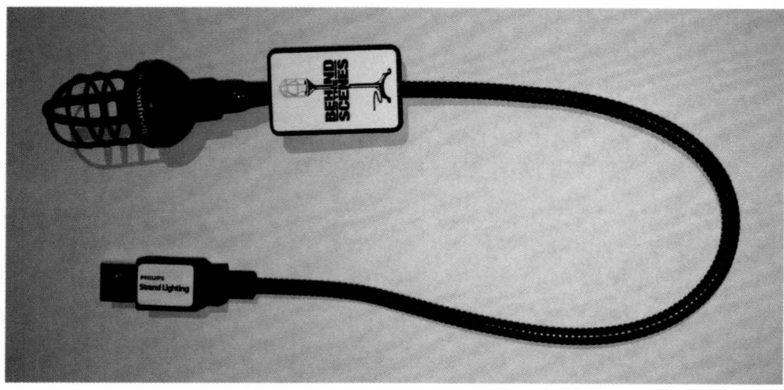

Figure 3.5 Behind the Scenes also offers a USB powered portable ghost light that comes with an LED light source. Photo courtesy of Lori Rubenstein, ESTA.

offers grants to help support industry professionals through crises including serious injury or illness (http://www.estafoundation.org/bts.htm).

The Costume Shop

The later costume chapters include specific strategies that can lead to a more sustainable shop. Use the information from your initial assessment to determine where to focus your strategies to meet green initiative objectives.

Costume shops encompass a number of activities beyond stitching costumes. Millinery, fabric painting and dyeing, shoe repair, make-up design, fittings, laundry and costume repair as well as stock storage may all take place in the same facility. The later costume shop chapters deal with sustainability in depth, but like the other production areas, the initial walk-through assessment can highlight points for attention.

Products that potentially impact water and air quality including aerosol sprays, detergents, and chemicals should be inventoried to determine if more benign substitutions are appropriate. For example, can spray hair color and hair spray be replaced with liquid or gel products that do not disperse into the air? If the costume area is frequently called upon to do craft oriented work, perhaps these tasks can be handled more effectively and safely in a designated space outside the costume shop that is shared with props.

Task lighting in the costume shop and make-up area needs to be cataloged to see if more energy efficient lamps are available for use. Costume shops seem to always be placed in windowless basement rooms. Therefore the need to evaluate and provide lighting control becomes even more important, because artificial light is the only option for most tasks. Because the costume shop may be open during dress rehearsals and performances to accommodate costume changes or any needed repairs, the lights in this shop may burn for more hours than most other production areas. Once the total usage time is tallied, it may be clear that use of motion sensor activated fixtures or adding switches to zone lights and running fewer fixtures at a time is a worthwhile investment. Adding switchable power strips to sewing machines and the work lights at each sewing station can also help limit power consumption.

Historically incandescent lamps have been popular at make-up stations in order to mimic stage lighting. Many stations also use a miniature lamp base socket which makes finding direct replacement lamps problematic. It may be possible to replace existing stations with sockets that will accept medium screw based lamps. The LED marketplace now includes products that provide warm light and a wide beam spread diffused by a frosted bulb. The Southern Theatre in Minneapolis has refitted their make-up stations with these lamps and the performers are pleased with the resulting light. Reducing the ambient room temperature with lamps that are not as hot is a happy by-product of the change.

Inventorying the costume, costume prop, shoe, and hat collection is probably one of the most daunting tasks imaginable. Making sure that storage allows the inventory to remain clean, vermin free, and easily identifiable and accessible is one of the keys to making sure the inventory can be reused. The shape and layout of each facility will determine the kinds of containers that can be used. Like each of the other shops, paths of egress used in emergency must always remain clear of stored items and stacked items cannot interfere with any sprinkler heads in the shop. Part of the walk-through assessment should include examining those specifics to determine if stock must be culled or moved to another room.

Ask the costume shop workers to catalog which tasks take the most time. Frequently the change that makes the work process more efficient is also greener. For example, replacing a vintage washer that uses an enormous amount of water and energy to deal with its small capacity loads can reduce the number of hours used for doing laundry and reduce environmental impact. Purchasing a high efficiency dryer with a steam feature doubles the benefits.

Assessing the Work Process

Sometimes simply following traditional practices without examining current technology leads to added expense and waste. One interesting example is the use of rechargeable batteries. Terry Gips, the keynote speaker at the May 2012 Sustainability in Theatre Conference held in Minneapolis, was stunned by the animated and lengthy discussion generated by a question about whether or not performance microphones could be powered with rechargeable batteries. For years, most companies that used microphones inserted new batteries at intermission in spite of the fact that the original batteries still had power. A number of industry professionals believed that rechargeable batteries were not compatible with use in live performances because of the danger the microphones would lose power during the show. Many participants were only convinced that rechargeable batteries might be reliable enough for a show, once they learned every microphone used at the conference was powered with rechargeable batteries. Thanks to the influence of the Broadway Green Alliance and its campaign to convince Broadway shows to make this switch, major productions ranging from Broadway musicals to Cirque de Soleil are now using rechargeable batteries in show microphones. This story underscores the need to examine common work processes and production practices.

Keep track of wasted resources from a few productions. By wasted resources, I mean materials intended for some aspect of the show that are never used because of some mishap in the execution process or items that are replaced before exhaustion *"because that is the way it has always been done here."* This may be a result of using materials without the structural integrity needed or poor planning so that the project cannot be completed in time to be used in tech and performance.

If unexpected waste is generated by the same task on each show, it may be a sign that volunteers or students do not understand assignments or need more supervision. Examples might range from the five gallons of paint that is muck instead of the warm brown needed for painting the set, the flats that are built 3-5/8" too tall or the stage lamps that burn out because someone touched the quartz envelope. It is easier to keep track of these kinds of errors if everyone understands the log is to discover what action needed to be taken, not to hold people accountable for their mistakes. Workers who are adequately trained and supervised by knowledgeable team leaders make fewer wasteful errors.

Ultimately examining the work flow and process can be as important as looking at the use of raw materials or the cost of the power and water bills. Once these initial baseline audits are completed, the Green Team should return to the initial vision of the sustainability initiative. Your detective work may have revealed information that requires refinement of the company's overall vision and objectives. It is time to start developing both procedural and financial strategies that will allow the company to meet those defined goals.

Funding Sources

How do you finance any sort of upgrades or improvements? Experienced sustainability consultants should be able to direct you to potential resources for financing if you are working with a green professional. Those possibilities may include rebate programs, private or publicly funded grants, low interest loans, or some combination of financing. There are some financial institutions that specialize in loans for sustainable improvements that essentially collateralize the loan by assuming it can be repaid with the utility savings created by the changes. No one can guarantee that your theatre will be awarded a grant or loan. Ultimately the financial history of the organization and how closely the theatre's plans align with the specifics of the grant or loan program will determine that possibility.

One colleague described the search for funding: "*Grant-writing is a big scary behemoth to most people.*" Grant-writing will always be time-consuming and perhaps labor-intensive, but it does not have to be frightening. Grant-writing takes time because it involves research to find the appropriate funding sources and to then gather all the requested statistics and materials to complete the required applications. You don't need to hire an expensive grant-writer in order to craft a strong application, but you do need to remember some key points.

Before you make a grant application, determine if it is a grant that requires matching funds from other sources. If you do not feel the theatre can raise the capital to match the grant funds, there is little point in spending the time on the application process.

Not every option is available in every city or town, but there are some common sources of funding:

- Large businesses and corporations may offer special project funding to not-for-profits, especially those organizations that serve the community in some way.
- Contact utility providers for information on rebates and special programs. Many will do energy audits for free and make recommendations—the caveat; the auditor may not be experienced with theatres.
- Contact state agencies charged with pollution control or energy conservation for information on funding programs.
- Contact local city and state politicians for tips on funding sources.
- Check city, county, state, and federal government sites for potential grants programs.
- Contact private foundations for a list of granting programs.

Be creative in determining whether or not the parameters of a fund meet your goals. Kim Bent, founder and co-Artistic Director of Lost Nation Theatre in Montpelier, Vermont, describes one program:

> *"There's a grant fund administered by the Vermont Arts Council called Cultural Facilities Grants. The total budgeted for these requests each year is about $200,000. Proposals are funded up to $20,000 for improving and up-grading historic public buildings. These are matching grants. Many communities put in*

requests for funding support to modernize the bathrooms in their town halls. However, the program will also fund other up-grades for such things as lighting systems, including the purchase of energy efficient fixtures and theater lights."

Being creative means knowing the criteria used for evaluation of the grant and focusing on those criteria when structuring your proposal. That information will be fully explained in the grant description. Do not apply for funding if the project doesn't meet grant guidelines. You cannot fool a funder into supporting a project that doesn't fit the type of work that they fund.

Many requests for funding, particularly for state grants, have to be submitted in online applications. In some instances, the funding application process is being streamlined via the adoption of a universal platform for almost all state agencies. An online application allows limited space to say as much as you can about your organization and the work you do. Be clear and concise.

Edit your grant writing as you would edit a story; spelling and grammar mistakes reflect poorly on the management of a company that could allow such mistakes to be submitted to a funder. Your web site is an adjunct to every grant you write, so make sure it is up-to-date and informative. Funders frequently look at web sites, often during the process of reading and discussing applications. The web page does not have to be fancy, but it does matter if it does not describe the company effectively or list the same officers as the grant application does.

There are some common elements to most grant proposals. You will almost certainly be asked to explain what makes your organization and its goals unique and deserving of financial support. This is usually described as a mission statement. Make sure your mission statement is strong, accurate, and concise and be certain that the details of your application support that mission.

One staffer at a state arts agency suggested:

"Read your work out loud to eliminate confusing descriptions—some funders do this in closed panel meetings when they find a grant difficult to understand. Share your grant writing with people who are not familiar with the workings of your organization, to make sure the "story" is clear."

Many granting agencies will want information about organizational outreach. These activities may include educational programs, talk-backs, and discounted tickets for certain groups or participation in community events. Many funders expect even small organizations to focus on some aspect(s) of outreach because in the end it's all about audience development, and community integration, an important issue for all arts organizations. If your company is not engaged in these activities now, there should be some consideration of integrating outreach activities in the overall mission of the organization.

Some work examples, support materials, or descriptions of successful projects that fulfilled that mission are usually requested as well. Depending on the agency and the specifics of the grant, documentation may include video clips of a production, production photos, a script, or other documents.

One grant peer panelist offers this advice:

"Unless you are asked to provide evaluative information within the body of the application, don't quote from reviews or newspaper notices. Most funders are trying to use their application processes to evaluate your organization, they don't care what someone else thinks about you (although support materials might include reviews, etc.)."

Almost every funding application will ask if the organization or individual has received other grants and may request an explanation of how money was spent to complete the funded project. This is usually a written narrative. All of this is background information, but it is an important part of the application.

One savvy grant analyst suggests that applicants "storyboard" their applications: He recommends beginning the process by devoting a single sheet of paper to each application question and then—working with others—brainstorming ideas in rough form to answer each question. These pages can then be condensed and organized to complete the final written application.

He is emphatic on some points:

> *"Focus on answering the questions asked in as much detail as possible; don't skew your answers to the perceived strengths of your organization or what you think a funder wants to hear. Your application is essentially an extended elevator speech: cut the excess and give the facts. Don't repeat the same information in different ways."*
>
> *"Funders are usually experienced professionals, so don't insult their intelligence by attempting to teach them about an art form through the application. Stick to the story of your company and what it does. Be specific in your details, and don't use acronyms unless you fully explain them. Don't try to impress your funders; there will always be better, stronger organizations out there. Although there is certainly competition in the grants world, you are competing, first, against yourself."*

He adds:

> *"Don't drop a lot of well-known names in an application; this won't impress funders. But do include the names of artists, however obscure, that work regularly with your organization. You never know who is known by whom. And don't ever answer a question "n/a." Always answer questions with at least a minimal sentence, e.g., "We do not currently use technology in our productions—we lack the capacity for this—but we are working with our technical director to expand the technical capacity of our theatre's resources so that we might soon be able to mount work with more sophisticated technical demands." Funders like to know that you are thinking about how to solve challenges and expand the current limitations of your organization."*

The project proposal is the most significant part of the written grant. In the grant work project can mean anything from a facilities upgrade to a single production. Make sure you frame your proposal in a manner that reflects the parameters specified by the granting organization. Different programs may limit funding to specific individual or organizational projects; others may allow funding to be directed toward general operations expenses or capital expenditures. You will have to state how the funds will be used and indicate how the expenditure meets the project goals.

Pay attention to all deadlines and all application requirements, such as support materials and budgets. When support materials are required, make sure you follow instructions on how to submit them—in hard copy or online. Don't undermine an otherwise strong application by submitting weak or incomplete support materials.

The more specific the information the better the odds of obtaining funds. For example, it is too general to request $10,000 to reduce the carbon footprint of the company. You must indicate each step in meeting the goal of carbon footprint reduction and give quantitative information about how the reduction will be achieved.

A legitimate researched budget for the project is usually required. Documentation for the budget figures, for example bid documents from potential vendors, may be included in the requested support materials. Be sure to include every requested piece of documentation.

One 20-year veteran of a large state agency that funds the theatre offers the following advice:

> *"Start the process early and read all the way through the guidelines for the grant application. The name of a grant category may be misleading and there is nothing more frustrating than completing a grant proposal, only to discover after the submission that your*

organization should have applied to a different program or that your proposed activity actually fits the parameters of another grant category. Private funding sources may have more leeway in determining whether or not a proposed project or activity meets the criteria for a particular grant. Governmental granting organizations are not noted for bending the rules regarding funding criteria and restrictions, especially when taxpayers' money is involved."

She adds, *"The instructions for the grant applications vary between funding entities. If you need clarification or assistance contact the granting organization or sponsor."*

Writing grants may never be fun or fast. Once you have determined the parameters of your sustainability initiative, it may be a necessity to meet your organizational goals. Hopefully this information will help you tackle the project with some confidence.

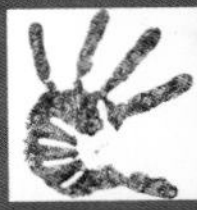

This segment of the baseline audit has focused on technical production areas and the facility. Other areas should be audited as well. The next chapter looks at administrative offices and the rehearsal process. Greening theatre requires a holistic focus that encompasses all participants in the process.

Chapter 4

The Forest View

Non-Technical Areas

Administrative and management personnel are organizational leaders and can be instrumental in supporting a sustainability strategic plan. These individuals also have a direct interface with your patrons and will be a conduit to funnel information about your green program to audience members and sponsors. Greening theatre production goes beyond the stage and shops. Look at every aspect of your operation to see where change can make an impact.

This book is about greener theatre production, so you may wonder why there is a chapter about the areas outside the design and technical theatre arena. Any sustainability initiative has to be embraced by all areas of the company. Administrative offices and the areas outside of production are often ignored in discussions about greening theatre. Anyone working in the main offices, house management, or performance preparation is an integral part of the production process. Without their efforts the company would not exist.

Administrative Areas

Offices

For many small companies or nomadic companies the administrative office may well be in someone's dining room instead of an entertainment venue. Fortunately, green changes are just as effective in a nontraditional setting as in a corporate office. Assessment is always the first step in each area, whether the evaluation is formal or informal. Don't forget to audit the offices associated with all technical and design areas as well.

Once again, Terry Gips, CEO of Sustainability Associates, can serve as an initial resource. He created and publicly offers a checklist based on the principles outlined in the Natural Step Framework. All of these changes are particularly well developed to address the issues in all of the non-technical areas of your company. See the Natural Step Framework checklist he has created for businesses in Appendix A. This checklist can be printed as long as correct attribution is maintained on all the documents.

Take a look around all offices, administrative and production. Start your evaluation by considering these questions:

- Are there recycling bins and are they in use?
- Are bulletin boards papered with flyers and reports that hardly anyone reads?
- Is there a stack of Styrofoam plates, paper napkins, and plastic utensils on the shelf above the microwave and fridge?
- Are mail slots filled to the brim with paper and third class mail that will eventually go straight into the garbage can?
- Are there volunteers stuffing envelopes or addressing paper brochures for the next quarterly mailing?
- How is staff publicizing shows and advertising ticket sales?

Save a Tree or Two

Almost all paper is made of a by-product material recycled in some way at the manufacturing level, although virgin sourced paper is still available. Recycled paper products are now offered that are the same quality as paper that has no recycled content, so there is no reason to not purchase recycled content products. Paper products that are manufactured from post-consumer waste are a greener choice. The higher the post-consumer waste recycled content, the more material that skips the landfill. There are also options to buy paper products that are manufactured from wood products grown in forests and on plantations that are managed with environmental concerns in mind. (See Chapter 7 for more information on forest certification systems.)

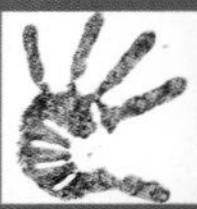

No-Cost Ways to Tame the Paper Monster

- Print double-sided when possible.
- Keep single-sided scrap paper and cut it into scratch pads.
- Use an erasable white board, a chalk board, or even a wall painted with chalkboard paint to post announcements and schedules. Any changes are only an eraser away.
- Recycle paper in the blue bins and avoid using brightly colored paper that cannot be recycled.
- Print documents or emails only if you must have a hard copy for specific reasons. Your staff is probably already receiving emails from environmentally conscious people or companies with this note at the bottom: "*Think about the environment. Please don't print this email unless you require a hard copy.*" Ask them to follow that instruction.
- Reuse envelopes whenever possible. At Lost Nation Theatre, paychecks are placed in onsite mailboxes instead of mailed. On the first payday, company members are asked to return the envelope to the office. Every subsequent paycheck is placed in the same envelope for the rest of the season.
- Any marketing offer that includes an envelope with a clear window and no marking can be reused for your own single mailings or in-house mail.
- Use direct deposit for paychecks and reimbursements. If paystubs are required this may not be possible, but many documents can be provided as digital copies.
- Enroll in online banking to pay bills—this eliminates both the paper bill and mailing the check for payment.
- If your company has investments as part of its endowment, check for online options with the brokerage company or financial advisor. Look for socially responsible funds for your investments.
- Scan any documents possible and use cloud storage as a backup for important information that might be lost in a catastrophic computer failure.

Recycling used paper is a good start, but it is a step not a goal. Controlling paper use is one easy way to limit waste. As always, common sense and specific needs of the task must be considered. Ultimately someone in the office is going to have to use paper for a legitimate reason. It is as inevitable as needing toilet paper in a bathroom.

Some corporate business offices institute a paper audit and track how much paper is used for regular tasks like annual reports, invoices, receipts, etc. Category specific documents are tracked as they move through the organization. A determination is rendered as to whether or not a hard copy is actually required to complete the specific task or share that particular information. If your administrative offices create enough documents, this can be a valuable study. Once that baseline is established, you can create specific goals for reduced paper use and evaluate the success of these efforts.

One caveat on moving toward fewer printed documents: I worked at an educational institution that decided to go almost paperless and put most documents online. Because the changeover was disorganized and chaos ensued. No one could find the significant documents and guidelines needed to perform assigned duties. A phone call looking for the correct file name and location information needed to access the document on the network might or might not garner the correct information.

If you take this step, create a master list that indicates which documents are digital and the file names. Post the master list to make the change to a paper-limited office work and avoid wasting everyone's time.

For smaller companies, the volume of paper created may not warrant this kind of audit or transformation in record keeping. However, in any setting, it is worthwhile to determine the kinds of paper documents currently in use and determine where reductions of printed copies are possible. It is easy to count how many reams of paper are used over a specific period of time and count how often the paper garbage can must be emptied in the same time period. Creating an office culture where people ask themselves if a print copy is required will reduce paper waste.

Beyond the Printer

Various kinds of document management systems are commercially available that allow all paper documents to be converted to electronic media and stored in a fraction of the space yet easily recalled if needed. Cloud storage or some other system backup is a wise choice if converting important documents to computer files.

Free Internet options like Dropbox and those associated with cloud storage systems allow groups to share and collaborate on documents without allowing public access to the files before distribution. Even simple word processing programs can eliminate multiple hard copies for work in progress. Each collaborator should use a different font color or the Review feature to add comments. File names must clearly indicate the revision number. If a check off sheet is included in the file it is even easier to determine who in the group has responded or edited the document.

In the past signed documents required a hard copy. Many software programs like Adobe now offer the option of electronic signatures. If you cannot afford the Adobe packages, less expensive software from companies like Docudesk offer the same capabilities. Make sure an electronic signature is considered legitimate and legally binding for the document in question.

Other options for reducing paper consumption and waste exist in administrative settings. Printer configuration on a network can lead to accidental printing errors, particularly if some of the computer users are in different rooms than the printer. The more options available on the printer, the more likely it is that the settings will be incorrect for a particular print run and the paper wasted. Make sure everyone on the network knows what the print options are, how to change the selections and the selected office default settings. Add a sign that sits on the printer labeled "Duplex On" on one side and "Duplex Off" on the other. We saved a lot of paper and color ink cartridges by communicating the problem to everyone using the networked printer and adding that simple sign. It ended the wasted print runs of double-sided color images that needed to be single-sided for use in design meetings. If there is a choice between black/white and color printing, make sure the standard default is black and white. Everyone who uses the printer should be informed of that choice.

Eliminate the Junk

In spite of the ease of digital communication, many marketing campaigns still rely on printed third class mail. Pity the costumer who is still getting catalogs from the Peek-a-boohoo Lingerie Company two years after ordering a garter belt for a show. Any order with a vendor will automatically add your information to their marketing database unless you opt out. Unfortunately some companies have expanded this practice to snagging your name if you log onto their web page but do not place an order. Once again you will have to opt out to be removed from the marketing lists.

Around 2008 the volume of unsolicited third class direct advertising mail began to be scrutinized by a number of groups. The United States Post Office began offering options to determine which catalogs and advertisements would be delivered to your home if you filled out a choice form online. According to the Direct Marketing Association (DMA) web site, the association announced its own green initiative called *Recycle Please* the same year by including a logo on the third class mail envelope, asking the recipient to recycle the mailed pieces. An interesting note, originally the Federal Trade Commission objected to use of the logo because it gave an "unfair advantage" to member businesses of the DMA that included the logo.

The DMA also initiated *The Green 15*, techniques that it recommended members use to become more environmentally responsible and create a green mission statement. Steps include using recycled content paper products and assessing the environmental management of the source of raw materials used to create the paper for their mailed catalogs and advertisements. Some cynics might suggest that the Direct Marketing Association's goals are self-serving since various *Green 15* documents also point out how many people are employed in the direct marketing chain and that shopping from catalogs and fliers is greener than driving to a store. The DMA is about promoting the businesses it serves and the green suggestions are valid whether you are the marketer or the customer (https://www.dmachoice.org/).

Individual companies that would take steps to limit junk mail for a fee are advertised online. While they probably do a terrific job, individuals can do this for themselves without using an outside business.

Consumers can eliminate junk mail in two ways. Go online to www.dmachoice.org to sign up online or download the land mail registration form from the web page. Using the land mail option does cost $1.00. This service used to be known as Mail Preference. Statistical research from a range of environmental groups suggests that 50% of all mail is still discarded. The best choice is to eliminate items you know you do not want and recycle anything else.

This action will eliminate unsolicited marketing and is intended for domestic not commercial addresses, but is worth a try for your theatre. It will not necessarily eliminate marketing from organizations you have done business with or if you signed up for a corporation's mailing list. Those vendors will have to be contacted individually. You can have each company member take care of his or her own junk mail or assign one person to do the honors.

Given the transition to e-marketing and the use of social media, one would assume the problem of unsolicited marketing would have decreased. The United States Environmental Protection Agency has been tracking municipal solid waste (garbage) for 30 years, including the amounts that go to landfills, are composted, are reclaimed through combustion to create energy, and are recycled. Its analysis for 2010 indicates that 72% of paper waste was recycled. Paper waste was still 28.5% of the 250 million tons of solid municipal waste generated in the United States. Some of that tonnage had to include junk mail. More good news, we are reclaiming more of everything and in general producing far less waste. A visit to the mailbox will indicate whether your office, home, or company is still contributing to the problem.

Magazines and informational mailing from industry colleagues and not-for-profit organizations, while not exactly "junk" mail, can build up just as quickly. Many trade publications offer free subscriptions upon request. Requesting an examination copy is easy. If the journal is not a good match for your interests, cancel the subscription. Contact each organization or publication directly and ask to be removed from their mailing list. This is not discourteous; it reduces waste and saves the publisher money.

Many businesses do not allow employees to have packages, subscriptions, or personal mail sent to the workplace. This limits the number of mailing lists that have the business address. It also eliminates the continuation of unsolicited mail once an employee leaves the company.

Most of us consider this issue a minor annoyance. An organization called Global Stewards (http://globalstewards.org/), an online source for sustainability tips, provides some interesting statistics. According to the organization's web site, 23 million acres of forest area was lost worldwide between 1990 and 2000. Loss of natural habitat is considered one of the biggest factors in extinction of species and plants. Nearly four billion trees worldwide are cut down each year for paper, representing about 35% of all harvested trees. Junk mail produces more greenhouse gas emissions than 2.8 million cars. Over 100 million trees and 28 billion gallons of water were used to produce US mail for just one year (www.globalstewards.org/junkmail.htm), an online source for sustainability tips, provides some interesting statistics. According to the organization's web site, 23 million acres of forest area was lost worldwide between 1990 and 2000. Loss of natural habitat is considered one of the biggest factors in extinction of species and plants. Nearly four billion trees worldwide are cut down each year for paper, representing about 35% of all harvested trees. Junk mail produces more greenhouse gas emissions than 2.8 million cars. Over 100 million trees and 28 billion gallons of water were used to produce US mail for just one year (www.globalstewards.org/junkmail.htm).

Given the potential impact of direct mailings on the environment, the effort to reduce junk mail is a worthwhile venture.

Creative Uses of Junk Mail

If your region includes an active visual arts community, plan a fundraising event around your move to limit junk mail. Invite artists to create works from junk mail and other waste materials. Place the created pieces in your lobby for a silent auction. This publicizes your company's move toward greener production, supports colleagues in the visual arts, and brings in monetary rewards as well. Or you could keep the materials and turn it into scenery if you can properly flame retardant treat it.

Amanda Nelson created the lovely piece *Kinkade* as well as several other installation art pieces from junk mail. While this kind of project is appealing, both as a piece of art and on an intellectual level, it requires as much planning and organization as any typical scenic element. Nelson says, "*It took a great deal of time and layout experimentation to find the visual composition. Then it took even more time and experimentation to figure out how to put everything together.*"

While the entire piece in a long view looks a great deal like a theatre backdrop, it is in fact created of smaller bundles to allow for disassembly and movement of the piece. According to Ms. Nelson, the entire piece of art weighs close to 300 pounds and is currently in individual boxes in her studio. Creating such an element as a lobby feature or a central part of a setting

Figure 4.1 *Kinkade* by Amanda Nelson. Photo courtesy of Amanda Nelson.

Figure 4.2 Detail of the binding of segments. Photo courtesy of Amanda Nelson.

makes a bold statement. Completing this kind of project requires ample time for planning and space for experimentation. However, adding an art piece using recycled paper to the public space in the theatre can create excitement about the sustainability initiative and be a constant reminder of the company's goals.

The Marketing Conundrum

A second facet of the junk mail conundrum is an examination of your company's own business practices. Many theatres have relied on direct mail campaigns to publicize the upcoming season and attract subscribers. You certainly don't want to be guilty of producing the same kind of clutter for potential patrons that you are trying to eliminate in your own offices.

Every theatre company can explore the use of social media for marketing and create digital communication paths with potential patrons. Replacing season brochures with digital media eliminates paper, printing costs, and mailing costs. Web content can be used as an advertisement for the current production by including interviews or video snippets of rehearsals online.

Replace volunteers stuffing envelopes with volunteers creating web pages and using social media. As you move to web-based exposure, check to see if your web hosting company is green. Certainly energy is required, but some web hosting companies like Fat Cow reduce their carbon footprint by using wind energy.

When creating a virtual presence instead of a paper one, consider the impact on customer service. There is a fine balance between making information and tickets available 24/7 and making the patrons feel like it is impossible to make contact with a human.

Post No Bills?

Show posters are strongly associated with theatre productions. At one time posters were as much an art form as an advertisement. Beautiful show posters are holdover of a tradition that evolved when there were few other advertising options. If your company has a web presence and you are using social media to your advantage perhaps that is a place to use digital posters.

If your company is not ready to let go of hard-copy posters and has a multiple show subscription option, consider a single season poster. I worked at a LORT company that created a single poster for the entire season. Unfortunately sometimes the poster had to be designed before the rights to all the shows were secured. A show title might be listed with performance dates and the caveat "or T.B.A." on the poster. If your season dates are contingent on a number of variables or you do not sell a subscription series the full season poster is not an effective option.

The history and strong association of posters with productions make some companies reluctant to eliminate them al together. Assess if posters are an effective advertising tool for your theatre, especially as more business and public areas restrict posting advertisements. Altering the size of print run may be a compromise solution if posters are important to your theatre's culture or identity. How many posters are left after the show to be thrown out? Could you print fewer posters? Can you use smaller posters to net the same advertising effect? If your company makes the hard decision to eliminate posters,

Make Social Media and Other Web Sites Work for You!

- Encourage potential patrons to "like" the company on social media.
- Encourage audience members to update their social media or send out communications when they are at the theatre for a show. Although you may want to reinforce that such activity should only happen in the lobby, the Guthrie Theatre in Minneapolis added specific seating sections for Tweeters during a performance in the 2013 season.
- Post publicity photos on your web page and offer them to anyone writing arts or news blogs in the community. Many web pages now allow you to watermark any photos you post.
- Explore use of blogging, Facebook, Pinterest, Foursquare and Meetup for each show and cast. Are live RSS feeds to your web site a possibility?
- Post videos of show segments or short interviews with well-known performers, directors, or designers on your web page to build interest in the upcoming production.
- If your local newspaper has moved to online circulation because of declining print sales, make sure your advertisements are included in the digital version.
- Consider radio and scrolling marquee advertising instead of hard copy mailings and print newspaper advertising.

share the reasons with your patrons and staff. This move toward sustainability can provide a positive image if the reasons are well publicized.

Low-Cost Options to Reduce Power Consumption

Concerns about power consumption should not be limited to the design and technical production areas. Consider the overall facility power use as well as that of any administrative offices. The production shops may not be open every day, but the box office and business office are probably staffed six days a week.

Transfer utilities to greener options if possible. This may mean moving to a cooperative utility company. When task lighting lamps need to be replaced, phase in compact fluorescent or LED lamps whenever possible. When possible, install a programmable thermostat on any environmental controls to limit power consumption.

Electronic equipment now includes products that are rated not only on energy consumption, but also on how easy it is to recycle the component parts. Look for greener equipment that is EPEAT® (Electronic Product Environmental Assessment Tool) registered when you need to replace electronics. The toxicity of the item, reduced energy usage, and ease of recycling are among the criteria that EPEAT uses to asses electronics.

Limit unnecessary power use. If you walk into a dark room and feel like a bunch of little red eyes are staring at you then there is a problem. Many appliances use standby power so they will turn on immediately. Turning the switch to *off* does not prevent this power draw. Some people refer to this additional power use as *Phantom Power*, which is actually a technical audio term related to powering microphones. It is also sometimes referred to as *Vampire Power* or *Phantom Draw*. Whatever you call it, the option wastes energy. Turn computers, printers, and office lights off at night instead of putting them to sleep. This requires cutting power to the item, not just flipping the switch to the off position. Segregate any electronics by using switchable power supplies or power strips so you do not have to unplug each individual cord. If there is a break room, add switchable power strips to coffee pots, microwaves, and any other appliances other than refrigerators that do not need power all the time. You probably don't need an accurate clock on every small appliance.

A colleague at a major regional theatre told me the company installed power strips for all the computers in the building. The theatre has a large staff and the company was able to see the reduction in its electric bill after taking this course of action.

Consider adding motion sensors to task lighting so that the lights do not stay on when the room is empty. This can be a particular saving in restrooms where lights might be left on for several days if no one is in the building for production work or performances. Make sure the sensors are of a good quality and can distinguish between an empty room and workers seated at desks who do not move around the room.

Vending machines are now available with similar devices called energy miser hardware. The refrigeration remains on to keep consumables cold, but the lights on the machine are turned off unless it is actually in use.

House Management and the Intersection with Patrons

Meeting the needs of your patrons has to be a priority. Make sure choices to be green do not make audience members uncomfortable. The intersection between house management and the patrons may create a balancing act between meeting audience expectations and supporting more environmentally conscious choices.

Paper programs create solid waste. However, you have to offer an option that meets audience expectations. If you are a booking house, there is no way to limit the sale of souvenir programs or control their manufacture and paper content. However, your own company's program can be a more environmentally responsible product. Use vegetable inks and post-consumer recycled stock to create show programs. Think carefully about the paper the program is printed on. Is it an easy-to-recycle paper product? Print fewer programs and collect them from patrons at the end of a performance. Most can be reused for several performances, saving on printing costs and reducing waste.

Theatres with a subscription season and a resident company can easily create a single season program. Some companies will add an insert for each show specifying the cast and creative team and crew. Others simply put all of this information into the initial printing run and forgo the separate inserts. These can be successfully recycled for use at multiple performances. For companies dependent on the income from advertising sales for the program, space could be sold on a season-long basis.

Lost Nation Theatre uses the season programs with inserts. They also create durable printed banners for major donors and show sponsors that are hung in the lobby. The company is well integrated in the community and many donors support the company for multiple seasons. These banners can be used for the entire season and then stored for use in the future. The program can use less paper and even sponsors who sign on after the program is printed are publicized and thanked in a uniform way.

One interesting alternative to a paper program is the "video program." Monitors in the lobby play a loop with show information including a brief spoken biography by each person who would have a biography in a paper program. This creative idea is an interesting alternative. However, unless the lobby is large it can create a bottleneck of patrons trying to enter the venue. If the technology and expertise are available there are ways to tweak this idea and use it in conjunction with smaller paper programs to reduce waste. Some companies have begun experimenting with programs that are available as downloads on patrons' smartphones. Trial and error may be the best way to determine what will work best for your particular audience and theatre. If something does not work as anticipated, you can always step back to the paper programs. Let your imagination be your guide.

Tickets

Figure 4.3 Lightspring/Shutterstock.

Some companies now use e-tickets on smartphones. If the majority of your patrons do not have the technology or there is a problem reading a single phone, a traffic jam can be created in the lobby. Remember the last time you went through security at the airport and someone's ticket bar code could not be scanned? Make sure the front of house staff has a plan in place to deal with this problem until the e-ticket system works seamlessly. The system does work; for example, Berkley Rep in San Francisco uses electronic vouchers and handles all season subscriptions online—eliminating paper waste of letters, brochures, and tickets.

If your company feels it cannot go electronic with tickets, is there some way to reduce waste by using thinner card stock to print tickets? Are laminated tickets that are collected and reused a possibility? Some companies have used clay poker chips for general admission houses that are then collected at the door and reused. Is there a way to recycle tickets that is easy and effective?

Someone has to do the accounting to balance tickets against income so don't make that job impossible. Larger venues and commercial and major regional companies need to have some sort of numbering system to get patrons into the correct seats. However, if you are a smaller company that uses festival seating, consider whether you need any kind of ticket at all.

The Concessions Stand

Bottled Water

One ubiquitous problem with greening theatre and almost any other setting: The plastic bottles of water. This problem of plastic bottled or canned liquid refreshment has been exacerbated by the change in some building codes that allows building owners to forgo water fountains if they provide vending machines or concession stands with beverages for sale. Anyone who has paid any attention to green information lately has seen information about the impact of bottled water. The plastic bottles cannot be easily reused because of the potential mimicry of plastics on some hormones.

They create a huge amount of waste, particularly when people cannot determine which identically labeled water bottle belongs to which person so both the water and the bottle end up being thrown away.

The shift to stainless steel water bottles has begun in some venues. Lea Asbell-Swanger, Assistant Director of the Penn State Center for the Performing Arts, talks about the problem. She says:

> *"We tried buying several large water reservoirs that allowed the cast and crew to refill personal, reusable water bottles. We placed water in backstage areas. The thought was that we would end up with only a few large plastic jugs that could be returned to the water supplier."*

She goes on, "*The test was not successful; cast members still brought their purchased plastic bottles to the theatre.*"

Figure 4.4 Plastic can be recycled, but many water bottles end up in landfills. Some of the water bottled in more exotic locales has to be shipped over great distances to reach the American market. Anibal Trejo/Shutterstock.

Why is bottled water such an issue for sustainability? According to the not-for-profit public interest organization Food & Water Watch, in 2009 almost 50% of the water sold in bottles is from the tap water in a municipal city supply. Since almost 75% of the plastic bottles used for water end up in a landfill, the financial and environmental impact of paying for a repackaged, municipally subsidized commodity seems problematic.

Some companies need income from refreshments to make a profit and audience members usually anticipate bottled water as an option at the concession stand. More than one colleague who attempted to eliminate bottled water from the concession area found that audiences complained bitterly. Lines at

Know What You Are Buying

Ever wonder what you are buying when you pay for that mobility and convenience? The Environmental Protection Agency has created a number of pamphlets called *The Water Health Series* including one titled *Bottled Water Basics* that was originally published in 2005. The EPA sets standards of acceptable contaminants in tap water under the terms of the Safe Drinking Water Act.

The Food and Drug Administration, under the specifics of the Federal Food, Drug, and Cosmetic Act, regulates bottled water as a food product. It applies standards of freedom from contaminants—chemical, radiological, microbial, and physical—to bottled water produced in the United States. Any bottled water originating internationally that is sold through interstate commerce in the United States is held to the same standards. Neither the EPA nor the FDA actually certifies bottled water, but certain language is set by each agency's regulatory standards.

Any bottled water must also include the name and address of the manufacturer, packer, or distributor, and the contents of the bottle. If you like bubbles, be aware that carbonated water, soda water, seltzer water, sparkling water, and tonic water are considered soft drinks, not bottled water, for purposes of regulation so these descriptions are not applicable to those consumer products.

The FDA regulation *21 CFR 165.110(a) (2)* defines the descriptions given to water from various sources. Those terms may mean something different than you assume. For example, spring water describes water from an underground source. It may flow to the surface at the point of collection—an actual spring—or it may be collected through a bore hole to the underground source. Drinking water is any potable water that is sealed in bottles. The only additions to the drinking water may be acceptable disinfectants or fluoride. In other words, you may be paying for water from another community's tap. "Glacier water" and "mountain water" are not regulated terms and may have nothing to do with the location of the water source in spite of the pretty pictures in the advertisements.

State or local jurisdictions approve water sources for bottled waters. The source and the finished bottled water are subject to testing, so the product is a safe choice. You have to decide if it is a smart choice (http://www/epa.gove/ogwdw/faq/pdf/fs_healthseries_bottledwater.pdf/).

water fountains can be long and a single swallow rarely satisfies a thirsty patron in the summer.

One consistently successful option is to keep kegs of water and serve it in compostable cups. Compostable cups can also be used for coffee or other beverages. Mugs or glasses that can be washed and disinfected are a possibility for any venue with a liquor license or bistro in the lobby, but for a smaller company the compostable cups, napkins, and plates are an easier answer. Clearly label the recycle bins for the compostable items to make the process work.

Composting can be handled through an offsite vendor that specializes in the service or by the company itself. Companies based in climates that include harsh winter conditions may not have the option of an outdoor composting site. However, indoor composting using worms is a possibility. Even some university dining halls have managed to install and maintain vermicomposting bins. Companies that specialize in children's theatre or offer backstage tours may find the novelty of worm composting intrigues visitors and sparks educational conversations about sustainability.

Waste from Concession Stands

Every food item sold at the concession stand has to be wrapped in some way, except fruit with a peel. Dealing with that garbage can be another issue. One success Asbell-Swanger had at Penn State was to collect candy wrappers from the audience for recycling. In addition to recycling candy wrappers from concessions purchased at a performance, patrons started bringing bags full of candy wrappers from home. Terracycle is the recycling organization the Penn State CPA works with. Terracycle specializes in Mars candy products and collects a number of other items for recycling as well. Terracycle's web page, www.terracycle.net/en-US/brigades/candy-wrapper-brigade.html, explains all the options. Terracycle is not the only organization that offers not-for-profit companies fundraising opportunities through recycling. Look online for other possibilities.

Look for Fair Trade coffee and organic treats for the concession stand. Consider limiting the number of food items available and make sure the garbage cans, recycling, and composting bins are clearly labeled. If catering for special events is a regular practice, look for a food service specialist that serves organic food and uses compostable supplies. Attendees recognize this reinforcement of the company's commitment to sustainability and it can offer a unique twist to fundraising events.

Some theatres, both commercial and not-for-profit organizations, which have liquor, beer, or wine licenses, depend on that income. Making a move from throw-away containers and plastic cups may be a huge logistical step. However, the earlier audits should have indicated the impact this choice would make and indicate if the results are worth the effort.

Restrooms

The audience members are guests in our theatre home and we need to make accommodations for their comfort and health. Examine choices for cleaning and personal care product in all facilities. Can you switch to unbleached recycled toilet paper and paper towels in the restrooms? Are low water use toilets and waterless urinals in place? If not, can you add a brick to the regular toilet tank to limit water consumption? One Minneapolis theatre, Brave New Workshop, includes recycling bins for the paper towels in its restroom facilities.

Is the soap in the restrooms biodegradable or some artificial antibacterial detergent loaded with chemical fragrance? According to industrial hygienist Monona Rossoll, fragrance is one of the least regulated and most potentially harmful chemical products in our daily environment. Can those expensive timed air freshener sprayers that take the breath away be replaced with more natural and environmentally friendly products? Containers of baking soda are one possibility and when the powder no longer absorbs odor, it can then be used as a cleaning product.

Eliminate artificial chemical based, fragranced cleaning products whenever possible. Don't fall into the trap of assuming anything labeled "green" or "natural" is a better choice. Many consumers are willing to pay more for products labeled organic or green, and big business has exploited the opportunity. Greenwashing is the term for labels that imply a more sustainable product but have no defined, regulated meaning. The problem is so prevalent that the Federal Trade Commission is improving guidelines about what claims can be advertised or included on product packaging. Changes in the FTC Green Guides include specific standards for what commonly used language like "recyclable," "nontoxic," and "compostable" really indicate about a product. Until terms like these are regulated, there is no standard meaning assigned to them and no process to verify if a product can legitimately use the description.

Baking soda and white vinegar are safer to use and everyone who made a volcano for their fourth grade science project knows to not use them together. Can your staff say the same thing about knowing which chemical cleaners can or cannot be used together? Apply these choices to all restrooms including facilities in the dressing room and green room.

Engage in preliminary research to make your choices. Commercially made cleaning products may be more convenient to use; just make sure the packaging is easy to understand. MSDS (or SDS) sheets are available on most products. Although the manufacturer or distributor is only required to make these documents available for employers to provide for workers, you can ask for them as a consumer. There is a way to find a balance between a clean and sanitary bathroom facility and using more earth friendly products.

A Word on Commuting

Travel of individuals has a tremendous impact on the environment and it is a problem area for every business, including theatres. This environmental impact of commuting is so significant that some states have even passed laws asking employers to encourage their workers to use public transit (http://apps.leg.wa.gov/rcw/default.aspx?cite=70.94.521).

Unfortunately, only communities with public transportation, sidewalks, and bike lanes can encourage individuals to leave the car at home. Some companies have offered ticket discounts for mass transit commuters. Providing a bike rack and allowing patrons to check bike helmets for free is another possibility that may encourage human-powered transportation.

Some companies and academic institutions have made financial arrangements with regular public transit providers to provide free rides for employees with proper identification. Others allow employees to buy discounted vouchers or passes for public transportation with a regular paycheck deduction. If your company is part of a larger organization it may be able to take advantage of this policy and have it encompass theatre ticket holders as well. In some cities a transit card for the rehearsal period and run of the show may be part of the show staff's compensation, particularly in nonpaying showcase situations. Remember, someone is paying for those seats on the bus, even if it is a discounted rate, so try to incentivize use of the public transit choice by accommodating bus and train schedules for your employees.

You can use social media and your web page to make public transit easy to use. Tourists or patrons who live in outlying neighborhoods may be unfamiliar with the public transit options where your theatre is located. In addition to showing maps, driving

Public transit options are more attractive if curtain times are selected to allow patrons and production personnel to easily catch the train or bus closest to the theatre. Even the most ardent environmentalist will have reservations about standing outside in the rain or snow to wait an hour for the next bus during off-peak hours. Another option is to leave the lobby café or bistro open long enough that patrons can wait in the lobby, lingering over a cup of coffee, instead of standing outside. However, balance the cost for paying staff to stay later for clean-up, especially in a unionized venue.

directions, and parking information include clear instructions on how to use public transportation to travel to the theatre. Include walking directions from the bus or train stop using street names and landmarks that are easy to spot after dark. When describing turning points use left and right as well as compass headings. Links to transit company schedules and any special instruction about how to purchase the fare ticket will help eliminate concerns about using unfamiliar modes of transportation. Car traffic contributes to environmental concerns. This problem cannot be fully addressed unless other convenient and safe options are available, a particular issue in rural areas and small towns.

Take a Look Outside

Contamination of runoff water from parking lots is also gaining focus in environmental stewardship. Several major theatres in urban areas have begun to address these questions in different ways. Lincoln Center in New York City has added a series of retaining pools that filter runoff water in natural ways. The courtyard fountains use this grey water and the water features add a contemplative and tranquil feeling to the area even when it is crowded with patrons. In settings with more car than foot traffic, similar natural filtration through retaining ponds has been added to deal with runoff from parking lots. A legitimate assessment of water runoff issues requires the expertise of a professional architect or building planner.

It is possible to make some changes that create a pleasant environment for patrons and have the added value of helping to protect the environment without the input of experts. If your theatre is a freestanding building it may include some lawn area and decorative plants as well as concrete walkways and seating areas. Think about what keeps that greenery alive and looking good. Is a lawn service spraying chemicals? Does the lawn require irrigation? As drought conditions spread to areas that have never had to deal with water shortage issues, water conservation is becoming a focus of sustainability. Can native plants or slow-growing native grasses that require less maintenance be introduced into these areas to limit chemical dispersion and the need for watering? If there are only small grassy areas, can the grass be replaced with rock gardens that require no watering or chemical intervention to prevent weeds or pests?

If public areas are littered with cigarette butts or garbage, experimentation to end this sort of litter may be in order. Addition of garbage cans or a recycling bin outside the building may be required or the existing receptacles may need to be moved to encourage use. Cigarette filters are more problematic. They are particularly harmful to birds and other wildlife. Whatever your feelings about smoking, realize that simply banning tobacco is probably not going to stop smokers from disposing of cigarette butts. Decide if the company is going to keep the area clean, or offer an alternative other than the ground.

Your investigation of environmental impact by the theatre should include the areas outside the building as well as the ones inside. Look for a balance between creating a pleasant atmosphere and manicured appearance that also supports your sustainability initiative.

The techniques described in this chapter should be applied to both administrative operations and production offices. As the company creates its green strategic plan, make sure any goals include the non-technical areas of your theatre company.

There is a third group that needs to be invested in the greening process: the performers and stage managers. The next chapter looks at greening the processes where those members of the company are involved.

Chapter 5

The Cast, Stage Managers, and Crew

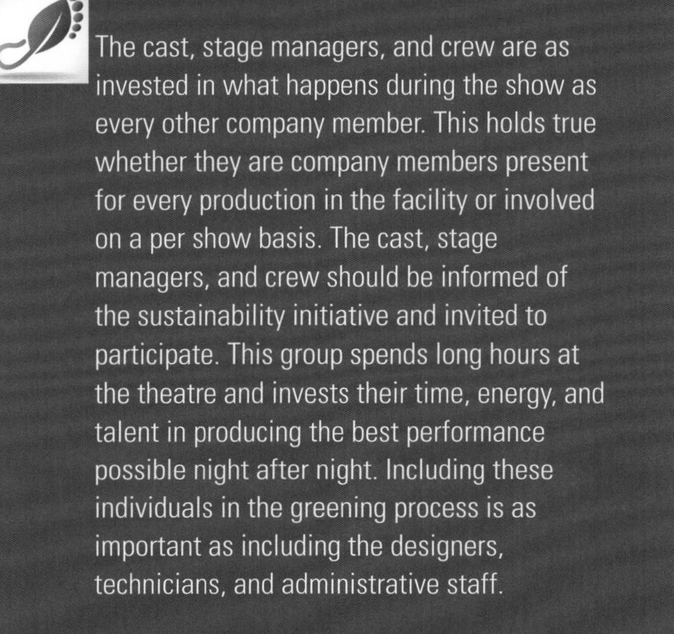

The cast, stage managers, and crew are as invested in what happens during the show as every other company member. This holds true whether they are company members present for every production in the facility or involved on a per show basis. The cast, stage managers, and crew should be informed of the sustainability initiative and invited to participate. This group spends long hours at the theatre and invests their time, energy, and talent in producing the best performance possible night after night. Including these individuals in the greening process is as important as including the designers, technicians, and administrative staff.

Recycling at the Theatre

The baseline waste audit has already given you some idea of how much waste is recycled. The "night shift," the cast, stage managers, and performers, may create a larger population than the people working behind the scenes on a given production. Securing their participation in the recycling program can have a tremendous impact on the amount of solid waste diverted from the landfill or incinerator. Recycling is an easy step to take and it is an even easier step to skip. At the end of a long rehearsal it can be tempting to avoid the extra 20 steps to the recycling bin because the contribution of a single can or bottle to the recycling seems insignificant. Publicize the potential impact of the cast and crew's contribution to the sustainability initiative.

After I began a sustainability initiative at one university theatre, I was continually surprised to find beverage cans and bottles in the regular garbage cans. Cast members left the stage after rehearsal by walking through the scene shop to exit the building. They, and the shop workers, were contributing drink containers, coffee cup lids that were recyclable plastic, and paper to the regular garbage cans, even when recycling signage was placed directly above the garbage cans.

I mentioned my frustration to colleague Erika Bailey-Johnson, the Sustainability Officer. She and some Environmental Studies students had done a physical audit of the paper and container recyclables mixed with garbage in one of the most active classroom buildings on campus and made some interesting discoveries.

They created an initial baseline analysis by counting recyclable cup lids and weighting recyclable containers and paper mixed in the garbage. They then made faculty and staff announcements and posted maps to recycling locations and did another audit. The percentage of recyclable material mixed with garbage was lowered. More recycling/garbage stations were added and some garbage-only containers removed from sites with heavy traffic. These simple changes led to an even lower percentage of mixed materials in the garbage when a second audit was completed.

The audit was repeated for three subsequent years and the percentages of recyclable material in the garbage remained reduced or even lowered each time. Publicized results of the waste audit raised the awareness of recycling options in the building. Maintaining stations that included recycling and garbage cans reduced the chances that someone would throw everything in the same can.

I noted through observation that the number of garbage cans on the path from the stage to the exterior door made it easy for people to ignore the option of recycling personal items. When the actors or carpenters were tired at the end of the day (or night) there was always a garbage can nearby and it was much easier to use that conveniently located container than to walk across the room to the recycling bins. When we moved the garbage cans away from the major traffic paths and added a single recycling bin close to the primary exit, recycling immediately improved.

Incidentally, I discovered the reverse was true for paper recycling. If the recycling bin for fiber and paper products was next to the garbage can, office workers separated trash and recyclables. When I separated the two containers, requiring the worker to step outside the office door to use the recycling receptacle, everything was thrown into the closer trash receptacle. Even though the can in the hall was less than ten feet away, no one walked out the door to use it.

The lesson from all this—if no one is doing the easy stuff like recycling cans and paper, try new techniques and bin locations to see if the volume of recycling grows. Make it easy for everyone to contribute to the greening process.

Prior to Performance

We tend to associate greening efforts with scenery and costume construction activities, saving energy and water in building operations and reducing the carbon footprint of stage lighting. The audition and rehearsal process are also an integral part of production and should be studied as closely as any other activity in the theatre.

The first phase is actually the pre-rehearsal period during the audition and casting process. The director, the stage management team, and hopeful performers are in the facility for extended periods of time before the show is actually cast and rehearsals begin. Starting to think about sustainability at this point will make it easier to keep things greener after the show company is formed and rehearsals begin on a regular basis. Think back to the 2008 carbon calculator cited in Chapter 2—even script printing and distribution for auditions should be considered in the greening process.

The second phase prior to performance is the pre-technical rehearsal period and the final third phase is the technical rehearsal, dress rehearsal, and preview phase of show development. Many opportunities exist in all three phases to limit the amount of solid waste produced by the company and cut down on energy consumption.

Auditions

Contact sheets and copies of sides are a part of the audition process even if an outside casting director is involved. In most situations the performers will provide résumés and headshots. The theatre will provide forms for the hopeful performers to list contact and availability information as part of the audition process. Normally a stage manager or an assistant will supervise the traffic of the auditioning performers. If a laptop is made available, it is possible to create a document that can be filled in on the computer by those auditioning. This needed information about each individual performer can be captured digitally and saved. A great deal of paper is eliminated and this choice offers consistency in the information gathered. Ask one of the assistant stage managers to supervise the process to insure that every copy of the document is in fact saved after it is filled out.

Post information about the company's green initiative and make it clear that the goal to move toward sustainability is not limited to the construction areas. Let auditioning performers indicate interest in serving on the theatre's "Green Team" on the same form where they indicate availability. If the cast understands that this is a long-term goal, they can become a part of the effort.

Auditions always require some printed material. Even if information is captured or sent digitally and the casting and stage director take all notes electronically, some items will probably have to be printed. Sides or script pages may be printed out for cold readings, especially in a school setting where students may not have a prepared audition piece. Limit the number of copies, use paper with 100% post-consumer recycled waste content and, once these pages are printed, file them and reuse them in the future.

The Rehearsal Period

Typically we approach the early rehearsal process and the technical rehearsals with a single-minded focus on whipping the

Some other steps to green the audition process include:

- Use dry/erase boards or chalkboards to communicate information and sign up performers in audition slots.
- Offer recycle bins for any beverage containers or paper waste.
- Schedule auditions so public transit is an option if it is available in your city.
- Offer to send scripts out as electronic files for initial reading if you are waiting for actor's editions from one of the publishers. Don't print out dozens of copies that will eventually be replaced by a bound printed version or thrown out if someone reads it for the audition, but is not cast.
- Indicate on the cast list that initialing not only indicts acceptance of the role, it indicates an understanding that communication will be digital and the performer is expected to check email for updates. I recommend using an email format only so broadcast emails can be sent out to everyone in a single action. Relying on texting takes up too much of the stage manager's time and energy.
- Do you want to collect paper headshots and résumés, or can the director rely on digital photos taken at the audition?
- If the ratio of performers auditioning to performers cast is high, it is worth measuring everyone and digitally recording the information along with a photo in an e-file. It saves travel and time for initial measurements by the costume shop.

Spend some time brainstorming with performers and crew for other ideas. They see what happens in the space at that time, usually long after most of the staff has left for the day. Their insights may bring a whole range of ideas to the table that would never be considered otherwise.

show into shape for opening night. Hours can be long and tiring no matter how much joy everyone takes in the creative process. It is the rare company where most of the participants do not have other demands on their time and energy. This ranges from the school theatre where both teachers and students must attend classes and meetings to meet the obligations that continue outside the production process to the company where almost everyone also has a day job from 9 to 5.

Even the company members who are actually employed full-time by the theatre have other obligations. Perhaps they are rehearsing one show in the daytime and performing another at night or finishing the designs for one production while in tech rehearsals or previews for a different show. Someone has to take reservations, put together the program and sell sponsorships, arrange for concessions, and complete grant applications to meet deadlines. With all of these distractions as well as the intense experience of creating a character, directing a production, or executing a design it is small wonder that sustainability is not a major focus in the rehearsal process. It is time to add sustainability to the list of concerns we associate with rehearsals.

Most engage in the rehearsal experience using the process learned in the early days of our theatre career. We cannot give a thought to how to apply our green initiative to rehearsal and tech period if we wait until we are in the process. There are too many other things that require our full attention in order to create a quality production. The solution is to take some time to consider areas that can be greened and make plans for change before auditions and rehearsals. Organization and communication are the keys to achieving this goal. Planning ahead also allows you to share any procedural changes with the company so members can make adjustments.

Company members who work another job will be eating on the run. Create a recycling station on one side of the stage with a receptacle for bottles and cans, one for fiber products, one for recyclable plastic ware, and a garbage can. Food is going to end up in the garbage can unless you are also composting, so make sure the trash is emptied daily. If you are serious about going green, request that no one bring in food in Styrofoam containers.

Encourage everyone to obtain a stainless steel water bottle that can be refilled or gift everyone with a bottle sporting the company logo. Individuals can label their bottles and you can sell additional bottles to the audience during intermission.

Figure 5.1 alexmillos/Shutterstock.

A lot of unneeded paper is generated during the rehearsal process. Even if you exclusively use 100% post-consumer content recycled paper, you can be even greener by limiting the amount of paper used. Some easy to make changes that can reduce the page count include:

- Send call lists and rehearsal schedules out via email or use Virtual Callboard. For this to be successful contact sheets must request email addresses and company members must know they are required to check that email address several times a day for important notices.
- Post the call sheet and costume fitting appointment lists on an erasable board. Make sure everyone knows where to look for these announcements and how last minute announcements are to be made.
- If the costumer and stage manager plan to text any late breaking changes, they need cell phone numbers and the cast members need to know to check their phones for this information.
- Many directors give cast members notes at the end of rehearsal, either passing out individual pages or reading his or her notes as performers scribble down the comments on note pads. This requires a fair amount of paper and can extend rehearsal time if notes are lengthy. If you are encouraging company members to use public transit, they have to know exactly when rehearsal will end. Is the director willing to send rehearsal notes via email to the individual cast members?
- If the work is a world premiere rewrites are inevitable. Look for a way to get the rewritten pages to everyone with less printing.
- Determine who needs specific design and technical plates and print those in an appropriate scale for the task. For example, the stage manager might want to borrow one large scale printout from the scene shop to tape out the floor, but prefer smaller 8.5"x11" printings to record blocking in rehearsal. Or the stage manager may be able to take notes in a PDF with a tablet or laptop since Adobe allows writing on the documents.

Sustainability During Tech Week

Lighting and sound level set, first tech, and dress/technical rehearsals can be long and tiring. Even if everyone performs his or her assigned tasks flawlessly, the process is time-consuming. The performers are faced with a range of new distractions including the stage going dark and it is the first time the stage crew, board operators, and fly personnel have rehearsed their tasks. Take the time to make a company announcement explaining any changes that will be instituted during tech week to green the tech rehearsal process. New company members will not have specific expectations of the agenda, but veterans of past productions will expect business as usual unless they are informed about changes. Tech week involves a number of people with different primary agendas for the time spent in the theatre. Consider each group and where they will work as you develop strategies for introducing sustainability into the technical rehearsal process.

Techniques to Consider

There are many documents that do not necessarily need to be printed in multiple copies. I served as scene designer on a multi-scene production with a lot of props changes. A clever assistant stage manager put a single flow chart on each side of the stage for the props crew. She then took pictures of each person's props onstage area with her cell phone. She sent the pictures to the crew member so s/he could take a quick peek right before the shift. In the past, a common technique for documenting television show set dressing in the environments that were used in each week's episode was to take a Polaroid photograph. When the set was put into place again, the crew could reference the Polaroid to ensure continuity in the look of the set. This use of a phone camera was a modern update of the old Polaroid practice.

Figure 5.2 Stage Manager Spencer Clouse prepares for technical rehearsals. Photo by Jessica Pribble.

To reduce the amount of water wasted in mopping the floor, find ways to limit the number of times mopping must occur. One of the easiest techniques is to provide a place for the cast to store rehearsal shoes—these don't have to be costume accessories—just shoes that they have not worn outside in the weather to get to rehearsal. As long as the performer changes out of street shoes before stepping on stage, you can limit the amount of dirt. This is particularly effective during the snow season where slush and salt or sand are tracked on stage or during any rainy period where dripping water and muddy footprints make the stage floor slippery for performers. If no one needs to lay on the floor or goes barefoot as a character, sweeping without mopping will keep the floor actor-friendly for several days.

Don't waste energy through unnecessary use of the lighting rig. Hopefully some thought has been given to finding an energy efficient solution for work lights. If rehearsals still require work lights and house lights to be run through the control console, create a single cue that is used exclusively for the rehearsals before tech week. If the console is newer and has features that allow parking dimmers, assign the work lights and house lights to a submaster after they have been parked at a reasonable level below full.

During tech week the light board operator may want to turn on the preset as soon as the channel check is complete so he or she can leave the booth and not return until places are called. Usually this occurs long before the house would open and the preset would be turned on. It wastes energy, uses up lamp life, and may fade darker color media over time. Make sure the stage manager calls for the preshow preset just before the house opens and the rig lights are not turned on before that time except for channel check.

During tech week some rehearsals will be stop-and-start processes instead of a smooth run through. At any time there is a pause to work out some technical aspect, to make a blocking change or work a bit, turn on the more efficient work lights and turn off the stage fixtures. Sometimes the pauses are brief, but over the course of the tech week—especially the 10-out-of-12 day—the energy usage adds up. Remember that not only the electricity used for the fixtures is involved. A full rig at a bright setting can raise the room temperature forcing the cooling system to use more energy.

If performers are using the theatre lobby as a secondary green room, make sure those lights are not left on all day or night as well. Make checking those switches a part of the stage manager's procedure to lock down the venue after rehearsal.

One way to keep the cast, stage managers, and crew engaged in the green initiative is to ask to elect an onstage Green Captain for the rehearsal and run period. The Broadway Green Alliance (BGA) developed the idea of using a Green Captain on shows. Each Captain brings the issue of being greener to other company members. They can also access the experts at the Broadway Green Alliance if anyone has ideas about green issues or questions about sustainability. At this point all of the shows running on Broadway have a Green Captain and they are being added at off-Broadway houses as well. At the USITT 2013 Conference in Milwaukee the Broadway Green Alliance announced its new College Captain program. Schools can sign up to participate and each College

Stage Manager Tech Week Checklists

For the Cast

- ☐ Use an erasable board for the costume grief list and call lists in the green room or make-up room.
- ☐ Provide pump hair spray and hair color to limit the use of propellants in the air.
- ☐ Only put lamps in the make-up mirrors actually being used or use LED direct replacements to reduce the heat generated.
- ☐ Avoid perfumed soaps or air fresheners and chemical cleaners in any confined space that the performers use.
- ☐ Keep heat down in the make-up area by ironing and steaming clothes in a separate room.
- ☐ Use LED lamps to provide adequate lighting that does not generate heat for any quick change areas and to light props tables and pass throughs that the performers use during the run.
- ☐ Provide a place for the cast to store deck shoes so they can change out of street shoes before going on stage during rehearsals and warm ups.

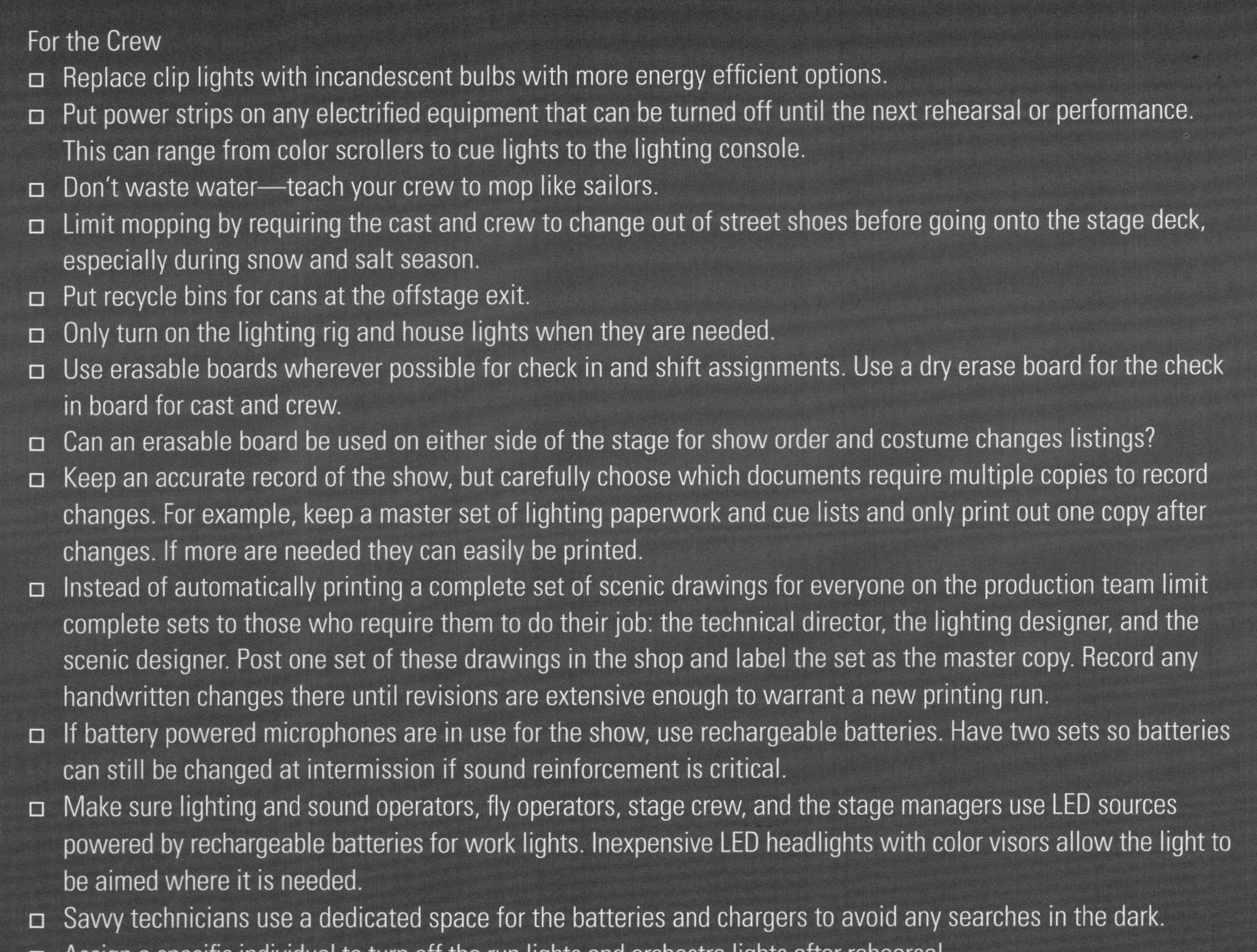

For the Crew

- ☐ Replace clip lights with incandescent bulbs with more energy efficient options.
- ☐ Put power strips on any electrified equipment that can be turned off until the next rehearsal or performance. This can range from color scrollers to cue lights to the lighting console.
- ☐ Don't waste water—teach your crew to mop like sailors.
- ☐ Limit mopping by requiring the cast and crew to change out of street shoes before going onto the stage deck, especially during snow and salt season.
- ☐ Put recycle bins for cans at the offstage exit.
- ☐ Only turn on the lighting rig and house lights when they are needed.
- ☐ Use erasable boards wherever possible for check in and shift assignments. Use a dry erase board for the check in board for cast and crew.
- ☐ Can an erasable board be used on either side of the stage for show order and costume changes listings?
- ☐ Keep an accurate record of the show, but carefully choose which documents require multiple copies to record changes. For example, keep a master set of lighting paperwork and cue lists and only print out one copy after changes. If more are needed they can easily be printed.
- ☐ Instead of automatically printing a complete set of scenic drawings for everyone on the production team limit complete sets to those who require them to do their job: the technical director, the lighting designer, and the scenic designer. Post one set of these drawings in the shop and label the set as the master copy. Record any handwritten changes there until revisions are extensive enough to warrant a new printing run.
- ☐ If battery powered microphones are in use for the show, use rechargeable batteries. Have two sets so batteries can still be changed at intermission if sound reinforcement is critical.
- ☐ Make sure lighting and sound operators, fly operators, stage crew, and the stage managers use LED sources powered by rechargeable batteries for work lights. Inexpensive LED headlights with color visors allow the light to be aimed where it is needed.
- ☐ Savvy technicians use a dedicated space for the batteries and chargers to avoid any searches in the dark.
- ☐ Assign a specific individual to turn off the run lights and orchestra lights after rehearsal.

Green Captain will be given a list of environmentally friendly practices that can be easily and immediately implemented; many are already used for Broadway productions.

If the company members elect a Green Team for their show or a College Green Captain joins the Broadway Green Alliance team, the entire group become engaged in the idea of sustainability and may start generating solutions. Look at a greener strategy developed by a student stage manager at Texas A&M described below. Maybe the cast, stage managers, and crew for your shows will be as inventive.

Photo courtesy of Madison O'Brien.

Figure 5.3 Madison O'Brien.

Almost Paper Free Stage Management: A Case Study

It is possible to reduce the paper used in stage management. Madison O'Brien, a senior in the Department of Performance Studies at Texas A&M University in College Station, TX, did just that for an academic research project.

Ms. O'Brien had stage managed 20 shows using the more traditional approaches so she was well versed in the process of stage management and had a clear understanding of the responsibilities associated with the work. In her project proposal she describes the role of stage manager:

> *"Stage managers provide centralized communication, organization, people management and task coordination in a theatrical environment. This study explores the advantages and disadvantages of new technology use in production. By using various forms of technology both made specifically for stage managers and adapted for a specific task I will judge how effective or in-effective various sectors of technology are at achieving their intended task."*
>
> *"A stage manager's job includes streamlining communication throughout the rehearsal and performance process, making announcements via e-mail and a callboard, revising scripts, and recording everything that may need to be referenced in the future by any member of the production team. The job description can be summed up as "central communicator" in that every piece of information is at some point passed through the stage manager, documented and sent to the respective persons."*

Since Instructional Assistant Professor Justin A. Miller joined the Texas A&M faculty three years ago, the Theatre Department has included a focus on sustainability and greening theatre production. Clearly this influence has expanded to the student body. Ms. O'Brien's experiment is one example.

Ms. O'Brien plans to pursue stage management as a career and had taken every available opportunity to learn more about the profession. She had never seen anyone attempt this process on a production beyond the casual statements made in passing about trying to reduce paper use in the production process. When asked why she decided to attempt this Herculean task, she answered:

> *"My interest first stemmed from the use of technology in stage management. Since with the realization that everything was becoming electronic it was obvious that eliminating paper would not only be green, but helpful to expand the boundaries of technology use as well."*

Her goal in the project was to both find green solutions and to assess if any of those options were detrimental to the stage management process of the show, *Prelude to a Kiss.*

The show was mounted in spring of 2012. Ms. O'Brien spent several months prior to the show examining options and experimenting with various technology solutions. As in all greening initiatives, organization and planning is a key to success. Two of the online resources she accessed for information are www.broadwaygreenalliance.com and www.smnetwork.org.

In addition to using the expected options—social media and email, Ms. O'Brien experimented with various iPad applications including ShowTool SM, iAnnotate, Time Calculator, NoteTaker HD, Pages, Numbers, and AutoCAD WS. She also subscribed to Virtual Callboard, an online resource she learned about at a regional USITT conference. It only costs $29 a month and does not require a long-term contract.

The process was almost paperless. I was particularly curious about how auditions and taking blocking notes were handled in a paperless process. Ms. O'Brien admitted that she was not able to eliminate paper in those two settings.

She explained that she had not yet begun her research on the technology when the audition process occurred. She added that she was not certain she wanted to eliminate paper at that point since the directors need that information for reference, particularly résumés and headshots. In the future she may try to keep contact sheets and all other information that is for her needs in electronic files, perhaps using a secure web site or email to collect the data.

She also discovered rather quickly that she was unable to use an electronic script to record blocking. Her preferred technique includes the use of symbols and abbreviations which was impossible without a hard-copy script. She also points out that the research project did not eliminate the need to do her job effectively even if there were technological mishaps. Therefore her assistant stage manager created a complete production book with hard copies of all up-to-date paperwork.

She was able to run the show completely on an iPad or Mac computer from the beginning of tech rehearsal through closing night. This eliminated the need for paper contact sheets, sign-in sheets, cue sheets, and reports.

Additional time was required to make sure all documents were up to date on the iPad. Cues for tech were loaded electronically and color coded in digital files. O'Brien relied on the MacBook during technical rehearsals to make any changes in cue placement or calling since the iPad uses a PDF reader that cannot be edited. During the run she switched to the iPad for calling the show.

Like any experienced stage manager, Ms. O'Brien also made contingency plans. She says, "*My assistant had a hardcopy script with all the cues on hand, but also carried my laptop and chargers so there were three alternative plans if technology failed.*"

Some additional expense is required to attempt this mode of stage management. Virtual Callboard has a modest monthly subscription fee. The iPad or other tablet may be an additional expense; however a reliable laptop or even desktop could be used to call the show if there is room in the booth. The time involved in transferring information into the computers could be mitigated by using a Dropbox program or cloud storage to speed up syncing information across computer platforms. For the experience to be successful, it also requires that the entire cast and crew have access to email, the web, and social media and are disciplined about accessing information frequently to find updates.

However, the process can eliminate a great deal of paper waste over the course of a season. Once the company is familiar with the process, it will be easier to use for each subsequent show.

Someone is probably thinking, is this really more effective than simply recycling the paper use in production? There is always an equation to be analyzed to determine the best course of action. Electronic equipment eventually faces its own disposal problems because of the potentially hazardous materials used to create computers and tablets. There is also a use of energy, although less than what is used to produce, transport, and recycle paper. Ms. O'Brien's experiment proves it is possible to dramatically reduce the creation of paper waste in theatrical production. It is an example well worth following if a theatre is committed to greening the production process. She did state that unless she found a better way to record information in a blocking script she would not be ready to try this process without backup. However, as more people test the technique, any flaws are sure to be addressed through experimentation and special app development.

Bold experimentation helps determine the validity of new ideas in greener theatre production. Each success creates the foundation for the next new idea.

Now that you have a deeper understanding of the issues involved in balancing sustainability and creating theatre, it is time to begin identifying strategies for change. Part II focuses on solutions to achieve both artistic and environmental goals.

Part II

Identifying Strategies for Greener Production

ASE/Shutterstock

Time to Make Greener Choices

Expanding our knowledge base about which construction techniques are environmentally friendly and what products are manufactured or harvested with conservation of natural resources in mind allows us to green the production and design process. Don't wait until the drawings are completed to consult with the technical staff and craftspeople building the show. Each individual's specific expertise may help find more sustainable choices as the visual elements evolve.

Take the process one step further and consider sustainability in the earliest conceptualization phase in order to balance the artistic needs of the show with environmental concerns. The season production calendar should reflect this desire to create more sustainable theatre by including time for the creative team to research and sample new materials and explore options to reuse existing stock. Selections that reduce use of virgin resources, reuse the existing inventory, and allow both whole elements and base materials to be recycled after the run are the greener choices.

Whatever choices you select, make sure they serve the needs of your particular company and make the best use of the available human and financial resources.

Chapter 6

Greener Scene Design

The Cradle to Cradle Philosophy

Most of us have been trained to view almost everything as disposable, from beverage cups to television sets. While the number of repair shops with skilled employees has diminished, the prices of repairs have increased. The more technology involved in how a product works the more difficult and expensive it is to repair. The easiest solution, and frequently most economical choice, is to throw it out and buy a new one.

Pundits have many theories to explain why this mentality is inculcated in the Western perspective. Some claim corporations have increased their profit margins by designing consumer products for obsolescence; instead of focusing on quality and product longevity to build a consumer base increased sales will come from replacement sales. Others blame both the overt advertising and the subtle marketing campaigns that encourage us to consume more and replace any item, even if it still functions, because it is no longer cutting edge.

Whatever the reason, all this consumption leads to waste that impacts both the environment and our wallets. Statistics from numerous sources suggest that almost 80% of most new purchases end up being thrown away by the consumer within six months. According to EPA statistics in 2010 the average American produced 4.43 pounds of garbage every day and recycled approximately 1.51 pounds of that total amount. Certainly any packaging for the new product ends up in the garbage immediately, but these statistics include everything from disposable coffee cups to tires to sofas to food scraps to plastic bags. The good news is that the percentage of solid waste recycled is actually an increase over past records (http://www.epa.gov/osw/nonhaz/municipal/pubs/msw_2010_rev_factsheet.pdf). Mentally review your own behavior over the last six months and see if experience supports these contentions.

The impact of buying new items is threefold for most consumer products—the impact of obtaining the raw material; the power to manufacture and transport the new product; and the waste when the old and new items are discarded. Whether the waste ends up in a landfill, is poured down the drain, or is incinerated, there is an environmental impact that in turn can affect nearby residents and local ecosystems.

Simply sorting items and placing them in blue bins at the curb does not totally address the problem. What most of us think of as recycling is, in fact, downcycling. Breaking down a product and reusing the material to make a new similar item would be true recycling, e.g. almost all glass that is recycled can be reclaimed and reused to make more glass.

Too often materials we think we are recycling are downcycled. Instead of being recycled in a manner that makes full use of the material, downcycling is the repeated reuse of a material in ever degrading forms that are recognized as being of inferior quality and less useful.

One of the most often cited resources that examines this question is *Cradle to Cradle: Remaking the Way We Make Things* by William McDonough and Michael Braungart published in 2002. The title makes reference to the term "*cradle to grave*" that is used in manufacturing to describe the lifecycle of a particular product.

The philosophy of sustainable design that is brilliantly described in the book centers on the ultimate goal for products to be produced in such a way that the source materials are not thrown out or downcycled in ever degrading forms. McDonough and Braungart advocate designing goods to avoid this practice. This is a "*cradle to cradle*" rather than a "*cradle to grave*" approach.

McDonough and Braungart recommend that technically based products, items that do not use biological raw materials, be manufactured in environmentally friendly ways and designed using products that can be reused or reclaimed for the fullest reuse. If the materials used for a product are not biologically based then the raw materials should be endlessly reusable in the current form to close the loop to the grave. They go on to suggest that in an ideal world, biologically based items should be made in a way that allows them to eventually be returned back into the ecosystem lifecycle and return to the earth. The entire concept of "waste" is questioned when design is based on these principles.

This is not a suggestion to stop recycling any materials. It is a call to look at whether or not there is a material that can be truly recycled instead of downcycled. Recycling is more than sending your products to a recycling facility; it also includes buying recycled products or reusing materials and resources instead of purchasing new whenever possible. The ultimate goal should be to close the loop and, instead of continuing to create waste, reusing all of the raw material or allowing it to decompose to the point that it returns to earth and contributes to the creation of new resources.

Almost all environmentalists, whatever their background and training, are calling for a mind shift that begins at the design phase for all products and buildings. This philosophy can be applied to theatre design as well as commercial and industrial design. Many of the raw materials used to create theatre are biodegradable; wood, natural fabrics, manila rope. Our most sustainable choice is not to simply make sure we use recyclable or biodegradable materials. Reuse is even more effective than recycling and can be facilitated through the construction materials and techniques we select. Reuse requires less energy and eliminates the need to dispose of or downcycle materials.

Greening theatre requires selecting raw materials that meet our production needs but are also recyclable and/or have been responsibly manufactured or harvested. It also means making choices that involve the fewest components that are potentially harmful to the environment and the people working with them. Finally, it means using a design process that uses the fewest new resources and eliminates the need to rebuild or remake elements or repaint the set because the design was not well thought out initially.

The greening process should not be limited to waste reduction or diversion from the landfill at the end of the run. Greening begins before the design and rehearsal process starts and involves all facets of the production.

Theatres need to adopt a "*cradle to cradle*" philosophy in order to become more sustainable. Like the commercial manufacturer, we must start with the design choices that support opportunities to reuse, reduce, and recycle. This plan will be reinforced in every segment that deals with design and execution of the design: scenery, costuming, and lighting.

Approaching the Design

This book is not a design text. There are a number of terrific books about the design process for scenery, lighting, sound, and costuming on the market and should be referred to if you need an in-depth discussion of design. What follows is a quick review of the major steps in the design process that will serve as a review.

- Start with the base of the performance piece. This may be the script for a drama or the score, libretto, and book for a musical. In dance, the choreography and music are the foundation. If you are working on an improvisation piece, performance art, or an organic piece of theatre, the concept may be the point of origin. Layers are added to this foundation as the director and designers discuss the piece and craft the message the performance should transmit to the audience. Eventually a production concept or message is developed.

- Engage in research and artistic exploration to develop the visual elements of the show. The conceptualization and exploration period should involve considering a range of visual options and focusing on the elements of design: line, color, texture, value, contrast, and shape instead of specific pieces of clothing or structural elements. Move from the evocative to the concrete instead of the reverse.
- Once the ideas sparked by collaborative discussions have coalesced, begin to work toward a more concrete design by sketching costumes, making scenic models, selecting sound samples, or creating visual graphics to support lighting ideas. It is only at this point that the physical needs of the design are articulated to accommodate the concept, style, and stage business of the piece.
- Imaginative design involves finding solutions that support all the preceding steps instead of relying only on the specifications given in stage descriptions of an acting edition. For example, the need for an entrance does not necessarily require the presence of a conventional door or the audience may understand levitation of the actor if the horizon line is obscured instead of actually flying the performer.
- Multiple meetings should be held to allow the design team, technical director, and staging director to discuss ideas and choose a specific design path. During this phase the overall visual concept is usually selected and designers move forward to create final designs. Ultimately these choices will support the needs of the performers and directors in the presentation of the piece as well as creating visually interesting images that support the overall theme and concept of the production.
- This collaborative process facilitates completion of the designs and starts the discussion about how to execute the designs within the resources available.

Less Paper, More Art

In the assessment section it was suggested that you keep track of how many pages of drawings really need to be printed. This can allow you to save on paper. The early creative process is one area where an enormous amount of paper may be used for communication of ideas. The design and the director or choreographer need to look at visual ideas to settle on an ultimate direction for the visual elements, part of the creative exploration process mentioned above.

Before easy access to digital information and color printers, this early process involved a lot of sketching and dragging heavy stacks of books into the design meetings to share imagery. I believe sketches and books are valuable communication tools and that designers should use them for design discussions. I am less sanguine about the new wave of Internet research that usually involves a lot of color prints to share imagery because a lot of that paper ends up in the recycling bin. Internet research has its place in design; but don't forget that books are still fabulous research tools as well. Designers who use web research can easily limit the number of hard copies used in early design discussions.

I frequently use PowerPoint to put together digital visual imagery, particularly initial exploratory visual ideas for my designs. This format can be easily shared with the rest of the creative team and any assistants. I can add comments on the images or in notes and so can anyone who wants to respond to something in particular. Anything from the web can be integrated into the presentation. In cases where members of the creative team are in different cities, the presentation can include scanned images of original work.

The other team members can view the PowerPoint at their convenience. The files are quite large so it may not be possible to email them directly to colleagues. There are free large file email services that allow you to send a download link to the recipient via email. The files can also be distributed with file sharing programs.

Once refined and updated as the design progresses, the presentation becomes a handy way to make design presentations to a large cast. At that point I also present the model, sketches, or renderings to the cast in conjunction with the PowerPoint. This technique can also be an effective tool in academic settings for design students working on paper projects for a class.

Other paperless options for sharing early visual communication engage social media. Pinterest allows users to attach visual images to digital bulletin boards. Web pages with the icon of a red pin in a box have a direct link to Pinterest to allow this pinning process, but almost any image can be added manually. Pinterest users can "grab" visual images from anywhere on the web or their computers and pin it to a specific board. Here is the social part of the media—any Pinterest user can view any other user's bulletin boards unless security is initiated to make the board invisible. Any Pinterest user who can see the bulletin board may pull images from it to repin on their own bulletin board or download, so I suggest not adding original art work to a bulletin board. The bulletin board creator can designate other Pinterest users who may pin things on a specific board, so that only the creative team may add pictures. Pinterest users can follow someone's board, similar to the way one selects to follow someone on Twitter. This keeps the follower posted on changes or additions to the images.

Each designer can start boards of images for a show. Since the number of boards is unlimited there can be a board per location, per scene, per act, or per character depending on the designer's needs. It is easy to start out with conceptual or abstract graphics that offer a range of disparate options supporting the production concept. The director or choreographer can easily grab and repin images to her board to indicate favorites and the entire production team can share ideas and art without being in the same room and without using a single piece of paper.

The Pinterest option can be applied in any design class as well. Students can use it to put together visual toolboxes or reference boards representing major movements in art, architecture, decor, or fashion. Completed projects can be presented in a smart classroom without printing anything. Pinterest is a great way to create an aggregate of visual information from a variety of sources. Each user can decide on the best way to document sources for imagery that might be further developed.

Another option for early communication uses the social media Delicious. Delicious organizes bookmarks using the list owner's specified tags. It can be used to share research from online sources. Once a user creates a Delicious account, later operating platforms like Windows 7 and Window 8 include a button for the tool bar that allows easy uploading of bookmarks while on the Internet. The bookmarked lists can be shared with any other Delicious user. Keeping track of attributions and citations from web-based sources can be much easier using Delicious, including keeping track of the sources used for any of the images that are kept on Pinterest.

> The collaboration process is the point where the designers and technicians should start making decisions that allow for reuse of existing stock and materials.

This is the time to plan the development of any newly constructed elements in a way that allows them to be created with reuse of the materials in mind. That may require an evolution in how the production team thinks about the design process. The entire creative staff has to buy into this reuse philosophy. Some team members can be fearful that a policy of promoting the reuse of stock items will somehow diminish the creativity that will be used to address their specific show. Integrating this philosophy at the design phase avoids asking someone to change his existing design to accommodate reuse. Approaching the design with both creativity and sustainability can serve a production as well as more traditional processes.

One advantage to adopting a collaborative production approach is the inevitable reminder to everyone that their contribution is a component of the greater whole, which in turn creates a more cohesive production. At each phase of design development the members of the creative team are encouraged to go back to the production concept and find the nucleus of the ideas that support the show.

This collaborative design process requires allocating an adequate period of time for the design and rehearsal process, well before the date for loading into the venue and starting tech rehearsals. When designers and directors are rushed in the development of a show, there is too often a tendency to adopt solutions that center on an initial idea or image. Flexibility to explore all of the options that might support a production concept in a unique way is abandoned in the name of expediency. Thoughts of reuse and repurposing are tabled in order to accommodate a truncated design and execution period.

This model is better served by having all of the designers be a part of the production concept and design development discussions from the first meeting. Otherwise the late hires are placed in the position of only being able to respond to, or even forced to work around, their colleagues' completed designs in other areas. Their options are restricted to what will work in the context of the already existing designs, which in turn may limit the options available to the director or choreographer.

Designers that have embraced a strategy to reuse stock elements or repurpose viable options from stock will have the time to develop their particular design with that goal in mind. I want to emphasize, again, that this doesn't mean that their artistic vision will be compromised or the design will be cut rate. This is not a suggestion that if the company is producing *Man of La Mancha* and the set designer wants an oversized dungeon door that she use the standard screen doors from *On Golden Pond* instead because they are in stock. However, if she peruses the physical inventory while she is still thinking about how the dungeon doors should look, an option may present itself. In my case it was 2′6″ wide x 10′ tall intricately cut out screens that had been an element in a production of *Cabaret*. They became the shutters for the dungeon doors and the rest of the dungeon door element was designed to incorporate them. Leftover pieces also made nifty panels for use in the church scene of the story.

Providing a complete and accurate inventory for designers is the first step. Ways to ensure that various stock items are reusable are specifically addressed in the following chapter. Many of those techniques center on construction choices in the execution of a design and selecting reasonable storage methods that allow access to undamaged components. Some examples of stock inventory include: Existing costumes and costume accessories, properties, gel color and lighting fixtures, scrap lumber from other productions, and stock scenic elements. Your inventories created in the early assessments provide a catalog of materials and already constructed elements available for reuse.

Designers and directors must always work within some unchangeable parameters. These may be the budget, the available labor resources, the production calendar and its integration with major holidays, or the configuration of the performance venue. The goal to reuse stock inventory or build items for deconstruction is simply one more parameter that has been added to the mix.

Many scene designers work in sketch or rendering format. While the ideas are presented in a fashion that suggests the three-dimensionality of the stage setting, they are usually not yet drawn in scale. At some point either a model or a floor plan and section in scale will have to be created to allow execution of the design. Other members of the production team need the information as well. The stage manager needs a scale floor plan to paint or tape out the footprint of the performance space in the rehearsal area. The director needs to know where entrances, exits, and furniture are located in order to fully block the show. The lighting designer needs scale drawings in order to create her light plot which places instruments in the venue to light the production.

The technical director or construction crew chief also needs scale drawings of the footprint and height of all scenic elements in order to build the set and place it in the venue. Architectural elements like a proscenium arch and venue amenities, including stage draperies for masking, must be integrated into the scale drawing for the setting to be placed on stage as the individual elements are attached to one another.

Your particular production process model will determine whether designs are fully completed before the technicians and crew chiefs executing the designs become involved. In some cases, the designer also creates all construction and technical drawings. Many of the construction specifications are determined in those drawings. In other theaters, the designer hands off the model, floor plan, and section to the technical director or shop foreman for the creation of working drawings. The third possibility is that those responsibilities are shared between the two positions. Whatever the production model, bringing the technical director into the mix as soon as possible will help facilitate reuse of existing elements and choosing greener construction materials.

Linking Sustainability in Development and Execution of the Design

Let's use scene design as an example for the integration of design and execution. Once the set design has progressed to this point it is possible to prioritize what aspects of the design are non-negotiable and which can be altered in size, finish, or style to allow creative reuse.

A Technical Director's Perspective

Technical Director Paul Brunner:

> *"Theatre is an exciting undertaking that often draws in people out of the pure joy, fun and gratification inherent in the process. Producing a stage production is also a serious endeavor with real costs and environmental impacts. The technical director has an important role to perform as to help create and support greener theatre."*

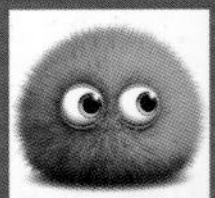

Engaging the Technical Director in the Design Process

Careful technical planning and construction allows for greener scenery construction. Under the purview of the technical director or technical production leader, the planning process should develop and include these key steps:

- The entire production team, including representatives of the scene shop, should take part in early conceptual meetings. The technical director and designers should work very closely to communicate the design, construction expectations, operation and movement of scenic elements, and types of scenic finishes.

- Everyone on the team should consider how stock platforms, flats, stairs, and other scenic and costume elements can be reused from previous productions. The technical director can support this effort. These elements can be more artistically incorporated into a design at this early stage in the process.
- Once a reasonable amount of information is available, the technical director and/or designer should create a preliminary cost estimate for the entire set.
  - Create a simple list that contains the number of sheets of wood products like plywood or hardboard, pieces of dressed lumber, and hardware like hinges or brackets. Count doors, molding, and any other specialty elements.
  - Multiply cost per number of unit type and a rough estimate will result.
  - Reused materials can be brought into account in this preliminary estimate. Eliminate the quantity of reusable materials from the cost equation. The cost savings of reusing materials quickly becomes evident to the entire production team.
  - Use this cost analysis review where there are other alternatives for reuse that can be sought.

Investigating Materials for Scenic Construction

The technical director is often the resident expert on materials and their uses. This is ever more important in greener theatre endeavors. If it's the job of a scenic designer to create scenery in a more sustainable manner, it is incumbent upon the technical director to have greener solutions for materials and construction processes. This is no small task. Because construction materials come from an enormous range of sources, a technical director must investigate what materials are available to them given their particular geographic location. Those closer to large metropolitan areas may have a much greater range of products available to them, while theatres in more remote locations may be at a disadvantage for obtaining unusual products. However, materials that are locally sourced are greener than materials that must travel great distances.

All of this work and communication is vital to providing a careful analysis of the set and materials within it. This is detailed work that requires time. It is best to provide at least several days, if not a week or more, to allow the technical director or design team to analyze the scenery and look for the best materials. Rushing the process almost guarantees a greater waste of time and materials. Professional scenic studios engage in this process constantly, and without it projects are more expensive and more mistakes are bound to happen.

Choices on execution of the design may be shared between the designer and the shop staff or it may be the job of the technical director to gather materials based on the specifications laid out by the designer. Thorough consideration should be given to the materials used in the construction of stage scenery. It can be a daunting task to meticulously research and assess potential construction products for sustainability and suitability. For a company without a permanent technical director, a dedicated space for a scene shop, and a committed core of technicians, the idea can be overwhelming. Make initial decisions about what kinds of scenic elements best serve the company and then evaluate the sustainability both environmentally and financially of particular materials.

It is possible to use almost any material for scenic construction; scenery can be constructed using materials ranging from retrofitting another company's old scenery to grabbing cardboard from the recycling bin. Imagination is the only limitation and many artists cite the use of unique salvaged materials as an example of "Reduce, Reuse, and Recycle." Most experienced designers and technicians agree that there may be issues centering on safety related to structural integrity or the ability to add effective flame retardant to some salvaged items. Be certain to consider these concerns when reusing materials.

Traditional construction materials used in scenery built from scratch for stock or use in a specific production offer some advantages. With new material, you know the source and should be able to determine its structural integrity. When scenery is constructed in a more uniform fashion it is easier to mix stock units with newly built pieces.

The traditional methods of scenic construction actually originated with companies planning to build a stock of possibilities for their shows. Theatrical performances were produced for centuries before anyone decided to build specific scenery for a specific show. These techniques offer a level of consistency that makes it easier to reuse pieces over and over again.

How to Choose the Best Materials

Determining the sustainability of a particular choice of material requires consideration of several factors. Initial considerations might include whether the material is from a renewable source that is created or harvested in a responsible fashion and whether it is possible to recycle or reuse the material if the scenery is not saved intact. Other considerations include how far the material has to be transported to reach the shop and if it is safe for the workers and the environment when the product is used to manufacture scenery. For example, does it create harmful particles when cut or toxic fumes when sprayed or heated? Is it difficult to dispose of the scrap material and does the product lend itself to being used up or is a great deal of unusable scrap created in the construction process?

The building trades have long been assessing construction materials for the amount of embodied energy to determine the sustainability of a particular material. Most sustainability writers describe embodied energy as the amount of energy that is required to obtain, create, and transport material.

This concept is sometimes further broken down into measurements of the initial indirect and direct embodied energy. The indirect embodied energy is a measure of the energy consumed in obtaining the raw material, transporting it to the location where it will be refined, and any manufacturing process energy required. Transporting the material to the consumer as well as the energy required in construction is measured to determine direct embodied energy.

If energy is required to maintain or repair the material once it is constructed into a building, architects and contractors usually describe this as recurring embodied energy. Sometimes the amount of energy consumed in recycling the material is also assessed and added to the total measure of embodied energy represented by materials. Determining which material is the greener choice can be daunting once the number of potential variables are considered.

Fortunately there is an available resource to help designers and technicians make more responsible choices. *Mo`olelo Green Theatre Choices Toolkit* is a 24-page document that evaluates and rates a range of commonly used theatre construction materials. This valuable resource was developed by Mo`olelo Performing Arts company in San Diego (Seema Sueko, Executive Artistic Director) through the A-ha! Program: *Think it, do it*, funded by Met Life and administered by Theatre Communications Group, the national organization for the American theatre. Mo`olelo Performing

Arts Company is happy to share its 24-page Toolkit. To request an electronic copy, complete the form on the web site at: http://moolelo.net/green.

The research and analysis for the ratings was conducted by Brown and Wilmanns Environmental, LLC (www.bw-environmental.com/index.html). According to Executive Artistic Director Sueko, the metric used to rate materials considered the following information:

- The Resources—this assessment includes embodied energy and ecosystem impact related to manufacturing or obtaining the material. Energy and water requirements and generation of waste were considerations. This was the most heavily weighted consideration.
- Human Health—this assessment is weighted less heavily and focuses on human health and safety during construction and interaction with the material during the run of the show. It also incorporates consideration of the impact throughout the material's lifecycle from cradle to grave.
- End of Show Fate—this assessment is also a sub-impact area and analyzes the material's end of life fate including the potential for recycling and any environmental impact if the material is disposed of after the run of the show.

Materials in the Toolkit are rated 0–4. The scale designations are:

4—Exceptional material
3—Good material
2—Material with as many negative as positive attributes
1—Materials with below average environmental and/or health and safety issues
0—Material should be avoided

See pages 000–000 to view three sample pages from the Toolkit. These pages illustrate the show the layout, rating system in use, and the specific information about each rated product. The example pages are the first page from three different material classifications that were rated. The entire document is more comprehensive and the printed sample represents a small percentage of the information contained in the entire document. Take the time to contact Mo`olelo Performing Arts Company for the completed Toolkit. It will be a tremendous asset in greening your production process.

The *Mo`olelo Green Choices Toolkit* is a reliable resource that helps jumpstart your knowledge and application of greener materials for performing arts it should not replace research into local and regionally specific materials that may not be included in the document.

Mo`olelo Performing Arts Company

Mo`olelo Performing Arts Company, self-described as a community-focused, socially-conscious, Equity theatre company with a commitment to represent a diverse range of voices onstage, began to address the issues of greener theatre production in 2006. On the organization's web site page titled *Green Mo`olelo* Executive Artistic Director Seema Sueko writes:

> *"... in 2006 we started realizing that our socially-conscious operations conflicted with the reality that theatre, as it is traditionally practiced, can be damaging to the environment. From the woods, paints, dyes, and energy used to the seasonal nature of theatre, our industry is consistently creating toxic waste at a high rate with each production."*

Mo`olelo addressed this issue by developing a green initiative in January 2007. One of the first steps was to create the *GREEN Theater Categories and Sustainable Guidelines* through consultation with Leadership in Energy and Environmental Design (LEED) accredited professional Preeti Gupta.

The company wanted to have a greater impact. In fall 2008 Mo`olelo received the MetLife/TCG *A-ha! Think it, Do it* grant to develop a tool to measure the environmental impact of production. In partnership with Brown & Willmanns Environmental LLC Mo`olelo developed the *Mo`olelo's Green Theater Choices Toolkit*. The Toolkit was completed in December 2009 and because it is freely given to requesting theatre companies it has been in use by theatre across the globe ever since.

Mo`olelo has continued to break ground in the arena of sustainable production. According to Ms. Sueko, in 2012 the company focused on creating a metric system to measure the environmental impact of each production. Spearheaded by Board Vice President and LEED accredited professional Alison M. Whitelaw and with consultation of LEED accredited professional Jeff Barr, they monitored the last two productions of that season and tested a pilot program that tracked the environmental life of all the materials used in production. Documentation included a record of the origin of the materials and how they were dealt with at the end of the run. Whitelaw states, "The notable result of this analysis was how much reuse of materials from other sources was involved in the construction of the set and how much diversion of materials from the landfill was achieved." Many items were repurposed or returned to inventory for future reuse.

Mo`olelo plans to refine the tools this season. The hope is that it will eventually be made to available to other companies and be as widely adopted as the *Mo`olelo Green Choices Toolkit*. Look for updates about Green Mo`olelo at http://moolelo.net/green/ to remain informed about their pioneering contributions to more sustainable theatre production.

Wood Products Scorecard

Score	Item	Pros and Cons
4	Wood products with recycled (PCR) content greater than 75%	+ Using wood products with a high recycled content reduces waste and greatly reduces the environmental and human health impacts related to the use of virgin forest products
4	Forest Stewardship Council (FSC) certified woods	+The Forest Stewardship Council (FSC) is recognized worldwide as an independent organization that establishes certification and labeling standards ensuring the sustainability of the management of forest products. Other parties certify forest management and/or wood products to the FSC standards. In addition to virgin wood certification, FSC standards are also available for recycled wood products
4	Cork	+Cork can be sustainably harvested in a low impact manner
4	Reclaimed wood or wood products	+ Reusing materials is even better than using materials with recycled content as there are almost no impacts related to the reprocessing of the materials. This reduces waste and greatly reduces the environmental and human health impacts related to harvesting and processing wood products
4	Homasote	+Homasote is a brand name generically cellulose-based fiber wallboard. Homasote is made up of recycled paper which is compressed and held together with a small amount of non-toxic PVA glue
3	Wood products with recycled (PCR) content between 10 and 75%	+ Using wood products with a moderate recycled content reduces waste and greatly reduces the environmental and human health impacts related to manufacturing virgin materials
3	Sustainable Forest Initiative (SFI) certified	+The Sustainable Forest Initiative (SFI) is an independent certification and standard setting organization focusing on U.S. and Canadian forests and ensuring that wood products are from well managed forests; originally established by the American forestry industry -On some issues SFI standards are less stringent than FSC
3	Canadian Standards Association (CSA) certified	+The Canadian Standards Association (CSA) is similar to SFI and focused exclusively on Canadian wood harvested from well managed forests -On some issues CSA standards are less stringent than FSC
3	American Tree Farm System (ATFS) certified	+The American Tree Farm System (ATFS) focuses on certifying the forestry practices of non-industrial private landowners in the U.S. -On some issues ATFS standards are less stringent than FSC

Mo`olelo Performing Arts Company is a participant in the A-ha! Program: Think it, Do it, funded by MetLife and administered by Theatre Communications Group, the national organization for the American theatre.

Glass, Ceramics, Earthen Materials Scorecard

	Item	Pros and Cons
4	Glass, ceramics, and mineral products with recycled content greater than 75%	+ Using materials with a high recycled content reduces waste and greatly reduces the environmental and human health impacts related to manufacturing virgin materials -None
4	Unfired clay products	+ These materials have very low resource requirements and envronmental impacts - Mining on very large scales for these clays can have a negative impact on local habitat
3	Glass, ceramics, and mineral products with recycled content between 10 and 75%	+ Using materials with a moderate recycled content reduces waste and greatly reduces the environmental and human health impacts related to manufacturing virgin materials
3	Beverage bottle glass (clear, brown, green)	+ These types of glass typically have a high recycle content which means that the mining impacts and energy requirements for producing virgin glass is reduced -Glass manufacture requires a significant amount of energy to melt raw materials for making glass; use of recycled glass in making new glass reduces the energy used in the manufacturing process
3	Gems (tourmaline, quartz, etc.)	+ These types of gemstones commonly do not require the removal and displacement of huge amounts of earth to produce and require almost no resources to process once found -Poor mining operations can still have negative impacts to habitat
3	Marble	+Marble does not require further processing after its initial quarry and cutting requirements -Quarry operations can have negative impacts on habitat
2	Fiberglass, non-formaldehyde resin coated	+Fiberglass can have high-recycled glass content, reducing the energy and processing requirements to produce new glass. Binders are typically used with fiberglass to maintain the functional integrity of the product (e.g., batt insulation, fiberglass mat); Non-formaldehyde resins eliminate the chance of the product off-gassing formaldehyde – a known human carcinogen -Fiberglass can irritate skin, eyes, nose and throat, and aggravate asthma and bronchitis
2	Glass, ceramics, and mineral products (other than bottles and jars), recycled up to 10%	+ Using materials with a low recycled content still reduces waste and reduces the environmental and human health impacts related to manufacturing virgin materials
2	Granite	+Durable material that can withstand extensive use with minimal wear -Dust from manufacturing processes, such as cutting, sanding, and polishing can result in exposure to crystalline silica, a carcinogen; some granite may also emit radon, a radioactive substance. Granite quarries may have an adverse effect on habitat

Mo`olelo Performing Arts Company is a participant in the A-ha! Program: Think it, Do it, funded by MetLife and administered by Theatre Communications Group, the national organization for the American theatre.

Textile Treatments and Colorants Scorecard

Score	Item	Pros and Cons
4	Sustainably sourced plant-based dyes and auxiliaries that meet GOTS requirements	+ Natural dyes sourced from sustainable sources can be a low impact way to color small quantities of textiles - Long-term colorfastness may be a problem
4	Undyed	+Undyed materials (ecru and colored cotton) have minimal impacts
3	Garment washing (wash only)	+Simple garment wash can reduce shrinkage and impart a degree of added softness with minimal impacts -Should be done at facility with adequate wastewater treatment
3	Low impact synthetic dyestuffs that meet GOTS requirements	+Low impact dyes generally use less water, fewer additional chemicals and fewer or no heavy metals in the dye stuff -These dyestuffs still require additional chemicals, water and heat, and wastewater treatment
3	Solution colored polymers	+Solution dyed (pigments added directly to the molten polymer) eliminate the water and energy use of traditional dye methods and there is no dye house wastewater to treat
2	Fabric sanding	+Sanding is a common textile treatment to mechanically soften the fabric and achieve a specific aesthetic -Sanding changes the physical structure of the fabric and can shorten its life. The process creates dust and waste.
2	Natural dyes from conventional sources	+ Natural dyes sourced from sustainable sources can be a low impact way to color small quantities of textiles -Conventional farming practices (synthetic pesticides and fertilizers) can have negative environmental and human health impacts
2	Procion dye	+ Specific dyestuff for cotton and other cellulosic fibers with high dye uptake
2	Softeners without VOCs	+Improves hand of fabric -Wide variety of softeners on the market; conventional products may have solvents that are volatile organic compounds (VOCs) contributing to air pollution
2	Synthrapol	+Detergent used as a pre-wash and post-wash for household dyeing -Contains isopropyl alcohol which can cause skin, eye, and mucous membrane irritation; the surfactant (detergent) is an ethoxylated compound; some of which are problematic in the environment
2	Water repellant waxes	+A reasonable alternative for water repellant treatments

Mo`olelo Performing Arts Company is a participant in the A-ha! Program: Think it, Do it, funded by MetLife and administered by Theatre Communications Group, the national organization for the American theatre.

Chapter 7

Selecting Scenery Materials and Construction Techniques

In this next chapter we are going to examine some commonly used construction materials as well as materials that may be less familiar. This is but a glimpse at available materials and cannot address every product. It does underscore the need to consider the pros and cons of materials and presents some common attributes that may be positive or negative in greener theatre.

Wood versus Metal

Wood is the primary material used in scenery today. It may seem counterintuitive to state that using a natural resource for scenery may be the most ecologically responsible choice. However, many agree that it is the truth. Lumber companies continue to improve methods for harvesting trees while reducing negative impact to the environment. In fact, most lumber companies operate within strict state and federal guidelines to protect the environment.

Figure 7.1 Sam72/Shutterstock.

Paul Brunner cites these facts in the discussion:

> *"Wood's greatest sustainable attribute is that it is the only construction material in wide use today which can be regrown. I think we overlook this important point. We can literally grow construction material in trees. When cut down and only when cut down, carbon is isolated within the tree fibers and locked away, known as carbon sequestering. Those trees are then replaced with seedlings, and those young trees grow faster than old-growth trees. Faster growing trees equals more carbon dioxide absorbed. That's a win-win situation."*

Table 1–3. Net carbon emissions in producing a tonne of various materials

Material	Net carbon emissions (kg C/t)[a,b]	Near-term net carbon emissions including carbon storage within material (kg C/t)[c,d]
Framing lumber	33	–457
Medium-density fiberboard (virgin fiber)	60	–382
Brick	88	88
Glass	154	154
Recycled steel (100% from scrap)	220	220
Concrete	265	265
Concrete[e]	291	291
Recycled aluminum (100% recycled content)	309	309
Steel (virgin)	694	694
Plastic	2,502	2,502
Aluminum (virgin)	4,532	4,532

[a]Values are based on life-cycle assessment and include gathering and processing of raw materials, primary and secondary processing, and transportation.
[b]Source: EPA (2006).
[c]From Bowyer and others (2008); a carbon content of 49% is assumed for wood.
[d]The carbon stored within wood will eventually be emitted back to the atmosphere at the end of the useful life of the wood product.
[e]Derived based on EPA value for concrete and consideration of additional steps involved in making blocks.

Figure 7.2 According to Table 1-3 from the *Wood Handbook: Wood as an Engineering Material*, wood had a negative net carbon value. From *Wood Handbook: Wood as an Engineering Material, GTR-113*, 2010, Ch. 1, p. 4.

Suggesting that wood has a negative net carbon value may seem puzzling, but it is true. First, trees absorb carbon dioxide through the process of photosynthesis. Their growth, powered by the sun, is exceedingly sustainable, naturally. Second, over half of the energy consumed in manufacturing wood products in the United States is from biomass (or bioenergy) typically from bark, sawdust, and other by-products. The wood products industry is the nation's leading producer and consumer of bioenergy (*Wood Handbook: Wood as an Engineering Material, GTR-113*, 2010, 1:2).

Consider alternative scenery materials. Plastics are derived from petroleum. While bauxite (aluminum ore) is one of the most abundant metals on earth, there is only a finite amount in the earth and we cannot grow more. The same holds true of steel (iron ore). Many sustainability philosophies underscore that limiting extraction of metals from the earth is a necessary step in restoring a more balanced ecosystem.

"Today, the net annual growth of commercial forests exceeds both the harvest and losses to insect, fire and disease by about 27 percent annually" (Chuck Leavell, *Forever Green: The History and Hope of the American Forest* (Atlanta: Longstreet), p61). This is a wonderful statistic, but great responsibility and care must still be taken so that we use wood as efficiently and as completely as possible.

Considerable ideological and political debate surrounds the use of trees and natural resources for human needs. Environmentalist Patrick Moore is co-founder of Greenpeace and the founder of Greenspirit (www.greenspirit.com) in 1991, a consultancy focusing on environmental policy and communications about natural resources, biodiversity, energy, and climate change. In his books and lectures Moore presents an argument that responsible use of trees is a necessary ingredient for a sustainable future. This argument counters more commonly held positions that less logging, and reduced use of wood, are critical to save forests and adjoining ecosystems and that more renewable alternatives should be sought.

Sustainability, and greener theatre, is rooted in an ever-changing body of science. This body of knowledge increases annually and is often clouded by polarizing views and arguments. Sustainability is a research field, a deeply held cause, and in some areas a high-profile political issue. Information about sustainability in the larger arena is useful to gain a better understanding of how sustainable practices can be applied to theatre.

How to Use Wood More Responsibly

Forest Certification Systems

Several organizations have developed forest certification systems. The systems set forth standards for forest management including stipulations for tree growth and harvesting as well as rules for verifying and certifying these practices. The guidelines vary from group to group and designate which wood and paper products may carry the organizational labels or be marketed as products of organizationally certified managed forests. The organizations update these standards periodically.

The Forest Stewardship Council (FSC) is the most well established group and is endorsed by a number of other environmentally responsible organizations including the World Wildlife Fund, the Sierra Club, and the Rainforest Alliance among others.

Figure 7.3 image courtesy of Forest Stewardship Council US

The Forest Stewardship Council (FSC) was established in 1993 by a range of individuals and groups independent of the lumber industry. The organization is known for forest management standards that protect the surrounding land and water. FSC standards prohibit direct impact on bodies of water from erosion and chemical runoff; protect old growth trees in regions where there are limited relic forests; and control use of harmful pesticides and herbicides and genetically modified trees in certified forests. The FSC standards also restrict conversion of forest land to other uses as well as requiring chain-of-custody evidence that allows determination of the forest-of-origin for products carrying the label. The FSC certifies forests around the globe.

The FSC is endorsed by a range of domestic and international large environmental groups and local community organizations. Additionally FSC standards require prior consent of indigenous peoples regarding forestry management on their lands and fully protect their traditions and customs. Other forest certification organizations include the Sustainable Forestry Initiative (SFI), the Canadian Standards Association (CSA), and the American Tree Farm System®.

Wood products certified by all these organizations include both hard, dressed lumber and sheet goods. Paper manufacturers can also have their products certified if the raw material used in production comes from a forest managed using one of the four systems. Some products will have stamps while others, such as the ATFS standards, may be more challenging to verify. These organizations are widely recognized to have transparent evaluation processes for the assessment of environmentally responsible growing and harvesting methods.

Figure 7.4 image courtesy of Sustainable Forestry Initiative

SFI was initially established in 1994 to provide a code of conduct for members of the American Forest and Paper Association. Use of third-party verification of practices for certification was added to the code in 1998. SFI adopted a label for products from managed forests in 2001 and in 2007 was incorporated as a certification entity separate from the American Forest and Paper Association. SFI addresses issues of water quality, biodiversity, and maintenance of wildlife habitat, as well as quick regeneration of trees. The 2010–2014 SFI operating standards for certification were developed through an open review process and continue to require independent, third-party audits for all certifications. SFI only certifies land in the United States.

Figure 7.5 image courtesy of the American Forest Foundation

The American Tree Farm System® (ATFS) includes 27 million acres of certified forestland managed by America's family forest owners who are meeting the highest standards of sustainability and managing their lands for water, wildlife, wood, and recreation. The organization is internationally recognized and it meets third-party certification standards. The ATFS certifies land that is privately held and is the largest and oldest organization to certify sustainable practices for family held woodlands.

The ATFS describes its work in the following way:

> *"For more than 70 years, ATFS has enhanced the quality of America's woodlands by giving forest owners the tools they need to keep their forests healthy and productive. Stemming the loss of America's woodlands is vital to our country's clean water and air, wildlife habitat, recreational activities, and producing the jobs, wood and paper products we all need."*

The Canadian Standards Association was an independent group founded in 1996 in response to forestry groups' desire to have a standardized certification system. It certifies land in Canada only. Look for wood that conforms to one of the following: Sustainable Forest Initiative (SFI), Canadian Standards Association (CSA), and the American Tree Farm System (ATFS) standards. Some debate has occurred over whether all certifications are equal. Some consider the SFI and ATFS certifications less desirable because the standards can be interpreted to allow more flexibility in forest management practices. There has been a call by some for allowing SFI and ATFS certification to be granted equal respect. LEED construction offers option certified wood credits for FSC or locally sourced lumber. This led to the ban on seeking LEED certification for state buildings in Georgia and Maine, by executive order of the Governors.

In spite of these concerns, use of wood carrying a symbol indicating it is from a forest that is managed with environmental concerns in mind is the best sustainable practice. It seems that selling lumber from sustainable managed forests would be a marketing coup for any supplier. Most have not chosen to exploit that opportunity. Many of the big box stores have information on their web pages outlining their corporate environmental plans that indicate they only sell wood products from managed forests. For example, in 1999 the Home Depot® made a very public commitment to eliminate wood products from endangered forests by 2002 (http://www.greenpeace.org/usa/en/media-center/news-releases/greenpeace-welcomes-the-home-d/). Several of the other big box stores including Lowe's® Home Improvement and Menards® sell some wood products that are certified by one or the other of these forest management systems as part of the regular inventory.

It can be difficult to find an employee at the local level who knows what, if any, of the wood products are certified. Only one person, an employee at a local Menards, even understood the question when I called around the Twin Cities for information. This particular store tries to keep a stock of standard construction lumber that is from certified managed forests. Multiple mills supply the lumber for resale and those mills may receive raw lumber from a number of forests. That makes tracking the information on each piece of wood difficult at the store level even if the raw lumber originated in a certified forest that includes a chain of custody. Allow some extra time to contact your local vendors to research the options available in your immediate area. Calls to the home office of a chain big box store may be involved.

Metals

Metals, in particular steel and aluminum, are used in scenery construction for theatre, television, and theme parks. Some regional theatres and opera companies regularly build their scenery using steel tubing. Steel tube is usually welded. If no one on your staff is trained and qualified as a welder, this should eliminate the option of steel scenery unless an expert can be hired, or the scenic elements are rented or borrowed.

Despite the added cost, steel is extremely durable and strong. There are places where steel is less expensive than wood, for example, a region with a history of steel manufacturing or a place where lumber is not readily available due to the climate or previous overharvesting.

For productions which travel, or that will encounter considerable use and abuse, steel is an ideal material. Steel is exceedingly durable for the rough conditions of trucking on touring shows. It is not susceptible to the same natural defects that wood is plagued with, such as knots, cupping, waning, or warping.

Aluminum lags behind steel in terms of applications for stage scenery. It is a wonderfully strong and lightweight material, but aluminum averages three times the cost of steel and is over three times weaker. It is used extensively for prefabricated truss (rock and roll truss) in arena and outdoor concert venues. Some venues, particularly road houses, use truss as a permanent front-of-house lighting system. Truss can also be rented from a number of theatrical vendors for use on a per show basis. Note that the reuse and recycling of steel consumes less energy than the reuse and recycling of aluminum.

The embodied energy necessary to manufacture steel and aluminum shapes verses wood is surprising. According to the USDA's Forest Products Laboratory's *Wood Handbook*, framing lumber has an embodied carbon content that is still only 10% of that of aluminum that is produced from 100% recycled material.

Recycling Scenery Materials

Most scenic materials are recyclable. Local and regional recycling options will dictate precisely how to do this. Depending on your location, there may be municipal options for recycling steel, wood, plastic, fiberboard and paper, glass and even compost materials. Many cities also have an e-waste recycling center and paint collection location available for recycling electronics and paint. In cities or towns where there is a green culture in place across the community, more recycling opportunities will be available.

When the research on recycling is done as part of the baseline audit, described in Chapter 2, check on construction material recycling as well. In many cases recycling that is deemed construction waste will have to be separated from regular recycling that might be associated with a home. A single piece of paper or one soft drink can mixed in with the construction waste to be recycled may change the classification to garbage.

Most often the recycler will require that the scenery be dismantled and classified by material; plastics in one container, steel in another, and wood in another. While wood recycling centers are gaining popularity, the process is more complex than simply melting down scrap steel in an iron mill for recycling. Wood that has been painted or which contains fasteners (staples, nails, screws) is not accepted for recycling. Additionally, most flame retardant products contain boric acid or inorganic salts, and when applied to stage scenery this can further reduce the wood's recyclability. However, the wood recycling process is becoming more prevalent and a greater number of options will be available in time.

Figure 7.6 Think outside of the box when considering available wood products for construction. antpkr/Shutterstock.

Wood: A World of Choices

Wood remains the most often selected construction material for scenery. Several factors probably contribute to this choice. In most areas lumber is less expensive than steel. Many of the stagehands at smaller companies have significantly more practice working with wood than metal. Welding and metal cutting require more specialized tools and safety concerns must be addressed when welding. Wood is recommended as a scenery construction product that contains the least embodied carbon when compared to aluminum and steel. Each piece of wood should be used efficiently to reduce waste and promote reuse.

Most people visualize standard dressed construction lumber—1x3 or 2x4 or 2x6—for framing and plywood and lauan for flat surfaces when scenery construction is mentioned. This is the standard model for many companies. However, there are other wood products that can be greener choices.

The lumber and boards commonly available at local hardware stores and home centers is called sawn dressed lumber. Wood in this form makes mediocre use of trees. Engineers have long sought ways to make more efficient use of natural resources and the result is a family of products called engineered wood products. These engineered products make more efficient use of trees to produce construction materials that are appropriate for building stage scenery.

Engineered Wood Products

Engineered wood products take the basic element of wood, the fiber, and use it to manufacture an enormous range of products. The same hard and soft woods that are used for dressed lumber are the base material, but many of the engineered composites can use mill scraps, waste wood, or tree

Figure 7.7 The storage rack of various engineered wood products in the Central Washington University scene shop. Photo by Jessica Pribble.

species that are not usually considered a structural product. Some veneers do require the use of whole logs. Since the size and shape of a tree is a minor consideration when harvesting trees for composites, versus the importance of a large, straight tree trunk for board lumber, engineered composites can make use of smaller and faster growing tree species. The wide variety of tree species used in these engineered wood panels results in a more balanced impact on forests and tree farms.

From plywood to laminated veneer lumber (LVL), these engineered products can help any stage set be more environmentally friendly. The most accessible materials suitable for stage scenery are engineered wood composite panels. These engineered wood panels are available in standard sheets of 4′ x 8′. Plywood, hardboard, and particle board are the panels most often stocked in scene shops. Most experienced theatre carpenters are familiar with at least some of these products. Gaining a greater understanding of a wide range of products and their basic properties can promote high quality scenery with efficient wood use and lowered environmental impact.

Engineered wood panels are made from wood fibers that have been mechanically processed and are classified by size. The fiber size defines the performance of the panel. Will it be a smooth finished surface ideal for painting? If so, very small fibers are needed. If a rough finish is desired, or a panel must have structural capabilities, then larger wood strands are used. The visual texture also relates to these principles. A panel with large strands of wood, roughly the size of a deck of cards, although there is a great deal of variation in shape and exact size, possesses more structural integrity. Engineered wood panels made with very small fibers and particles resembling saw dust and sand have poor structural capacity. These are better suited to scenic applications where great strength is not needed such as flat coverings and facings on platforms and stairs.

Theatre already makes wide use of these products in the form of plywood, oriented strand board (OSB), Masonite hardboard, and medium-density fiberboard (MDF). Too often particle board, fiber board, and to a lesser extent OSB are avoided in scenery, but all of these products efficiently use wood as a base raw material.

Inaccurate information and assumptions about these products have limited their use in theatre. Structurally, OSB conforms to national standards for span ratings and structural integrity just like plywood. More OSB is used in housing construction than plywood annually, yet plywood is usually preferred for theatrical scenery.

The least favorable attribute of engineered wood panels is that they are heavier than board lumber. As the wood fibers get smaller, the panel becomes denser because of the adhesives and resins used to hold the fibers. Dealing with the added weight is the trade-off for using a product that can use the raw material of trees more efficiently.

There is a green certification for engineered wood products. The Eco-Certified Composite™ (ECC) Sustainability

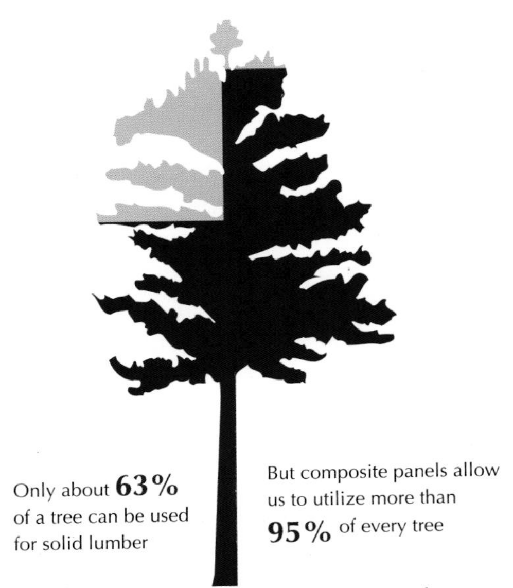

Only about 63% of a tree can be used for solid lumber
But composite panels allow us to utilize more than 95% of every tree
We aren't cutting more trees to make composite wood products—**we're making better use of the ones we already have**

Figure 7.8 Engineered wood products, such as plywood, oriented strand board (OSB), hardboard, medium-density fiberboard all make use of up to 95% of a tree. Courtesy of: Composite Panel Association (CPA) *Green by Nature* Flier (www.pbmdf.com).

Standard is the voluntary industry standard developed by the Composite Panel Association (CPA). It replaces the older CPA Environmentally Preferable Product (EPP) specification and voluntary certification program, established in 2002. The CPA web page describes the certification standard:

> *"ECC Certification is available to individual manufacturing plants and requires an on-site qualification audit and subsequent annual audits. Unfinished composite panel products must first comply with the stringent California Air Resources Board (CARB) formaldehyde emissions regulation before being considered for other ECC criteria. Qualified plants must then meet at least three of the following requirements:*
>
> - *Carbon Footprint – The plant shall demonstrate that the panel's carbon store offsets its cradle-to-gate carbon footprint as determined in kg-CO_2 equivalents of greenhouse gas (GHG) emissions. Each plant shall use the CPA Carbon Calculator to determine if a panel performs as a carbon sink resulting in overall net carbon storage.*
> - *Local and Renewable Resource – At least 85% of total annual wood fiber used shall be sourced within 250 miles (402 km) of the manufacturing plant.*
> - *Recycled/Recovered – Use a minimum of 75% recycled or recovered fiber; OR at least 50% recycled or recovered fiber AND a minimum of 5% post-consumer fiber. Percentages shall be calculated on a weight basis as measured in bone dry tons (bdt).*
> - *Sustainability – The plant shall document that greater than 97% fiber furnish brought on-site to manufacture panels is either converted into panels or other non-waste products.*
> - *Wood Sourcing – The plant shall hold a valid assessment and certificate from a certifying agency recognized by CPA such as the Forest Stewardship Council (FSC—Controlled Wood Standard or Chain of Custody Standard) or the Sustainable Forestry Initiative (SFI—Fiber Sourcing Standard).*
>
> *(http://www.compositepanel.org/cpa-green/go-ecc-green.html)"*

Veneer-Based Panels

Plywood

The largest fibers in composite wood panels are veneers which are thin but often wide layers. These fibers are the building blocks for plywood. The veneers are glued together with resins

Figure 7.9 A top view of plywood grain. Brandon Blinkenberg/Shutterstock.

Figure 7.10 Side view of stacked plywood. Note the visible ply layers. Marcus Turner/Shutterstock.

which produce a strong and stiff panel with great structural capabilities. Plywood is used for everything from furniture and cabinetry to flooring and decking in homes.

Plywood is the most recognizable engineered wood product used in scene shops. It is a panel product commonly available in 4′ x 8′ sheets in thicknesses from 1/4″ to 1-1/4″. By ripping 3/4″ thick plywood along its 8′ length into strips 2 1/2″ wide, one can quickly create 8′ long plywood strips. These "boards" can be the same size and shape of 1″ x 3″ sawn lumber and cost less per piece.

The sheet size also makes it possible to rip to any width, for example 5-1/4″ to provide framing for a 6″ tall platform without additional legs. (Refer to Appendix A for construction information about building a platform with a plywood frame.)

The grade of plywood used will affect the quality and strength, but even CD/X and Sturd-I-Floor® plywood, which are considered among the lower-grade plywoods commonly used in theatre, can be used in this way. Higher grade plywood with smoother face grains or including more layers (plys) are ideal, but can be cost prohibitive. Marine plywood is a specific product that will perform well in moist or humid settings. Plywood can be used in place of any 1″x 3″ boards on a span of 8′or less. While on the surface it may seem inconsequential, this small change in construction results in a much more thorough use of tree fibers through the use of an engineered wood product.

A scene shop can stock a smaller variety of materials by reducing or even eliminating 1-by board lumber if it uses plywood in varying widths for most scenery. Scenic carpenters may cut sheets of plywood into any width desired for a project.

Chris Fretts, Indiana Repertory Theatre Technical Director, has used 3/4″ 7 ply or 7 layer Underlayment Plywood as the primary scenery framing material for many years. At first, this was due to the declining quality of #2 pine board lumber. The plywood offers a straight, high quality material so there is no need to add an additional 10% to every lumber order to cover the material that is not straight enough to use in construction. Using a table saw, the plywood can be ripped to any width for a project. Fewer widths and lengths of pine boards need to be ordered. Everything is streamlined, from ordering materials through construction.

In situations where the framing requires a span longer than 8 feet in length, the Indiana Rep shop uses a higher quality lumber such as poplar. Fretts points out that "*the higher cost for this limited quantity of lumber is balanced by the less expensive plywood framing.*"

Figure 7.11 A close-up view of oriented strand board (OSB). Prapann/Shutterstock.

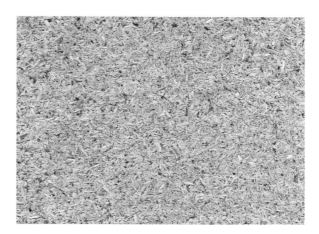

Figure 7.12 A close-up view of particle board. photocell/Shutterstock.

Oriented Strand Board or OSB

OSB is a close cousin to plywood. Made of large flakes or strands or wood, OSB is made by adding resin to the strands which are then oriented along the same direction. When the resin cures under heat and pressure, the strands are glued together and reinforce one another in a fashion similar to the plys in plywood. The resulting OSB panel is heavier than plywood but just as strong. OSB is available in 4′ x 8′ sheets with thicknesses from 1/4″ to 1-1/4″ thick.

OSB should not be confused with the product Flakeboard®. Flakeboard is a trade name under which a variety of wood products are manufactured. Generic flakeboard is made with randomly oriented strands and does not conform to standard structural ratings. OSB and plywood are the only engineered wood panel products that are designed for structural use.

Particle-Based Panels

Particle Board

Particle board is made of wood particles. The particles are similar to coarse sand or may even resemble small flakes. When mixed with resin the resulting particle board sheet is very flat, hard, and heavy. Particle board is most commonly found in furniture and subflooring and in some cabinetry. Available most commonly in thicknesses ranging from 3/8″ to 1-1/2″, particle board has never gained favor for use as a scenery construction material. It is generally considered to be too heavy and brittle for stage scenery, but many applications are viable in small stage furniture and properties. The panels are textured with a coarse finish and corners and edges can break off easily when moved.

Fiberboards

Medium Density Fiberboard or MDF

MDF may very well be one of the greenest wood products available today for scenery construction. Wood is processed to very small fibers, resembling coarse hair. When mixed with synthetic resin and pressed into panels the fibers virtually disappear, resulting in an extremely smooth and homogenous surface. MDF is not light, but it takes paint very well and remains flat and smooth when cut and shaped with traditional wood-working equipment. MDF does not have the brittle

Figure 7.13 A top view of medium density fiberboard (MDF). Photo courtesy of Paul Brunner.

Figure 7.14 A side view of medium density fiberboard (MDF). Photo courtesy of Paul Brunner.

characteristics of particle board, but it is as heavy, or heavier, per sheet. Generally, it is more durable and far better for scenic finishes, though the weight must be considered.

When cut, MDF will off-gas potentially harmful byproducts. Proper ventilation must be considered when working with any engineered wood products, particularly MDF. Manufacturers are constantly researching ways to reduce harmful off-gases while maintaining the characteristics that have made MDF so popular. Both "low-formaldehyde" and "no-added formaldehyde" MDF products are available today.

Hardboard (Masonite)

Hardboard (or Masonite) is the most common finish decking material for stages and platforms. Available in 1/8" and 1/4" thicknesses, it is commonly sold at most lumber stores for a reasonable price. It is hard, dense, and durable. Hardboard is one of the oldest engineered wood products and it is manufactured with wood fibers in a wet-panel screening process. This screening process is evident on the back side of some panels where it is common to find a textured finish. This process makes use of naturally occurring wood lignin. Lignin will act as a thermosetting adhesive which greatly reduces the need to incorporate additional formaldehyde-based adhesives making hardboard a low health hazard to humans. [Forest Products Society, *Wood Handbook: Wood as an Engineering Material* (Madison, Wisconsin, 2011), 11:13]

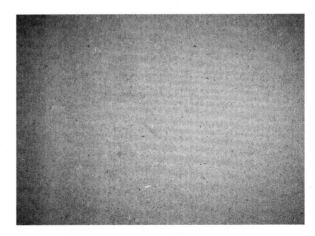

Figure 7.15 Close-up view of Masonite or hardboard. nuttakit/Shutterstock.

Experienced scenic artists usually let the product rest flat for 24 hours before base coating. Base paint both sides of each sheet of hardboard before it is installed on a platform or stage. Allow the first side to dry completely, then paint the second side. If not, the sheets will warp and buckle causing tripping hazards and an unsightly visual result.

While standard and tempered hardboard are most commonly available, ANSI (135.4) identifies a total of five different classifications for hardboard. Oil is infused into the particles when tempered Masonite is manufactured to make the product more water resistant. Each will react differently when painted. Once the sheets are properly primed and base coated they hold up well, but it can be difficult to get a smooth priming layer when using latex paints.

Cellulosic Fiberboard

Another wood composite common to theatre is fiberboard (cellulosic fiberboard). Considered one of the first wood composites ever developed, fiberboard is commonly known as a black 1/2″ insulation board. Also known under the trade name Celotex®, fiberboard is very inexpensive and is an effective sound reduction panel. When placed between hardboard and the plywood or OSB platform structure, it softens heavy footfalls and reduces sharp noises made by shoes and other footwear. Fiberboard becomes a dusty airborne hazard when cut, but it can be a useful texturing and carving material.

Homasote

The product named Homasote is similar to fiberboard. Developed in the early twentieth century, Homasote is a more attractive product than standard fiberboard. It is made almost entirely from recycled paper. The fibrous dust created when cutting the Homasote is less irritating to the skin than regular fiberboard dust.

While non-structural, Homasote is a widely available recycled product that has a wealth of applications for stage scenery. It has been widely used in the building trades for decades. The Homasote Company manufactures 18 different

Figure 7.16 The edges of homasote are easily damaged. Photo by Jessica Pribble.

products which contain anywhere from 55% to 98% post-consumer recycled content (http://www.homasote.com/). Ask your lumber supplier which products they keep in stock. Sound Barrier 440 is a commonly available version of the product and contains 98% recycled content by weight.

Homasote is typically four to six times more expensive than fiberboard, but its unique characteristics make it desirable for theatre. It is denser than cellulosic fiberboard, making it more ridged and easier to handle and work with. Also, because it is designed to be a sound-deadening panel, specific information is available as to the effectiveness of sound reduction.

Lauan

Lauan, frequently misspelled luan, is a commonly used product with a complicated history. The name comes from the giant red and white lauan or Philippine mahogany trees from which the face layers were originally harvested. It has now become a generic name for any tropical hardwood plywood. The raw material originates from tropical forests. There are now dozens of different trees in Asia's tropical forests from which lauan is made. The differences in surface color from one sheet to another can be attributed to this wide range of trees.

These forests are largely unregulated with little to no national or international oversight. New production techniques have also allowed the use of trees other than the original lauan trees and environmental groups fear that forests from the Amazon to Central Africa will ultimately be impacted. Destructive logging techniques and poor forestry management damage the rainforests when lauan is harvested using traditional methods. Environmental organizations including Greenpeace and the Rain Forest Action Network began calling for limits on the use of lauan in the building trades in the mid 1990s. The entertainment industry should follow suit.

Lauan is smooth and tight faced-grained plywood that is very stiff, almost to the point of being brittle, and lightweight. It is inexpensive and locally available at most lumber stores. Lauan is widely used in North America as a lightweight and thin hard-cover for theatrical flats and walls.

Theatre and television shops have searched for decades for a greener material with similar characteristics to replace lauan. A product called ScenicPly looked like a terrific alternative to lauan. Long time art director Garvin Eddy and some colleagues formed a group called EcoScenic and worked with a research and manufacturing team based in Oregon to create ScenicPly. The product was manufactured in the United States using wood products from FSC certified forests. It was available for purchase in limited areas in California and the Pacific Northwest.

Mr. Eddy has now joined the faculty at the University of British Columbia. He says:

> *"We have also been engaging a number of wood and sustainability scientists at the University of British Columbia to research and develop new products for specific use in theatre. They are really on the cutting edge of this type of research and are working a new cheaper and much greener version of ScenicPly as we speak."*

Another product named *RevolutionPly®* is being sold by Patriot Timber Products, a company based in North Carolina (http://www.patriottimber.com/lauan_plywood.html). The patent for RevolutionPly is pending. It is made from plantation grown and/or sustainably managed wood sources, making it a much greener choice than traditional lauan. While there is no chain of custody for this product, which is manufactured in China, all of the manufacturing plants are members of the World Wildlife Fund Global Forest and Trade Network. The embodied energy created by transporting the product is comparable to the impact of importing traditional lauan.

According to Patriot Timber Products, the company has supplied RevolutionPly for scenic construction to several theatre and film crews shooting in the region. The company also supplies the product to Lowe's Home Improvement stores nationally. The chain carries the product in the 1/4" x 4' x 8' size. It is called utility board, utility panel, or utility plywood at the Lowe's retail stores. The Lowe's employees at your local store may not recognize it by the trademarked name RevolutionPly.

The local Saint Paul, Minnesota, Lowe's carries the product for $19.95 a sheet. The lumber and building materials manager there, Dan Farrand, told me that every Lowe's carries different products depending on the needs of its local market. However, Lowe's product numbers are the same from store to store. If your local Lowe's does not carry RevolutionPly you can ask for product #80246 as a special order if you want enough of the product. Call your local store to see if they carry the product and ask them to confirm that it is supplied by Patriot Timber to make sure you are getting the correct product. Plan ahead to allow adequate time for a special order. See http://www.patriottimber.com/revolutionply.htm, Patriot Timber's web site, for more information on RevolutionPly including a video about the product.

The concerns over rainforest destruction have led to exploration and experimentation in manufacturing to find more sustainable replacements for traditional lauan. Reducing or eliminating the use of rainforest sourced tropical hardwood lauan in scenic construction is one of the most important steps you can take in greening your productions.

Paperboards

Industrial paperboard products also offer alternatives to lauan for designers and technical directors wishing to engage in more sustainable practices. Paperboard is used for packaging, book binding, signage and graphics, and arts and crafts. It is available in a wide range of thicknesses and finishes. Niagara Fiberboard, Inc. (www.niagarafiberboard.com/) manufactures several products including Upsonite, Easy Curve, and Universal, all made with a large percentage of recycled paper. The exact percentage of recycled material, and the portions of post-consumer recycled content in these products are not currently available from Niagara Fiberboard.

These industrial paperboard panels are well suited to stage scenery. Upsonite (also known as Upson Board) is available in 3/16", 1/4", and 3/8" thicknesses. It has a smooth two-sided white paper finish and is available in 4′ x 8′ sheets. Easy Curve is similar and manufactured to accommodate irregular curves and can be rolled into columns approaching 12 inches in diameter. Universal is a general-purpose panel with a smooth, off-white finish on both sides. It is available in 0.075" and 3/16" thicknesses. For outdoor use, Niagara Fiberboard also sells an all-weather board.

Paper-based fiberboards are similar in characteristics to stiff cardboard, but with a smooth surface. When painted these panels may wrinkle slightly because they will absorb water. Additional framing may be needed to ensure a co-planar surface, and wet-blend paint treatments may not produce quality results.

New products continuously hit the market. ECOR, manufacturer of advanced environmental composites, sells FlatCOR, WaveCOR, and HoneyCOR panels (http://www.ecorglobal.com/products.html). These are made from three-dimensional molded wood pulp and fibers. The panels are very lightweight and hold great promise for stage scenery. As with all new products, cost and availability are limiting factors for a vast majority of theatres.

Cardboard

Cardboard is actually a more generic term that can refer to products made from a variety of paper pulp based materials. It is readily available for reuse. The version most often used in scenic construction is corrugated cardboard.

Figure 7.17 Cardboard is another paper product that can be used to build scenery. Aykut Erdogdu/Shutterstock.

Honeycomb cardboard products are available, but will probably be eclipsed by the engineered fiberboard honeycomb products. This cardboard product uses an interior honeycomb that unfolds into a sheet of hexagon shaped cells. It is then glued between two sheets of thinner cardboard or liner. Smaller panels that are already glued together are also available from commercial vendors that sell packing and shipping materials. It is used by shippers to fill up voids in packaging to prevent the product from shifting. It is also available manufactured from 100% recycled content. The product itself is also recyclable.

The result is an amazingly sturdy piece of scenery that is lighter than most wood products, if you can get the right product and use it safely and correctly. Unfortunately the preformed panels cannot be bent easily. The original manufacturer seems to be out of business and the product in the rated structural form is hard to come by these days. There are ways to treat the product to make it flame retardant although painting it can be problematic, especially if you are using the newer products that use water soluble wheat paste to be more environmentally friendly. Wetting the product reactivates the wheat paste. If you are building your own panels from scratch the synthetic adhesives vary as to their ease of use and environmental friendliness. Check the MSDS or SDS carefully for information and instructions.

A few other caveats—the strength of the product is determined by the size of the honeycomb, not the thickness of the product so that is a mindset change from working with wood and steel. The product is not made for structural support although it is used to support objects in shipping. On one manufacturer's web page I saw an incredible claim of strength per square foot. When I called to check the validity, I was told the figure was an inaccuracy from the web site builder. Ask for test results to prove the actual capacity of the material if using it for structural scenery. If you make the panels yourself it is very difficult to keep the honeycomb in the exact configuration without getting adhesive on it before you are ready to place it and I found painting it required using some sort of encapsulation first. Like rigid foams, the thickness of the panel is predetermined and lamination or gluing of some kind is needed to build up depth. If you use an adhesive, the material is no longer totally biodegradable and may not be recyclable depending on the rules at your cardboard reclamation center. If you have never used the honeycomb before, due diligence in research is important. The technical directors I polled all suggested that stress skinned platforms made more sense if you were looking for a way to create a lighter, thinner platform that did not have to be cantilevered.

Corrugated cardboard is easily used for scenic elements. It can be flame retardant treated and painted, although specific techniques are required to avoid warping. George L. Pettit, a designer out of California, has long used the material for scenic elements. He has shared his expertise in a downloadable online resource titled *CORTEC: Corrugated Cardboard Technology for the Theatre*. (http://www.cortecscenery.com/). His guide is split into two segments and includes amazing pictures of the work he has created. If you are considering using cardboard for scenery, it is a resource that should be examined.

Effectively flame retardant treating any paper product for the stage is a significant concern. There are commercially available FR treatments available from theatrical vendors that meet this goal. It is incumbent on the user to read and follow all of the instructions to be certain that the treatment is correctly applied.

Large sheets are needed for bigger scenic elements and in spite of the volume of cardboard that enters the waste stream, it can be difficult to find as many large sheets as a project requires. However, finding enough cardboard to face the platforms is usually not a problem. If there are artistic concerns about the quality of the look that can be achieved, limit use of the cardboard for facings on the upstage side of the platforms. There is less buckling if the FR treatment and paint are applied with the cardboard flat on the floor. Let each coat of both products dry completely on one side before turning the cardboard over and FR treating and/or painting the other side. If the cardboard facings are removed carefully at strike, the pieces can go into stock for use on future productions. Think about how many facings a show normally uses and count the number of wood sheet goods that can be eliminated from use on a production.

Synthetic Materials

Foams and Plastics

Rigid foam is a material that offers options for sculpting and creating unusually shaped pieces. Certain plastics, whether flat material or PVC pipe, can be formed into three-dimensional scenic elements as well. There are some recycling centers that take foam and plastic but they are hard to locate and usually only take scrap pieces. Once the material has been coated and painted, like wood and paper, it is a less likely candidate for recycling.

From an ecological standpoint there are some problems. The manufacture of foam and plastic has environmental consequences and the products do not biodegrade. There are further safety issues from the potential for off-gassing when heated, for example using a hot knife to cut rigid foam. When cold cut, the crumbling pieces of rigid foam are usually too large to be inhaled, so that is some comfort. However with both plastic and rigid foam there are issues of storing both the raw material and the finished props or scenic element. If there is a fire or explosion there are potential health issues from the products of combustion, the possibility of melting materials sticking to skin, and the fact that these fires can be difficult to contain because the synthetic materials burn so quickly.

On stage, the materials must be adequately flame retardant treated. With rigid foam this usually requires encapsulating the foam element with a flame retardant coating before painting. Once the show is over, storage of the items for reuse may be complicated by the need to protect the material from damage.

Because rigid foams are so light compared to wood or steel scenery there are some companies that elect to use full sheets of the material as a base material for vertical scenery, creating a kind of flat. Unless the foam has been treated in such a way that the authority having jurisdiction deems it to not be a fire hazard, this is a poor choice for safety and, given the nature of the material, one of the least green choices possible.

Paper-covered foamcore board is a standard material for use in special events scenery. Gaterboard® is one trade name and many are familiar with the product as simply foamcore board. The material is lightweight and easy to manipulate in construction, requiring only an Exacta or utility knife. It is available in a range of sizes from the small pieces sold at office supply box stores for display use to the cases of 4′ x 10′ sheets in various thicknesses.

The product is even less green than rigid foam. It has all the same problems. However, the coating on the paper covering doesn't allow it to be easily painted with anything by spray paint. Even airbrushing with water-based paint requires some sort of priming coat of an aerosol spray or liquid paint that is not water soluble. Foamcore scenery and decoration is almost always a disposable finished product because the material is relatively inexpensive and does not store well. The pieces get dinged, crushed, dented, or destroyed easily. Those traits may make it a reasonable choice for a special event where everything must be personalized or trademarked in some way. However, it is not a green choice.

Putting it all Together

Fasteners

How the base materials are joined impacts the sustainability of scenic elements. Stage scenery can be assembled with any number of fasteners. Nails, staples, and screws are only a few of the options. Fasteners driven with pneumatic tools are popular in many shops because they speed up the construction process. As industrial tools, pneumatic tools are efficient and clean, although compressor noise can be a sound pollution problem in some shops. Their use in recent decades has greatly increased the ability to produce strong lightweight scenery in less time.

Their downfall is during scenery strike. Nails, staples, and other small-wire fasteners are time-consuming to remove from wood. Professional and student carpenters alike are left frustrated with the tedious process of trying to pull out these pneumatic fasteners to reuse wood from stage sets. Some theatres can spend the time and extra effort to pull staples out of wood. While this is ideal, it is not a likely model for professional theatres who must pay per-hour for labor or companies who rent performance facilities and work against the clock to vacate the venue. More often than not, the choice is made to consign the material to the landfill than to take the time to fully clean it for reuse.

While wood that is screwed together is easier to deconstruct, the widespread use of drywall screws is not necessarily the best answer for scenery. Drywall screws are available at any local hardware store or home center and they are commonly used in almost every scenic studio. The use of these screws in stage scenery is directly proportional with improvements in cordless tool technology. The 1990s saw great improvements in both battery and cordless tool technology, and once these tools became affordable for most theatres there was no looking back. Operating these tools is simple, and the installation and removal of screws is very easy.

The principal of drywall screws could be a great way to easily reuse wood from production to production. However, there are two faults with drywall screws. First, they take far longer to install than the split second it takes to pull the trigger on a pneumatic stapler and install a staple. Scenery can be built much faster with pneumatic tools and a range of scenic shops stay away from screws for that reason. Second, drywall screws are not designed for load-bearing situations. They are intended to hold up drywall. Because theatrical scenery is built to be lightweight and portable, the framing and fasteners are extremely important. Drywall screws may be used in certain flat and wall constructions, but they should be avoided on any weight-bearing structure. Platforms are susceptible to forces that are magnitudes higher than intended for drywall screws.

Fortunately, there are better options that address the inherent weaknesses of drywall screws. Replacing drywall screws altogether is possible. Particleboard screws look almost identical to drywall screws but are made of hardened steel. They most often have a black phosphate coating. This makes them both strong and well suited to theatre. Particleboard screws can cost anywhere from two to four times more than drywall screws, posing a budgetary challenge to some theatres. They are not commonly available at local hardware stores, but they are available through industrial supply vendors (Fastenal, McMaster-Carr, Grainger, etc.) who specialize in offering a wide range of fasteners to broad industry. Particleboard screws are almost identical to drywall screws in appearance and use but offer far greater strength. They are an ideal choice for strong and durable scenery construction and also promote easy reuse and material salvage during strike.

An option that is more widely available is deck screws. Designed for use on residential decks and patios, deck screws are made of hardened steel and are far stronger than drywall screws. Available in most hardware stores in a wide range of colors and styles, deck screws are a promising alternative to drywall screws. They can be used in more situations where scenery must be structural. They can be used and reused until their driver tips are stripped or thick with paint. No matter which fastener is used, any wood connection or joint that you anticipate will receive a force or structural load that is at or greater than the weight of an average person (150–200 lbs.) requires great care and attention to detail.

Glues and Adhesives

Glues and adhesives have an important function in stage scenery. When used in accordance with the manufacturer's recommendations, glues can add strength where it is needed most. All too often glues and adhesives are used "just in case" in conjunction with fasteners that do not need additional support or adhesion. Adding glue or adhesive will not make up for low quality construction materials or subpar carpentry in the cases where better support is needed.

To be specific, glues are all natural products while adhesives are synthetic. Any product which is purchased as a liquid in a bottle or tube is actually a synthetic adhesive. These terms are used interchangeably today to describe a product which holds two materials together. Glues are rooted firmly in traditional scenery construction and historic painting techniques. Glue is a commonly accepted reference and the most common glues for stage scenery are white glue, yellow glue, and a rather wide range of construction adhesives (or mastics). Commonly available in most any hardware store, these products are very effective when actually needed.

Glues get in the way of recycling scenery. Many scenic studios will apply glue to almost every wood joint to ensure a strong and stable connection. Flat and platform coverings are also often glued to ensure that the covering material stays firmly attached to the frame and to reduce the likelihood of squeaks. Where staples and nails are used, glue can be an important component for a strong joint. Frustration occurs when trying to dismantle scenery and salvage materials for reuse. Extra effort and additional tools are required to break apart the scenery. A joint that was glued together with good intentions often results in extra time during strike and, when anything is broken apart, the salvaged materials will almost always be damaged in some way. The banging and hitting needed to break apart pieces of wood often cracks and mars the wood. Glue does not help save materials for reuse. It hinders the process by requiring additional effort when the glue was probably not necessary to begin with.

Greener theatre requires that we reconsider when and how glue is used in scenery construction. Certain structural situations arise which require a proper nail-glued joint. But, these situations come up very seldom in most stage sets. The joints illustrated, the lap joint with screws, the butt joint with screws, and the joint between two 1″ pieces of steel tubing, are common to stage scenery and do not need glue when the proper fastener is used.

If the application of glue is reduced in stage scenery, then the fasteners are more important than ever. The fastener length should be at least two times the thickness of material being attached. For example, consider attaching a 1″x 3″ pine board lengthwise edge to edge. The 1″x3″ is 3/4″ thick. Two-times 3/4″ equals 1-1/2″. The minimum fastener length is at least 1-1/2″. You can also illustrate this by simply stacking to pieces of the material and measuring the sum. This will yield a strong and efficient joint.

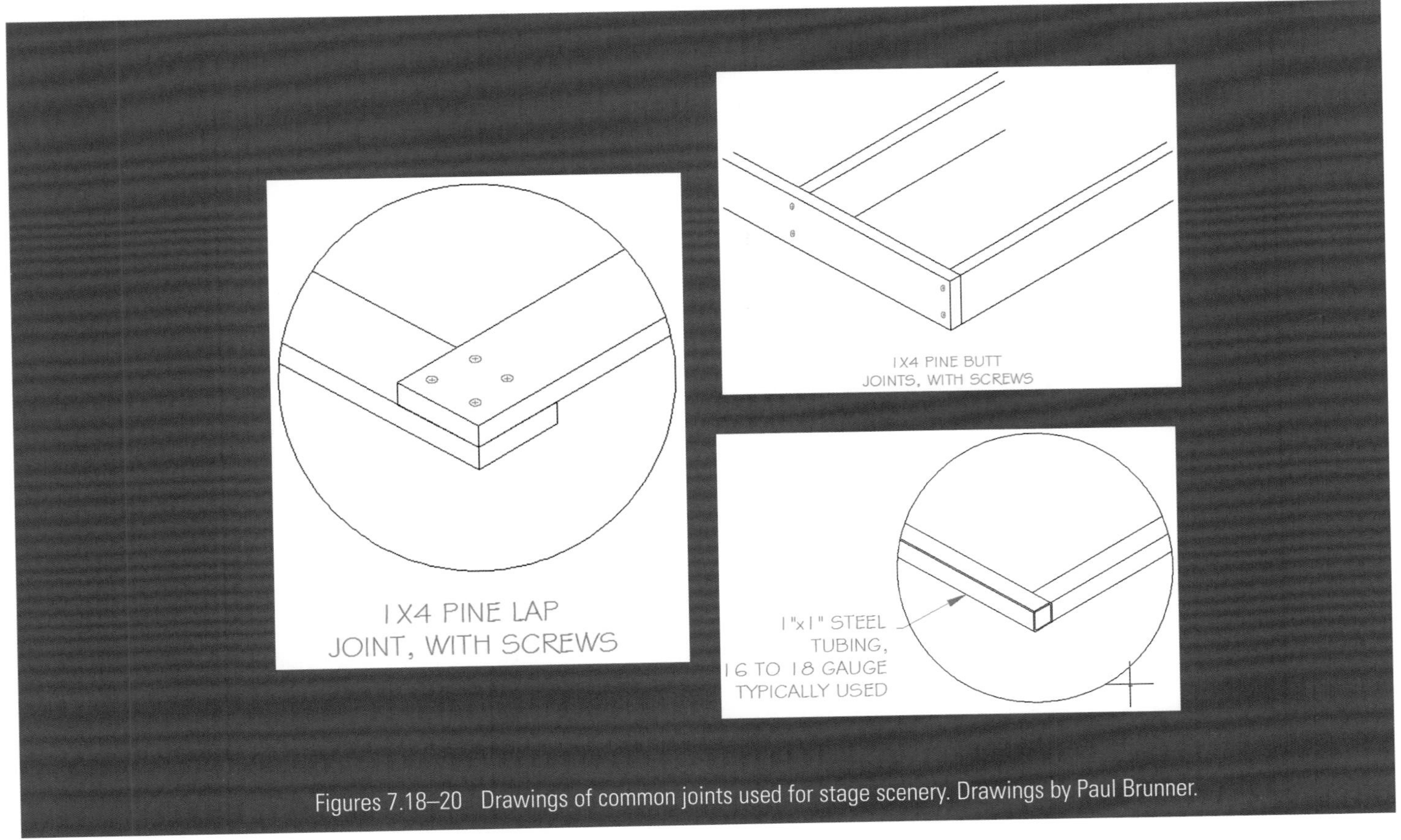

Figures 7.18–20 Drawings of common joints used for stage scenery. Drawings by Paul Brunner.

Figure 7.21 A 2"x 2" corner bracket. Photo by P. Brunner.

If strong decking screws are used to fasten wood framing together, then the glue adds almost no strength to the joints. Also, a small investment in corner brackets will yield even greater recycling opportunities.

This corner bracket is installed with two 3/4" long screws which provide great strength and rigidity. During strike, the screws can be removed and reused, along with the bracket and all pieces of wood. By installing a screw on the board face, the wood's strength is retained. Typical screwed joints require the screw to pass through one piece of wood and enter the second piece of wood's end grain. The grain tends to split apart and results in a weaker join versus screws installed perpendicular to the face grain. Brackets such as these installed with the proper screws and no glue provide a sustainable method for modern scenery construction with minimal impact to design.

Construction Techniques for Traditional Scenic Elements

Choice of materials, fasteners, and construction are all factors in determining whether or not scenery is reusable or recyclable. How the component elements are built and attach to each other is just as important. It is impossible to offer instructions for the best way to build every item. Hopefully these examples will spark your imagination and allow you to find building solutions that support deconstruction and storage. Every company's circumstances will impact the possibility of using specific suggestions, and storage space is one of the most influential factors. As with other aspects of greening production, planning ahead is the key to making deconstruction a possibility.

Vertical Elements

Even if shows do not have realistic settings or walls, there are usually vertical elements. Flats are the most common. There are a myriad of possibilities. The easiest choice is to try to build basic units to a standard size. The late Ralph G. Allen, noted theatre historian, suggested that historically the real limit on the width of flattage was the average width of a train boxcar door because that was how most show scenery was moved. Fortunately most contemporary companies are not constrained by this parameter.

For many years flats were normally covered in muslin. Soft-cover flats come to modern stagecraft from the traditional methods of historic production techniques. This stagecraft choice allowed for flats of almost any height and width. For those working in intimate spaces the need for tall flats is minimal, but in larger venues it is not odd to see flats over 20 feet tall. A hard face would be a problem for building, floating, and traditional moving techniques with flats this tall.

Soft-cover flats allow for a different range of scene painting techniques and looks than a hard-cover flat. Until the 1980s it was not uncommon to see scene paint mixed in a shop using a hot plate and dry pigment and animal glue. Some professional scenic artists still use this technique. (See Chapter 8 for more information on sustainability in scene painting.) Soft-cover flats are easy to store because the unit is only 3/4" thick and the frame can be recovered if the flat is made correctly. For some companies soft-cover flats, whatever the height, may be a

The scenic designer can reuse and recycle elements using many techniques

- Use furniture inventories to select existing chairs, tables, rugs, counters, and/or appliances from the theatre stock.
- When finalizing the lengths and height of walls, doors, and staircases, select measurements that match existing pieces. If every flat in the inventory is already 8′ or 12′ tall, don't decide that the set has to be 10′-6″ tall unless there is a compelling and unavoidable reason for that choice. Not only does this allow for reuse, it means that any newly constructed pieces match existing inventory options.
- Use regular shapes for floors and platforms whenever possible so the fewest additional elements have to be constructed. Check the size of flats with door and window openings and stock windows and doors before establishing the size of these opening in the set.
- Base any drops or scrims in this show on the items already in stock if at all possible.
- Unless the show is a piece that will be built offsite by a commercial scene shop allow the technical director or master carpenter to participate in choices of how items will be executed and sized. If the suggestions will impact the quality of the design or diminish support of the concept, you are always free to refuse the modification suggested.
- Avoid last-minute changes that may be costly in terms of time, money, and sustainability by planning every aspect of the scene design. This includes accounting for storage of offstage pieces when not in use as well as requirements to meet safety codes about width of egress route, dropping the fire curtain to seal with the floor, and visibility of emergency exits. This is part of the designer's responsibility.
- Stock sizes for scenery are frequently determined by common sizes for building materials. For example, hard-cover flats are typically in a size related to the 4′ x 8′ size of the sheet goods used to cover them. The same is true for platforms that have plywood or other sheet good lids. Those sheet materials usually come in a 4′ x 8′ size.
- While soft-cover flats can be any height, their width is limited by both common sense and the width of the fabric. You don't want to try to store flats so wide that they rip themselves apart—6′ is usually as wide as you can build without some issue for taller flats. Muslin is available in a variety of widths, but if you buy 10′ wide goods you can cover two 4′ wide flats out of each length of fabric cut from the bolt or bale.
- When purchasing fabric that will be painted, it is tempting to order muslin that is already treated with flame retardant. However, you will probably find the goods harder to paint effectively and this leads to waste as well as frustration.

greener choice because the thinner, lighter unit allows storage for reuse. That must be weighed against the environmental issues related to how cotton is grown and where it is shipped from (see Chapter 10 for this discussion). Most of the wide muslin sold in the United States is transported from Asia.

Hard-cover or "Hollywood" flats use the framing, usually 1x3, on its side instead of flat and are skinned with a sheet good for a hard surface. Originally 1/8" lauan skins were used, but those have become extraordinarily difficult to find and a 1/4" sheet good is most commonly used. These units were ideal for television for a variety of reasons. Taller flats were not needed which meant that it was quick to build flats using sheet goods. The construction technique made the flats self-supporting when joined at turning points so additional stage braces were not needed. It was also easy to remove units to accommodate camera shots if needed.

Hollywood flats probably became popular in theatre for a variety of reasons. Designers and carpenters became more familiar with the technique as the cross over between video, film, and theatre increased. As more converted spaces and low ceilings venues developed, these flats addressed some of the space issues because additional bracing was not needed. Also the more intimate venue put the audience much closer and in many cases demanded painting changes. Many realistic materials are easier to paint on a hard-cover flat. The materials section above has outlined the problem with using lauan, but some alternatives are suggested. The flats take up more room, but are sturdier to store and self-supporting when in use.

Companies that need taller flats may build the frame like a soft-cover flat or a Hollywood flat and use a hard cover. The horizontal seam created by using more than one sheet of material must be addressed, but all the vertical seams must be hidden as well unless you only create sets painted with a striped wallpaper effect.

In working with students or less experienced carpenters one source of waste comes from inaccuracy in measurements because dress lumber is not a full 3" wide. If the shop chooses to buy wider boards and rip them down to width, this error can be eliminated by ripping the material to a true 3" width. The other, and perhaps better, possibility is to spend a little time making sure everyone can read a tape measure and use fractions in basic math.

Decks

Decks are usually created by joining platforms. There are alternatives. Some shops use long trestles to support lids. Others build parallels instead of platforms so that the units take up less storage space. In either case the height of the supporting unit is fixed by the framing and stacking lids must be used to change the height of the playing space. A number of stagecraft texts give explicit instructions on how to build these units. Some technical directors use hanging joists like they are laying a floor in a house so that the boards used for the floor can be easily pulled up, stored, and reused.

Platforms are commonly used because they can be legged to various heights and the construction process is not as difficult as the techniques used to build parallels or trestles. The platforms and legs of various heights can be stored after the show and used over and over again. Legs are usually bolted to the platform. If a jig is created to drill the initial holes so that the same pattern is used on every platform, the framing will last longer. Multiple holes in the framing are one common way that platforms are compromised and must be replaced. Reusable units are the greener choice.

Triscuits: One Version of Stress-Skinned Platforms

Triscuit platforms are one easily reusable option that makes wise use of the construction materials. With apologies to Nabisco, the name was given to the units because the shape resembled the crackers. Triscuit platforms were first introduced in 1993 as part of the USITT Technology Exhibit Catalog by Evan D. Gelick. Today they have gained acceptance at numerous regional and academic theatres as a remarkably rugged and durable platform. Their construction is very specific, but when done properly the resulting platform will far outlast traditional methods.

Triscuits are designed using an approach detailed in the *Plywood Design Specification, supplement number three*, by the Engineered Wood Association. The arithmetic behind these platforms is dense, but for those who wish to design custom stress-skin platforms the approach is explained in the text, *Structural Design for the Stage*, by Alys Holden and Bronislaw Sammler.

Stress-skin platforms are entirely glued structures. A plywood top deck is glued to a frame and an additional sheet of plywood is glued to the underside of the framing creating a sandwich style platform. Glued connections between the framing and the top and bottom plywood skins ensure a critical transfer of structural stress through the entire panel and mimic the efficient capabilities of an I-beam. The platform is far thinner than traditional platforms and retains the minimum weight capacity of roughly 50 lbs. per square foot, or the capacity of traditional 2″ x 4″ or 1″ x 6″ framed platforms.

Figure 7.22 is a framing drawing for a Triscuit platform. A larger version is included in Appendix B.

The interior framing is designed to be 5/4″ pine (said as "five-quarter"), a high-quality wood virtually free of knots and other defects. Today, this wood is expensive and difficult to obtain. A variation on this framing incorporates 2-inch-wide strips of 2-by (2″ x 4″, 2″x 6″, etc.), a far more commonly available wood. The added thickness, from 5/4″ to 1 ½″, further ensures proper structural performance. Note the double-ended arrow which indicates the correct plywood grain orientation. Plywood face-grain and the framing must be parallel and travel in the same direction. This ensures the maximum stiffness since a majority of wood fibers are working together in the same direction. Overlooking this important step negates the capacity of the platform.

A Triscuit platform is actually 3′-11 7/8″ by 3′-11 7/8″ square. This accounts for the saw kerf when cutting a 4′ x 8′ sheet of plywood in half. Additionally, when installing Triscuits a 1/8″ gap is maintained between platforms to eliminate

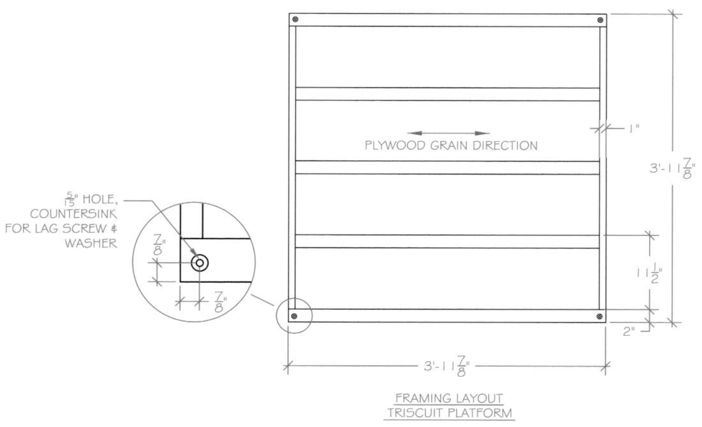

Figure 7.22 This thinner platform has the same structural integrity as a traditional 2″ x 6″ or 1″ x 6″ framed unit when built correctly. Drawing by Paul Brunner.

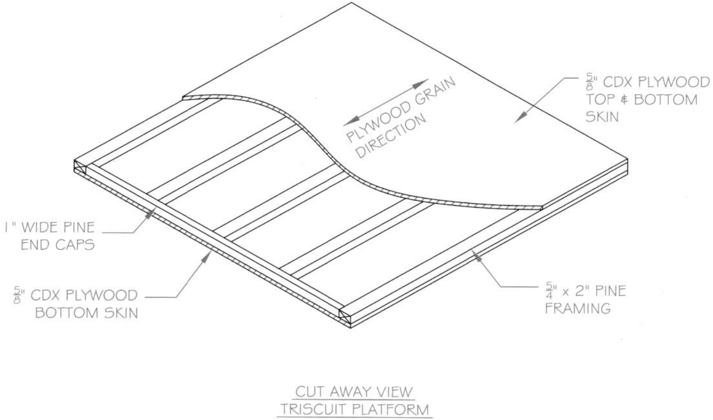

Figure 7.23 A Triscuit platform is actually 3′-11 7/8″ by 3′-11 7/8″ square. This accounts for the saw kerf when cutting a 4x8 sheet of plywood in half. See Appendix B for a larger version of this drawing. Drawing by Paul Brunner.

squeaks. A 3/8" hole is drilled into the four corners to secure the platform to a stud wall with a 5/16" or 1/4", three-inch lag screw.

This highlights an advantage to these platforms, in that one can install and fasten each platform from above. No longer will it be necessary to crawl underneath platforms to secure them to one another. The gray bars indicate stud walls in relationship to the platform. All wood fibers, those of the framing and the top/bottom plywood sheets, are spanning the four-foot distance making every effective use of the wood.

Triscuits are tried and trusted platforms. Variations on Triscuit include the "Texas Triscuit," a steel-framed 4-foot by 4-foot platform decked with 5/8" plywood that is actually not a stress-skin at all. It does share similar positive attributes to the original Triscuit by maintaining a thin profile (framed with 1 1/2" square, 16 gauge steel mechanical tubing, plus the 5/8" plywood decking, 2 1/8" overall thickness) and remains durable over many years. Steel will add cost and carbon footprint to the initial investment, but durability is a reasonable trade-off.

Some technical directors have made stress-skin platforms using common insulation foams (white beadboard foam, pink or blue foam) to replace the interior framing. This reduces the construction time and cost while increasing the sound deadening properties of the platform. However, the actual strength properties of such a panel are indeterminate and no specific method exists to analyze this sort of structure. Trial and error is necessary.

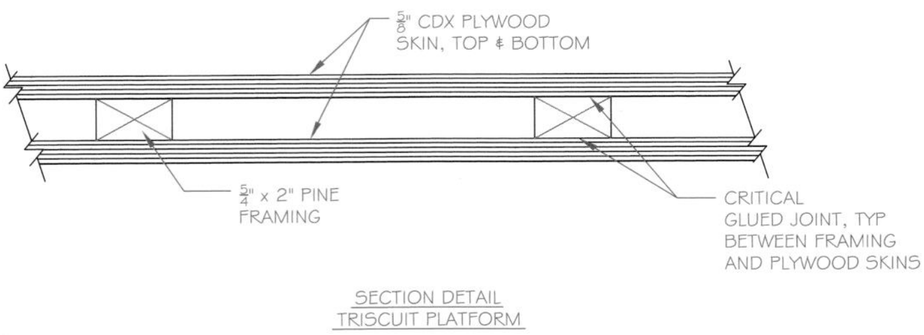

Figure 7.24 This detail drawing shows a side view. See Appendix B for a larger version of the drawing. Drawing courtesy of Paul Brunner.

Step Units

Constructed step units that use permanent carriages are difficult to store. A new step unit must be built for each height needed. In the *Stock Scenery Handbook* Bill Raoul offers an alternative construction technique that used flat frames for the risers. See Appendix B for layout and construction information.

Triscuit platforms possess the following attributes which make them a sustainable choice for stock scenery:

- The wood frame and plywood top/bottom skins work together for an exceedingly thin and efficient structural member which is a very efficient use of wood.
- The thin profile (2-3/8" to 2-3/4") is half the thickness of regular platforms maximizing storage space.
- This platform style lasts longer than traditional platforms due to its entirely closed construction. Framing is enclosed within the top/bottom plywood skins so no damage can result from framing getting caught on one another when handling and stacking.
- Installation and strike is faster and safer; fasteners are installed from above eliminating the need to crawl beneath platforms.
- Dense construction reduces hollow noise for more realistic sounding footfalls. This eliminates the need for any sound-deadening material on platforms.
- The 1/8" gap between platforms virtually eliminates squeaks for a quieter platform deck.

This construction technique is a sustainable choice for a variety of reasons. The stair units can be broken down into flat carriages and treads for more effective storage. The individual elements can be reused in multiple-height step units. Instead of building a whole new step unit, you simply add or subtract risers built to incremental heights for a shorter or longer stair run. The shape of the tread determines if the unit is straight or curved stairs and the direction and degree of the curve. Integrating this technique into construction can significantly reduce the amount of lumber consumed per show because of the versatility in supporting various designs and the ease of reuse.

Figure 7.25 The curved steps use the framing described above. The facings are made from cardboard and are base coated. Photo by EEJ.

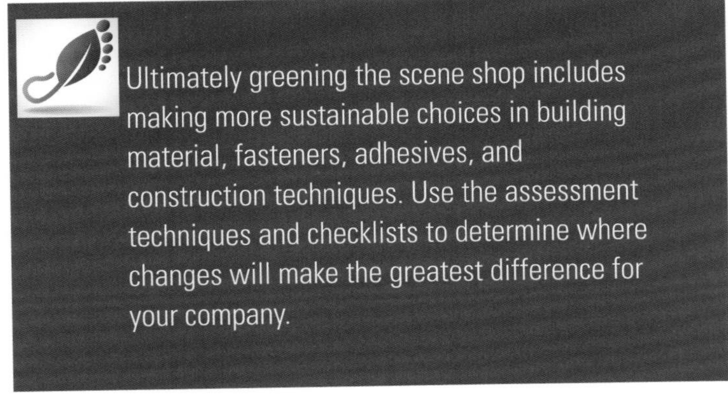

Ultimately greening the scene shop includes making more sustainable choices in building material, fasteners, adhesives, and construction techniques. Use the assessment techniques and checklists to determine where changes will make the greatest difference for your company.

Chapter 8

The Paint Shop

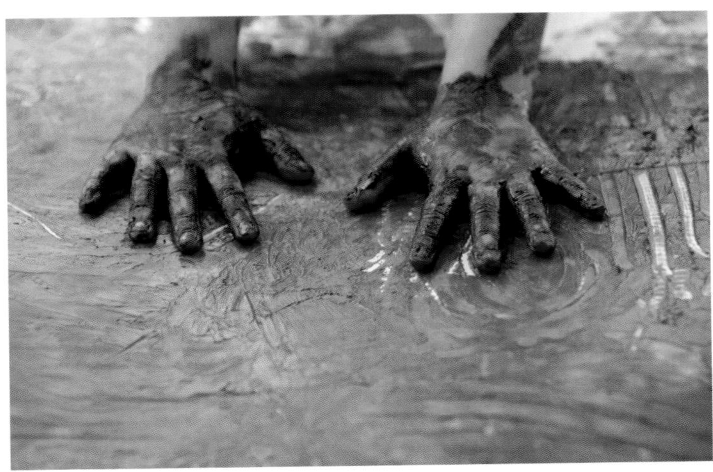

Figure 8.1 holbox/Shutterstock.

There are as many different labor divisions and work space configurations as there are companies producing theatre. Some theatres have separate paint shops and dedicated scenic artists while others have a single work space and a unified crew that performs every production task. Other situations may make use of any available labor, experienced or not, for painting projects. This chapter is geared toward the less experienced scenic artist, but I hope it sparks ideas that allow the working professional scenic artist make the paint shop greener.

Whatever the division of labor, thoughtful decisions in the paint shop can make a significant difference in greening your productions. Issues about the environmental impact of paint for permanent structures have long been under discussion in the building trades. Think back to all the warnings about lead paint, for example. Theatrical productions usually do not use the same finish materials as general contractors, even if the finished temporary settings create the illusion of a realistic environment. As Ian Garrett eloquently states in his essay "Theatrical Production's Carbon Footprint":

> *"A Doll's House is not your house. Theatre artists don't build homes—Nora's and Torvald's for example—we build worlds. We rarely use the actual materials we portray on stage. We create facsimiles that read at a distance as the real thing because of time, money, and expense."*
>
> In *Readings in Ecology and Performance* edited by Wendy Aarons and Theresa J. May (New York: Palgrave Macmillan, 2012), 201.

Even in intimate spaces where the audience can touch the performers, inexpensive building materials are generally used for construction and painted or coated to appear to be more expensive and usually more durable: Masonite for marble or plywood for oak. This illusion is created through the use of various kinds of paints and coatings.

Paint has been with us for centuries. Early man painted cave walls with paint made from charcoal or dirt mixed with spit and animal fat. Historians hypothesize that paint was applied with brushing, smearing, dabbing, and spraying techniques using the available natural tools like twigs and feathers, even creating sprays by blowing paint through hollow bones.

Early painters used dyes made from plant or animal sources or pigments from earth and minerals to create color. The sources are not that different today, except that many colors have been created from synthetic products to mimic what were originally colors from organic or mineral sources.

The original paint palette was limited. Look at recreations of early Egyptian architecture and you will see six colors: white, black, blue, red, yellow, and green (http://www.webexhibits.org/pigments/intro/early.html). Fortunately a broader range of options are available for the contemporary scenic artist.

What is Paint?

Paint is comprised of a pigment for color, a binder to adhere the pigment to the painted surface, and a vehicle that allows application of the paint by holding the first two components in suspension. Pigments may be from natural sources—hence the description earth tones or mineral colors. Pigments may also be synthetic. Binders include acrylics, polyurethanes, epoxy, and natural sources like casein and animal or vegetable glue products. In addition to holding the components together and to the painted surface, binders help the product cure. During the drying process, the solvent or liquid vehicle evaporates. The curing process makes the paint durable; curing is the bonding of the components to create a polymer. A filler may be added to give the paint body. A product called Dutch Whiting, a chalk based filler, used to be a very popular additive for paints mixed in the shop with dry pigment and animal glue. Other fillers include clays and talc. Commercially manufactured paints still include fillers in the formula.

Historically there were a variety of recipes for paint pigments, most of which were actually concocted by the artist as he or she was working. These include the now exotic sounding options like egg tempera and old fashioned milk paint that could be dissolved off the kitchen table with vinegar for a real spring cleaning. If you can find a copy of the out-of-print book *Formulas for Painters* by Robert Massey, it contains intriguing options for mixing your own paint.

Even as late as the 1990s many scenic artists used powdered dry pigments and aniline dyes suspended in solutions that included binders that were cooked in the shop on a hot plate. Professionals who specialize in scene painting still practice these techniques for particular applications. Having any powder form of a pigment, however benign the source of the colorant—and many of them were not—led to instances of the powder accidentally becoming airborne. Health and safety of the painters was a concern (see Monona Rossol's book *The Artist's Complete Health and Safety Guide*).

When first developed in the 1850s synthetic aniline dyes were prized for the brilliance of color they made possible. Take the time to investigate the chemical processes that were used to create aniline dyes and it won't be a surprise to learn that those dyes were considered toxic if ingested, or absorbed through the skin. Even the inhaled vapors could be harmful. These dyes have been replaced in most instances by much safer water based products which some scenic artists, including Cobalt Studios co-founder and teacher Rachel Keebler, refer to as "faux" dyes.

Paints may use an oil based solvent. Oil paints are usually designated as hazardous materials by local regulation and require specialized disposal techniques due to the potential environmental impact if the paint leaches into the soil and enters the water. Potential health and safety issues are also connected with these paint formulas. Clean-up of tools involves turpentine or some substitute, like mineral spirits. Turpentine is a plant based product, but it is not a green material. Turpentine soaked rags are flammable and exposure to the fumes should be limited for health reasons. Disposal must also meet local regulatory standards.

Oil based paints and sealers require long dry periods in dust free environments if the finish is to remain unmarred and clean. That fact alone makes those products unsuitable for use in most shops or theatres. Professional scenic artists do work with oil based products for the finishes created; for example products like Fabulon for floors that will take great abuse from moving scenery or Break-Through!® for special applications. Commercial shops that build and paint trade shows frequently use oil based lacquers to create a specific look or to create finishes with higher durability for long run extravaganzas or touring exhibits. Those shops also have the equipment and facilities needed to use the products safely. The Occupational Health and Safety Administration (OSHA) generate the applicable standards. Additional standards of environmental responsibility are outlined by the EPA and administered by the local authority having jurisdiction. For the less experienced scenic artist there are few instances where a safer and more eco-friendly option will not meet the needs of the project.

Paint that uses a water vehicle is frequently described as water based. In fact, water based implies that the paint will dissolve in water, like children's paints and markers that will wash out of their clothes and the living room carpet, even if it has already dried or cured. Paints with a casein based binder, like Rosco's Iddings Deep Colors®, can be reactivated with water and washed off nonporous surfaces.

Water borne means the product will not dissolve in water once it cures, even though you can clean up most of the tools with soap and water. Because of labeling and advertising we tend to use the terms interchangeably even though they do not mean the same exact thing. The terms are used to distinguish these paints from the oil based products but can be misleading if you don't know the difference. Dried scenic paint will not wash out of your clothing.

Paint in a Can

I prefer using paints formulated for scenic applications. There are some cases where it may make more financial sense to purchase good quality flat latex for base coating, material specific primers, or products formulated for construction applications, for example water borne polyurethane sealers. Certainly Jaxsan®, a coating for waterproofing and providing thermal insulation on roofs, was not created for theatre application. However, it has become a commonly used product in paint shops for creating texture. Because of the popularity, some theatrical vendors are also stocking Jaxsan.

Some theatre groups feel it is less expensive to buy cheap paint at big box or discount stores, especially discounted mis-mixed custom colors. It is worth doing an in-depth analysis of costs to see if it really is cheaper. For theatres in cities where there is not local vendor who carries scene paint, the shipping charges have to be calculated into the price to determine the true cost. Vendors usually discount scene paint prices based on the size of the order. If it is possible to make a stocking order at the beginning of the season and have everything trucked in on a palette, the cost may not be that different from buying paint a can at a time from the big box store.

Ask your theatrical vendor what possibilities are available to reduce shipping rates. Many suppliers are willing to work with the customer on large orders. There may be handling and packing charges that increase the shipping costs. Ask the vendor to specify any additional costs. You want to be aware of any handling charges before placing the order, but the fact that additional fees may apply should be no surprise. Paints, coatings, and sealers travel better when shipped in boxes that include inserts or other void fillers to hold the cans in place. That packaging must be purchased by the vendor and employees paid to pack the paint appropriately.

Most vendors will not ship paint on a Friday during the winter months in cold climates. The paint is more likely to freeze if it is sitting in the shipper's distribution terminal over the weekend. Repeated freezing can compromise the quality and performance of paints, coatings, and sealers. Plan your order so you do not have to pay for overnight freight or pay overtime to the painters because the paint order could not ship over the weekend.

Companies that buy paint on a per show basis may find some comfort in being able to run to the store to purchase one more can of paint at any time. There is always the chance of the runner accidentally picking up a can of paint that is a glossy finish instead of flat color or buying the cheapest white paint available which may not have adequate binder. Anyone who has finished painting the floor black at 3 a.m. and realized that half of it is flat black and half of it is semi-gloss black knows the pain of this mistake. Similarly, anyone who has ever rented an apartment with white walls where the paint wipes off at a touch even after drying, is familiar with the problems of paint with poor binding qualities.

Scene Paint versus House Paint

My preference for scene paint versus house paint may come from learning to design and paint before the proliferation of computer generated renderings. Since scenic paints come in colors that are analogous to studio artist colors, it is easier to exactly match the color in the rendering. Most interior house paints do not come in the full range of colors used for sets, and if a vibrant color requires custom mixing it may not be any

Figure 8.2 Photo by Jessica Pribble.

cheaper than a gallon of scene paint in the correct color. Part of the paint's cost is determined by the cost of the pigment and rich vibrant colors require a great deal of pigment.

Quality scene paints are designed to be thinned in varying proportions and still maintain brilliance of color and adhere to the material painted. They are also formulated with the understanding that flame retardant products may be used in conjunction with the paint. House paint is formulated to be used out of the can according to the instructions on the label. There is less waste when the scenic artist can mix colors with confidence that the paints will remain in suspension together and can have a good idea of what will happen when particular colors are blended to create a third color. The availability of most scenic paint lines and colors in gallons, quarts, and for some specialty colors even pints, allows purchase of smaller quantities of scene paint for accent colors. Theatre is a tiny niche market when compared to the building trades. In my experience, paints manufactured for painting scenery are going to be more effective and user friendly than products created for an entirely different application.

Since it is impossible to discuss every paint and coating product on the market, focus in this chapter is on paints commonly used in theatre settings. This assumption of common usage is based on anecdotal evidence from personal experience, discussions with other professional charge artists and scene painters, not statistical analysis of data.

The sustainability checklist discouraged the use of any paints or coating treatments that require personal protection devices or special solvents. However, this is only the first step in making the paint shop greener. The type of paint selected and the embodied energy in manufacturing and transporting that product are part of the impact.

How the paint is applied, thinned, stored, disposed of, and how the application tools are cleaned are all part of the total environmental impact of the painting process. Prudent choices protect air quality both in the workplace and the environment and help prevent water contamination as well as protecting the people working in the shop or performance venue.

Low Volatile Organic Compounds (VOC) Paints

Advertising campaigns by household paint manufacturers remind us all that low VOC paint is more desirable. Unfortunately most of the advertisements do not consider if the consumer has any idea what VOC actually means. The Environmental Protection Agency (EPA) posted a definition on the Internet at http://www.epa.gov/ttn/naaqs/ozone/ozonetech/def_voc.htm.

As of March 31, 2009 the EPA announced that according to 40 CFR 51.100(s):

> *"Definition – Volatile organic compounds (VOC)*
>
> *(s) "Volatile organic compounds (VOC)" means any compound of carbon, excluding carbon monoxide, carbon dioxide, carbonic acid, metallic carbides or carbonates, and ammonium carbonate, which participates in atmospheric photochemical reactions."*

This definition is followed by a long list of organic compounds that are excluded from regulation because they have been found to not react to sunlight. The information above is only an excerpt of the EPA regulation. You can find the entire definition on the web page listed above if you are interested in a little more chemistry.

In case this definition does not clear anything up for you, the EPA has some simpler language as well on another web page, http://www.epa.gov/airquality/ozonepollution/.

> *"Ground level or "bad" ozone is not emitted directly into the air, but is created by chemical reactions between oxides of nitrogen (NOx) and volatile organic compounds (VOC) in the presence of sunlight. Emissions from industrial facilities and electric utilities, motor vehicle exhaust, gasoline vapors, and chemical solvents are some of the major sources of NOx and VOC."*

This may seem counterintuitive since there is huge concern over the loss of the ozone layer in the atmosphere. While ozone is a protection in the atmosphere, it has a negative impact close to the ground. It can cause respiratory issues for people and harm plant life. Studies have linked the presence of VOCs to certain cancers, renal damage, and impaired brain function. Several studies have cited paint and paint related products as the second highest source of VOC in the air, exceeded only by automobiles as a source. Recent estimates place paint's contribution at approximately 11 billion pounds per year.

VOCs are described as volatile because the organic compounds have a tendency to not remain in the liquid or solid state in certain instances—for example, when exposed to sunlight, VOCs turn to a gaseous state and are released in the air. This behavior is part of what makes the liquid in paint evaporate so the paint can dry and cure. The most off-gassing occurs when the paint is first applied and drying, but the vapors can be released for months as the paint cures. Anyone who has painted a room or closet understands this experience. Occupants are exposed to the vapors throughout the process of curing.

VOCs were considered essential to the function of paint because the chemical reaction involved allowed the curing process to happen more quickly. Solvents have been the highest contributor of VOCs, although VOCs may be present in the binder or pigment as well. Paint that does not evaporate does not dry and cure. The conundrum becomes obvious once you understand the role of VOCs in paint.

Low VOC house paint was not widely available outside of California for many years. Consumer awareness has increased the national availability of low VOC house paints and although it is usually very expensive per gallon, competition is bringing the cost down. Some low VOC paints do not apply as expected; this application quality is referred to as the hand of the paint. Quality of the hand describes if the paint flows easily from the brush and covers the painted surface evenly with each brush stroke. Not all brands of low VOC paints have this problem. Create samples to test the hand of any paint or coating product you have not used before.

The change to lower VOCs products has been ongoing. Paints that are advertised as low-VOCs by reputable dealers and manufacturers contain 50 g/L (grams per liter) of VOCs or lower. However, the actual EPA standard for both latex and oil based paints is higher. For a paint to qualify as low VOC, it must have less than 5 g/L (http://ecofriendlybuilder.com/Eco-Paints-and-Finishes/Low-VOC-Paint.aspx).

Keep in mind that the numbers cited on the paint label may be measurements taken before the paint's pigment or any additives are added, both of which can contribute more VOCs. Although we are now accustomed to hearing about low VOC paint, many newer air quality regulations actually now refer to Hazardous Air Pollutants (HAPs). This new distinction has probably arisen because different VOCs have different levels of environmental impact.

Several different methods are used to calculate the VOCs or HAPs in paint and the processes are complex. The Paints and Coatings Resource Center has an explanation of the various methodologies online, http://www.paintcenter.org/newcalc.cfm. Most of us are dependent on the MSDS or the can label for the VOC information. Remember to look for other potentially harmfully additives as well. Even low VOC paints may include formaldehyde or some sort of bacterial or fungal inhibitors. In spite of those caveats, low VOC paint is still the greener choice whether you are using specially formulated scenic paint or a building trade product.

Being Green at Sculptural Arts Coatings. Inc.

Figure 8.3 Photo courtesy of Sculptural Arts Coatings.

Some companies have made environmental concerns part of the corporate culture from their inception. John Saari, creator of the Sculptural Arts' product lines, describes the environmental philosophy at the company:

"Since 1991, in everything that we've done, the focus was always to deliver the best quality paints and coatings with the best possible health and safety ratings so our products were formulated with this as a number one objective. If you have the best health and safety ratings, it actually follows that the products can be created with lowest volatile organic compounds".

"Even in our packaging: while others were sending cans of paint or such in boxes with large EPS foam fills to protect the cans, we were the first to introduce cardboard inserts that could be reused from package to package and then recycled easily. When additional packaging was necessary we reused newspapers for the additional protection – recycling and reusing is a part of what we do."

He adds:

"It is a conscious choice to deliver a quality product with great body and good hand in application. We worked for more than two years preparing to meet the current California Standards with modifications and alterations. Some products such as the Sculpt or Coat and Plastic Varnish have been low VOC from inception and required very little tweaking."

There are a number of lines of scene paints. Some of the most well-known include the Rosco lines: Off Broadway®, Iddings Deep Colors®, and the Super Saturated® lines and Sculptural Arts Artist's Choice® line. Other brands include the Muralo Vogue Deep Colors® line, Mann Brothers' Studio Paint®, and Cal-Western Artists Acrylics®. All of these companies sell paints nationally, including California, where there are very specific regulations regarding VOC paint emissions, and have low VOC products available. Many, if not all the colors in several lines of scene paint are low VOC including Rosco's Iddings Deep Colors, Mann Brothers' Color Themes, Cal-Western Paints' Artists Acrylics and, of course, Sculptural Arts Coatings' Artist's Choice.

There are additional numerous entertainment paint and coating products designed for specific effects ranging from paints that react to black light, phosphorescent paints and paints designed to be used for specific effects in film and television like Chroma key colors and Ultimatte super flat paints that blend with matching fabrics and tape. An examination of the MSDS or SDS will indicate the quantity of VOC content. There are also a range of industrial products used by experienced scenic artists for special applications and projects that require the finish to stand up to long runs, outdoor weather conditions, and touring or repeated use in exhibit and trade show conditions. Each of these has their own unique characteristics and cautions. When using these more specialized products read the instructions, the SDS information, and contact the manufacturer or vendor for answers to any questions on handling, use, storage, and disposal.

VOCs have gotten the most consistent public attention. Realize that other paint ingredients, including pigment, may be considered as hazardous materials or potentially harmful to human health. Hence the importance of using the health and safety precautions stated on the MSDS or SDS.

Green Seal$_{TM}$ is one certification that guarantees safer paint. Green Seal is a not-for-profit that evaluates a range of products. The organization bases credentialing—use of the Green Seal—on scientific standards. Paints with the Green Seal offer lower VOC levels and must meet specific standards that prohibit the use of specified chemical compounds that include carcinogens, reproductive toxins, heavy metals, and formaldehyde. The list of forbidden ingredients lists specific chemicals not general categories (http://www.greenseal.org/FindGreenSealProductsandServices).

Figure 8.4 Image courtesy of Brielle H. Welzer, Green Seal.

Another certification program is offered through Greenguard Environmental Institute. The organization was founded in 2001 with a stated mission of protecting "human health and quality of life by improving indoor air quality and reducing chemical exposure." The group with acquired by UL Environment, a division of Underwriters Laboratories (UL) in 2011 (http://www.greenguard.org/en/index.aspx).

Be aware that although some brands have not sought certification, the company may still be committed to not using any chemicals on the EPA's list of toxic chemicals or products. If you particularly like a product that has not announced a green certification, investigate the company's green credentials and product information. You may find the company is "walking the walk" even if they have not considered the advantage of "talking the talk."

Spray Paint, or at Least Finding a Greener One

Traditional aerosol spray paint has been around for years. Because of its popularity with taggers, some urban areas restrict sales of spray paint to individuals over 18 years of age. These older products may be fast and convenient, but the environmental impact is not worth the ease of use. Most spray paints are oil based products and have a high VOC content. Between the product and the propellant, the user is exposed to potentially harmful chemical products. The same spray feature that makes it cover surfaces quickly also means that anyone nearby is exposed to the product, whether they made the choice to use it or not.

Anyone who considers that speed of use and lack of water needed in clean-up an advantage of spray paint should consider two points. In order to create any sort of specific image with spray paint, time-consuming friskets or other masking are required to protect the surrounding area from paint overspray. And while water is not needed to clean a brush, the can must be discarded according to existing regulations. It can take you longer to dispose of a partial or empty can of spray paint than it will ever take to clean a brush. Most manufacturers' cans cannot be easily recycled and end up in a landfill. Special solvents are required to make the cans of most aerosol spray paints recyclable. Manufactures have been attempting to address these drawbacks. Several companies now market a water based latex spray paint that is labeled low VOC.

One relatively new brand of spray paint, Plutonium™ Paint, seems to be more ecofriendly than many other brands. I have not had an opportunity to use the product myself since seeing it mentioned on LinkedIn by another member of the Scenic Designers and Fabricators Group. My research turned up only a few reviews, all fairly positive. One caveat: most of the reviews were not written by theatre scenic artists and the product is listed under "street art" products by at least one online outlet.

Still the possibilities are interesting. According to the manufacturer's web page, http://www.plutoniumpaint.com/, the product reduces the carbon footprint of the aerosol spray by 50% when compared to traditional spray paints because it uses a 70% pigment load and 30% propellant load. This means fewer hydrocarbons in each can, although most manufacturers have switched to less damaging forms of hydrocarbon propellants in aerosols. The paint is a modified automotive acrylic lacquer base that dries in three to five minutes. According to the company's web page the tin free spray cans are also recyclable. It is available from reputable online sources, including Dick Blick Art Supply.

Take Responsibility for Health and Safety

Take the time to carefully read the warnings and instructions for this or any similar product. Pay particular attention to the manufacturer's specifications on reactivity with flame retardant products and any safety measures that require use of personal protection devices. This caveat applies to any paint, coating, or sealing product by any manufacturer whether it is a spray or in a can.

No product is guaranteed safe if not used in the way which it was proscribed by the manufacturer. If you cannot take the appropriate environmental and worker health and safety precautions, don't be irresponsible. Find an alternative product that can be used safely. Aerosol spray paint requires use of adequate ventilation systems and personal protection devices, including respirators with the correct filtration system, to protect both the user, air quality in the workplace and the environment.

Some paint and scene shops have spray areas or booths that are designed to meet the recommended practices for use of sprays. If these standards have not been met, you should not use the products.

Taking the project outdoors does not eliminate the hazards. *It simply exposes a different group of people to the potential health and safety hazards.* Look at the MSDS (SDS) for any

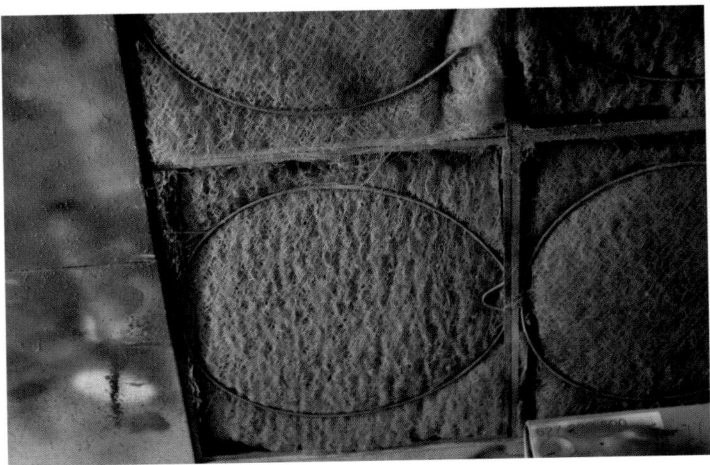

Figure 8.5 Spray booth wall at Central Washington University. Photo by Jessica Pribble.

popular spray paint in any color. Potential side effects of overexposure will probably include: nausea, headache, dizziness, redness or itching of eyes and skin, and nervous depression. Extreme overexposure may result in unconsciousness or death. The chronic health hazards may include permanent brain and nervous system damage.

Some may argue that the MSDS (SDS) for many canned liquid paints will include similar warnings of potential side effects or health problems from overexposure, depending on the exact composition of the paint. However, it is much easier to reduce exposure of a contained liquid that you can see while you are using it. And because it is applied in a more controlled manner that does not include propellants, the painter is less likely to expose bystanders to the safety hazards. If you are really unlucky, you will accidentally spray paint things that were never intended to be painted: Cars, buildings, grass, shrubbery, passersby on the sidewalk. Getting spray paint off of an object is not nearly as easy as unintentionally painting something or someone.

Replacing Spray Paint

Limiting use of spray paint does not have to compromise artistic quality. Savvy painters realize there are options available that eliminate the need for spray paint in most instances. Some painters or props people depend on spray paint to create metallic effects. They may be reluctant to use the liquid metallic scene paints because those made with metal powders are reactive with FR products. Look for metallic color scene paints made from mica platelets that do not have this issue if reactivity with FR treatments is a concern.

Others may have had unsatisfactory color or coverage results from the liquid metallic scene paints. This issue can be addressed by using appropriate base coat colors. The scenery usually requires an initial primer coat or base coat before moving to the color base coat for a metallic finish. Start with white before moving to the colored base and metallic finish coat.

Coatings for Nonporous Surfaces

Spray paint has been the go-to choice for many painters who need to either base coat or paint construction materials that canned water based paints will not readily adhere to; plastic, metal, and soft and rigid foam are common examples. In other instances reused scenery or props may already have been painted with oil based paints or glossy top coat treatments or have an unusual shape that makes brush painting time consuming. There are water borne primers and painting tools that can be used instead and eliminate the need for spray paint.

Scene paint manufacturers have created a range of coating that will adhere to nonporous material and create a hard encapsulating coating or a more flexible finish that allows soft surfaces to be brush painted while maintaining "squeezability." Examples include Sculptural Arts Sculpt or Coat and Tough 'n White and the Rosco products Flexcoat, Foamcoat, Tough Prime, and Crystal Gel. Commercial paint stores also provide a range of water based primers for nonporous surfaces that work

Painting Metallic Finishes

- For golden metallic base coat a flat yellow ochre or golden yellow. Let it dry completely before painting on the metallic.
- White and lighter yellows will provide good highlights. Washes of purple, black, or some combination will create shadow colors on the dried metallic gold paints.
- For silver tones base with a flat grey latex. Choose the base coat value carefully; a light grey will produce brighter silver than a dark grey. Let it dry completely before painting on the metallic.
- Use white or light grey for highlights and black for shadows and highlight on the dried silver paint.

on surfaces ranging from roto-cast plastic to glass. Explain what you are painting and specify that you want to use a water based or water borne flat latex or acrylic paint on top of the primer.

At Indiana Repertory Theatre in Indianapolis, charge artist Claire Dana frequently primes plastics like PVC with white polyvinyl glues (think Elmer's) and paper. She has successfully used bogus paper and kraft paper, but prefers newsprint because the thin material rarely shows overlap seams. The process is nontoxic and paints well once the coating is dry. It also provides a reuse for paper products that might normally be thrown out.

Read the instructions for any coating product, particularly for drying time before applying a second coat, and clean-up instructions as well as SDS for any product before using it. Perform sample tests before tackling the final project.

Replacement Tools for Spray Paint

Paint application tools other than aerosols exist for creating a mist or spray ranging from electric and air spray guns, air brushes for small surfaces and hand pumped sprayers. Hand pumped sprayers and small air brushes require very thin paint. This may mean multiple passes of thinner paint for an opaque coat. Externally powered sprayers using air compressors or electricity require more practice for perfect results, but can use thicker paint requiring fewer coats.

Commercial spray guns that run on air or electricity are also available but if the paint is atomized there are specific requirements for personal protection equipment and safe use.

Figure 8.6 Use of an airless sprayer in a confined space. Lakeview Images/Shutterstock.

When the spray is that fine, it can penetrate your skin. There are many different manufacturers and versions including a product called an airless sprayer. There are also sprayers that are pumped up with compressors and are then detached to allow the painter to move around.

Misted coats of paint may be desirable for more than color coverage. Multiple spatter coats can tone colors, create a sense of shadow, aging, or dirt on painted surfaces. Misted color can add texture to faux finishes and natural surfaces or simply make flat color walls less reflective so the scenery looks more realistic under stage lights. For floors painted to look like a nonspecific material, multiple coats of colored spatter may be used to make the floor color more responsive to different colors of stage lighting or create discreet playing areas that only become obvious when the lighting emphasizes the spatter.

It is, of course, possible to hand spatter with liquid paint using a brush. Using a sprayer can make the task much faster and allow for more control on the size and consistency of the individual drops of paint. Using a spray tool is a better ergonomic choice than hand spattering.

Many of the hand pumped sprayers are manufactured for use in agricultural industry, not to spray paint. Larger pump sprayers are frequently referred to generically as Hudson sprayers. Hudson is a manufacturer. There are other brands in use, but it is a case of a manufacturer becoming a generic reference like the name Kleenex® for any brand of tissues. These units may hold up to several gallons. The reservoir may need to have more air pumped into it periodically to maintain a consistent spray pattern. Both these and powered sprayers require the user to thoroughly understand the instructions.

Hand sprayers are suitable for spattering, grading washes, toning or texturing, and creating patterns or effects. Examples include the use of stencils for patterns and spraying though lace to create an abstracted wall paper pattern. There are also hand painting techniques that can eliminate the use of any sprayer to add texture that replaces spatter or toning sprayers such as sponging, rag rolling, or stippling. See scene painting books for more information on those techniques.

Figure 8.7 Using a Gloria floretta hand sprayer to add spatter to painted rocks. Photo by EEJ.

Smaller hand held sprayers usually carry 1.5 quarts of liquid. Inexpensive sprayers are available in garden, hardware, and paint stores. Some are of a quality that allows them to be considered disposable—better than aerosol spray paint, but not exactly sustainable either. Many experienced scene artists prefer the sturdier all plastic P50 hand sprayer or the Gloria Floretta brand hand sprayers which have some metal parts. If properly cleaned these particular brands will work for years.

Eliminating Other Aerosols

A technical note: It was already mentioned in Chapter 7 that we tend to use the terms adhesive and glue interchangeably. Glues are produced from animal or plant sources and adhesives

Using Hand Held or Hudson Sprayers

- No sprayer will survive long if you are not vigilant about cleaning it out with water as soon as you have finished spraying.
- Paint for hand sprayer must be low viscosity, about the consistency of skim milk.
- A clear water based sealing product can be added to the mixture for greater durability. I personally like Rosco Clear® in gloss or flat for this purpose.
- While cheesecloth can be used for straining paint, cheap nylon net bags from the paint store are better choices for spray mixes to prevent clogs and uneven spray. Cheesecloth can leave lint in the paint that clogs the nozzle.
- Experiment with sealers not only for look but also for walkability. Some gloss sealers can be slick even when dry. Do not believe the theatre lore that pouring a regular soft drink on the floor will make it less slippery. Soda will just make the floor sticky and attract pests.
- Keep a damp sea sponge in a bucket of clean water on hand to catch any drips for vertical units. Wring the sponge out until it is barely damp before using it.
- For short run productions, I will spray multiple light layers of sealer. The floor finish is durable enough for a four- to six-week tech and run period as long as there is little or no rolling scenery or tap dancing. The spray process is faster, and it avoids some of the more distressing and common problems with brushing or rolling sealer onto a floor like bubbling, visible application strokes, and cloudiness.

are synthetic. While understanding this distinction may lead you to greener, safer choices don't let it be your only guide. Natural does not necessarily mean harmless.

Various spray adhesives are the probably the second most commonly used aerosols in the paint shop. People frequently reach for the spray can when adhering unlike materials or creating temporary bonds. Explore other solutions. The range of potential replacements depends on the specific application. Ask yourself if regular white polyvinyl glue or adhesive will take care of the bond. If having the adhesive dry to a white opaque color is a problem, there are flexible liquid products, like Rosco Flexbond®, that dry so clear they can be used as pigment binders. Modern glues and adhesives provide some of the strongest bonds possible when the product appropriate to the materials to be bonded is selected.

Hot glue (actually an adhesive product) is nontoxic if used appropriately; however the little sticks and guns frequently do not offer strong bonds. Chip versions of the glue are available that can be melted in a larger container and used to glue larger pieces of material. Ascertain that the melting temperature of the glue is not high enough to damage the materials being glued. Warning—hot glue will burn your skin. It will do considerable skin damage if you try to remove the glue from your body while it is still hot and will burn you if you let it cool before peeling it off. Use this option with great caution and only if there is not another reasonable solution.

One safe and fun alternative is to use wheat paste glue, especially for temporary applications. Water reactivates the binder, making it an ideal choice for mounting stickers, posters, or pictures that need to be removed without damaging the surface they were attached to for the show. In spite of grade school art class memories, the paste is usually made from whole wheat flour, although bleached flour can be used as well. The less processed flour is stickier as anyone who has made whole wheat bread can attest. Some other whole grain flours work as well, but that requires experimentation.

Dissolve the flour in boiling water or hot water, usually some proportion based on four cups of flour to one gallon of water. Some crafting recipes add vanilla extract, essential oils, and a variety of other additional ingredients. These additives have no impact on the adhesion; they just make the glue smell good until it spoils. The paste should be sealed in a jar and refrigerated. Small quantities are best since wheat paste has a limited shelf life that is determined by climate, time of year, how long it is out of the fridge, and so on. Commercially packaged dry wheat paste is available that only needs water added. The premixed powder will usually contain some additive to keep bugs and rodents from eating it, so it is not as sustainable a choice as homemade.

The Painting Process

There are several fabulous scene painting books available that will give tips, techniques, and explanations of equipment and processes. Sustainability is about avoiding waste, protecting the air quality, avoiding potential water contamination, and recycling and reusing resources instead of putting them into landfills, so techniques and processes are only discussed as they relate to greening efforts.

If paint elevations or rendering are available, pull out the sheet of reusable acetate and tape it over the rendering to protect the original artwork. Mixed samples can be tested on the acetate for a match to the rendering. A scenic artist's job is to match the paint on the set to the color on the rendering. Designers can avoid waste by not only assessing the color match against the rendering but by making sure the paint colors look as intended under gelled stage lights. The wise scene designer makes sure the lighting and costume designers have paint swatches or chips in time to assess the interaction of their palette with hers. When things don't work in tech, someone has to make a change that requires extra work and the use of more materials.

Savvy painters know one of the easiest techniques to avoid waste through mis-mixed paint color is to accurately record the proportions of each test formula as it is mixed and sampled. Keep a written list of the formula for each paint name where it is easily accessible but unlikely to be painted or drenched with water. Write the formula on the side of the bucket as well. The formula can list the proportions of each color and any additional binder by actual liquid measures. At the sample stage this might be in tablespoons or cups. In the final formula it might be gallons or portions of a gallon. Translate the formula in proportions based on the sample. For example if one cup of Emerald Green paint is mixed with two cups of White for the appropriate color; the final formula is one part Emerald Green: two parts White/not thinned.

Many experienced charge artists use a digital scale to measure the proportion of the ingredients instead of the liquid measure method. You don't want to waste paint trying to match a color you have already created and tested.

Even if you plan to use the color in glazes or washes, mix a concentrated color. Record the proportion of water to paint for the thinned mixture. If colors throughout the design are closely linked and different viscosities of the same color are needed, you want to use some portion of the concentrate to mix related tints or tones. In that case the formula for a tint using the concentrate might read one part Brick Red Concentrate: one part White: two parts Water, or the weight of each component.

Adding water to paint increases the opportunity to introduce bacteria which will make the paint start to decompose. When shops cooked animal glue on a hot plate and mixed their own paint decomposition was a significant issue. It was not unusual to add liquid Lysol® to retard the growth of bacteria or Oil of Wintergreen to mask the smell when the paint started to go blinky. If you use Oil of Wintergreen, remember it is toxic if ingested. Even with contemporary synthetics it is not uncommon to see painters put essential oil on a Band-Aid® and place it on the top of the can to help mask any smell that may develop over time.

It takes significantly longer for commercial scene paints to spoil; most have strong preservatives. As health and safety have been introduced in the workplace, those preservatives have

Mixing Paint Successfully

- Let the test sample dry completely before deciding it is the perfect color. Colors mixed with a lot of white paint will dry lighter than the wet color. Dark tones may dry darker than you expect.
- If the scenery will be sealed, test the samples by adding sealer after they dry. Most sealers take paint back to the wet color when applied.
- Once the color mix is selected create a small batch that can be used for paint chips and to test painting techniques.
- Create paint samples large enough to adequately reflect color if you are testing swatches under the stage lights. Professional scenic artists usually paint exactly what is on the rendering. If you are also the scenic designer, you may want to perform this test and the lighting designer probably will want to look at scenery color under stage lights to test gel colors as well.
- Once the color is finalized, mix the amount that will be needed for the show.
- Label both the lid and side of the bucket with the name of the paint—usually what it will be used for on the set—as well as the formula.
- Only use paint buckets that either have lids or can be sealed in some way to keep mixed paint from drying out. In a pinch, a wet cloth can be "sealed" over the top of the bucket.
- Adding plastic wrap to the opening can compensate for a bucket lid that will not tighten down. Watch out for spills since the lid is not actually sealed.
- If there is a small paint spill (the instructions on MSDS or SDS are for major spills, not the gallon bucket that was kicked over) put sawdust on top of the wet paint and vacuum it up with a wet/dry vac. I have even absorbed wet paint out of carpet using this technique.
- Always use a clean scoop, brush, and bucket when mixing paint to be certain that unadulterated colors are not contaminated with other paint colors!

Sustainability at Cobalt Studios

The dynamic and talented Rachel Keebler is a co-founder of Cobalt Studios, probably the most respected training programs for scenic artists in the United States. She and colleague Howard Jones started Cobalt 25 years ago. At the 2013 USITT Conference the two were awarded the USITT Special Citation Award for 25 years of Service and Training of Scenic Artists at Cobalt Studios sponsored by the Education Commission. Cobalt teaches students with many hours of classwork and by having them work on projects that are realized productions. Cobalt also offers numerous short-term workshops and master classes taught by skilled professionals.

When asked about more sustainable practices for paint shops Keebler replied:

> *"If I could, we would go back to a lot of the older processes, always using soft cover flats and animal glues so we could wash them off and reuse them. I would use paper mache instead of rigid foam. And instead of shipping wet paint around all the country, it would be more sustainable to mix local water with pigment and shop made glue."*

Some 95% of the work at Cobalt is painted drops. Keebler prefers to start with FR treated or IFR materials whether they are synthetic or muslin. "*More and more we are working on IFR scrims and poly cycs.*" She adds:

> *"Frequently the problem with FR muslin is sealing and shrinking it so it takes paint properly. We deal with this problem by creating a supersize of starch and animal glue mixed together; both products are heat friendly and the heat helps with both the sealing and the shrinking."*

The IFR synthetics are treated differently because they do not need sizing. Keebler says, "*We just paint right on it with an ink, Prochemical Liquid Decorator Color. I call it a faux dye; it is water based product with finely ground pigment.*"

Greener choices made at Cobalt Studios include replacing more damaging dyes with water based products whenever possible and, for the few times they must use them, replacing turpentine with mineral spirits or odorless terpenoids. One plan for the future is the installation of a grey water system for cleaning buckets.

Cobalt has addressed the paint disposal issue in a unique way. She had a table built that had a wire inset instead of a solid top. Previously used bogus paper serves as a liner for the wire grid, similar to the way that newspaper is used to line bird cages. Leftover paint that cannot be used for another application is poured through the top of the table. The paint solids are filtered out by the bogus paper. When all the liquid evaporates the bogus paper dries out. When the bogus paper is so dirty that it cannot filter out any more solids, it is disposed of as solid waste. Keebler notes, "*It saves filling slop cans with kitty litter and sending them to the landfill.*"

Like any other commercial setting, productivity and greening the process have to go hand in hand. Realistically, Cobalt Studios or any other paint shop has to provide what the customer or designer wants, and greener choices have to serve that work process.

Go to the Cobalt Studio website, http://www.cobaltstudios.net/, for more information on the training program, workshops, and available rental stock.

changed over time to significantly safer chemicals than the original choices which included mercury. Eventually any open paint will decompose. Just straining it will not remedy the issue, and any paint that smells spoiled in the can will continue to smell bad when it dries on the scenery; another reason to limit the amount of leftover product from mixing.

Tools and Accessories

It is rare to have a place to paint scenery that is not used for other purposes. Usually drop cloths or some sort of masking is required to protect the floor and adjacent areas. Whether you use bogus paper, brown kraft paper, plastic, or canvas these drop cloths can be reused. The first impulse is usually to discard anything other than fabric drop cloths. If the paper or plastic is dry, shake any large paint chips off of it, and store it for reuse.

Metal paint cans are reusable if the rim is kept clean so dried product does not prevent a good seal. Avoid scratching off the protective interior coating because that will allow rust to form in the can. Excess paint can be cleaned out with the small foam brushes available at paint stores. Some painters put holes in the rim with small finish nails to allow excess paint to drip through into the can, but there is a danger of cutting your fingers if the hole has a ragged edge. Partially used cans with clean rims can be tightly sealed and stored upside down to avoid air entering the can. Take special note of the tightly sealed description.

Plastic buckets with lids are for sale at every paint store and most big box home improvement stores. Before spending money on those, investigate possibilities for recycling cast-offs from another business. Some coffee shops and bakeries get butter and similar products in 2.5 quart plastic containers with handles and lids. Most are thrown out or recycled by those shops, so they are happy to give them away for other uses. These buckets are large enough to mix paint in easily without being cumbersome. Check any restaurants or cafés to see if they have a similar option available. Any kind of paint will eventually start to dry up or spoil. Keeping it sealed when not in use to avoid evaporation and contamination will delay the inevitable.

The work process on individual shows will determine what greener choices are possible. For example, I hardly ever use roller trays or plastic liners when painting floors. Instead I put the paint in five-gallon buckets and hang a roller screen on the inside to avoid throwing out plastic liners or washing the roller pans. If a lot of scenery is going to be based or painted the same color so rollers and brushes will be used over several days, save some water by wrapping them in plastic bags at the end of the shift. They won't dry out overnight and can be reused without cleaning.

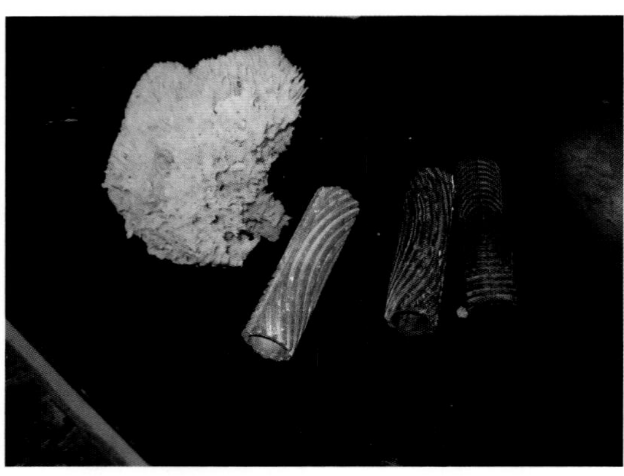

Brushes, specialty tools, sea sponges, rollers, and trays are the other mainstay of any paint shop.
Figure 8.8 A sea sponge and wood graining tools. Photo by EEJ.

A similar technique works for roller skins. York University Assistant Professor James McKernan has created YouTube videos of a paint prewash station for rollers. The original roller skin prewash station was developed by a film painter who visited York and further refined by David Rayfield. The videos show construction of the refined version that is in use at York University. The prewash station uses two five-gallon buckets. The built prewash station simply joins everything together into a single package that can be put on a cart and rolled to the sink. However, the process could be recreated with two five-gallon buckets on the floor.

The first bucket is partially filled with water. The lid is not reattached. The second bucket has a lid with a 4" circle cut in the top. After the skins, still mounted on the roller, are scraped to remove excess useable paint, they are rinsed in the first bucket. This water can be used until it will not rinse off anymore paint.

Cleaning Up Paint Tools

Prewashing tools can limit overall water use. Water for the initial cleaning can be used over and over again until it is almost paint itself. Then use a final clean wash and rinse cycle to finish the process. This process works well with brushes and any specialty paint tools. Special tip, do not use soap to wash sea sponges. They will suds forever. Instead, keep the sponges in a bucket of water that is changed periodically throughout the work day. Do a final rinse at the end of the shift.

Never leave brushes standing in water or paint. It splays the bristles and can cause the glue holding the bristles in the ferrule, the metal housing that holds the bristles together and attaches them to the brush handle, to swell. Brush any excess paint or water off on the edge of the can or bucket and lay the brush sideways. Rinse the brush in a water bucket if it might dry before you use it again on the project.

- At the end of the day or shift, scrape any excess color off the brush back into the bucket.
- Set up a larger bucket partially filled with clean water. Agitate the brushes, one at a time, in the bucket as a prewash. By the end of the clean-up this bucket will be more like paint than water and should be disposed of as paint, not simply poured down the drain.
- Set up a second bucket with a dollop of soap, Ivory liquid, or your preferred product and agitate the almost clean brushes in this bucket.
- Rinse in clean water at the sink or in a bucket. Reshape the bristles and hang up with the bristles pointing toward the floor to dry.

The skin is then removed from the roller and attached to a spinner. It is then inserted into the second bucket and spun to remove paint water before being taken to the sink for a final cleaning (http://www.yorku.ca/tags/Theatre_Artisan_Green_Skills/Paint_Conservation.html).

Roller skins particularly waste a lot of water when thoroughly cleaned. A patented product called *The Spinout Roller Cleaner and Buffer* cuts down on the amount of water needed and limits spray while cleaning. It originated for use in the commercial painting industry but has found its way into the inventory of theatrical vendors as well. Unless the water is captured and filtered for disposal, you are putting paint water into the system. However, if it is used for the final rinse after a prewash station has been used, the waste water has very little paint in it.

The use of prewash stations is particularly useful for shops that lack an easy to access slop sink. Water with a significant amount of waste paint in it, like the water used in these kinds of wash stations, should be disposed of as paint, not water.

Other options to limit use of clean water or white water in the paint shop include collecting rain water or grey water if

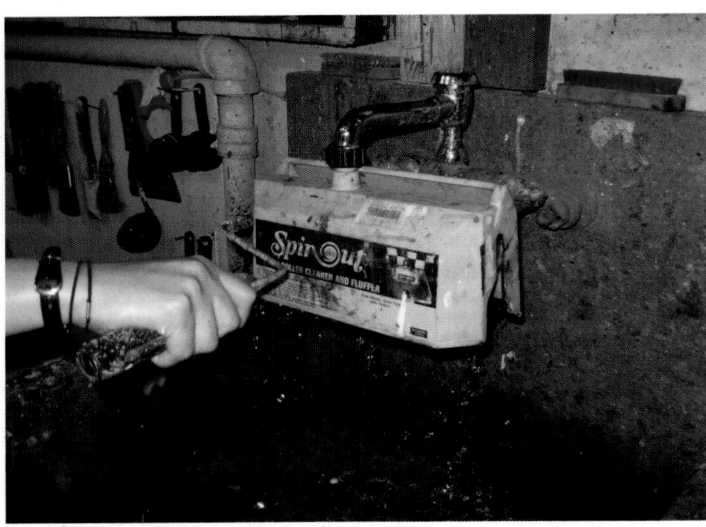

FIGURE 8.9 The *Spinout* decreases the water needed to clean roller skins thoroughly. Photo by EEJ.

possible for cleaning paint tools (and mopping the floors). Look for ways to limit the amount of clean water used in the clean-up process.

Disposal of Paint and Related Products

Resource Conservation and Recovery Act (RCRA) 40 CFR 261 is the standard that establishes the criteria for identifying hazardous waste and specifying appropriate disposal. The local AHJ will administer that standard and tell you what actions you must take to be in compliance when disposing of paint and solvent waste.

The first step in greener disposal of paint is to avoid creating excess paint that will become waste. Most paint labels indicate the surface coverage that can be expected. Many break that information down by application method. While these manufacturer's figures can be assumed to describe the best possible outcome, the information can be used as a reasonable starting point. I usually mix 10% more to compensate for possible differences between the ideal and actual results. Take the time to determine how many square feet of scenery need to be painted with each color and use the coverage information as a guide to how much color to mix.

After the scenery has been painted and touch-up kits (small individual labeled cans of each paint color to take care of any nicks or mars that occur during the run) are prepared, any leftover paint can be stored for use on future shows. If the company does very few productions or lacks any space to store leftover paint, donate the leftover paint to other theatre companies or organizations that can use it. Habitat for Humanity projects and community organizations may be delighted to have the paint.

If a new show will be painted within a few months, the paint may be useful as it is, especially if formulas are available to mix more of the same color. Otherwise similar colors can be mixed into larger buckets for base coating and back painting new scenery. I usually end up with two large buckets post show; one is labeled "Not Quite White" and the other "Almost Black." Don't be surprised that there will be a lot more dark paint than light paint. Be sure to strain any big chunks out of the paint before combining it in the slop buckets.

Paint should never be thrown down the drain. It is not good for the plumbing and it can contaminate groundwater. Most municipalities have rules that require many paint products to be collected as hazardous waste per RCRA. Water borne latex and acrylic paints are usually not considered hazardous materials. The best choice is to find another organization that will accept the paint as a donation or give it to an individual. Though few and far between, there are commercial companies that accept leftover latex paint and recycle it into new paint.

Even if you are using water borne products that do not require specialized disposal, no one wants wet paint slopping around in the garbage. It must be dried out or solidified in some way that does not involve freezing. Once the temperature goes back up the frozen paint will liquefy again. Leaving the bucket

Avoid Buckets of the Wrong Color

There are few things more disheartening than realizing several gallons of new paint have been used to make five gallons of a color that cannot be used for the show or successfully tinted, mixed, or otherwise transformed into a useable color. Testing samples and writing down formulas for the colors makes this less likely. However, even if the formula is perfect, mistakes that are hard to correct can be made when making larger batches if the person mixing does not know common characteristics of latex paints.

- Create the samples and carefully record the formulas before starting to mix large batches.
- When mixing color add small quantities of dark paint to lighter colors. If paint is too light a small quantity of the darker color with change the value. It can take gallons of white to lighten a too-dark color.
- If the above error has already occurred, pour off a small amount of the dark color and use it to start the process again—mixing dark paint into light paint.
- If you are working with a variety of brands and compositions of paint, experiment with small quantities first to make sure the pigments will remain in suspension in the mixed content solutions.
- Create thinner washes and glazes from concentrated premixed paint colors. If too much water is in the solution in the beginning, a lot of paint will have to be added to reach the correct viscosity and a large quantity of the thinned mix left over.
- Always avoid contaminating the unadulterated paint, no matter how many measuring cups, brushes, or buckets it takes. Put the paint for mixing in a new bucket instead of using the original container. This makes it easier to avoid accidentally putting other colors in the original buckets. Using a measuring cup or ladle instead of pouring paint from the can will help keep the rim clean for a tight seal.

open will allow the water to evaporate; although this never seems to happen as quickly when you are trying to dry the paint out as when someone accidentally leaves the lid off the can. Clay kitty litter is an inexpensive absorbent material that can be used to "solidify" paint as well. When water evaporates and the paint litter mixture dries, it can be placed in the garbage. Investigate the local laws concerning disposal of the paints you have selected.

Like every other area of production, the steps to a greener paint shop center on Reduce, Reuse, and Recycle. Meticulous planning is a no-cost way to save time, money, and material resources by reducing waste in the paint shop. Scene painting is one of the areas where an audit of the work process can help move to a more sustainable process. If any paint is waste because it was unacceptable as opposed to left over, try to determine what went wrong and created this waste.

Special Safety Note: Storage of Flammable and Combustible Products

If you still have any aerosols or flammables in the paint shop, you should have a Flammable and Combustible storage cabinet. This is not simply a metal cabinet. Criteria for the appropriate storage cabinet are established by NFPA Flammable Liquid Storage Code #30 and OSHA standard 1910.10.

If the shop does not contain a flammables cabinet or you do not know what needs to be placed in the flammables cabinet; make an appointment with the institutional safety officer, the individual responsible for safety in your organization, or the Authority Having Jurisdiction for accurate information. Certain items should be stored in flammable cabinets for the safety of workers and first responders in the case of an emergency.

Figure 8.10 Flammables cabinets should only be open when retrieving an item from inside. Photo by Jessica Pribble.

Take the time to think through paint and decorative processes and select the products that have the least impact on the environment while still meeting the needs of the show to reduce potential air and water contamination and the use of natural resources.

Chapter 9

Greener Stage Lighting Design and Technology

Figure 9.1 The stage lighting rig, no matter how large or small, is a place where changes can have a dramatic impact on greening production. Valerii Ivashchenko/Shutterstock.

The stage lighting rig, no matter how large or small, is a place where changes can have a dramatic impact on greening production.

This is not a lighting design or lighting stagecraft book. Since it is geared to a broad audience, enough information about equipment and design is offered to allow readers whose expertise is not in stage lighting to make greener choices and to understand the tips offered. More comprehensive and in-depth information is available in a number of excellent textbooks, blogs, and manufacturer and vendor web pages.

In recent years there has been a great deal of attention on lighting as a possible area to reduce a theatre's carbon footprint.

The publicity about the elimination of lower wattage, inefficient incandescent lamps reinforced the concept. Governmental concerns about environmental stewardship are a huge step forward in green thinking. Unfortunately the focus has only been on technology and efficiency without acknowledgment of the broader range of concerns, particularly the quality of the light. Almost everyone has certain expectations about the quality of light a source will provide.

The next time you are in a hotel where the chain has clearly made lighting changes to be greener, step into the bathroom and think about whether you have ever looked worse in your life. Ask yourself if the nightstand lamp would allow you to read a newspaper in bed without a flashlight. You don't have to be a lighting designer to recognize that a light source is not adequate to the task for which it is being used. Color rendering and intensity have to be considered along with energy use.

Direct replacement compact fluorescents were touted as the answer to reducing energy consumption in domestic and industrial lighting. They are more efficient than incandescent bulbs and the goal of reducing use of electricity was the only criteria considered. Over time discussion has developed because the limited spectrum of compact fluorescents does not produce light that is as visually appealing to most people as the incandescent bulbs they replaced. This limited spectrum also impacts the color of the objects being lit.

Concerns beyond aesthetics have emerged as well. The presence of mercury in this widely used consumer product has made the use of these direct replacement lamps more controversial than anticipated. Questions about how the electronic ballasts of the compact fluorescents may impact power distribution systems as the use becomes widespread have also been posed.

Basics of Lamps

Incandescent Lamps

Traditional stage lighting luminaires (fixtures) used incandescent lamps and then moved to the improved incandescent tungsten-halogen lamps. Older incandescent stage lamps with the traditional filament are enormous compared to more contemporary, slimline, tungsten-halogen lamps.

The oldest incandescent lamps worked like the ones used in domestic settings. They create light because the electricity heats the lamp filament until it glows. The filament does not catch on fire because the glass globe is either filled with an inert gas or is a vacuum without air. Traditional incandescent lamps are inefficient because much of the power consumed is converted to heat. Only about 8% of the energy consumed is converted to light according to the Philips Lighting University web page (http://www.lighting.philips.com/main/connect/lighting_university/). Incandescent lamps are terribly inefficient. On the other hand they are cheap, work with a variety of power sources and controls, including stage dimmers and lighting consoles, and offer a full enough spectrum of light to render color accurately.

This level of inefficiency is what has led to the legislation to stop the use and manufacture of incandescent lamps in some parts of Europe and more recently in the United States. The incandescent lamps that are being phased out and will no longer be manufactured are mostly smaller bulbs. This may have an impact on the availability of bulbs that are used in house lights, task lights, and general illumination areas of the venue.

Tungsten-Halogen Lamps

A number of specialty lamps are excluded from the manufacturing ban at this time, including most of the tungsten-halogen or T-H stage lamps in common use. Tungsten-halogen lamps still operate on the principle of incandescence, heating the filament until it glows. However they are more efficient than the older incandescent because of something called the tungsten cycle. The tungsten filament evaporates into the halogen gas as it heats. When the lamp is turned off and the filament cools, the tungsten solidifies on the filament. These lamps are slightly more efficient than older traditional incandescents, converting approximately 12% of the electricity to visible light (http://www.lighting.philips.com/main/connect/lighting_university/).

T-H lamps create significantly more heat than traditional incandescent lamps. The globe surrounding the lamp is made of quartz and if touched the oil from skin will likely cause a lamp failure as it burns into the globe. Most electricians know these lamps according to their American National Standards Institute (ANSI) three-letter code: HPL, FEL, BTL and so on. In this case, the code is a description with no rational basis for the letters chosen, not a regulatory code. The three-letter description identifies lamp specifics including the length and shape of the filament, the height of the envelope, and the kind of base.

Arc Lamps

Fixtures with arc lamps are also widely used in the entertainment industry, particularly in follow spots, intelligent or robotic units, and high wattage stage lights. These lamps are significantly brighter than T-H lamps. In this case, the electricity jumps a gap between two contacts in the lamp to create light. This method of producing light means they perform differently than incandescent lamps. Arc lamps require a mechanical dimmer or douser since decreasing the power will eventually prevent the electricity from crossing the gap to create light. These units are always drawing full power unless turned completely off. There may be a lag time between powering down and being able to restrike the lamp.

The appearance of the white light from each of these kinds of lamps is different and that difference is described as color temperature. Color temperature is measured in degrees Kelvin (K). The lower the color temperature the warmer the white light from the source appears. There is no scientific or industry standard definition of the terms cool or warm light, although we often see the terms used as descriptions of lamp color. Natural daylight is around 6,500K and appears more white or cooler than incandescent or T-H lamp light which is usually in the range of 2,800K to 3,200K. A Xenon Arc lamp is usually in the 5000K range.

LED or Light-Emitting Diode Lamps

LED or light-emitting diode technology has also created a new option in stage lighting. One industry response to environmental concerns has been to focus on equipment that uses an LED light source. LED units operate on a totally different principle than the lamps mentioned above and can appear very different visually. Color is not created by adding color media in most cases; it is created by altering the chemistry of the crystal sandwich comprising the solid-state semiconductors that we call LEDs.

Instead of installing a lamp into a socket, the LEDs are often integral to the luminaire itself, which usually includes a power supply to drive the LEDs, optics to reflect or refract the light, and a heat sink to dissipate the heat generated by the LEDs. Although the beam of light itself is fairly cool, the process of generating light from LEDs does produce some heat within the emitters, which can affect their longevity if not properly managed. LEDs operate for significantly longer periods of time and consume far less electricity than a conventional unit. A conventional T-H lamp will last around 2000 hours and an LED can last as long as 50,000 hours or more. LED lamps are available in a range of colors as well as color temperatures from warm white to cool white.

Viewers usually have an emotional response to the color temperature of light. This is particularly true of watching incandescent lamps dim—we are accustomed to seeing the light moving into an even warmer range as power to the unit is decreased to dim the light. Even more importantly the perceived color temperature of the white light can impact the colored light created by adding color media to the luminaire.

Many lighting designers familiar with conventional stage lighting units are accustomed to thinking of brightness in terms of the foot candles generated by a particular unit using a particular wattage lamp. Most have expectations that a stage fixture will produce light in a particular color temperature range, usually warmer light. Part of this expectation is based on experience with units in the field. Photometric data supplied by the manufacturer or collected into industry sources; for example, Robert Mumm's *Photometric Handbook*, also impacts designer expectations. (Mumm's book was last updated in 1997, but if your company has older fixtures, the information is there.)

Lumens are the more current standard unit of measure. It indicates how much light is contained in a certain area. Luminous flux measures how the human eye responds to the wavelengths present. The candela is a measure of luminance or how much light the unit is generating directly at the source and lux measures illuminance or how much of the light makes it to the object being lit. Efficiency ratings currently used in legislation and manufacturer's descriptions of products are usually expressed in luminous efficacy measured in lumens per watt (lm/W).

One way to make lamps more efficient is to make units that produce more wavelengths in a particular portion of the spectrum that the human eye is more responsive to; the yellow/green end of the visible spectrum—fluorescents are an older example of this manufacturing technique. The lime green color used for indicator lights on electronics is a wavelength that the human eye most easily sees. A theoretical light fixture that produces only these wavelengths could have an incredible efficacy of as much as 600 lumens per watt. However, the quality of the lighting and color-rendering ability would be atrocious. Greening your stage lighting system also requires examination of more than instrument efficiency.

If all goals rest only on efficiency, then there is no incentive to look at other properties of the light produced. A similar analogy is if low cost is the only goal in manufacturing a consumer product, is there an incentive to be concerned about durability, how well the product does its job, or the work environment where it is manufactured? It is incumbent on the end user to look beyond the single barometer of a high lumen per watt rating and make sure that the LED unit meets all of the goals she deems important.

As you make choices for the lighting in your venue, look beyond the initial enticements of the rebates and lower wattages. Consider all of the aspects related to lighting usage in the facility with a long-term point of view. As more direct replacement LED options come into the marketplace, they may become a better choice than compact fluorescents for task lighting even if the initial cost is higher.

The same considerations should be examined for every upgrade to more efficient lighting whether it is in the lobby marquee, the dressing room make-up mirrors, or the luminaires used to light the productions. Just as there is no one-size-fits-all answer for a sustainability initiative, there is no single lighting product that can meet the artistic and practical use requirements of every facility.

A Review of Common Stage Lighting Fixtures

Understanding the basics of stage luminaires and how they create light is the first step to making greener lighting choices. The explanations below are very basic descriptions. Consult a stage lighting text for more information about why the luminaires function in the ways described. The two most basic categories of luminaires were conventional and automated fixtures.

Conventional stage lights must be manually focused. Changes in color media, and change in the shape or quality of the beam of light, can only occur when an electrician is working at the unit. Conventional luminaires may be wash fixtures that cover a broad expanse of the stage with a soft-edged beam of light that fades out or spotlights that cover a confined area of the stage and have a more distinct edge to the pool of light.

Ellipsoidal reflector spotlights or ERS that may be known by brand or model names including Leko® (now used generically), Shakespeare®, Source Four®, SPX®, are conventional fixtures commonly used in the front of house (FOH). These fixtures are further identified by size specifications that help indicate the size and intensity of the beam of light each produces; for example 6 x 9 in older ERS units or by the beam

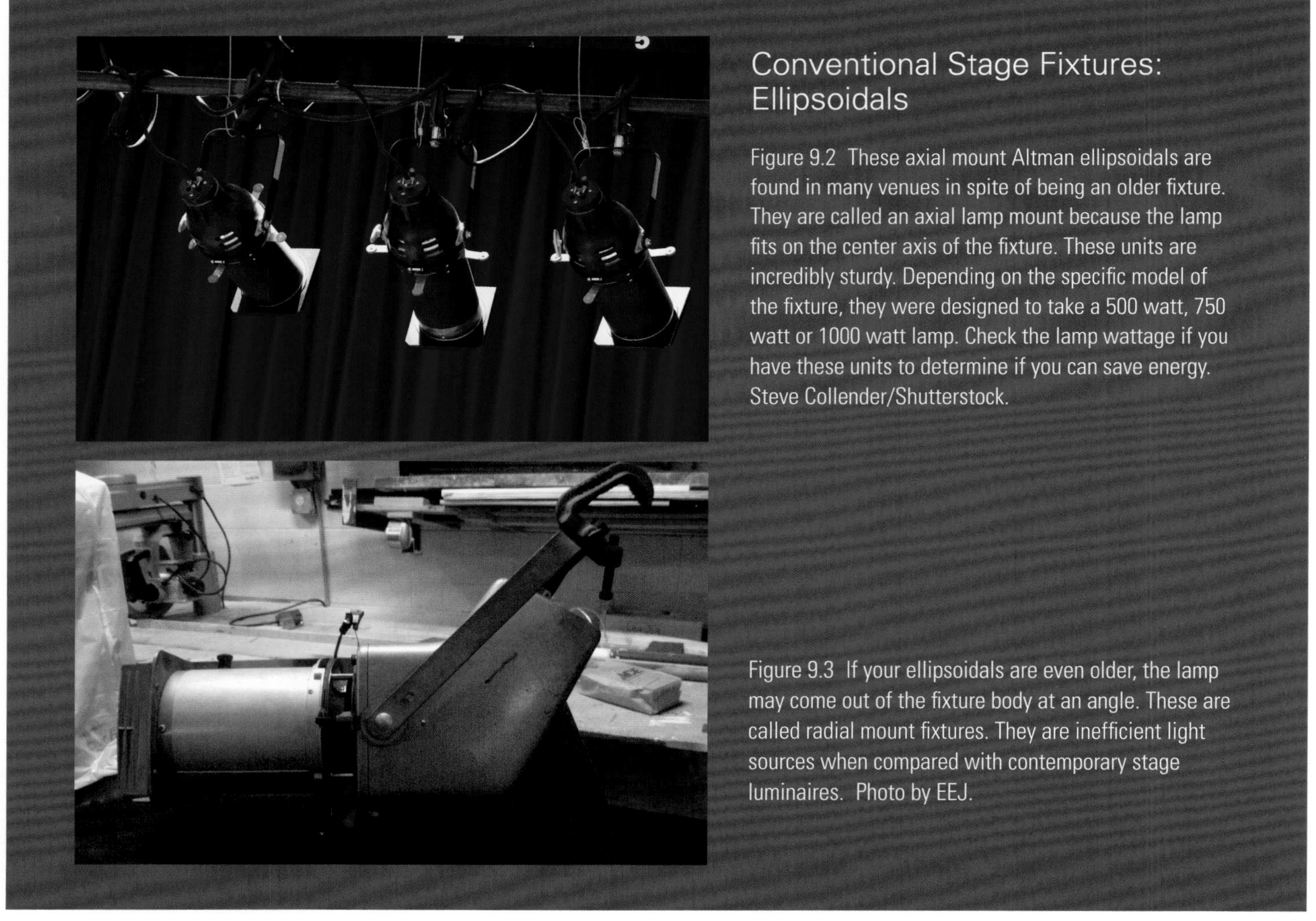

Conventional Stage Fixtures: Ellipsoidals

Figure 9.2 These axial mount Altman ellipsoidals are found in many venues in spite of being an older fixture. They are called an axial lamp mount because the lamp fits on the center axis of the fixture. These units are incredibly sturdy. Depending on the specific model of the fixture, they were designed to take a 500 watt, 750 watt or 1000 watt lamp. Check the lamp wattage if you have these units to determine if you can save energy. Steve Collender/Shutterstock.

Figure 9.3 If your ellipsoidals are even older, the lamp may come out of the fixture body at an angle. These are called radial mount fixtures. They are inefficient light sources when compared with contemporary stage luminaires. Photo by EEJ.

angle size 30° of newer ERS luminaires. Beam angle specifies the size of the pool of light created by the fixture.

The two-number designation for older units tells you first the diameter of the lens, 6″ in the example given. The second number, 9″ in the example, is the focal length which is determined by the distance of the lamp from the lens. The shorter the focal length, the wider the area covered by the pool of light. The light is actually a three-dimensional cone, but if you were to draw it on a piece of paper and measure the angle with a protractor, that degree would tell you the size of the beam. The lower the angle number, the narrower the cone of light and the further away it can be placed from the object being lit.

Ellipsoidal reflector spotlights create a coherent beam of light that can be seen as a well-defined circle with a hard edge. Since the beam of light is sharply defined it can be shaped with the shutters inside the fixture or using templates or gobos that are placed inside the unit to create shadows. The light is also coherent enough to allow the use of slides when

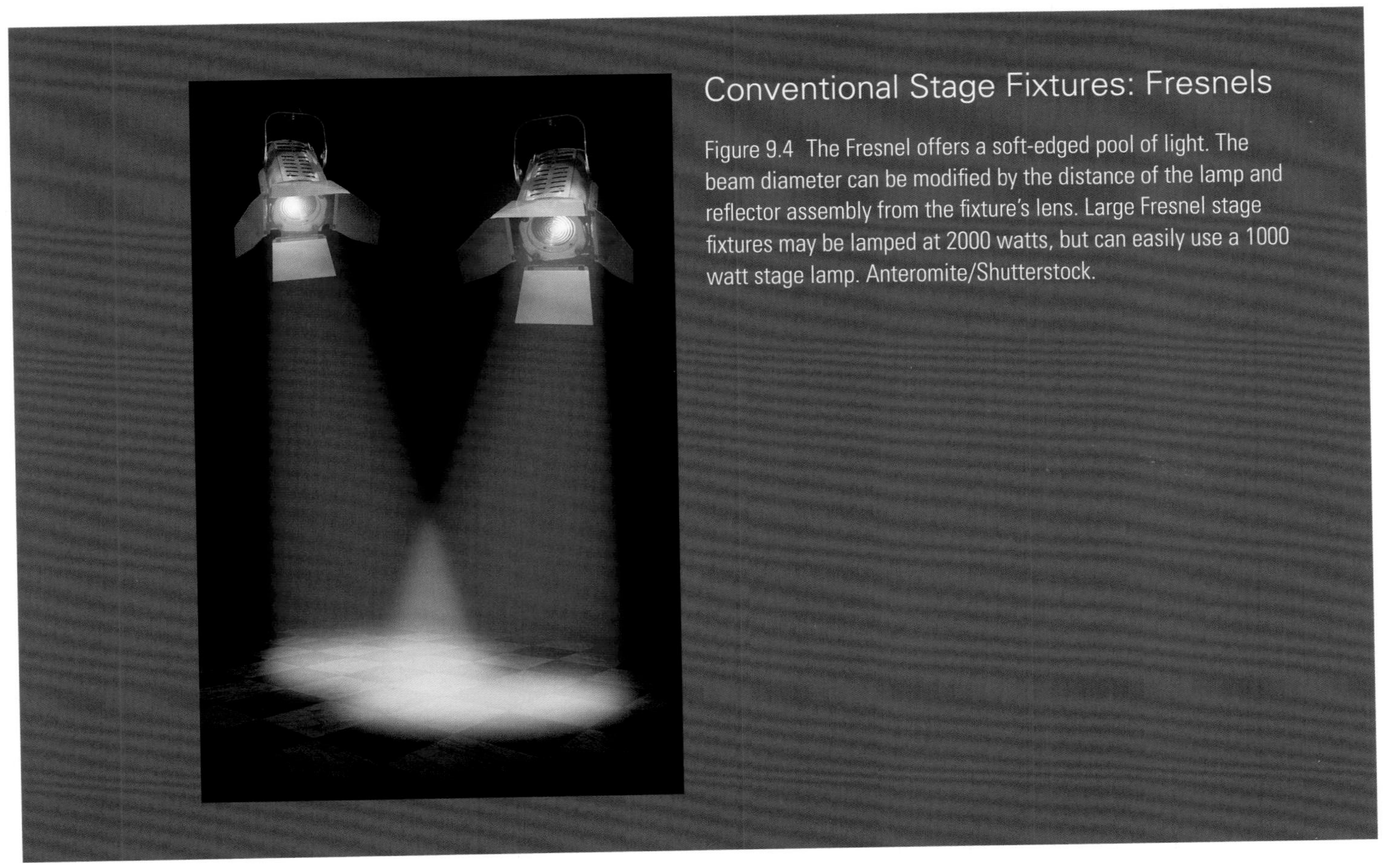

Conventional Stage Fixtures: Fresnels

Figure 9.4 The Fresnel offers a soft-edged pool of light. The beam diameter can be modified by the distance of the lamp and reflector assembly from the fixture's lens. Large Fresnel stage fixtures may be lamped at 2000 watts, but can easily use a 1000 watt stage lamp. Anteromite/Shutterstock.

accessories like the Rosco Image Pro are added to the unit. (http://www.rosco.com/lighting/ipro.cfm).

Fresnels are common conventional wash units. The unique lens shape allows the light to have a softer edge but remain coherent enough to travel long distances and still be seen as a beam. Lighthouses use Fresnel lenses. The beam of light from a Fresnel cannot be shaped in the same way and ERS beam can, but the Fresnel fixture allows for an adjustable beam spread. In other words, the Fresnel can be placed in spot focus to create a very bright and compact pool of light or it can be flooded to increase the beam angle. This produces a much softer-edged, dimmer pool of light that covers a greater stage area in light that feathers off at the edges. Frequently Fresnels are first identified by the manufacturer; Altman, Source Four, Philips, or Arri, for example, because so many companies make them. The diameter of the lens is used as a second descriptive qualifier to indicate the size of the fixture. Typically, the larger the fixture, the more area it can cover onstage and the higher the wattage of the lamp inside.

A third workhorse of the theatre is the PAR Can. Traditional PAR Cans are sometimes called "Deep Throat PARS" to distinguish them from the newer, more compact hybrid PAR units such as the Source 4 Par® and the Altman Star * PAR®. The hybrid units use the same T-H lamp as ellipsoidals manufactured by the same company, but produce a pool of light that mimics the oval shape of the original PAR Can.

These units create an oval pool of light that can be oriented upstage to downstage or stage left to stage right. These units are defined by the wattage of the lamp and a designation indicating the size of the pool of light. Many of the lamps commonly used in traditional PAR Cans are included in the incandescent ban. Users will have to find the more expensive

Conventional Stage Fixtures: PAR Cans

Figure 9.5 Traditional PAR Cans use the lens of the sealed lamp to control the size of the oval pool light created. The lack of a fixture lens makes them light for touring and quick to focus since they simply need to be pointed and locked in place by the electricians. Fedor Selivanov/ Shutterstock.

Figure 9.6 An ETC Source Four® Par with its multiple lenses. Photo by EEJ.

T-H replacement version of the lamps. The Source Four Par® and Source Four Parnel® are modifications of the old fashioned PAR Can that bridge the world of allowing multiple sized oval beams from the unit and using the Source Four technologies that allows maximum efficiency from a single lamp. In this case, instead of changing the lamp for a different size oval, the user replaces the front lenses of the unit.

One other common group of stage lighting fixtures is found in many venues; wash fixtures without lenses that are used to light large swathes of the stage or vertical scenery. Lenses refract light and limit how wide the beam of light becomes as it moves away from the fixture. Strip lights have multiple lamps in a single body and are effective for lighting broad expanses of stage or cycloramas. Scoops are large single units that can fulfill the same functions and are also commonly used as work lights in venues.

Because conventional fixtures use incandescent lamps they dim easily allowing remote control of intensity. However without the addition of accessories; color, focus, or where the fixture is aimed, the shape of the beam produced, or how defined the edge of the pool of lights is, can only be altered by a stagehand at the individual unit. An accessory may be required to change a mentioned attribute.

Automated or Intelligent Fixtures

Automated fixtures, also known as intelligent fixtures or movers, allow the user to make changes to a variety of specifics. These include focus, color, projected pattern and movement of that pattern, intensity, definition of the edge of the beam of light, and shape of the beam or some combination of these attributes which may be controlled remotely. If the entire fixture pans and tilts it is called a moving head. These units usually have a greater number of automated attributes. Some automated fixtures have a single mirror that may move inside or in front of the unit and only the focus of the light can be changed from the control board. There are many different combinations of automated attributes.

Automated units are broadly divided into wash units that cover large areas with light or profiles that can provide a defined discreet beam.

The flexibility offered by automated lighting fixtures means that fewer individual lighting units can create the same number of possible looks as more conventional fixtures. However, automated fixtures may use discharge or arc lamps that are dimmed mechanically instead by decreasing the amount of electricity going to the lamp. These lamps are more efficient than incandescent lamps in terms of the percentage of electricity converted to visible light. Because the color is produced inside the luminaire there is less waste of color media. This does not necessarily mean that automated units are greener.

The units draw a great deal of power whenever they are powered on, even if no visible light is hitting the stage. This is referred to as the quiescent load. It is not uncommon to see quiescent loads of over 800 watts for automated fixtures. That is energy consumed all the time, before the lamp actually

Figure 9.7 Automated moving head lighting fixtures in use at an outdoor performance venue. vvoe/Shutterstock.

strikes to create any visible light. Because the units are large and heavy and include a multitude of internal parts there is a great deal of embodied energy in the unit as well. There are applications where automated luminaires are the most sustainable choice because they exactly meet the needs of a company or production with the fewest fixtures. There are automated units that use incandescent lamps in order to blend more effectively with conventional fixtures in the rig.

LED light source units are available in both wash and profile units that have attributes similar to the conventional fixtures mentioned above. The profiles can use shutters for framing and many can accept patterns or gobos and some of the wash units offer the option of a spot or flood of the light beam. Automated fixture models using LED arrays are also available from a number of manufacturers. Later in this chapter there is a more complete discussion of LED stage lighting fixtures including suggestions to determine if they are the best option for your company.

Making the Most of the Equipment You Already Have

The first step in greening your stage lighting is to get the most out of what you already own and identify where gaps exist in the inventory. Lighting is usually an integral part of any production unless you are doing a workshop reading or performing a show for radio broadcast. Low-cost or no-cost greener choices are possible without the financial costs of replacing equipment. An audit of your stage lighting equipment means it is time for another inventory spreadsheet. Greening your stage lighting will be more efficient with an accurate inventory that only includes useable fixtures.

The Lighting Equipment Audit

You should tally power consumption as well as counting fixtures and lamps. Ultimately you may end up estimating a portion of the electricity used by your lighting rig. Do this by determining the potential total wattage of the existing fixture inventory. Include stage lights that are damaged in the inventory if they can be repaired and reasonably used in production. In addition to counting the models and focal lengths of the units, keep track of the lamp wattage and ANSI code. Chapter 2 more fully describes these kinds of audit and inventory practices.

You probably have a number of instruments that can only be used from one specific hanging position. In most traditional proscenium venues there are only enough instruments of the correct focal length to hang in each available position in the front of house (FOH). For example, if there is a balcony rail, a catwalk, or a box boom position, it is usually far enough from the proscenium arch that the focal length and beam spread of the lighting unit is much narrower than that of units used in the upstage hanging positions. These FOH positions may be far enough apart that each uses a different focal length as well. Since most of these luminaires produce a beam of light too narrow to use on stage, they don't move too much and are probably all used every show.

The units used on the stage may be able to be used from a number of hanging positions including temporary vertical trees or booms or ladders if dance concerts are part of the season. Count all of these units by type and focal length or manufacturer and model. Record the lamp wattages in use as well. The older your fixtures, particularly ellipsoidals, the more likely they are to all be lamped at 1000 watts. If you have never taken this step and depend on an inexperienced hang and focus crew, you may have a variety of lamps wattages installed in fixtures of the same type. This discrepancy can impact the quality of lighting in productions.

Don't bother to count archaic fixtures that are never used. Strip down the metal and glass and recycle those materials. Lenses and bases may be reusable as repair parts. Determine if damaged fixtures are so old that repair parts are not available. These should be broken down and recycled as well. The fact that some lighting fixtures have remained viable for use long after parts for repair are available is a testament to the durability of the original products.

Even if you have only newer units, you may be able to reduce the wattage of lamps used in any venue with a low ceiling. The closer the stage fixture is to the performer being lit, the shorter the throw distance. Throw distance is the length of the linear route from the lens to the performer. The shorter that distance, the less the beam of light can spread out and the brighter it is. For example, many ETC Source Four® fixtures are lamped at 750 watts even though the HPL lamps used are

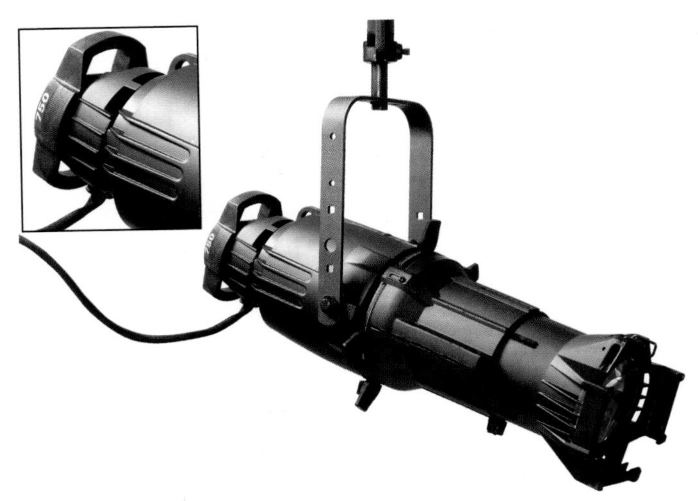

Figure 9.8 A Source Four 750 watt ellipsoidal. The designation 750 on side of the cap of the unit means it can accommodate a lamp at that higher wattage, not that you have to use that wattage. Russell Shively/Shutterstock.

available in 575 and 375 wattages as well. In smaller venues with short throw distances, these wattages may be a better choice.

Track it all. Looking over old paperwork or plots may help you determine the average number of each type of unit hung for shows. If you have a rep plot, you can count the units in place to get raw data.

You don't know how often each luminaire was turned on and what power level it will run at in each lighting cue, so this is not a scientifically accurate measure. However, you can total up the number of potential watts by multiplying the lamp wattages used by the number of hours the rig is in use to reach an average on power consumption. This technique should also make you aware of opportunities when you can save electricity by turning off the stage lights and use general task lighting.

Determine if lower wattage T-H replacement lamps are available and will provide adequate visibility for productions. Talk with the manufacturer or your theatrical vendor to determine which lamps are suitable for your specific fixtures. A lamp has to do more than simply fit into the fixture socket. If the lamp is the wrong length or the filament the wrong shape to work with the unit's reflector, it will not operate as designed. Having all stage lighting fixtures operate at peak efficiency is the more sustainable choice. How many watts of electricity use can you potentially save by making those changes?

Also calculate how many potential watts you could save by switching to more recently manufactured luminaires that use lower wattage lamps. For example, replacing older 1000 luminaires with newer units designed to use 575 watts offers a potential savings of 425 watts per unit. Typically you will discover that while you save watts by replacing old fixtures, you lose nothing in intensity by moving to newer units. In fact, you may be able to run the newer units at lower levels to achieve the same look because they are more efficient.

Asbestos Cords

If you have fixtures with asbestos cords there is a twofold problem. First, they will certainly be old enough to be very inefficient, but more importantly there are health and safety issues. OSHA standards only define asbestos as a health hazard when it is "friable"—meaning it can be reduced into smaller pieces of particulate matter that will be ingested into the lungs. However, many industrial hygienists, most notably theatre expert Monona Rossoll, say that even having the units hanging in storage raises measureable asbestos particulate matter in the air. Every time the units are moved to be rehung or focused, the cords may release asbestos. Wrapping the cords in tape or adding another covering, sometimes referred to as spaghetti, over the asbestos cords is not a solution. Neither is painting the cords.

Asbestos removal must be addressed by someone qualified in asbestos abatement. Removal of hazardous waste is usually priced by the pound. Only the cords are problematic, so have the asbestos abatement team dispose of the caps only. You can dispose of the metal body and glass lenses by either storing parts for repairs or recycling. Some venues choose to rewire these fixtures after the old cords are removed. Any unit old enough to still have an asbestos cords is probably not worth the cost and effort of rewiring.

This brings us to another issue—any instrument manufactured with an asbestos cord was designed to use the incandescent lamps produced at the time. These lamps did not generate the heat that a modern lamp is capable of producing. Just because a lamp fits in the socket, does not mean it is an appropriate direct replacement. The reflector is not as efficient so you generate a lot more heat without a great deal more light. Units of this vintage should be replaced for a host of reasons.

Paying for new lamps or new fixtures is always an issue. There are various grant programs and rebates from companies that can help defray those costs. The fact that there are both safety and energy efficiency issues may make it possible to secure a grant for an equipment upgrade. If the fixtures are older, determine if the dimming and control board are of similar age. It is desirable to upgrade that equipment at the same time, and may be necessary in order to be able to use newer fixtures. Documentation of both safety and sustainability issues may be an asset in trying to raise capital for new units either from administrators or grant-funding entities. See Chapter 2 for ideas on funding sources.

Operating dimmers and luminaires at their peak efficiency means that you get more lumens per watt. Simply stated, peak efficiency means that equipment produces the most useable light possible for the amount of power consumed.

Getting the Best Performance from Dimmers

If your dimmers are electronic, most of the operating components are the same whether they are digital or analog. Only the control module that receives and acts on instructions from the lighting board is different. Dimmers attached to an analog control module must receive a constant signal to know the amount of electricity to send to the lighting fixtures. If you have analog dimmers there will be a control cable from the back on the lighting console to each dimmer so that a constant signal can be maintained or a conversion box that translates the digital signal from your board to instructions that the analog dimmers can understand.

Digital dimmers know their address or name, to put it in the simplest terms. Once a digital dimmer receives an instruction it continues to follow the instruction until a new one is received. In the case of a digital board attached to digital dimmers, there is usually only one cable coming from the back of the console to the dimmers. Conversion or translation boxes also exist that allow analog boards to talk to digital dimmers.

Most experienced stage electricians believe that digital dimmers are more responsive and energy efficient than analog dimmers. Some analog dimmers can be upgraded with digital command modules either from the manufacturer or third party vendors like Johnson Controls. Some brands of older analog dimmers are sturdy, high quality products that have long life spans. Replacement of the control module costs a great deal less than replacing the entire dimmer rack. Very little equipment has to be removed, disposed of, or rewired. Consult with a theatrical supplier who does dimmer installation work or another qualified person to determine if this is a good option for the equipment in your venue and to determine what manufacturer's equipment best suits your needs.

Whether your dimmers are individual packs, small rolling racks, or large, high density racks, the entire unit is cooled by fans that draw air into the dimmers to dissipate heat. Most of these fans do not filter the air. This allows dust and dirt to be drawn into the electronics as well, much like the fan that cools a desktop computer. Dimmers need to be cleaned by vacuuming or blowing air through them on occasion to eliminate that debris. The presence of dust bunnies will compromise dimmer operation.

If the dimmers do have air filters on the enclosure door these can be removed and washed with water, the same way you can wash a window air conditioner air filter. Allow the filters to dry fully before replacing them in the rack.

Before engaging in any of these activities, *turn off the power to the dimmers.* This requires more than simply flipping the circuit breakers of the dimmer or turning off the board.

Figure 9.9 A locked out power source. Harry H. Marsh/Shutterstock.

Turn off the power to the dimmers where it enters the building. Depending on the electrical codes in your region, there may be a power feed disconnect close to the rack that allows you to turn them off without cutting other power in the building. If the power feed control (usually a large box with a physical handle that you pull) is not close by, you may need to have someone from custodial staff or facilities maintenance help you find the power disconnect. The power feed should be locked out and tagged out while you are working so no one can turn the power back on while you are working. There is an OSHA standard about lock out/tag out on power sources (http://www.osha.gov/OshDoc/data_General_Facts/factsheet-lockout-tagout.pdf). Whoever performs this task should fully understand the process and follow the standard to the letter, even if unpaid volunteers instead of employees are involved. If you do not understand any of the terminology or descriptions in this paragraph, contact a theatrical vendor or a licensed electrician to assist you. Do not become a competitor for a Darwin Award by taking a chance with your life and hoping for the best.

If there is an accessible power box that feeds the dimmers, you should be throwing that handle to the off position at the end of each day. Otherwise the dimmers will continue to draw power, even when the board is not turned on. This power draw is the quiescent load. Other lighting equipment including arc lamps and moving units and some lighting accessories may also draw a quiescent load when not in use and should be physically disconnected from power feeds by a switch or unplugging.

If the dimmers in your facility are so antiquated that they are direct control resistance dimmers, a great deal of power is wasted every time they are turned on. Most resistance dimmers found in older facilities are round with either dial faces or individual handles. They always draw full power when operating and the energy going to the fixtures is limited by introducing a material that is resistant to the flow of electricity into the circuit. Energy that is not converted to light is converted to heat. Even if you are only using a fraction of the power to actually produce light at a low level, you are consuming every available watt while you do it.

How can you tell if you have resistance dimmers? If you have to move individual handles and the audience sees any changes made at the lighting controls as they happen, you probably have resistance dimmers. There is not a control board per se because each dimmer is actually part of the electrical circuit that includes the lighting fixture. Control equipment of this vintage should be replaced as quickly as possible and the energy savings might mean huge rebates from the utility supplier. Resistance dimmers are unlikely to serve your artistic goals or support high production standards. They heat up the work area and waste energy.

Electronic dimmers are connected to a remote lighting console. Preset or computerized lighting consoles use a low voltage signal to send instructions to the dimmers and control the amount of power that is sent to the lighting fixture, which in turn control brightness of incandescent or tungsten-halogen (TH) fixtures. This distinction may also be useful in determining whether you have electronic or resistance dimmers. New dimming products that use solid state technology to control stage lighting fixtures are being introduced to the theatre market as well.

Design Practices

Like all the other production areas, the lighting design itself is a place where choices can make the process greener. Our audiences, and perhaps even we as designers, have come to expect a certain level of spectacle in theatre. In a presentation with Richard Cadena on *Greener Lighting* sponsored by the Broadway Green Alliance, well-known lighting designer and sustainability advocate James Bedell described this tendency as "the arms race." The technology has to serve the art, not replace it.

Greener lighting design involves making the best use of the available equipment and not adding in equipment that does not serve the design. That frequently means taking the time to look at the luminaires' photometric information and calculating how many fixtures you really need to light the space and where they should be placed. If you do not know how to use a section view of a theatre to perform this task, see the latest edition of Steve Shelley's book, *A Practical Guide to Stage Lighting*, for guidance.

Careful crafting of a design concept and predetermining how the lighting will reveal or emphasize moments on stage is a part of the lighting design process. Effective planning of the design in advance is usually more efficient than trying to design on the fly by simply responding to rehearsals or techs. Sharing your plans with the rest of the creative team is an equally important part of the lighting design development. If the first technical rehearsal is when you decide what the lighting cues will look like, you are not doing your job as a lighting designer.

Are LED Fixtures the Best Choice for Your Company?

Most theatres cannot afford to replace their entire lighting systems, even if grants and other supplemental funds can be obtained. Don't misunderstand my point; LED fixtures and more efficient conventional units can be a marvelous sustainable choice for a venue, especially if the entire inventory can be upgraded to more efficient luminaires.

However, the new stage lights are like any other highly publicized new technological gadget. If the product does not meet your needs, you don't know that you can depend on the vendor and/or manufacturer supplying the equipment for support when needed, you don't fully understand how to use the equipment effectively, or you can't afford it, the purchase is not a sustainable choice. If you spent more time selecting a cell phone plan or deciding which new computer tablet to purchase, you have just gambled a lot of money on your new lighting system. Evaluate any technology upgrade to determine that it meets your needs.

Patrick Hudson wrote a wonderful blog on *Cue to Cue*: "LED stage lighting fixtures: are they worth it?" (cuetocue.offstagejobs.com/?p=898). This and other articles from Backstage.com remain as reference material. As of May 2013 the original blog is no longer updated. The new blog by Patrick Hudson is (http://topofshow.com/). The July 29, 2012 article answers that question: "*Short answer: maybe. Longer answer: it depends on why you are purchasing new gear, and what your use is going to be.*" He clearly lays out some of the pluses and minuses of the newer technology—the blog is worth a read if you are considering LED units. Hudson thinks they can be a perfect option for some companies but says, "*whether or not you should purchase LED fixtures for the possible cost savings comes down to how, and how much, your venue tends to use its lighting gear.*"

If you do not use the stage lighting equipment long enough and often enough for a reasonable ROI, it may not be the best choice. It is equally important to make sure that the investment meets your artistic goals by producing a quality of light that meets your production team's and audience's visual expectations. An informed decision depends on your understanding how the LEDs operate.

Understanding LEDs

The first step in happily using LED fixtures is to understand that the use of solid state electronics means that the performance differs from that of a familiar conventional fixture. LED units fall into several color types. There are units that include red, blue, green, and amber (RBGA), including the Altman Stage Lighting, Inc. Spectra Cycs or Spectra Star Pars. Some manufacturers use only the red, blue, green (RBG) LEDs or red, blue, green, and white LEDs.

Designers might expect the fixtures using the primary colors of light to exactly mimic the performance of strip lights with primary gel colors, but not all wavelengths of white light are present in the beam from the unit. This can be a huge visual difference from the familiar strip lights that start out with a perceived white source that covers most of the entire visible spectrum.

Wash and profile units are also available with white LED light engines. The white units may be tunable to produce a range of color temperatures like the Philips Color Kinetic IntelliWhite fixtures or the Strong Neeva units. Others like the Robert Juliat TIBO and ZEP have one warm color temperature that allows them to integrate with incandescent fixtures. Gel or other color media can be used with white LED fixtures to color the beam, but it should be noted that because the spectral output of most white LEDs is significantly different than that from a typical incandescent bulb, surprising and unpredictable differences in color media performance can sometimes result.

Electronic Theatre Controls, Inc. (ETC) offers several different white profiles with different color temperatures designed to integrate with daylight or conventional T-H units. It has also introduced units from the Selador Line that use the x7 Color System™ which includes LEDs that produce color in seven different wavelengths in each individual luminaire. This greater range of LEDs in the array means that a broader range of wavelengths from the spectrum of visible light are present in the beam from the fixture. This allows greater flexibility in color mixing from each unit and better color rendering of costumes, scenery, and performers on stage from the beam of light.

It is impossible to list the attributes and names of every manufacturer's LED unit. The ones mentioned are a sampling of products available on the market at the time of writing. By the publication date of this book, these manufacturers may have improved or replaced these lines and many more from other companies will be on the market. Most theatres are accustomed to buying luminaires piecemeal as money becomes available. Rapid improvements in LED technology mean that keeping color and intensity consistent between old and new fixtures is more challenging with LED units than conventional fixtures.

Color and white LEDs are produced in a very complex manufacturing process, not unlike the one used to produce computer microprocessors, and there is apparently as much artistry as there is science in the process. Unlike a manufactured lamp or a color filter that has a specified tolerance that leads to a uniform color from each item with the same specifications, LED color may vary from batch to batch. The issue is compounded by the fact that LEDs are usually purchased from an outside source instead of manufactured at the company where the luminaires are manufactured. Some models by the same manufacturer might produce very different colors of light if they were not manufactured in the same batch. Fixture manufacturers purchase LEDs within given ranges or "bins" of colors and brightness. These differences in brightness and color can be a big deal. The company buys a range of bins and then might combine LEDs from different bins to get an overall mix that is consistent from unit to unit. It is difficult to maintain the same "recipe" over time, because the LEDs coming off the manufacturing line tend to get brighter and brighter, and the bins may not have the same exact mix of chips every time.

Different manufacturers have addressed this issue in different ways. For example, Philips Lighting uses a proprietary process called "Optibin" to maintain an optimal range of color consistency across manufactured products. Some manufacturers include an optical sensor at the LED array that takes a real-time read-out of the color generated.

According to LED Product Manager at ETC, Rob Gerlach, the company has adopted a different approach. He says:

> *"We build fixtures with a mix of LEDs that is as consistent as we can make it; then during assembly we put each fixture on a spectrometer. That spectrometer measures each color of LEDs one at a time and stores the spectral information within a chip on the LED array. The end user gives the fixture a desired color setting and the fixture on its own figures out the best way to achieve the color, given the specific spectral output of its LED array. Instead of the designer needing to give the unit different levels channel by channel, she can simply tell it the desired end result and the fixture does the work of creating the right look."*

This solution enhances consistency and makes it easier to integrate newer units with previously purchased inventory.

Since LED fixtures of the same model may produce light with different spectral content, it is possible that colored objects will be rendered differently or that the designer is asking for a color that is possible in one unit and not in the unit next to it. There may not always be absolute precision from fixture to fixture. One argument against the use of LED fixtures is that they do not render color as well as T-H lamps. While this is not true of all LED fixtures, it is difficult to determine simply looking at ratings on a piece of paper.

The Color Rendering Index (CRI) is a quantitative scale that measures a light source's ability to show color in the same way that natural light (actually an idealized black-body radiator at a specified color temperature) does. The higher the score on the scale of 0 to 100, the better the color rendering index of a source. For example, a lamp that produces monochromatic output like a sodium vapor lamp would have a score of 0. Incandescent lamps have a score of nearly 100.

Unfortunately, the test always uses the same color swatches. A company wanting to boost a product rating can choose to manufacture a unit that produces light geared to reading those swatches; just as it can produce a unit with LED wavelengths that show a high lumen per watt efficiency. Other tests are in development to measure color rendering, including one from the National Institute of Standards and Technology (NIST) called the Color Quality Scale (CQS). It is another quantitative scale.

Rob Gerlach outlines some of the problems to be solved before it is a reliable tool:

> *"NIST has a preliminary version of a metric meant to replace CRI, but the Color Quality Scale does not penalize a light source for rendering colors in a more vivid way than they're rendered by the reference source, e.g., natural sunlight. The reasoning behind this is that some manufacturers claim that more vivid color is always a good thing".*
>
> *"I argue that this is a highly subjective assertion and that unnaturally vivid color rendering introduces uncertainty and can lead to undesirable results, particularly in the world of entertainment lighting, where a designer needs complete control over the way that colored objects are illuminated. It may be difficult to find an LED source that produces very deep red wavelengths, because these wavelengths don't count for much in terms of lumens, so efficacy takes a hit. Most LED fixtures artificially boost red by producing more of the short wavelengths in the orangey red range instead of the really deep red tones that are critical in illuminating skin, rendering natural materials like wood and giving people and scenery a healthy, rich look. You can get a high CQS score by designing a fixture's output to meet the requirements of this specific metric, but this doesn't necessarily guarantee performance that is identical to an incandescent lamp."*

In the case of LED performance, a cut sheet cannot tell the whole story as easily as it can in the case of a conventional unit. Matthew Armendariz-Kerr from ETC says succinctly, "*Additive color mixing is a nuanced problem. Numbers alone cannot tell the story.*"

The lp/W rating is another number that can be potentially misleading. There is no doubt that any well designed LED unit will have a more efficient performance than an incandescent unit when this kind of efficiency is analyzed. When considering a particular LED product, ask if that rating is based on the lumens at the lighting array or the number of lumens on stage after the light has passed through the optical elements of the unit. Not surprising, the number of lumens will be higher at the array than after the light has been refracted several times. This rating only addresses the efficacy of turning electricity into visible light. The rating does not quantify the embodied energy of the unit—what it took to manufacture it and truck it to the point of sales. Nor does it address if there is a quiescent load involved in the unit, something common with intelligent fixtures that use LEDs. Note those intelligent units would have a similar quiescent load if they used another type of lamp as well.

The individual LEDs are grouped together on a printed circuit board called an LED array. In the earliest fixtures this circuit board could not be replaced. Even if the light maintains its intensity and integrity for 50,000 hours, no one wants to throw it away. Almost every quality unit can have that array replaced now.

Some LED units will dim on proprietary control systems and some will work with the familiar stage lighting control language DMX 512 using an Ethernet system. The more complex the unit, generally the more channels it takes to control. The units that work on existing consoles function like any other addressable accessories. Even if the LED unit responds to DMX control, it will require constant power like a scroller or other common DMX addressable accessory.

Some common accessories will run on an electronic stage dimmer set to full power or even respond to dimming. Others will not. Manufacturers are developing stage dimming racks that can accommodate hybrid rigs that include conventional fixtures, automated units, and LED fixtures. There are also individual dimmer modules like the ETC Sensor3 Rack and its Sensor3 ThruPower Modules. The modules include a switch on the front that allows the user to bypass the dimmer components and have full power directly from the circuit breaker to the circuit.

Units that require proprietorial control can be much more difficult to integrate into a system that is using conventional fixtures and an existing console. The manufacturers that have always specialized in entertainment lighting are going to be more likely to offer support for this process because they will understand the specific problems.

Even though we can see an LED fixture fade up or down, it does not operate like an incandescent lamp. Unlike tungsten units, LEDs respond to instructions in a few milliseconds. There is no thermal inertia from the lamp filament, and designers have grown accustomed to seeing that lag. Gerlach describes the problem more specifically:

> *"LED level changes are nearly instantaneous, or what we might call "steppy". It takes a high level of processing within a fixture to balance that out, since there is not enough bandwidth in a control protocol like DMX 512, to give the high resolution needed to deal with this from the control end. DMX updates only as much as 40 times per second and that is not nearly fast enough to avoid "steppiness" when dimming an LED, so the fixture has to fill in the space between each step. The bit resolution of the instrument can give you a sense of the capacity of the light to respond to the system. However, it is the software in the unit that will ultimately determine how it behaves in response to commands."*

Pros and Cons of LED Units

The controversy about whether or not LED units can serve theatre effectively reminds me of the initial responses to flat field ellipsoidals when they were introduced to the market. Designers were accustomed to overlapping the beams of light from units that had an intensity fall off at the edges of the beam. Some designers could not imagine creating a wash of light with luminaires that offered an even field of light across the entire beam. Responses included,

> *"They are perfect for gobos as a special application, but you could never light an entire show with them."*

Now the fixtures that offer a flat field of light are considered the gold standard of ellipsoidals and most theatres want them in the inventory. It takes time to integrate any new technology, especially into an art form. Theatre is a small niche market, but the manufacturers and vendors that serve the entertainment industry will continue to solve the problems in any viable technology until it serves the art created.

While the available LED options keep improving, there are potential drawbacks to the purchase and/or use of LED units on stage if you do not research the purchase carefully. One important consideration with LED stage fixtures is that they are initially very expensive and it can take some time to recoup that cost even with rebates. If your rig is not in use many hours every day, the savings on the electric bill may not be significant enough to offset the cost. There is a learning curve to using the fixtures and how steep it is depends on your experience, the console you own, and the fixtures you purchase. It can be difficult to integrate units buying only a few at a time and still create a consistent look because the technology changes so quickly.

Several years ago the biggest problem seemed to be not being able to get an intense enough light from an LED source. Solutions are addressing that problem. Well-known lighting designer Richard Cadena has articulated the rule of thumb that LED units double in brightness about every two months.

Consistency of color from fixture to fixture of the same model manufactured by the same company is another potential issue. Cadena suggests that the color answer may lie in finding a way to create white light that is a good balance of color temperature and light quality with LED sources and then using gel or other color media just like a conventional fixture. Time will tell if this is in fact the trend that emerges in the next year. The number of white LED profiles suggests that manufacturers are moving in this direction.

The newest generation of high quality LED fixtures has addressed the initial problems of pixilated color and multiple shadows. For example, the Philips Selecon PL line has introduced an internal optical unit that "homogenizes" the beam and creates light that looks like a single point source lamp.

The inability of some LED units to fade in and out of cues like incandescent lamps is another problem that seems to be in the past. Units from a number of manufacturers now dim well, even in comparison to an incandescent fixture. At the national USITT 2013 conference in Milwaukee, the quality of light from the LED units on the trade show floor was amazing.

On the plus side, LED fixtures are a unique tool that can serve the design. They are more sustainable because they use less power to operate and may offer more options in a single unit than is possible in a conventional fixture without additional accessories. Because the light does not generate as much heat performers will be more comfortable and there should be some savings on air conditioning costs.

Perhaps more importantly, there is a conscious effort by established fixture manufacturers to make LED fixtures that perform in ways that are familiar to lighting designers and stage electricians. The major lighting manufacturers are also working toward the goal of creating lines of LED units that will integrate with their existing incandescent fixtures, both conventional and automated, just as most created automated units that would integrate with their conventional units. As these developments reach the market, the learning curve for using LED units will diminish and it will be easier to integrate the new technology into entertainment lighting design.

A personal note: Because my initial recommendation is not that everyone should find a way to purchase new LED units to make productions greener, I feared some people might assume that I am prejudiced against the technology. I think LED units are a potentially tremendous option to support the artistry of lighting design and reduce the theatre's carbon foot print. I have used red, blue, green, amber color wash units as

Savvy designers offered these tips on selecting LED units for purchase:

- Determine your real needs. Will RBGA wash units for toning and cycs be the best choice or do you need warm white LED fixtures that can take color media and be integrated into your existing rig?
- See the units in person. Do not rely on reviews or cut sheets for a final decision.
- It can be difficult to determine how a unit will dim. Make sure you see the unit perform and evaluate it across the entire curve. If possible see it in conjunction with a conventional fixture.
- Ask to see how the unit dims on fades of different speed from 0.1 second to 120 seconds.
- Have a person stand in front of the unit while it is dimming.
- Choose the unit with the dimming profile you want. Rewriting the profile on the board is not going to make that huge a difference.
- Heat Sinks are an important part of the LED fixture. Any fixture that feels very lightweight may not have adequate heat sinks.
- Buy fixtures manufactured by a company that you trust and work through a vendor that you have established a relationship with prior to this purchase.

color toners and to light scenery and cycloramas with beautiful results. I have also used white tunable LED fixtures in architectural applications and been very pleased with the results.

I have not used LED profile fixtures to light performers' faces because the option has not been available at any of the venues where I have designed, but I will certainly seize the first opportunity that presents itself. LED fixtures are another design option; another tool to create a specific look and integrate into a lighting design.

The following images are of some of the LED stage fixtures available at the time of writing. The goal is to show some of the variations currently on the market. By the time this book publishes the LED equipment on the market will probably look similar but be brighter and better.

This is not meant to be an exhaustive gallery of every LED stage light available. Not every manufacturer is represented and no manufacturer's complete line is shown.

All of the units shown have a lamp life of up to 50,000 hours. Not every feature about each unit is articulated due to limited space. Descriptions are not identical due to differences in marketing materials and cut sheets which are written to emphasize the unique features of each manufacturer's equipment. Look at manufacturer's cut sheets for more information, but remember no amount of information on paper can eliminate the need to see the fixtures perform, preferably integrated into a rig instead of as a single light in the show room or at a trade show booth.

LED Profile Fixtures

Figure 9.10 The Strong Neeva is a profile spotlight that uses a 60 watt LED source. It is available as RGBA, RGBW, or tunable white unit. Neeva is an RGBA, RGBW, or tunable white LED luminaire. It has a fixed beam angle of 26°. Photo courtesy of Ballentyne-Strong.

Figures 9.11 and 9.12 The two images on the left are Profil LED fixtures manufctured by Robert Juliat. The top unit is the ZEP Profile. It has a 150 watt LED source and can be controlled by DMX. It is a 28° to 54° Zoom. The 3200° K color temperature creates a neutral white light. The bottom unit is the TIBO, a 75 watt LED fixture. It is a 30to 45° zoom, but can be configured for a 15° to 35° option. At 3000°K it has a slightly warmer white light than the ZEP. Photos courtesy of Robert Juliat Lighting.

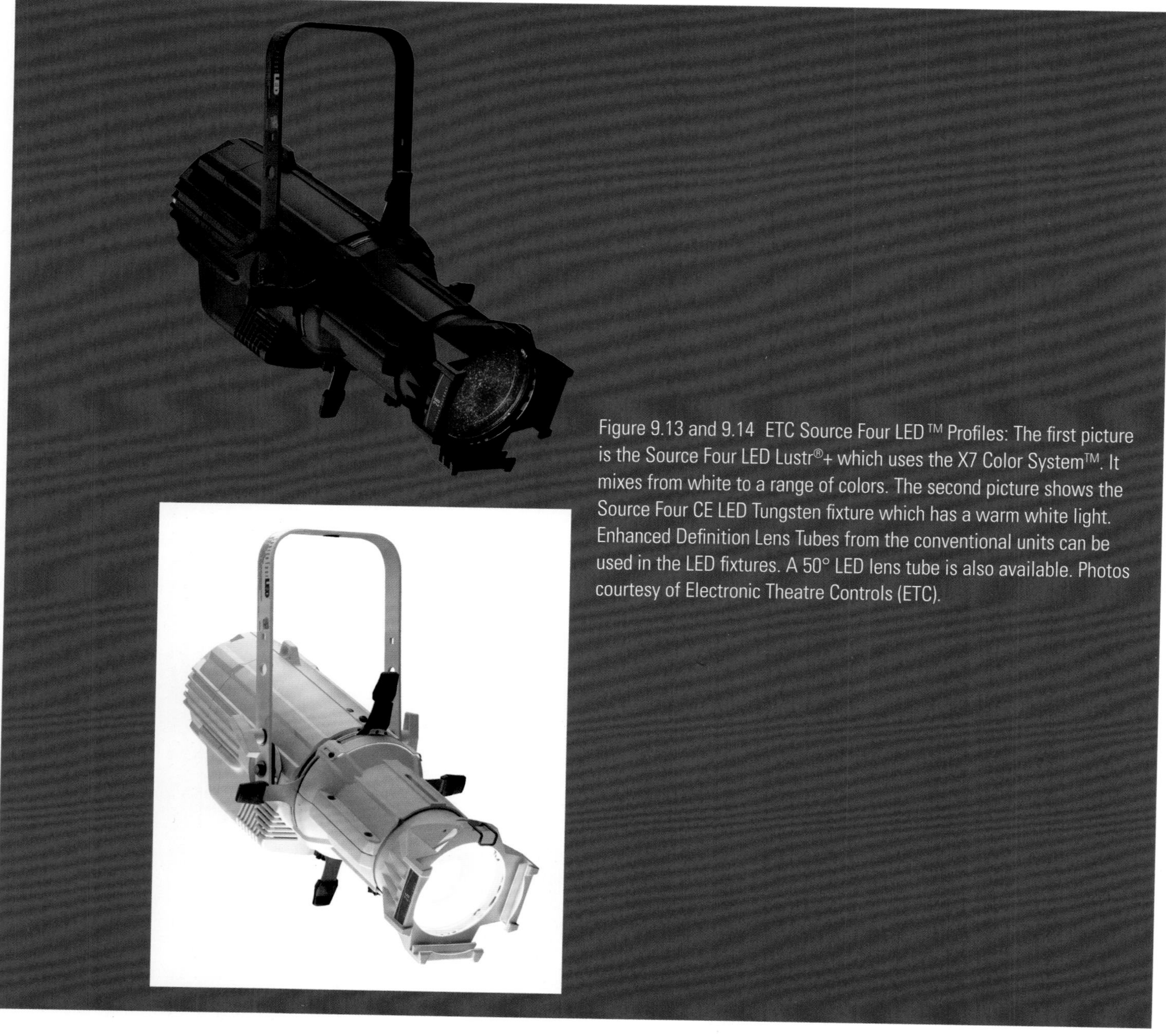

Figure 9.13 and 9.14 ETC Source Four LED ™ Profiles: The first picture is the Source Four LED Lustr®+ which uses the X7 Color System™. It mixes from white to a range of colors. The second picture shows the Source Four CE LED Tungsten fixture which has a warm white light. Enhanced Definition Lens Tubes from the conventional units can be used in the LED fixtures. A 50° LED lens tube is also available. Photos courtesy of Electronic Theatre Controls (ETC).

LED Wash Fixtures

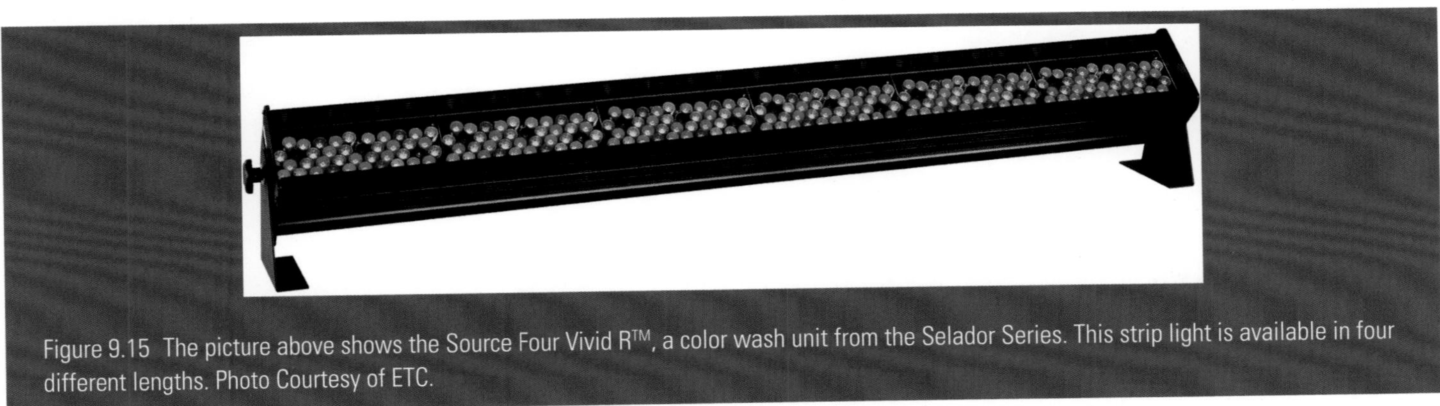

Figure 9.15 The picture above shows the Source Four Vivid R™, a color wash unit from the Selador Series. This strip light is available in four different lengths. Photo Courtesy of ETC.

Figure 9.16 Pictured above is the Desire$_{TM}$ D60. It includes options to change profile and performance settings to accommodate a range of lighting functions. Both of the Desire and Source Vivid R use the X7 Color System for color mixing and have a 50,000 hour light sources. Photos Courtesy of ETC.

Figure 9.17 The 100 watt Spectra Star*Par is an update of the old fashioned PAR Can. The use of red, green, blue, amber LEDs allows for color mixing. This LED fixtures uses different lenses to change the beam size. {Photo courtesy of Altman Stage Lighting, Inc.}

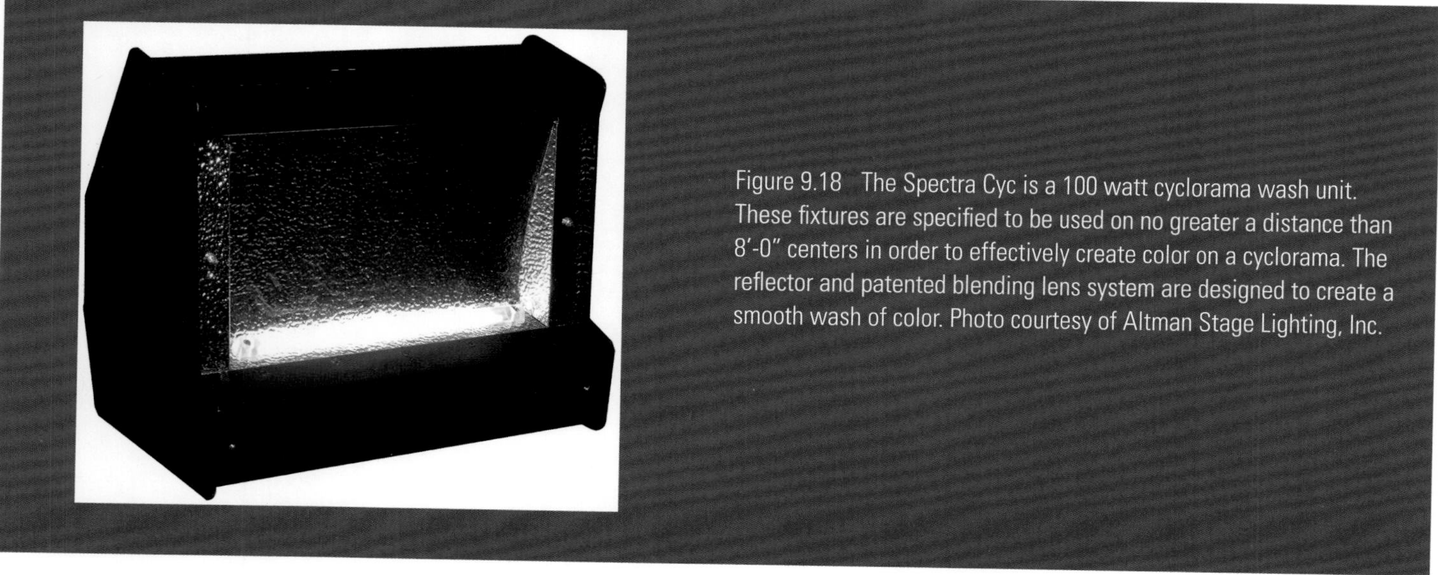

Figure 9.18 The Spectra Cyc is a 100 watt cyclorama wash unit. These fixtures are specified to be used on no greater a distance than 8′-0″ centers in order to effectively create color on a cyclorama. The reflector and patented blending lens system are designed to create a smooth wash of color. Photo courtesy of Altman Stage Lighting, Inc.

The similarity in outer appearance to the manufacturer's conventional versions of these fixtures makes it easy to assume they will function exactly like their conventional counterparts. LED fixtures are a possibility that can serve design and green your productions; only you can determine if they are a good choice for your situation.

If your company is not in a position to make this kind of purchase it is still possible to reduce your carbon footprint by maintaining your existing equipment so that it operates at peak efficiency and choosing lamp wattages wisely instead of potentially over-lighting the space.

Chapter 10

Costume Design

The Crossroad of Ecology and Artistic Expression

> *The tree which moves some to tears of joy is in the eyes of others only a green thing that stands in the way. Some see nature all ridicule and deformity . . . and some scarce see nature at all. But to the eyes of the man of imagination, nature is imagination itself.*
>
> William Blake

A shift toward environmental stewardship and greening work practices has occurred. This thread is woven throughout our stories and modern myths. Ecology is a central theme in several extremely popular animated children's movies, as well as the one of the top grossing films of all time. As designers, we help tell these stories, but we can also become part of them.

Learning to evaluate where sustainability serves your artistic expression is one of the great tasks of designing in the twenty-first century. Costume design lends itself to sustainability because there are so many different ways to complete the tasks we perform. Almost without exception, costume designers employ elements of sustainability in the work they do for reasons completely unrelated to green initiatives. It is simply impossible to costume on a budget without using second-hand or stock pieces.

Yet, as Chapter 1 pointed out, a one-size-fits-all sustainability plan will serve neither all kinds of designers nor all kinds of productions. Some productions will lend themselves naturally to alternative dye techniques while others will be easy to costume from stock. The company with a full staff of stitchers, drapers, and crafts people will make different choices than the small company with one costumer who handles everything from design to laundry.

Design Philosophy

There is an ideological divide in the philosophy of design which comes to a head in any discussion of how to begin a design process. In short, this divide centers on when the limitations of reality should enter the design process. Whether it is the physics of the space, finances, or how a garment stays on the body, the day-to-day demands of production will eventually enter the equation. When initially imagining the look of a production, should we as designers be concerned with how a garment is constructed, or how large the workforce will be? Should we design around stock that exists, or does this restrict the potential design? How do we expand the boundaries of imagination and artistic expression if the pedestrian considerations of stock pantaloons and petticoats are crowding our minds?

Wherever you fall on the spectrum of idealism and pragmatism, there are ways to make your designs more sustainable. Whether you choose to build versatility into constructed costumes to allow reuse, limit the number of new pieces, allow the existing stock at your theatre to influence your color palette, or attempt to purchase only recycled fabric, each production allows some kind of green initiative.

When compared to other design areas, costuming may differ substantially in its approach to sustainability. A flat is a flat regardless of who is standing in front of it. A gobo is a gobo regardless of the color or intensity of the light which shines through it. The pieces in costuming are less interchangeable. While I would love it to be otherwise, you simply cannot retrim the same pair of trousers for every show. A bare stage does not evoke the same audience response as a naked actor. On the flip side, if the scene shop needs a flat, they must build it. If the costume designer needs a blouse, he might purchase it new, rent it, or find it second-hand; options which are seldom available to the scenic designer. Thus our sustainability methodologies are different than some of our colleagues.

Most of the actions we can take to improve the ecological impact of costuming will happen in the costume shop, after the design work is done. But we cannot ignore the beginning of the process. The costume designer sets the length of the race. We decide how hard we are going to have to fight to reach the finish line in time.

Adding sustainability to the parameters of costume design can feel like yet one more limitation. Budgets are already tight. Work hours are long. It is easy to lose sight of what we are trying to do. It is easy to start focusing on daily concerns and forget the goal. Ultimately, we support the story, reveal character, and converse in a common visual language with our audience. If we lose sight of this, we are lost.

> Embracing sustainability and greener production should not diminish the power and artistry of our work. Mediocre design defeats the goal. Just as every set should not consist of an empty stage, not every costume design should be second-hand modern dress. We must serve the spirit of the play.

Organic Design: An Alternative to the Traditional Design Process

We have all come to costume design by different routes. Some of us have little or no formal training or simply rely on our expertise in related areas, like directing or acting, to tell us what costumes should look like. Others have formal training and credentials: A BFA or an MFA, regional-theatre experience, or credits as an assistant to a seasoned professional. Some of us have worked extensively as costume shop managers or make-up artists and gradually transitioned into design. Still others have come from the worlds of fashion and fine art. Many of us depend on students and volunteers to help execute designs, while others have the support of professional stitchers and drapers. Some render, some design through conversation, and others work sculpturally to design garments. It is impossible to lay out a single sustainable-design philosophy which allows us all to work to our potential. Instead, I will tell you my story.

I was baptized into costume design in the storefront theatres of Chicago after graduating with a BA degree in theatre that focused primarily on directing. Typical costume budgets were under $500. With all the time in the world (something I never had and, let's be honest, no one ever does), I still would not have been able to afford to build or buy all new pieces for the shows I was designing. I became so proficient at second-hand shopping that I could tell you, based on the title of the show, which of the 20-plus resale outlets I frequented would supply the production. I cut apart old prom dresses for the satin or crinoline, filled my bathtub with Chinese tea to antique wedding dresses, and pieced together 1930s productions from once-loved Laura Ashley discards. It did not occur to me that this was environmentally savvy or good for the earth. It was a matter of necessity—necessity breeding invention.

Yet, resale shops and Chinese tea go a long way toward limiting the waste of a production. Not only does that 15-year-old prom dress cost less than buying the fabric from which it is made; it does not use raw materials and petrochemicals, reinforce sweatshop labor models, create the chemical ridden waste water, or require shipping the fabric from Asia. The original creation of the dress did all those things. The damage is done. The embodied carbon footprint of the garment has already been incurred. Giving that dress a second life prevents me from adding another carbon footprint.

Working with nothing, I learned to be an artist of occasion, allowing available resources to inspire my work and leaving me with a rather flexible design philosophy. Walking the streets of Chicago, inspiration was everywhere. Boutique clothing stores, art museums, second-hand shops, antique stores, and quirky cafés constantly informed my design sensibilities. If I needed ideas, I spent my lunch break at high-end department stores, art galleries, or parks.

Working in this way prepared me to problem solve nontraditional theatre pieces and take on increasing complex design challenges, but did not adequately prepare me to work in a traditional theatre model. Enter graduate school. Graduate school was a painful experience of relearning classic design methodology. While I grew enormously as a practitioner, I suffered a complete loss of the free flow of ideas and inspirations that had driven my choices as a designer up to that point. I found the rigidity of the classic design model imposed on each production served neither the designers personally nor the production.

Organic directing has become a widely accepted way to craft a play. I have worked with directors who block the show from start to finish before rehearsal and those who drop all their preconceptions of the show at the first rehearsal. There were multiple systems for effective theatrical process, but can you design organically using the directors' method as a potential model, a mode of work which allows for adaptation, evolution, and change?

Just to be clear, I am using organic here to refer to the organic work model, I am not talking about designing with materials that have been labeled "organic." Well, not yet anyway. Rather soon, these ideas are going to become interdependent. But let's not get ahead of ourselves.

As we move away from twentieth-century realism, more strain is put on our traditional design processes. The status quo must adapt in order to meet these nontraditional educational forms. Devised work, ensemble-based processes, and technology-driven theatre are increasingly prevalent. We must learn to bring that same spirit into our designs. It is fundamentally necessary that we open up theatrical design to nontraditional processes. This move will help us incorporate sustainable practices into our work.

Organic design requires that we build a sense of trust. We must balance the many needs of the production with the needs of the process. We must discover ways to keep a shop full of workers busy until we know all the answers. It's certainly easier when you are a one-person shop. Balancing the sense of discovery and process with very real deadlines in order for others to complete their work is something we will all discover on our journey.

Before you all start shouting because you think I am recommending we stop rendering, building garments, and dyeing fabric, rest assured I am suggesting nothing of the sort. I am not recommending that costumes not be fully designed until opening night. I am simply asking that the process be as adaptable as the project. If *The Tempest* can be designed an infinite number of ways, the process for getting there can take an infinite number of paths. It simply requires clarity, specificity, and communication. Design should be a journey in the same way directing is a journey. In fact, adequate organization and preplanning are what allow us to respond to the discoveries made in rehearsal so the design can evolve for as long as time allows. This same organization and attention to detail are what allow us to seize any opportunity for greener choices.

When you own the process, when it is organic, it is easy to allow sustainable practices into the mix because they are not fighting the status quo. Every production will be different. It is not important that you adopt every sustainable option in every production; indeed no designers can and still serve the show. As you become more comfortable with the benefits of sustainable design and the products available to you, you will be able to decrease the potentially damaging ecological impact and reduce the carbon footprint of your productions. Sustainability is a journey, not a destination.

How Clothing is Made (as Simply as Possible)

Before we can talk about sustainability in costume design we need to understand the full impact of manufacturing the material we utilize. While many of us know what fiber content and processing mean, we may not appreciate how these things affect the environment and, in turn, our individual sustainability goals.

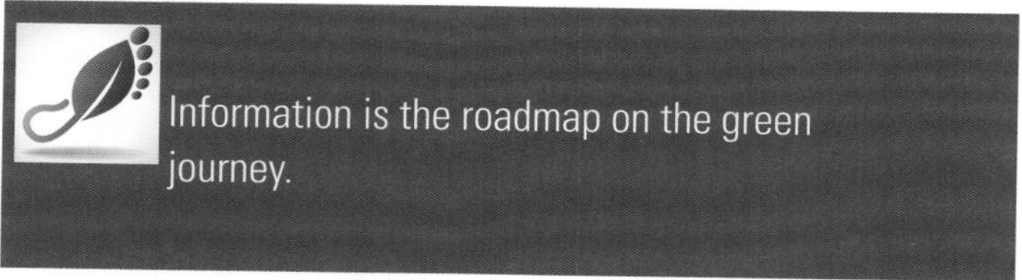

Information is the roadmap on the green journey.

Cloth—the First Challenge

Making cloth is bad for the environment. That might sound like an overstatement, but it is not. There is simply no good news about cloth production. We pay a heavy environmental price for our clothing, especially cheap disposable clothing.

Raw Materials and Processing

Cotton: Standard agricultural methods for growing cotton are extremely toxic. While we think of wearing cotton as the simplest way to dress "green," estimates suggest that cotton fields soak up almost 25% of the world's pesticides. In addition to its susceptibility to pests, cotton requires extensive fertilization. Contamination of ground and surface water by fertilizer is frequently the result of crop management used in cotton agriculture. The heavy use of these chemicals contributes to heavy metal contamination in the soil.

Figure 10.1 Cotton fields are treated with an enormous quantity of pesticides. gkuna/Shutterstock.

While demand for sustainably and organically produced cotton is growing, the infrastructure is simply not large enough to meet demand. This is a problem with almost all organic agriculture. Small organic farms frequently cannot support the potential demands of the commercial marketplace because of the labor-intensive practices involved. When available, most organic cotton comes from overseas where oversight and regulation are more lax. Shipping and import tariffs add to the price consumers pay.

The Organic Consumers Association articulates the problem:

> *"Besides being highly subsidized, cotton is the most toxic crop in the world. Cotton uses more than twenty-five percent of all the insecticides in the world and 12% of all the pesticides. Cotton growers use 25% of all the pesticides used in the US. Yet cotton is farmed on only 3% of the world's farmland. California is one of the only states where farmers are required to provide pesticide use reports. The California EPA (Cal EPA) reported that only 15 chemicals accounted for 77% of the pesticides used on cotton from 1989 to 1998 and that these were some of the most toxic chemicals in the world. Cal EPA and US EPA analyses illustrate that seven of these fifteen most used cotton chemicals were probable cancer-causing pesticides, eight caused tumors and five caused mutations. Twelve of the top fifteen cotton pesticides in California caused birth defects, ten caused multiple birth defects, and thirteen were toxic or very toxic to fish or birds or both."*
>
> *(http://www.organicconsumers.org/clothes/224subsidies.cfm)*

Wool and silk: Raising livestock, animal or insect, for use in commercial fabric manufacturing has all the pitfalls of farming for meat. Trimming costs for commercial wool production leads to poor living conditions for animals, the use of industrial feed (which in itself uses petrochemicals like fertilizers and pesticides to grow and requires shipping fossil fuels), and extensive pesticides to control fur-loving vermin. Silkworms are raised from eggs and must be anesthetized inside their cocoons before they can become moths in order to manufacture silk. Questions about animal quality of life are clear, but the ecological ramifications of raising animals for the sake of making clothing should give one pause as well.

Organic and free-range wool products are available, although they tend to be primarily cottage industries. Some silk manufacturers try mitigating these issues by making clothing from collecting the discarded cocoons of wild silkworms. Quantities of these materials are small and the collection is labor intensive, making these products both rare and expensive.

After the Harvest

Refining is the next major step after harvesting the raw material. Turning commercial cotton, wool, and linen into thread or yarn starts with bathing or irradiating the material to ensure that no creepy crawlies have hitched a ride. The system for transforming the material into thread or yarn is typically automated involving a series of cleaning machines, carders, spinners, and extruders. While this process does not require significant chemical input, it can take two full days of electricity for the base material to come out the other end of the machinery on a spool. In the case of silk, after the silkworm has been boiled to prevent it from breaking through its cocoon, and to remove the sticky residue which holds the cocoon together the strand is unwoven and spun with other silk filaments to make thread.

Figure 10.2 Cocoons for silkworms. ermess/Shutterstock.

Figure 10.3 Cotton threads being combined onto reels at the factory. Humannet/Shutterstock

Man-Made Materials

Rayon: Rayon is a semi-synthetic material which comes from making cellulose, or plant fiber, into fabric. Rayon can come from any number of plants like bamboo, new-growth, and old-growth trees. At first blush, this seems ideal, but the intensive processing required for the transformation makes it a less-than-ideal final product.

The standard refining process to make wood pulp into thread includes immersion in a caustic soda bath, pressing between rollers, crumbling, mixing with carbon disulfide in a vat, dissolving in yet another caustic solution, filtering, degassing, extruding (like making tiny homemade spaghetti), bathing in sulfuric acid, stretching, washing—this time to remove instead of add chemicals, and cutting. All of this is after the processed cellulose has already been extracted from the plant.

Polyester. Polyester is produced almost exclusively from non-renewable petrochemical sources. Not only the raw materials, but also the processing is dangerous for the environment. It is not locally sourced, contributes directly to oil dependency, and once discarded polyester takes thousands of years to decompose.

While production bypasses the problems of pesticide and animal use, noxious chemicals are used in refining to transform oil into long thin polymers of weavable plastic. Although many different ways of making polyester exist, here is a general description.

First dimethyl terephthalate reacts with ethylene glycol at a temperature of 300–400°F. The resulting alcohol is combined with terephthalic acid at nearly 500°F. At this point, the molten polyester is extruded to form long thin sheets. The polyester is cooled until brittle, and broken into pieces. The pieces are then melted again at over 500°F and spun out into long thin strands, stretched and brought together to produce the thread. Other chemicals may be added to make the fabric easier to dye and to decrease flammability.

Figure 10.4 Spinning thread in a textile mill. Rehan Qureshi/Shutterstock.

Once the raw material has been made into thread, several additional steps are needed before the garment arrives in your neighborhood store. These include making the threads into fabric, treating the fabric with dyes, print jobs, and, of course, apparel construction.

Weaving and Dyeing

Figure 10.5 Once the threads are formed the fibers are then woven into cloth. While most cloth production is now in the hands of computers, the weaving industry still employs many people of all ages at low wages. Sirichai Manmoh/Shutterstock.

Figure 10.6 Either before or after the thread is woven, it will likely see one or more dye or chemical baths. paul prescott/Shutterstock.

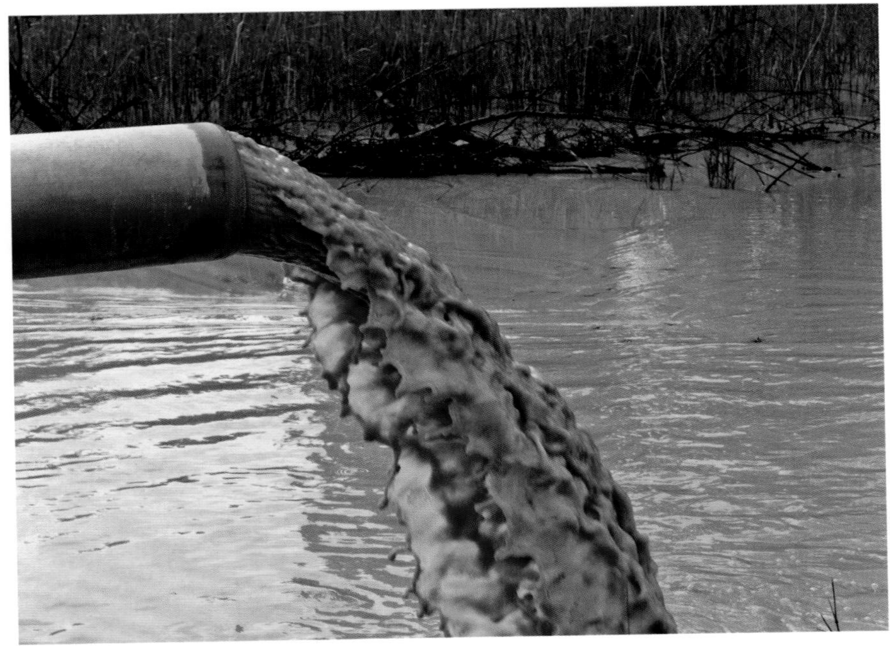

Figure 10.7 Waste water from a factory pours into a river. Dragana Gerasmoski/Shutterstock.

Printing and Sizing

Printing and sizing involve a number of additional chemical additives and baths. Hundreds of dyeing techniques and practices are used commercially. Aside from the chemicals in the pigments themselves, there are mordants, the chemical binding agents which help the pigment to adhere to the cloth, resists which prevent the pigment from adhering to the fibers, and sizing to keep the fabric from warping out of shape to name a few. Each of these steps may include caustic chemicals and several hundred gallons of waste water.

Cutting and Stitching

For every factory with safe working conditions and fair wages, there are likely hundreds more that fall short in one or both areas. The garment industry helps industrialize nations and allow their citizens access to better opportunities, but often the price is very high. Each garment you purchase helps to reinforce the working model of the corporations that helped it reach you. Long work hours and low pay are standard, but many factories also have child labor, worker intimidation, dangerous working conditions, limited access to healthcare, and strenuous deadlines. Conditions inside garment factories deserve far more attention than I can give them here. However, it is important to remember when discussing the full karmic price of what we wear.

Shipping

There is more to shipping than simply factory to store. The raw material must move from field to thread factory, factory to mill, mill to dye factory, dye factory to garment factory, factory to distribution center, to another distribution center closer to its destination, to store, to you. Some destinations could be side by side or housed in a single building, but each step might also be halfway around the world. While the label doesn't tell you where your garment has been, you can expect it has traveled extensively.

According to the United States Department of Agriculture's Economic Research Service:

> *"About 30 percent of the world's consumption of cotton fiber crosses international borders before processing, a larger share than for wheat, corn, soybeans, or rice. Through trade in yarn, fabric, and clothing, much of the world's cotton again crosses international borders at least once more before reaching the final consumer."*
>
> *(www.ers.usda.gov/topics/crops/cotton-wool/background.aspx)*

Looking at each step individually shows that the amount of embodied energy in every piece of clothing is astounding. The cost in resources goes far beyond the amount of fabric used to cut and sew the individual garment. Considering the source of the garment from beginning to end is as important as deciding what to do with it at the end of the run.

Strategies

Regardless of your design strategy, once the design is on paper, your work as a designer is not done. Ergo, your opportunities to think sustainably are not done either. My mother likes to say that your money is the most powerful vote you have. Whether it is a modest $100 or many thousands of dollars, those votes can be cast for sustainable, renewable, and non-toxic products. In the end, companies exist to sell us what we will buy. The louder and more frequently we say we want green products, the more they will be made available to us. Here are some ways you can cast your vote and help reduce waste.

Organic Fabric

Buying organic fabric is expensive. The market is young and small; the processing is labor intensive. Add to the mix the fact

Purchasing Close to Home

The popular refrain, "Think Globally, Act Locally" is an important touchstone for thinking about how to acquire the necessary materials for any project. For most of us, whether we work in a rural or urban environment, any supplies we need will have traveled many thousands of miles before getting to our door. It is almost impossible to fathom the many stops a bolt of fabric or package of buttons makes on its way to us. One of the ways we can shorten that journey is to buy as close to the source as possible. For materials which we need in quantity, we can search out wholesalers and bulk distributers who are able, not only to catch our desired product further up the transportation stream, but also to offer us a considerable discount. Using wardrobe supply companies also dramatically reduces packaging. Instead of large snaps coming five to a piece of cardboard, they can be acquired by the gross in a reusable plastic bag. Cheaper in the long run, more efficient packaging, and sent directly to your door. What's not to like?

Based on your location, it may be possible to find a wardrobe supply house in your area. Though many are located in New

York or Los Angeles, prominent suppliers also exist in cities such as Cincinnati, Atlanta, and other regional hubs. This often reduces the shipping time and price in addition to lowering the environmental impact of that final leg of the trip. While it is unrealistic to be expected to predict all the needs of your season, when you can afford to do so order back stock of frequently used items to minimize shipping and packaging on future orders. Notions and other small items are ideal bulk purchases because they require very little storage space.

For some of us, "Act Locally" is more realistic than for others. Living in rural Washington state, I reminisce regularly about my days in Chicago when fabric warehouses, artist boutiques, and box craft stores were just a train ride away. These days, 40 miles of highway and three mountain passes separate me from my closest "fabric stores." These are poorly stocked shadows of the stores I remember from my life in the city. Even here, however, there are opportunities to support both local business and environmental causes. A little leg work has uncovered local leather suppliers and sustainable wool products; products I feel comfortable purchasing when I know the animals were well cared for during their lifetime.

that organic farming has a reputation for paying fair wages, and the transition from conventional farming is costly and time consuming, it is no surprise that, by the yard, fabric manufactured from organic materials can easily cost twice the price of standard material. However, fabrics and yarns made from organic material are gaining ground and slowly becoming more competitive. Garment construction materials are coming in an ever-increasing variety of colors, weights, and patterns. Finding what you need is not as effortless as walking into a national chain store and pointing, but a little education in fabric weaves and finishes opens up an almost endless sea of organic possibilities via the Internet.

If we as consumers do not purchase these products to help the industry grow, it will never be able to build the necessary foundation to be financially competitive. It may not be logistically or financially possible to costume an entire show with organic fabric. Perhaps a single character, or a set of matching shirts, is all you can afford. It is important to make an effort, small or large, with every production. The entrepreneurs and business people of the organic market will put your investment to work. You may find with your next production the options are less limited in style and price.

Even organic fabric is not waste or chemical free. The organic label simple means that the fiber, often cotton, was grown without the use of synthetic pesticides and fertilizers. There are several other ways in which the producers of a piece of cloth may or may not have adopted additional sustainable practices. These include dyeing, printing, finishing, and packaging. Many organic fabric purveyors are committed to using low impact processing, however simply using the label "organic" does not require them to do so. A little research goes a long way to better understanding what your fabric has been through.

Recycling Options

Pulling From Stock

I like to start pulling from stock early in the design process, just after the design team has settled on the premise of the production. I use stock as a source of inspiration, to get a tangible sense of period, and to infuse the design with life. While I end up restocking the majority of what I pull on these early days, I have created a mental catalog to assist me in the rest of my design process. If I am serving as shop foreman for another designer, I can show him available options that might be incorporated into show designs. Pulling early keeps everyone thinking about available pieces as details of the production are refined.

Designing Versatility

In order to reduce the use of raw materials, always ask "Can a single garment serve more than one function?" For example, in a recent production of *Little Women*, I discovered we needed to build a new petticoat for Jo to achieve the appropriate length. Instead of just building a standard petticoat, we built a ruffled cotton skirt which doubled as part of a beach outfit later in the play. Combining this with a vest from the opening scene, I eliminated an entire look from the build list. I hear some of you out there saying, "That's not sustainability, that's just good design." You are right, of course. Good practical design and sustainability are often one and the same. The point is to make these choices consciously.

Tips for Shopping the Show

One of the easiest places to find second-hand and handmade items for production is the Internet. In order to reduce the bulk of shipping, you can ask for your items to be minimally packaged, combine items into a single shipment, or save the packaging for future use. All other things being equal make a point of buying products which have minimal or recyclable packaging.

When you are shopping in stores, use nylon or canvas shopping bags instead of disposable bags. Schedule your shopping trips in advance and create an exhaustive shopping list to limit driving. Ask other areas, like props or scenery, if they would like to join you.

Shopping a Show

Thinking about your process for shopping from the source of the products to the materials used to create the textiles and clothing you purchase can help you meet your sustainability goals.

Second-Hand Shopping

Our disposable culture has created an elaborate industry both for consignment shops and not-for-profits reselling our discarded items. While not every show can be costumed from the racks of thrift stores, there are often surprises to be found.

Old sheets and blankets can become mock-ups and garments. The fabric from an old skirt can be reimagined into a vest, blouse, or scarf. The lived-in quality of second-hand clothing limits the need to distress off-the-rack clothing, eliminating both hours of work and the expense of giving clothing a lived-in look. The choice gives a comfortable and relaxed feel to production and can eliminate the need to use new materials to create garments that are then damaged to look worn.

One problem with second-hand shops is that returns are often limited or simply not allowed. At the end of a show, you might end up with several pieces that never made it on stage but cannot be returned. I often chalk this up to the process and donate the pieces back to the store and get a tax credit. If it is helpful, use the pieces to increase your stock. If you plan to use

Quick Tips for Newbie Renters

- Prices—when you are budgeting for rentals, be sure you have tallied all the additional costs. The rental fee does not typically include shipping, return shipping, pulling fees, or cleaning costs. Depending on distance and volume, these can double the out-of-pocket expense of rentals. Many rental agencies require deposits for a portion of the replacement costs of the garments. Be sure your producing organization is prepared to cover these costs upfront. Also, make sure the rental company will refund the rental fee for any garment returned before opening night.
- Alterations—this is an important point. Most rental agreements limit the alterations that can be done to the garment and require that all work be reversed before the garment is returned. Think twice before renting something which will require substantial reworking for your production. Any alteration which will permanently alter the garment is typically forbidden.
- Timing—most rental houses will allow you some time to fit the clothing and discover whether it will work for your purposes. Whether or not the measurements are accurate, not every garment will look and feel like you are expecting. Allow enough time to deploy your plan B if the garment does not live up to expectations. Be sure your rental contract has enough time at the beginning for fittings and also for cleaning and repairs at the end of the run.
- Shipping—if you cannot pick up your garments in person, allow time for them to travel. Finding rental houses in your region helps both reduce time and also the ecological impact of the journey. When the garments arrive, be sure to keep all the packing materials to use when returning at the end of the run.
- Quirks—each company is different. The rules for one will likely be different than the rules for the next. Be sure you know the specific rules for the rental organization you are using.
- If you depend on volunteer or student labor, be certain there is an easy way to distinguish rental garments from owned stock to avoid losing pieces or a mistake in alterations involving cutting fabric.

the same shop repeatedly, you may be able to negotiate a special arrangement; perhaps mentions of the charity in the season program for return privileges. Look for win-win arrangements. Some places allow exchanges within seven days. Whenever possible, I schedule fittings as close to my shopping trip as possible so that I can make the most of these exchange opportunities.

Rentals

Rentals come in two basic types: renting on a piece-by-piece basis and renting entire shows. As a designer, I tend to shy away from renting entire shows. After all, what are you hiring me for? On the other hand, my expertise allows the company to make the best use of every dollar because I am qualified to evaluate how appropriate the rental garments will be or request substitutions. Even on a piece-by-piece basis, renting can be an amazing resource. There are certainly environmental costs to rentals (particularly shipping and dry cleaning), but in terms of reuse and recycle, rentals score very high.

I am constantly amazed how few people are utilizing rental opportunities. Those of us in education often make the case that rentals limit students' learning opportunities. Do not ignore the educational opportunity of learning from how other stitchers or drapers are constructing costumes. Looking inside professionally tailored garments has given me ideas of how to improve my draping skills. When we build less, we have the luxury of more time to build better. When a production requires six frock coats, if you can rent three and build three, you both increase your stock and have the time to ensure what you make is built to last.

Reciprocal Agreements

If you are working for a community or high school program, it is likely that you can create agreements with others in your area to pull freely from each other's stock. Theatres in a region working at a similar level, such as universities or community theatres, can benefit from an "I scratch your back you scratch mine" rental attitude. Reciprocal agreements allow two companies to pull from each other's stock without incurring rental and stocking fees. This, in essence, doubles the size of your stock. You should still have a contract which spells out your expectations for one another and keep detailed records of which pieces are being used. Just because you are not paying to rent something, does not mean that you should treat the piece with any less respect than you would a rental house piece. Look at some of the examples of reciprocal and sharing agreements described in the earlier chapters for ideas of how to develop your own costume consortium.

The Human Connection

Sustainability is wrapped up with local business initiatives, safety protocols, and community outreach programs. While this many-headed beast may, at times, be difficult to untangle, all these things have one simple thing in common; improving quality of life. Something I like to call the human connection. It is not at all surprising that an action or product that is good for the environment is also likely to be good for the community and the worker.

Supporting Local Business

Building community is about sharing the burden. Caring for the earth requires conscientiousness, effort, and time. While I am happy to take on the task when I can, I do not always have the luxury of time. This is where your community can help. To survive against the megastores, small businesses need to offer something you can't get at larger outlets. They often band together to support other small businesses, offer better customer service, and stock unique merchandise. If you need something specific, chances are your local small business owner knows where to get it. If you want fair trade items, a small business is more likely to have them for you. At small local businesses, the store management usually has the power to reach barter agreements or make exceptions for you in contrast to the big box store where management is far removed from the sales floor.

Just as it is important to support organic wool and cotton suppliers, we should have active relationships with our area business people. They are the gatekeepers of information. They are more likely to stock the green alternatives you seek and to be able to order them for you. Whether we order fabric, buy garments, or hire a cobbler, we are helping to support local commerce and the American economy.

The Community of Designers

This sense of community should extend to the designers in your area as well. Get to know other people in your field who work in your area. It is easy to feel isolated working long hours tucked away in the basement of a building. Build a sense of community. Get to know the people who can help you get the answers to your questions, who might have sustainable sources, and who share your goals to sustain and enhance the theatre design experience. We are often too quick to think of our colleagues as our competitors. We are all painfully aware of the problems facing the theatre and, instead of banding together, we become territorial. This might seem obliquely related to sustainability, but the opposite is true. When we share with and support the members of our community, we are better able to meet the challenging goals of sustainability together.

Sustainability for the Freelance Designer

Freelance designers have a unique set of challenges when they consider how to achieve a more sustainable work environment. They often have a very limited knowledge of a company's stock and resources. We deal with distance, both between ourselves and the theatre and often between our regular suppliers and the theatre. You must develop relationships with suppliers who are local to the theatre company instead of your design studio. Take advantage of Internet resources like the USITT Costuming Listserve to ask other designers who live or work in the area for suggestions. An Internet search may also reveal consortiums or theatres in the region where rentals are possible.

Travel

As a resident or freelance designer, personal travel is a major consideration. A gas-efficient vehicle will help you spend your budget or your paycheck effectively.

While I know this is extreme, I once clocked 4000 miles in seven weeks designing for a company in the mountains of New Hampshire. When you add the 1,500 miles each way I traveled to get to the job, it's a wonder I finished the summer with a cent to my name. Even with my 38 mpg hatchback, there is no way to justify that kind of ecological impact for a single member of the team, even if I was costume designer, shop manager, and wardrobe chief. One of the reasons so much driving fell to me is that I had such a gas-efficient vehicle. While it is appalling to think I used nearly 200 gallons of gas, an SUV would have easily consumed twice that.

Aside from the expensive lesson of making sure travel compensation is included in a contract, I learned several important ecological lessons. Better planning would have led to longer, more exhaustive trips to town instead of heading out each morning with a list of things to pick up before work. While I sometimes drove other company members to the theatre, we could easily have consolidated the number of cars with a simple schedule of when we were leaving in the morning and when we would return at night.

As a freelance designer, travel can mean more than shopping trips. For out-of-town designers, especially from across the country, there is huge ecological impact traveling for pulling, fittings, and dress rehearsals. An out-of-town designer might travel back and forth three or more times for a single production. Flights, lodging, and meals all have environmental impact. If you are renting a car, be sure it is the most efficient car that will do what you need. Ask for lodging with a kitchenette so you can prepare your own meals. Is it possible to travel by train or public transportation for some of your meetings? Can you attend production meetings via teleconferencing? Are there other company members in your area who might be interested in carpooling with you? Make the company equally responsible for considering sustainability. Would it be more environmentally and fiscally responsible if they rented a hybrid automobile for several weeks at a time and set specific times and dates for shopping trips? If they have an accurate inventory and cast measurements, would it make more sense to preplan purchasing and ship fabric and supplies to the theatre from a vendor? You may be able to think of a number of other options based on your own experiences in far-flung places.

Respecting the Practices of Others

In some ways, you work for yourself as a freelance designer. In other ways, you are a guest in someone else's home. Getting the shops you work for to understand your desire for sustainability will encourage the company to find ways to improve their practices. Coming in from the outside demanding substantial changes to the way they work is not a great plan for being hired back. Each company will be at a different place in their sustainability journey. They may be safety minded. In that case, you may have more success addressing sustainability issues which coincide with improved worker safety. Most companies with limited resources will be keen to adopt practices which save them money.

You may not be able to control what happens at all. Clear communication is the best possible tool for an efficient work environment. This extends to how you want things done. Lead by example. Get a sense of what sustainable practices the company has in place. You may find if you ask for very simple accommodations in advance a large impact can be made.

Pre-Design Checklist

- Check the following list as you begin a design process to help remind you of your options.
- Do you have extra material on hand which can be incorporated into your design?
- Do you have period-appropriate clothing in stock?
- Have other local theatres in your area done similar productions recently?
- What other rental options are available in your area?
- Are organic or naturally derived products available?
- Is there a local business to supply what you need?
- Can you use available products to complete your renderings?
- Can this garment serve more than one purpose?
- What is the reuse potential of the garment? Is it worth having in stock?

The costume designer plays a significant role in the sustainability efforts of a production. No matter what style design you do, you can improve your sustainability goals and reduce your carbon footprint by thinking about these issues from the beginning of the process. Preplanning is efficient not only in time management but also in reducing your environmental impact. While not every option is available or appropriate in every instance, you can make a substantial impact by adopting simple changes.

Chapter 11

Costume Construction

Sustainability for the Human Element

Costumers are among the savviest people I know, although I admit a certain bias. I am constantly amazed by their fortitude, imagination, and tenacity. Because most everyone gets dressed in the morning, there is a sense that "anyone" can be a costumer. Indeed, truly great design looks natural and effortless. Anyone who has had a hand in it knows this to be the furthest thing from the truth. Costuming lives at the crossroads of high art and everyday living. Costumers bridge the gap between production and performance. Amongst technicians, we have the unique position of constant interaction with the cast because our work requires their presence and participation at many stages. Costume shops are constantly in the know, not because we are gossips (although sometimes we may be), but because we require communication with all production areas to do our work.

The human element complicates costuming to such an extent that out-of-the-box thinking and on-the-fly problem solving are prerequisites for doing our work. We have been caring for the needs of people, from their egos to their allergies, for so long that many healthy and sustainable practices have become commonplace because they serve the largest number of people effectively. Seasoned costumers will find many of the sustainable practices here already in place in their shops. Indeed, they are so ingrained in our daily operations as to appear common sense.

We save leftover bits of garment trim and buttons to use on accessories or hats. We keep patterns and scrap paper to take notes. We cut old undershirts into dust rags and use our pencils until they are nubs. We maintain a stock to use in the future. We know high-tech and low-tech ways to solve many of our most challenging problems.

Costumers are keepers of the arts-and-crafts movement. The diversity of materials we employ and the varieties of skills we master are staggering. As such, finding large, simple solutions to sustainability issues is not realistic. Greening the production side of costuming often happens in small practical pieces. Unlike our colleagues in scenery and properties, it is difficult for us to see the consequences of waste production at the end of a show. It is not in the dumpster or garbage bins. Every costume stock, however, has a corner of ill-conceived and unusable things destined for donation.

The results of most insidious processes we take part in are neatly washed down the drain and evaporated into the air. It can feel so distant, so abstract, to count gallons of water we never see, and concern ourselves with air quality and river water on other continents. Yet, our shrinking resources and expanding expenses tell us that we need to think globally.

Assessing the Situation

Getting a clear picture of the environmental impact of the products we purchase and the processes we complete can be very difficult (see Chapter 2 for more complete assessment information). Tracing every purchase back to its source is nearly impossible. Because manufacturers are not forthcoming with information and we cannot grow the cotton ourselves, we make decisions blindly. We assume or infer basic pieces of information about what we are purchasing. Not everything requires a stab in the dark.

We do have some tools to evaluate our environmental impact including MSDS or SDS sheets, water meters, and air-quality meters. We can count the products we use and the volume of materials we go through. Whether you know the exact environmental impact of a bolt of muslin or not, you can assume the impact is halved if you consume half as much.

The Forest View Assessment

- ☐ Look at previous budgets. The areas where you spend the most money (on product, not labor) will be areas making the largest environmental impact. While the proportions may not be exact, those numbers can serve as guideposts. For example, travel, shipping, and material all have an impact on both finances and ecology.
- ☐ Check MSDS or SDS sheets to be sure you are using products as directed. Product use and disposal regulations not only protect your health, they can limit environmental exposure. There is a strong correlation between practices which are good for your health and those that are good for the environment.
- ☐ Assign a member of your shop as the environmental steward or Green Captain. This person is responsible for making sure that shop equipment and lights are turned off when not in use. The steward also ensures recycling is available, collected, and sent to the appropriate place.

Standing on the Shoulders of Giants

One of the great things about sustainability in costuming is that we can make use of the many strategies and products already in place for the popular domestic and commercial green initiatives. We deal with many environmental challenges that already have researched alternatives. There's no need to reinvent the wheel. A quick Internet search will provide anything from recipes for homemade soap to workshops and instructions for plant-based dyes. The recycled paper, blue bins, and Internet file-sharing sites adopted by so many offices fit perfectly into the costume shop.

The Office (Briefly)

The conservation initiatives of the costume shop's office closely parallel those of the front office (see Chapter 4 for specifics).

Figure 11.1 Organized inventory of patterns and stock are kept in notebooks divided by style and period. Photo by Jessica Pribble.

However, the most important advice I can give to improve the sustainability of the costume office is good organization and appropriate documentation.

We have invested a great deal of time meticulously organizing and digitizing our catalog collection. During this process, we realized that simply putting pictures in a digital file was not enough, we needed detailed information as well. Now, a cursory glance at our catalog tells us what the company owns, what sizes are available, and where the pieces are located. Having this information at our fingertips allows us to efficiently track and use products and supplies, reducing the possibility of time and material waste.

Pattern Alteration: Building Costumes for Reuse

In the throes of a production schedule, it can be very difficult to think about constructing garments for future use. Before pulling out the Ginghers scissors, remember the time and effort you will save in the future by constructing this garment for alteration. Certain construction techniques allow costumes to be more readily used in future productions. Use these ideas to make the theatre's inventory of constructed costumes meet the goal of sustainable reuse.

Muslin: The Basics

As costumers, we use muslin for everything from draping and mock-ups to pressing clothes, rehearsal clothes, and ironing board covers. If you do not already do so, there are many ways to repurpose a single piece of muslin to get maximum benefit.

Reduce, Reuse, and Recycle Muslin

1. Mock-ups are full-scale prototypes of costumes built out of a cheap or readily available fabric (typically muslin) that we use to perfect a pattern before cutting the final fabric. When constructing mock-ups, most seams can be sewn using a long stitch length. This facilitates both adjustment in the fitting and also deconstruction at the end of its life. While it might seem wasteful, be sure to cut your mock-up on the straight-of-grain. Because of the loose weave of most muslin, even the slightest bias will change the fit and increase the risk of cutting the final garment too small.
2. When the mock-up has completed its life as a draping tool, use the material for a number of alternative purposes. I occasionally send the mock-up into rehearsal so the actor can get accustomed to wearing something the shape and length of his final costume. This is especially useful for productions that have high levels of physical action, costumes that "do tricks," or sets with numerous stairs, levels, or obstacles.
3. When a completed mock-up is not needed in rehearsal, you can save it for use in future rehearsals. At a university, mock-ups are often prized for use in period-style acting classes and workshop productions.
   If you have no other use for the mock-up, it can be deconstructed and saved as scrap fabric. While you may cut your large mock-ups directly from the bolt, smaller pieces can be cut from the scraps of old mock-ups.

Because of the volume of muslin we consume at Central Washington University, we find it helpful to keep three boxes of used muslin pieces under the draping table; one each for small, medium, and large scraps. If you regularly use different weights of muslin, you might find that your boxes are designated light-, medium-, and heavy weight.

The scene shop often has muslin scraps from flat construction that are too small for their needs. If you take leftover fabric from scenery, ask if the manufacturer has pretreated it with flame retardant as that may not be the best choice for clothing which makes contact with skin.

In addition to use in future mock-ups, we use scrap muslin for sewing samples in costume technology classes, pressing cloths at the ironing boards, flat-lining fabric, rehearsal handkerchiefs, and a myriad of other practical uses. Once the sizing has been washed out, muslin scraps become absorbent enough to use as cleaning cloths or rags. A single piece of muslin might have 10 or 12 incarnations before finally retiring to the fabric recycling bin.

Building for Reuse: Getting More Mileage from Constructed Costumes

When you choose to build a garment, it is important that you get as much mileage out of the garment as possible. However, the needs of a production often dictate that the piece be very specific in its design. There are several ways that costumers build costumes to achieve the most versatility and potential without short-changing the current production. The possibilities fall into three basic categories: building for alterability, temporary distressing, and trim.

Easy Alterations to Allow Reuse

Building additional seam allowances into the garment's construction is the most basic way to ensure the garment can be manipulated to fit another actor. This can be especially important with body-hugging and tailored garments which are designed to show off the specific actor's body. Vests and Victorian bodices come immediately to mind.

Working from a commercial pattern can make this process difficult, as the patterns are designed to be stitched a given distance from the cut edge without a marked stitch line to follow. Additionally, it can be difficult for the novice to discern which sides of a pattern are the appropriate places to add width to the seam allowances because patterns are rarely labeled to indicate where the seam will eventually hit on the body.

When you are working from a commercial pattern, it is labor intensive to add additional seam allowances, especially when it means reorganizing how the pieces lay out on the fabric. Plus, the rewards of your work will not be reaped until some unspecified date in the future. Ask yourself, how much potential does this piece have for reuse? If I know the garment is destined for substantial, irreversible distressing or is being made from an unusual or nontraditional material, I save myself the time and resources by cutting it as indicated on the pattern. When I know a certain period comes up regularly or the piece is universally useful, the time to create larger seam allowances for future refitting is always well spent.

One caveat: Not every seam of a bodice or dress can or should retain copious seam allowance. Curved seams such as princess or fiddle-back seams will not lie properly if extra seam allowance is maintained. Any seam that curves dramatically or requires easing will likely prove problematic. These seams are often cut or slit closer than even standard seam allowances in order to function properly. Other vertical seams, however, can prove ideal locations for additional alteration opportunities.

Figure 11.2 Adding additional seam allowance to a commercial pattern. Photo courtesy of Jessica Pribble.

In horizontal seams, there tends to be less need for variation in width to accommodate future refitting. Actors vary less in height than girth, and therefore the internal horizontal seams tend be less important. In fact, there are often fewer horizontal seams in the structure of garments than vertical.

Variations in performers' heights tend to be distributed evenly while girth can be concentrated in individual areas of the body. Two men might wear the same size trousers but a barrel chest will give one a very different vest size. Shoulder seams and hems are the best places to add as much seam allowance as the garment will comfortably hide because the variation in actors' heights and build (not weight) is often in these areas.

Building Common Garments to Accommodate Refitting

Vests

In addition to the original 1/2" or 5/8" seam allowance indicated in a pattern, I cut an extra inch of seam allowance in the side seams (SS) of any vest or bodice I build. This allows the garment to increase four full inches in girth and maintain its overall structure. If there is a center back seam (CB), I will add an inch there as well. This allows you to compensate for a more or less rigid posture of performers who may wear the garment in the future. I try to add 1/2" of seam allowance at the shoulder seam, allowing for an inch of difference in height or slope at the shoulder.

Jackets and Bodices

Jackets and bodices can benefit from the same additional seam allowances as a vest. However, if the torso of a jacket is let out at the SS, it will increase the size of the armscye, the seam where the arm of the garment meets the side of it. Thus, an equal amount of seam allowance should be added to the sleeve seams. This applies more readily to garments which are tailored to the body, than those with a boxier cut. Historically, this has meant womenswear benefited more from this alteration technique than menswear, but the hard and fast rules of garment tailoring are starting to shift.

If a box cut jacket needs to be let out substantially, it is probably time to purchase or build a new jacket. Jacket alterations are extremely common because adjusting the sleeve hem is the most often needed change. If the sleeve will handle it, I cut an additional two inches of seam allowance at the sleeve hem.

A special tip—stitching darts in women's vests and bodices: When stitching a dart on a side seam with extended seam allowance, be sure to only stitch the dart to the original cut line. If you continue the angle of the dart into the extended seam allowance, it will force the side seam to buckle.

Trousers and Skirts

The CB seam of a pair of trousers is another common area for alterations. I leave as much as two inches of seam allowance in this area. While the CB seam of a pair of trousers is a great place for extra seam allowance, the curve down to the crotch will not easily tolerate additional bulk. Gradually increase the seam allowance from the most severe part of the curve to the waistline.

Any additional seam allowance added to the vertical seams of trousers should be reflected in the waistband. While adding seam allowance to the CB seam is the most obvious solution, many commercial patterns simply do not have seams there. Tucking the additional seam allowance back at the ends will work if the closures do not include buttonholes or machine-pressed snaps which cannot easily be undone. If there is not a CB seam, add the extra seam allowance to the end of the waistband without these closures. This solution only works if the waistband is a uniform width.

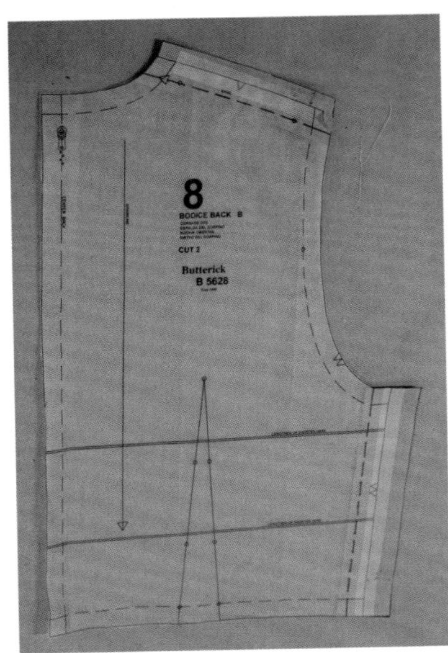

Figure 11.3 Use the original cut line on the pattern to stitch the dart. Photo Courtesy of Jessica Pribble.

Shaped waistbands typically have a side seam. If not, you can create one. Adding a seam to the waistband at the side seam is less visible than CB and allows you to hide extra seam allowance where the bulk will be less obvious. While there is not always a line on your waistband pattern piece labeled side seam, the pattern typically has a notch to indicate where the waistband crosses the side seam of the garment. You can simply cut the pattern in two pieces at this point. Be sure to add the standard 5/8" seam allowance plus whatever additional seam allowances you added at CB to these pieces. Stitch them together on the original cut line and continue constructing the garment as if the seam did not exist.

The SS and inseams of trousers and the SS of skirts can often handle additional seam allowance as well, particularly below the bottom edge of the pocket. I don't recommend reserving enough fabric to turn peg leg trousers to boot cut, but an inch at each seam will accommodate a wide variety of leg shapes and muscle development. I find this is especially important if the pants are made from fabrics with minimal elasticity.

Adding additional hem gives the trousers the option of adding a cuff in the future as well as accommodating a taller actor. When too much fabric is turned up at the hem of either a skirt or a pair of trousers, the garment does not move as it should and the stitches used may start to strain under the weight of the fabric and become visible. Therefore, it is very important not to sacrifice the aesthetic of your current production for potential future applications. The maximum turn-up will vary dramatically based on the cut of the garment and weight of the fabric. More than four inches is often a recipe for frustration. If this is at all overwhelming, you can reap 90% of the benefits by simply adding an inch of seam allowance to the side seams and two inches to the hem of every garment that will tolerate it.

Lining and Seam Finishing

Once a garment has enough seam allowance to be alterable, it is important to make sure those seams are accessible to you once the garment is completed. When lining a jacket or vest it can be helpful to flatline the lining at the side and shoulder seams, sewing those two pieces together with wrong sides together, instead of finishing the lining entirely. Simply surging the edges of the fabric and the lining together before stitching the side seams is the easiest way to finish the seam without encasing it inside the lining. However, this only works if the audience doesn't see the inside of the garment.

You should decide on the best technique based on the level of theatre you are producing and your need for reusable stock. For jackets, it sometimes makes sense to either partially line or leave the lining open at the bottom edge. A swing tack will secure the lining in place, preventing it from riding up and out of place while leaving easy access to the seams for future alteration.

If you are just starting out with constructing garments from patterns or you have never closely analyzed a commercial pattern before, the following instructions may help you add additional seam allowances.

1. Start by collecting materials. This will include the supplies you normally use to trace and mark your patterns like wax pencils, wax tracing paper, a tracing wheel, a graphite pencil, straight pins, and your commercial pattern. In addition, you will need a 2″ wide clear plastic ruler.
2. Before laying the pattern out on the fabric, I recommend marking each pattern piece with the seam allowance that will be added. When working with bodices and vests, locate the pattern piece marked bodice/vest front. If the line drawing of the garment on the pattern envelope has a vertical seam running from either the shoulder seam or the armscye to the waist, you will find multiple pattern pieces usually marked center front (CF) and side front (SF) and center back (CB) and side back (SB) respectively. With a graphite pencil, write + 1/2″ at the shoulder seam of CF and CB. (Usually the SF and SB pieces terminate somewhere in the armscye. If they continue up the shoulder, + 1/2″ should be marked on the shoulder seam of the SF and SB of these pieces as well.) Next, mark the side seams of both SF and SB with +1″. Continue marking the additional seam allowance desired on all the additional pieces in your pattern.
3. Prepare your fabric as you normally would and begin laying out your pattern pieces, leaving additional space where your pieces indicate. Laying out your pattern on the fabric, you may discover that the additional seam allowance renders the map in your pattern impossible to follow. As long as you have purchased enough fabric, perhaps more than is indicated on the back of the pattern, this should not matter. Just be sure to lay your pattern pieces out on grain matching any patterns as you would otherwise have done. When your pattern is pinned down, trace around the outside, and transfer all markings as you would normally have done. Before removing the pattern pieces, use your clear plastic ruler to extend the edges of the pattern piece the specified amount. Mark this line in a contrasting color. Extend the perpendicular lines at a 90° angle at each corner to make a new corner with your extended seam allowance.

Cut out all pieces on the outermost line. Disregard all added seam allowance and use the original marked line as though it were the cut line. This marked line should not be used as a stitch line. For clarity, use your clear plastic ruler to mark the stitch line (typically 5/8″ from the original cut line) on the piece using a contrasting color. This often clears up any confusion the stitchery may have regarding where to stitch.

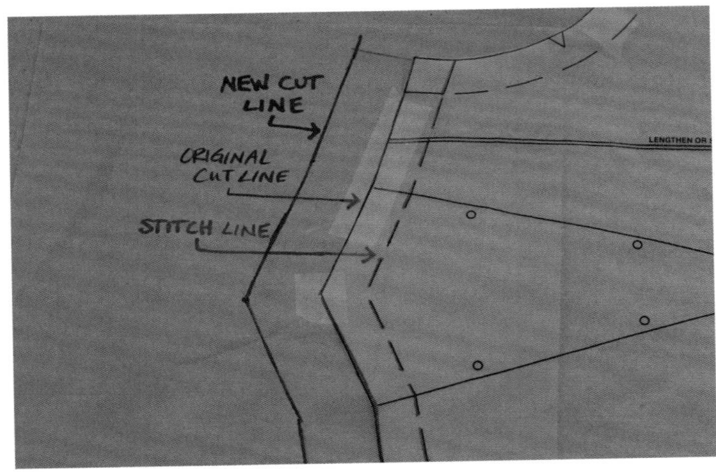

Figure 11.4 Example of altered pattern piece. Photo courtesy of Jessica Pribble.

Temporary Distressing: Removable Wear and Tear

Nothing sells the authenticity of a costume design better than distressing. Distressing, or the act of making clothing appear used, worn, or "lived in," helps convey the time, place, economic status, and past action. In short, it is essential to properly clothe many characters. Yet, as costumers, it can be disappointing to "ruin" perfectly good clothing, especially if we are building up our stock or hoping to limit our carbon footprint. While some plays dictate clothing that is beyond repair, at other times we can adopt temporary or reversible distressing techniques to limit damage to the base garment.

Distressing Products

Vaseline and glycerin are regularly used to create sweat and pit stains. Many make-up products like Ben Nye's Texas Dirt and Plain's Dust can be adhered to cloth using either of these washable products. There are water-soluble distressing products called Schmutz Sticks available designed to simulate everything from grass stains to rock dust. Each of these products is designed to wash out of most materials. A test on scrap fabric may be in order. Products like Texas Dirt are designed to come in contact with actor's skin, sweat, and body heat. Therefore they are safer for the performers than any paints and pigments meant to cure on a canvas.

Fabric Additions

There are several ways to create the illusion of a worn spot or frayed hem in a garment. The first is the simple addition of a patch. Following the grain of the original piece with a distressed patch of the same fabric can give a garment the appearance of distressing without an obvious patch. In a proscenium house, the distance will often make the transition disappear. If the patch can be stitched on inconspicuously, from a distance it will appear that whatever distressing is on the patch is part of the garment. It is particularly effective if the distressing is located in the center of the patch, but not along the edges. The patch will blend into the base material. Because patches and stitch lines are attached to the garment without inflicting any structural damage, this style of distressing is particularly effective. While thin fabrics work best, any light- or medium-weight fabric can work as long as the grain as well as any pattern or texture is matched as closely as possible.

Often making a garment look distressed involves fraying hems and cuffs. If you have additional material it can be simple to add a faux edge to a skirt or pant leg. Many fabrics come with selvedge, or the factory edge, that is naturally frayed as it comes off the loom. Otherwise, a long strip of the fabric can be cut and deconstructed to look like an unfinished edge. These long narrow strips of fabric can be sewn to the inside of the existing hem. The desired edge should extend below the hem of the garment and be stitched as close to the edge as possible. The hidden edge of this internal trim should be cross-stitched or blind-hemmed up as needed. This type of distressing works particularly well on fabrics which are either rough or busy enough to mask the transition from one fabric to the other, as well as garments which have decorative finishes like cuffs and trim.

Reinventing a Garment with Removable Trim

True stock costume pieces like a well-tailored pair of men's trousers, a simple vest, or a white blouse can make several appearances in a season without reminding the audience of previous productions. One of the best ways to accomplish this is with the use of removable trim. Whether the piece is dressed up with gold braid or "worn" down with distressed trim, a costume piece has many lives. Changing decorative closures and adding or removing lace or ruffles can have the same impact.

Whether you are using distressed or immaculate trim, it is important to attach the trim in a way that is structurally sound, but easy to remove in the future. Often, trim can be attached with a long machine stitch or a couple of discreet rows of running stitches. Heavy trim should be attached to lighter fabric at the seams, where the seam allowance can help support the weight. If you need to attach trim to the middle of a garment, I recommend placing a piece of twill tape on the inside of the garment and stitching through the three layers. This helps prevent the fabric from stretching and reinforces the stitches so that they do not pull holes in the fabric.

Garments are often resized without removing trim, so be sure the additional seam allowance you have added to the garment is reflected in the trim. At the least, your trim should have a seam where the garment has a seam. It may be possible to either open the seam in the garment and insert the additional trim, or fold the trim back on itself and stitch it down topically. Successfully hiding the extra trim on the garment depends on its thickness. If leaving extra trim on the garment is unsightly, remember to set aside several inches of trim to store with the garment when it returns to stock.

When I am finishing the edge of a garment with bias tape, particularly armscyes or neck-edges, I will wrap the pieces individually and then sew the garment together at the shoulder and side seams. This makes it fast and easy to make adjustments at those seams without having to remove the bias.

Each garment we build should be judged for its value in the general stock of the company. Realistically, many garments have little potential for reuse even before taking seam allowance and trimming practices into consideration. For garments that are likely to be used in many productions, spending additional time and effort on construction can help you build a versatile and valuable stock. While it is a small step ecologically, it is crucial to long-term sustainability.

Wardrobe: Caring for the Production and the Planet

Many of the most practical and immediate improvements that can be made in costume production come with the way we care for and maintain the garments. This is a central area where we take cues from the domestic green initiatives. Earth friendlier detergents and surface cleaners have been on the shelves of stores ranging from natural food stores to mega-grocery chains for almost 20 years. There is always the issue of "greenwashing" so don't take the package at face value without some additional research.

Momentum continues to build, and customers have started voting with their money. Each time I go looking for a green alternative to a wardrobe product, I find one. In fact, I usually find several. The options are out there. A better understanding of what chemicals are involved in typical wardrobe duties can help you make decisions about what to use.

Dressing Rooms: Creating Sanctuary

Dressing rooms are, to many actors, a sacred space; a place for mental as well as physical preparation. It has often been my experience, however, that these spaces are hot, cramped, poorly ventilated, and chemical ridden. Fighting the heat to apply one's stage make-up is a mentally defeating proposition. Many of the products and processes that make dressing rooms unbearable are the same ones that harm the environment.

Dressing Room Lighting

Mirror lights typically consist of 6–12 incandescent lamps simulating stage lighting which traditionally comes from incandescent lamps at multiple angles. Chapter 9 pointed out how inefficient incandescent lamps are. The bulbs convert more electricity to heat than they do to light. We know this from the push toward more sustainable light bulbs in our homes.

In an enclosed space like a dressing room where each of 12 stations can have as many as 12 lamps burning, it gets hot very quickly. More energy efficient lighting in dressing rooms could easily lower the temperature ten degrees.

Yet this strategy is often met with resistance and skepticism especially by those concerned with theatrical make-up. The art of applying theatrical make-up has everything to do with the lighting design and proximity to the audience. The conversion from incandescent to more energy-efficient light sources in domestic applications has outpaced the conversion in theatrical lighting. There is a great debate about the impact that converting dressing room mirror lights to compact florescent bulbs will have on the make-up technician's ability to correctly apply color and shadow. As LED lighting improves and expands, this issue should eventually resolve itself. Several versions of these lighting options already exist. I recommend

Figure 11.5 Actress Carly Squires Hutchison prepares to go on stage. Photo by Jessica Pribble.

Figure 11.6 Damon Runnals, General Manager of the Southern Theatre in Minneapolis, has found LED lamps that work remarkably well in the dressing rooms. They are 7 watt soft edge warm white lamps named the PAGEANT™ LED from Light Emitting Designs. They provide good visibility and color rendering without heating up the dressing room. Photo by EEJ.

discussing an ideal lamp color temperature range with your lighting designer and looking for appropriate lamps in your price range. LED lamps are the coolest burning and the least expensive to run. Finding lamps that will serve as direct replacements in existing make-up stations due to the small lamp base and the need for a diffuse source has caused many to shy away from LEDs. However, as the lamps improve, more companies are actually changing out the mirror sockets to accommodate their use.

If the color bulb you are looking for is not available or is not affordable, there are other solutions. One option is to buy the best bulbs you can afford and apply stage make-up as if there has been no change. The designer can respond to any issues during notes. This is the way most designers have dealt with the pre-existing variation in dressing room to stage lighting. The second is to leave one or two stations stocked with incandescent light where actors can test colors and intensities and return to their stations to complete application under fluorescents. Because the fluorescents are not full spectrum lamps, simply adding color media will not correct the problem.

If each station is not operated by an individual control switch, remove the incandescent lamps from any unused stations. Even if every socket in the room has a bulb in it, heat can be reduced if an individual is tasked with turning off the make-up lights when places are called.

One final idea; at CWU, we have a small number of theatrical lighting instruments hung at the far end of each dressing room which we turn on briefly before curtain. The actors can see themselves standing in full stage light and make appropriate adjustments.

As well as compensating for variations in style between make-up and stage lighting, this affords us two additional benefits. First, it allows us to gel the light specifically for each show; making this the closest substitution for the actual stage lights as possible. Second, and equally important for an educational environment, it forces the performer to stand and look at themselves from a distance. They see something closer to what the audience will see. This allows the most egregious application errors to be caught before the actor enters the stage.

Reducing the heat of incandescent lighting may actually have unexpected make-up application benefits. Actors will be cooler so the make-up will set more quickly and accurately, remaining as applied instead of sliding down the face. Reapplication will be reduced with the reduction of sweating saving both time and product. Any prosthetics will apply more securely as well.

Additionally, more privacy is possible if the dressing-room doors remain closed. We can eliminate the use of box fans in the space and put less strain on the building's heating/cooling system. Less sweat means less work for the wardrobe crew, less make-up on collars and cuffs, less wear to the costumes, a better smelling dressing room, and a generally nicer place to work.

If the dressing room does not include a spray area, aerosol hair coloring, hair spray, and antiperspirant should not be applied in its confines. Hopefully you can shift away from using these products but if they must be used, do not fumigate the dressing space with them.

Laundry: Clean Clothes, Filthy Water

Figure 11.7 One of the less glamorous tasks of wardrobe managers is the laundry. Diego Cervo/Shutterstock.

Costume shops do a lot of laundry. We start by prewashing fabrics to remove sizing and ward off garment shrinkage. We wash fabric as part of the dye process, and we wash to refresh clothing when it comes out of storage. We launder to make sure the actors have passably clean clothing for every performance, and we wash again at strike to prepare clothing for storage. A single piece of cloth used in a two-week academic run might end up in 15 washing-machine loads. In a conventional washer, those 15 loads can add up to well over 600 gallons of water.

Because of the volume, changes in our laundry habits have the potential to have a major impact in both the fiscal and ecological arenas. Washers and dryers are specifically discussed in the segment about machinery in the costume shop, but laundry products and aids must be addressed as well.

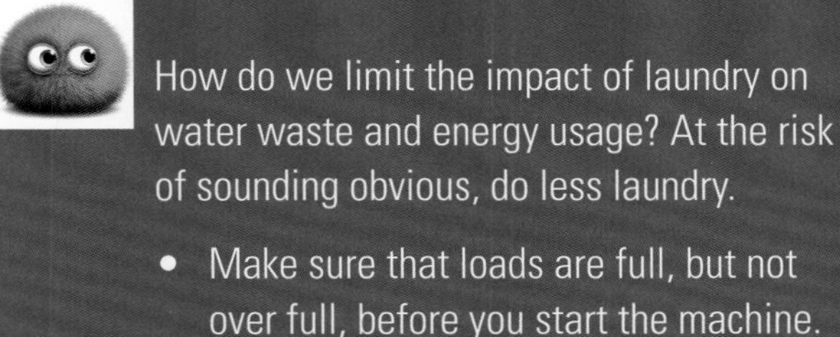

How do we limit the impact of laundry on water waste and energy usage? At the risk of sounding obvious, do less laundry.

- Make sure that loads are full, but not over full, before you start the machine.
- Save towels and other heavily soiled items for a separate load so that you can run your mixed loads on shorter, gentler cycles.
- Run your machine with cold water whenever possible.
- Adjust your settings for the size and style of load you are doing. If you must wash a load with just undershirts and socks, set the machine to small load, cold water.
- Adjust the amount of detergent you use to fit the load you are doing.

The Laundry List

When I began writing this chapter, it occurred to me that I had no clear understanding of what laundry detergent is. Sure, I've been responsible for washing my own clothing since I was 12. I've been a wardrobe mistress for countless productions. I have completed the age-old ritual of washing clothing thousands of times. Sure, I know about perfumes, dyes, and the existence of color-safe bleach. But when it came to the actual composition of my everyday detergent, it might have been fairy dust and angel tears for all I knew. In the box below is a layman's description of what I discovered.

Choosing the Right Detergent for You

So, how do you get your clothes clean without the "laundry list" of chemicals? How do you know which detergent is right for your needs? One of the first things to take into consideration is the kind of laundry you are doing. If you are working at an outdoor summer stock, you will have serious dirt to contend with. If you are washing for a Victorian costume drama, your concerns will be largely removing stage make-up and keeping your cottons looking fresh and starched. Of course, the material you are washing can be very important too.

If you are using a conventional washer, only use as much detergent as you need to get the work done. We all want our clothes to come out clean, but adding extra detergent isn't usually required. High-efficiency washers require detergents that are less sudsy than traditional detergents. These detergents are marked with an "HE" logo letting you know that they are safe for use in these machines. Simply preventing overuse of our current detergents would save untold gallons of chemicals

More than suds, detergent is not one thing. Standard laundry detergents contain several types of chemicals which are combined to increase the product's effectiveness:

- *Builders*, or what we refer to as water softeners, can make up a large percentage of the mass of a detergent. They are designed to deactivate calcium and other minerals in the water which can leave deposits. This allows the other active ingredients to do their work.
- *Surfactants* bind to dirt and oil and also to water, helping pull the stain away from the cloth.
- *Bleaches* help clean organic plant material stains from your laundry. Most color-safe laundry detergents use a hydrogen peroxide process which is enhanced by an activator like tetraacetylethylenediamine.
- *Enzymes*: Some detergents also use enzymes. Enzymatic agents help break down heavy protein and carbohydrate stains. The old truism that spitting on a blood spot will prevent it from staining comes from the presence of these enzymes in your saliva.
- *Optical Brighteners*: While not used as a cleaning agent, optical brighteners are common additives in detergent giving the appearance of cleaner colors and brighter whites by absorbing ultraviolet light and emitting blue light. Optical brighteners are what give your white shirts that desired glow and make many detergents black light reactive.
- *Additional Additives*: The ingredient list doesn't stop there. A detergent might have chemicals designed to prevent loose dye from adhering to other garments and chemicals to prevent the detergent from harming the machine. Several additional chemicals help to differentiate one brand from another including perfumes and dyes.

from entering the waterways. Here are some other choices to consider. These suggestions are in order of increasing environmental stewardship.

- Concentrated Detergents: Simply reducing packaging and transportation costs helps the environment. Two-in-One, Triple-Concentrated, or even Four-Times concentrations are available for most national brands. Some brands have gel packs of super-concentrated detergent which dissolve in the water. This will assure that you only use the amount of detergent required to do the job.
- Fragrance- and Dye-Free: If you have not already done so, you can switch your detergent to fragrance- and dye-free. This removes several unregulated chemicals from the water supply, but is the same detergent you are familiar with and mixes with the water in your machine to create exactly the same cleaning action. Many costumers have already adopted this practice out of personal preference or deference to the myriad preferences and allergies of their actors.
- Phosphate-Free: One of the most egregious disrupters of the ecosystem in detergent is the use of phosphate-based builders or water softeners. A popular builder is sodium triphosphate which, when released into the environment in waste water, disrupts the ecosystem by overfeeding algae which crowds out larger freshwater marine life. Many governmental agencies around the world are starting to limit or disallow phosphate use in detergents. While the handwriting may not be on the wall for Americans yet, it is not difficult to find a phosphate-free option.
- Naturally Derived: The many ingredients in detergent including surfactants and enzymes can be either man-made or naturally derived. Several plants have natural surfactant qualities which can be harvested and used as detergents. Palm and coconut are commonly used in naturally derived laundry soaps. Reviews of these products tend to be very positive with the exception of whites never coming out as white as synthetic detergents. This happens not because of the cleaning action, but due to the absence of artificial optical brighteners. These optical brighteners do little to actually clean the cloth, but reflect light to increase the appearance of whiter material.

  Most national grocery chains and health-food stores carry several brands of naturally derived detergents. Because the water softeners in naturally derived detergents are often milder, the hardness of your water may have a larger impact on the success of a specific detergent in your area. Experiment with a couple of brands before deciding which one works the best for you. Consider supplementing these products with a tablespoon of baking soda or washing soda to soften water.
- Castile or Hemp Soap: There are a myriad of traditional organic soaps on the market which can be used to assist in laundering clothing. While soaps contain a surfactant to help get your laundry clean, they do not contain a builder to prepare the water. Their success may be contingent on the hardness of your water. In areas with harder water, larger quantities of these products will be required to do the work. I find castile, hemp, or plain Ivory® soap work better than detergent for hand washing.
- Soap Nuts or Berries: Members of the tree genus *Sapindus* are commonly referred to as soapnut or soapberry trees because their fruit's hull contains a naturally occurring surfactant. These plants have been used to wash clothes for centuries by both Native American and Asian populations. For modern appliance washing, the fruits are dried and placed in a small sachet which, when added to your laundry, releases the surfactant into the machine and washes your clothes. These are both naturally organic and minimally processed. A small handful of these berries will wash approximately six loads of laundry. While not always readily available in your hometown, soap nuts are easily purchased on the Internet.
- DIY Detergent: The industrious among you might be interested in making your own detergent. If so, you will find countless recipes and pieces of advice on the Internet.

Most of the recipes I have come across include a bar of your favorite soap, washing soda (a harsher chemical related to baking soda), borax, and water. Remember washing soda is more caustic than baking soda and can be a skin and eye irritant. While somewhat labor intensive, making your own detergent gives you the confidence of knowing exactly what has gone into your laundry. You can add scent with essential oils, adjust the water softener to meet the needs of your area, and save an incredible amount of money over conventional organic or naturally derived options. This is probably the best way to use organic bar soap in the washer.

Jack and the Bean Stalk

I tried to keep my skepticism at bay, but when researching soap nuts I kept seeing Jack throwing magic beans into the washing machine. I had visions of beanstalks growing out of my washer with glowing white t-shirts unfurling like new leaves.

I had to try it. A week later, out came my first load. And, while I discovered a distinct lack of giants in the sky, I also noted a distinct lack of scent. I am already a perfume- and dye-free detergent user, so the lack of perfume came as no surprise. I was struck by a lack of any smell at all. My laundry didn't smell musty, chemically, or sweaty. It didn't smell like me. It did not smell like sunshine after the rain. It had no scent. I'm quite certain I had never smelled just fabric before. I recommend using the soak option on the washer to allow the nuts time to release their washing properties.

While it remains to be seen whether soap berries can tackle my husband's marathon running, my everyday work clothes came out better than ever.

The Price of "Cleaner" Laundry

Price is always a consideration when shopping for products that will be purchased regularly. After a cursory Internet search, I was stunned to find that I could find Tide for approximately $0.25 per load (in the form of a huge double-concentrated container and as 6x-concentrated pouches) and Seventh Generation 4x Free and Clear for under $0.27 per load. In fact, I found the Seventh Generation product at half that price, but it seemed to be a one-time special offer. The Seventh Generation product is sold in a compostable paper-based container which uses 66% less plastic than standard packaging. There is a joke here about "my two cents."

The soap nuts I purchased averaged out to $0.14 per load including shipping but would have decreased in price substantially had I purchased a larger volume. Following the directions for using Dr. Bronner's Liquid Castile Soap as laundry detergent costs just under $1/load. However, if you use it as an ingredient in homemade detergent, the cost drops dramatically. Homemade detergent is by far the cheapest. Depending on the soap and essential oil you buy, you can spend less than $0.05/load. Of course, that does not factor in the time and energy that went into making the product.

Spot Cleaning

The universal offender to wardrobe cleanliness is stage make-up which somehow manages to get everywhere. Each commercial product comes with directions for treating and removing stains. Depending on which product you use, I recommend some experimentation. While I have by no means exhausted my options, I have never found anything to be more successful at removing cream stage make-up than a plastic bristled brush and a bar of Ivory soap. Scrub some soap onto the stain with water, let it sit for 20 minutes, scrub again and rinse. Works like a charm on both cotton and synthetics.

There are also commercially marketed enzyme-based and soap-nut-based stain removers as well as the old standbys involving baking soda or lemons on white fabric. The Biokleen products are particularly effective at removing dried organic stains.

Fabric Softeners

A traditional next step in the laundry process is to use fabric softener in order to reduce static cling and improve the smell and texture of the garments. Fabric softeners come either in liquid as a washing machine additive or a fiber sheet for the dryer. The chemicals in fabric softener coat your fabric in order to reduce the build-up of static electricity and make it feel softer to the touch. Traditional fabric softeners can rub off of clothing and expose you and your actors to such toxic chemicals as formaldehyde and chloroform.

If you use dryer sheets, be aware that the chemicals may build up on your dryer lint screen and limit air flow in the dryer. Take your lint trap to the sink and see if water will run through it. If not, give it a good cleaning with soap and water, and blame those dryer sheets.

Like detergents, fabric softeners have several alternatives.

- *Use less fabric softener*. Natural fibers do not develop static cling in the dryer. If you divide your loads into natural and man-made materials you can do away with fabric softeners in the natural fiber loads. Tear your dryer sheets in half and use fewer per load.
- *Switch to scent-free and naturally derived fabric softeners*: As with detergent, fabric softener comes without artificial scents and dyes. Several familiar companies sell fabric softener and dryer sheets derived from soy and other natural materials.
- *Hang clothing to dry*. Either directly from the washer or when the clothing in the dryer is just slightly damp, remove them and hang them to dry. The longer clothing remains in the dryer, the more it tends to develop static electricity.
- *Invest in dryer balls*. Instead of using dryer sheets, just throw these reusable fabric softening balls in the dryer with your clothing. They lift and separate the laundry, decreasing drying time and preventing electrical build-up. A pair of spikey plastic dryer balls cost under $10. If you miss the scent of fabric softener, you can buy PVC-free dryer balls with a refillable compartment for specially designed essential oil paper cartridges. This style will cost you $25 plus cartridges. Still, cheaper than dryer sheets over time. PVC-free means less off-gassing from the hot plastic in the dryer balls. You can even personalize the scent of your laundry. Like most reusable devices, dryer balls pay for themselves quickly. Dryer balls need not be made from plastic at all. Dryer balls made of wool from recycled sweaters and socks are available online and at many natural food co-ops. Using these eliminates the plastic off-gassing when heated and they are made of recycled materials.
- *White Vinegar*. In lieu of adding anything to the dryer, you can add white vinegar to the final rinse in the washer instead. It will remove excess soap and soften your laundry. The smell of the vinegar dissipates entirely in the dryer so you won't smell like salad dressing.

Dry Cleaning: A Chemical Bath for Your Clothes

Dry cleaning isn't really dry at all. Instead of washing your clothing in water and detergent, dry cleaners give your clothing a bath in liquid chemicals.

Perchloroethylene, also known as PERC in the industry, is the most commonly available dry-cleaning chemical. According to the Center for Disease Control, approximately 85% of dry cleaners use this particular solvent in their processing. Exposure to PERC may lead directly to several types of cancer, renal failure, and breathing problems. Low-level exposure, such as what you will find in ground water or what will be absorbed through your skin from wearing dry-cleaned clothing, has never been directly linked to adverse human reactions. Low-level long-term exposure, such as what would be experienced by someone working in the dry-cleaning industry, has been linked to many of the health issues listed above.

While modern dry cleaners use a filtration system to clean and reuse the PERC, substantial amounts of it remain in the clothing after it is removed from the machine. This residual chemical content may be released into the air by the pressing machine or come off on the person wearing the garment. You have probably smelled it in your closet after removing the plastic from your freshly cleaned clothes.

There are several considerations as to whether or not a piece of clothing needs dry cleaning. Is there a water-cleaning method to will deliver the same results? If a greatcoat is worn onto the stage, then removed and hung for the remainder of the scene, did the garment really receive enough human contact to require dry cleaning? Simply reducing the amount of dry cleaning required can make a major environmental impact.

While certain garments may not need to be dry cleaned, many costumes made from fine wools or mixed materials can only safely be cleaned without water. Assuming they need more than a quick spritz with vodka, what then?

Wet Cleaning: Before the invention of PERC and other dry-cleaning chemicals, cleaners would often divide clothing into two piles. The first (made largely of synthetics) would go to the dry cleaner. The natural fibers would be wet cleaned, or, as I like to call it, washed. Modern wet cleaning is simply a version of the kind of washing you would be doing at home except the machines have special settings that allow the cleaner to specify how the garment should be treated in order to protect it from damage or shrinkage. Some dry-cleaning facilities offer wet cleaning services, in addition to their water-free services. This service reduces the number of garments coming in contact with PERC. Hand washing can be very time-consuming. Wet cleaning allows you to leave that work to someone else.

Greener Dry Cleaning: While PERC may be the standard dry-cleaning chemical, it is by no means the only solvent used for dry cleaning. A nationwide group of cleaners under the umbrella GreenEarth Cleaning use a nontoxic silicone-based solvent to replace PERC. Unlike PERC, liquid silicone breaks down into sand, water, and carbon dioxide if released into the environment. If you have ever had the experience of having expensive buttons or trim melted by the dry cleaner, this may be the product for you. Customers report substantially lower incidents of this kind of damage. Because costumers often need to dry-clean exotic or unusual materials, it is comforting to know that a service exists with a lower likelihood of catastrophe. Hundreds of GreenEarth Cleaners exist throughout the United States, mostly in well-populated areas. You can find more information and a list of cleaners near you at www.greenearthcleaning.com.

In-Home Dry Cleaning: After researching home dry-cleaning kits, it is my assessment that they are rather ill named. It appears the majority of what they do is bake a pleasant scent into dry-clean-only clothes. In addition to having the same unregulated perfume chemicals as detergents and fabric softeners, they do not typically remove much dirt from the cloth. At-home dry-cleaning bags seem ideal for freshening up a blouse that has spent too much time in the musty storage area. A tumble in the dryer with a slightly damp washcloth and a couple drops of essential oil, however, would probably achieve the same goal.

Febreze®: To Spray or Not to Spray

Cheaper, faster, and at least somewhat successful at removing armpit funk, Febreze and its imitators are standard alternatives to dry cleaning for many of us in the theatre. I can't be alone in loathing the way they smell. I'm often struck by the fact that we are happy to use perfume- and dye-free detergents for our actors, but daily spray their clothing with these same chemicals.

In order to remove the smell from clothing, household odor-eliminating sprays often contain volatile organic compounds and known carcinogens. Research indicates regular exposure can have damaging effects on the lungs and respiratory system. Additionally, the packaging is often inefficient and expensive. Alternatives are so easy, so numerous, and so inexpensive, you will start to wonder why you ever paid for these chemicals in the first place.

Vodka: Before the invention and distribution of Febreze by Procter & Gamble in the 1990s, wardrobe supervisors and costume shop managers were getting along just fine with a combination of cheap vodka and water for freshening clothes, not drinking. Alcohol can destroy odor-causing bacteria and break down water insoluble residues. It is also completely sustainable, minus the packaging. Vodka contains no chemicals that adversely affect the environment, and is 100% biodegradable. I have used both a 50% vodka solution of two parts water to one part vodka successfully. Using distilled or filtered water will prevent the spray from depositing minerals on your clothing and allows the vodka to better do its work.

The reduction in odor can be complemented by the addition of an essential oil to mask any residual unpleasantness. I have found that adding a woodsy smell has the added benefit of making it less desirable as a beverage for young members of the wardrobe crew. Another great wardrobe freshener can be made from two cups of water, ¼ cup of baking soda, ¼ cup of vodka, and a few drops of an essential oil. This has the advantage of using less vodka per batch, but the batches must be made up (or at least the baking soda added) just prior to use. It is important with any spray to spot check the fabric to ensure that the product will not stain or discolor the garment.

If it is impossible to get or keep alcohol in your work environment, you can save money and chemical exposure by diluting your Febreze 50%. You can limit packaging by saving your old bottles and buy the larger refills at the store.

Lysol Alternatives

When it is absolutely necessary to disinfect an item, a time when you might use a product like Lysol, there are sounder solutions available. We often disinfect hats and shoes, for example, in the course of a run and during strike.

Shoes: Placing a small satchel full of baking soda in each shoe after a performance will absorb residual moisture and neutralize odor. These satchels can be reused for many performances before replacing the baking soda. We often replace the insoles in shoes when they are given to a new actor. Washable insoles reduce (if not eliminate) the need for disposable inserts.

Hats: The brim or inside of a hat can be sanitized with a straight alcohol wipe or spray. When disinfecting non-porous surfaces, a vinegar and water solution will also work. The smell from vinegar will completely dissipate given enough time, but I tend to reserve it for non-porous surfaces, in case timing becomes a factor.

Surface Cleaning

Wardrobe supervision is an art which requires balancing the needs of many people and personalities. It requires some waste to get the job done. However, there is a great deal we can do with the products we buy and the way we present our options. With whatever wardrobe supplies you choose to use, you can take small steps in reducing your carbon footprint by avoiding aerosol containers, buying refillable applicators with bulk bottles, and using the products with discretion.

Prioritizing

While we would love to implement as many sustainable practices as possible, realistically these changes will be taken one step at a time. Allow your company time to adopt the practices and fully appreciate their benefits. Because we begin each journey with a single step, here is a way to decide where to begin.

Priority Checklist

Start with the changes that will impact worker safety.

- ☐ Remove and properly dispose of harsh chemicals.
- ☐ Clean air ducts and vents.
- ☐ Properly store and label the remaining chemicals.
- ☐ Limit dry cleaning and aerosolized chemicals.

Next, make changes which will reap the most benefit for the smallest effort.

- ☐ Make sure your recycling services are complete.
- ☐ Buy naturally derived and organically grown supplies.

Follow with immediate cost-saving measures.

- ☐ Reuse on-hand materials.
- ☐ Limit paper consumption.
- ☐ Organize stock to limit crushed items.
- ☐ Make your own detergents and cleaning supplies.
- ☐ Buy in bulk or in appropriately sized batches.

Finish with choices which will help with future savings.

- ☐ Build for reuse.
- ☐ Replace efficient workstation lighting.
- ☐ Limit the purchasing of dry-clean-only materials and garments.
- ☐ Purchase energy efficient machinery.
- ☐ Learn temporary distressing techniques.

Chapter 12

Costume Crafts, Make-Up, and Storage

Costume Crafts

Under the umbrella of the costume shop, there is more than just constructing and maintaining clothing. We work with dyeing, weaving, millinery, jewelry, cosmetics, wigs, and shoe repair. Each of these areas employs materials and chemicals beyond the standard needle and thread. Each chemical we employ must be not only properly used, but also safely and effectively stored. Because the potential products are so numerous, I cannot realistically cover every one. Instead, I will focus on the most popular and give overviews of other groups.

Fabric Dyes

Dyeing clothing has a bad rap. Synthetic fabric dyes often use heavy metals and other toxic chemicals to complete the task. It is easy to see the pollution as we pour a pot of used dye water down the drain. Some dyes contain phosphates and known carcinogens with the understanding that the level of exposure is low enough to mitigate the individual human risk. The MSDS (SDS) and the dye box do not address the cumulative effect that multiple costume shops dyeing fabric have on the environment. With the water required to dye the garment, rinse away the extra dye, and clean the machine, it is easy to use over 100 gallons of water for even a medium-size dye project.

You might wonder how anyone could justify a traditional dye project. It is important to remember that the alternatives take their toll on the environment as well. It might seem counterintuitive, but sometimes a conventional dye job can have the smallest environmental impact. If you have a piece

Figure 12.1 ADA_photo/Shutterstock.

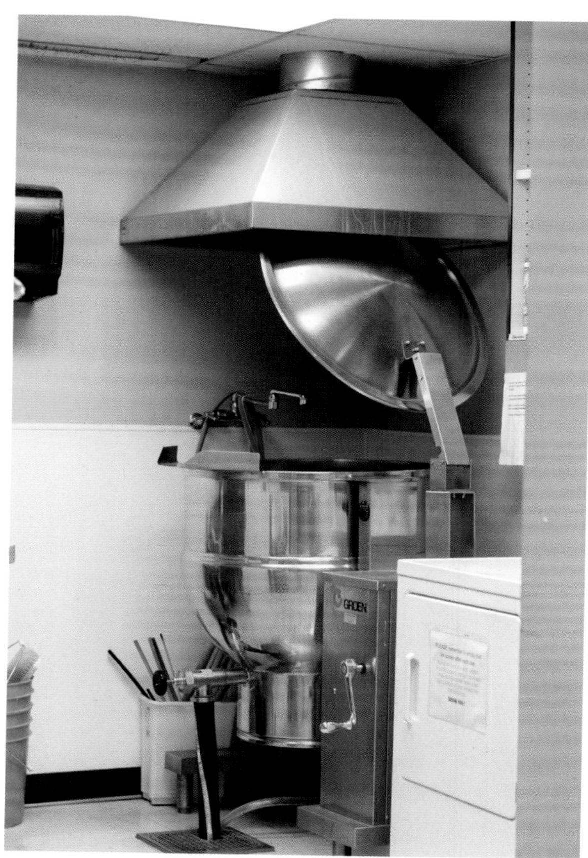

Figure 12.2 Dye vats require adequate venting to prevent fume buildup. Photo by Jessica Pribble.

in stock that will become the piece you need with a simple dye job, do it. The alternative may mean buying a garment which has to be grown, cleaned, woven, dyed, stitched, and shipped. One dye bath is less environmentally taxing than creating an entire garment, as long as you dispose of the dye water appropriately. Dyeing can open up a world of possibilities for your clothing. Reimagining stock and second-hand pieces are an obvious way to limit the pollution of production.

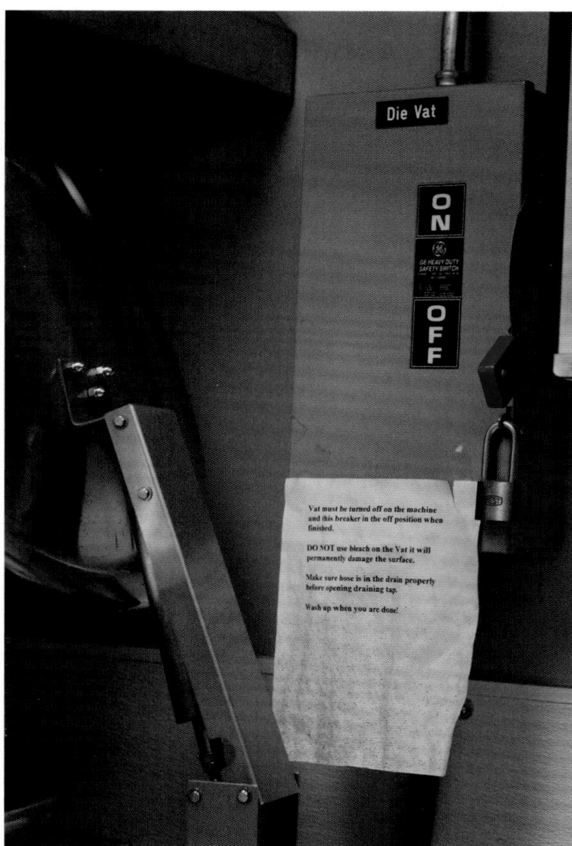

Figure 12.3 Locking out the dye vat when it is not in use is a wise safety measure. Photo by Jessica Pribble.

Types of Natural-Fiber Synthetic Dye

Not all dye baths are created equal, in either effectiveness or ecological impact. There are simple steps you can take to limit the waste of your traditional dye projects. First, make sure the dye you are using is designed for the fiber content of your garment. In order to do that, check out the different types of dyes you can use in the box below.

Dye Basics

- *Acid Dye*: Acid dyes are used to dye protein (think animal) based fibers: Wool, alpaca, and silk. Acid dye is not, as you might be imagining, necessarily a caustic or dangerous dye process. The dye functions best in an acidic pH environment meaning that a weak acid such as vinegar is used as an activator.
- *Direct Dye*: Direct dyes are used on celluloid (think plant) fibers: cotton, linen, and rayon. They will weakly dye protein-based fibers as well. Direct dyes are hot-water dyes, which are not the most effective or long-lasting dyes on the market. They are, however, inexpensive and, as such, they are standard ingredients in all-purpose dyes.
- *Fiber-Reactive Dyes*: Fiber-reactive dyes are cold-water dyes, which bond permanently with celluloid fibers. They are brighter, longer

lasting and generally more effective for dying than their direct-dye alternatives. Fiber-reactive dyes require the use of soda ash (non-toxic sodium carbonate).

- *All-Purpose Dyes*: All-purpose dyes are a combination of acid dyes and direct dyes designed to be at least somewhat effective on a large array of fibers. The most ubiquitous all-purpose dye is RIT.

In order to prevent huge amounts of wasted dye from going down the drain, be sure to choose a dye that works for your fabric. All-purpose dyes are ideal for use on garments that have mixed natural-fiber content. However, a natural/synthetic blend can be better served by the dye designed specifically for the natural fiber in question. For example, all-purpose dye is ideally suited to a cotton/wool blend. For a cotton/poly blend, however, you might be better served choosing a fiber-reactive dye. When you use all-purpose dye on 100%-cotton garments, the acid dye content goes directly down the drain.

SPECIAL TIP: When heating water for a small dye job, use an electric kettle instead of an open burner. The water will heat faster, and it will use less electricity.

Natural Dyes

For thousands of years, people have been using naturally occurring materials to color their clothing. It has only been in the last 150 years that synthetic dyes have become available. While it is certainly easier to find a box of RIT dye, it is not the only option available. Plant-based dyes can create a wide variety of both subtle and vibrant colors.

If you live near a major metropolitan area, you may be able to find a natural-dye store in the area. These products are also available online. The natural-dye market is small and since the products have an organic base, availability may depend on the growing season. The pigment might come from a flower, tree, nut, or insect.

In order for most natural dyes to adhere to fabric, they will need some assistance. Natural-dye processes use two products. One part is the pigment and the other is the mordant. Mordants are chemicals or substances that help the dye adhere to the fabric.

Using natural materials in a dye bath is still not a one-size-fits-all process. Depending on the pigment you are using to dye and the fiber content of your fabric, you will need to select a specific temperature, quantity, and mordant. Mordants run the gamut from heavy metal baths to salt water. Make sure the mordant you are using meets your sustainability goals. The last thing you want is to replace one toxic process with another.

Most of us are not in a position to wander the wilderness picking plants to use in our dyeing practices. We need more immediate and consistent alternatives. When we can't collect our own dyes, we can certainly purchase them. Several online sources will provide you with everything you need to complete your natural-dye products. Most dye sources will provide you with a basic recipe to get you started.

Tea and Coffee Staining

Due to the tannic acid, a box of loose leaf tea is all you need to create a wide array of brown dye hues. Tea staining has a long history in the theatre for aging anything from clothing to window coverings to paper props. You can achieve all sorts of variation by changing the type of tea, the water temperature

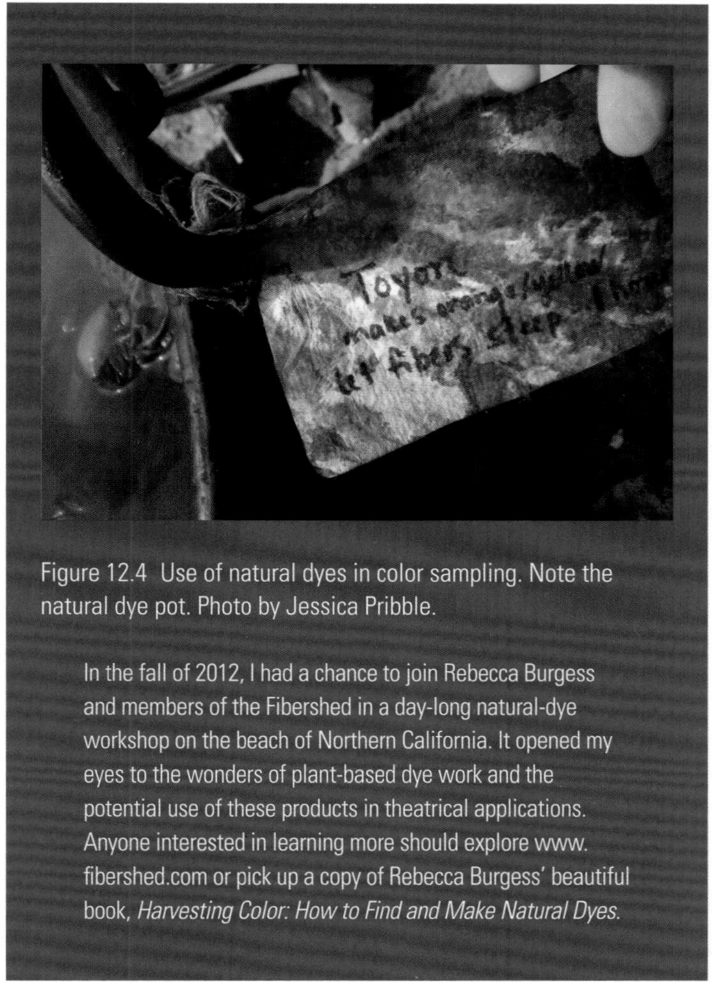

Figure 12.4 Use of natural dyes in color sampling. Note the natural dye pot. Photo by Jessica Pribble.

In the fall of 2012, I had a chance to join Rebecca Burgess and members of the Fibershed in a day-long natural-dye workshop on the beach of Northern California. It opened my eyes to the wonders of plant-based dye work and the potential use of these products in theatrical applications. Anyone interested in learning more should explore www.fibershed.com or pick up a copy of Rebecca Burgess' beautiful book, *Harvesting Color: How to Find and Make Natural Dyes.*

and the length of exposure. The most potent tea I have found is Lapsang Souchong. I originally bought it to drink, only to discover I don't enjoy smoked tea. What it lacked for me in palette-pleasing flavor, however, it more than made up for in dye potential. It may leave the garments smelling like they have been dried over a wood fire, but the color possibilities are worth it.

Adhesives, Aerosols, and Other Off-Gassers

Air quality is a major consideration in the craft shop. Worker safety dramatically improves with proper ventilation, appropriate safety gear, and a reduction in toxic chemicals. When not properly cared for, costume craft shops can be some of the most toxic environments in the theatre. Reducing the number of chemicals in the shop can help create a safer, cleaner working environment for everyone. Please remember that nothing here should be considered an appropriate alternative to a proper certified safety inspection and analysis.

Adhesives

When purchasing glue, be sure that it is designed for the specific task you have in mind. Many glues have naturally derived alternatives or come in nontoxic versions. There is really no such thing as sustainable wonder glue that meets all needs. Wheat paste may work for some applications, but it will not provide a strong enough bond for heavier materials.

Use adhesives responsibly; make sure you purchase the glue you need in the appropriate size container. If you use a great quantity, purchase in large bottles. For glues you use infrequently, be sure to buy smaller containers that will not let the products dry out before you have a chance to use it. When I buy superglue, I always buy the single application tubes. I find these tubes typically last me about three applications which are as long as the applicator stays unclogged and the glue resists drying out. While the packaging seems wasteful at first blush, I tend to get as much use from a smaller package as I would a larger one.

Many adhesives, even after they dry, off-gas. Be sure that any glue that will be near an actor's face, such as in a crown or mask, is completely non-toxic. For some products, you can forgo the use of glue altogether. Papier mâché for example, can be made with just flour and water wheat paste.

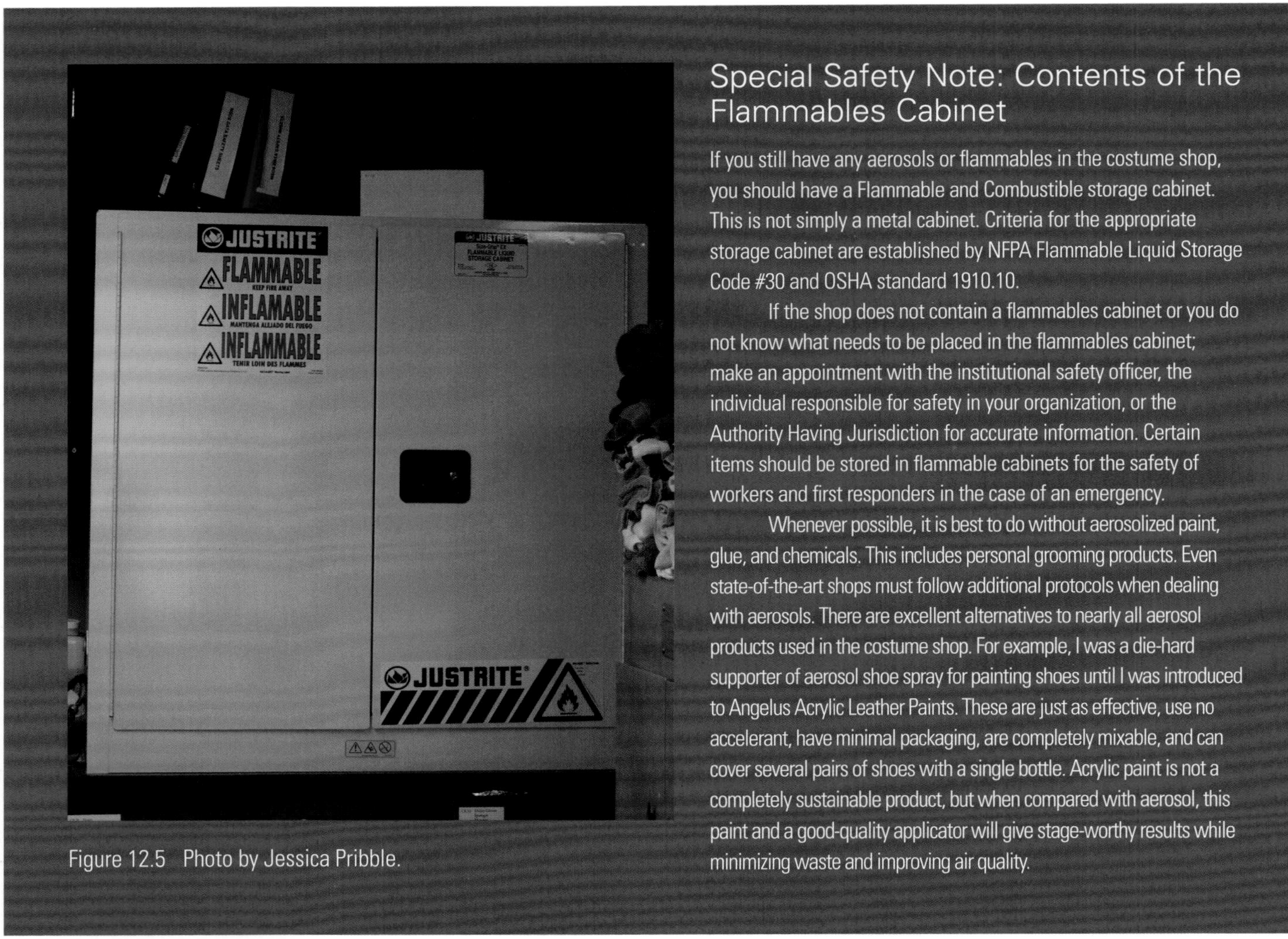

Figure 12.5 Photo by Jessica Pribble.

Special Safety Note: Contents of the Flammables Cabinet

If you still have any aerosols or flammables in the costume shop, you should have a Flammable and Combustible storage cabinet. This is not simply a metal cabinet. Criteria for the appropriate storage cabinet are established by NFPA Flammable Liquid Storage Code #30 and OSHA standard 1910.10.

If the shop does not contain a flammables cabinet or you do not know what needs to be placed in the flammables cabinet; make an appointment with the institutional safety officer, the individual responsible for safety in your organization, or the Authority Having Jurisdiction for accurate information. Certain items should be stored in flammable cabinets for the safety of workers and first responders in the case of an emergency.

Whenever possible, it is best to do without aerosolized paint, glue, and chemicals. This includes personal grooming products. Even state-of-the-art shops must follow additional protocols when dealing with aerosols. There are excellent alternatives to nearly all aerosol products used in the costume shop. For example, I was a die-hard supporter of aerosol shoe spray for painting shoes until I was introduced to Angelus Acrylic Leather Paints. These are just as effective, use no accelerant, have minimal packaging, are completely mixable, and can cover several pairs of shoes with a single bottle. Acrylic paint is not a completely sustainable product, but when compared with aerosol, this paint and a good-quality applicator will give stage-worthy results while minimizing waste and improving air quality.

Cobblers

Actors are hard on their feet and our shoes. For some productions, characters are moving, running, and dancing for two hours straight. They require total security in their footwear. We, as designers, usually desire a look that can make that security difficult. One of the ways we compensate for asking actors to dance in heels or period shoes is to glue rubber with added traction to the bottom of the shoes. In this situation, the actor's safety is paramount. Less effective options can cause serious injuries.

Most shoe rubber is sourced from wardrobe supply companies. I encourage you, when possible, to supplement this with locally sourced rubber. Here in Ellensburg, our local tire store provides used car-tire inner tubes free of charge. Because this product lacks the additional surface grooves of traditional shoe rubber and comes in only one color, it is not ideal for all applications. However, we have found it useful for period shoes and musicals with a modest amount of dancing. In order to adhere this product to the shoe permanently, it is especially important to score to rubber extensively before attaching to the shoe. This is an easy way to recycle a material headed for the landfill, remove the slipperiness from period shoes, and never open your wallet.

Care for the shoes you already own to extend their life. Take shoes to the cobbler before the actor has worn all the way through the leather. Resoling a pair of old shoes is an excellent way to support a local cottage industry, save money, and limit the use of new material. Develop a relationship with your local cobbler. You may find the price is very reasonable for repeat business. Purchasing quality footwear and properly caring for it improves actor safety, improves the look of your design, and increases your stock.

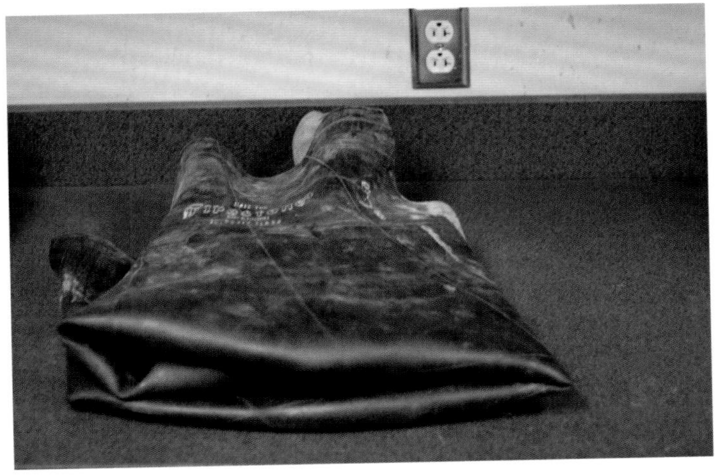

Figure 12.6 Tire rubber can be locally sourced. Photo by Jessica Pribble.

Machinery: Caring for What We Have

Two fundamental criteria should be considered when evaluating the sustainability of a new machine: energy efficiency and longevity. Depending on the machine, one criterion may be more important than the other. For example, looking at a domestic sewing machine for energy efficiency requires considering whether that machine is capable of doing all the things you want it to do. The efficiency comes into play when you consider whether or not you will need to purchase a second machine to perform tasks the first machine cannot. Relatively speaking, the energy consumption difference between types of domestic sewing machines is low because of their small size and similar operation. Washing machines, on the other hand, are designed to do one thing. The efficiency will be graded on how much energy and water it consumes.

Take into consideration the ROI, or how quickly the reduced utility costs start to pay for the machine to tell you if it is worth the additional initial investment. While some machines certainly require less energy than others, also consider initial purchase price and the longevity of the machine. Disposable sewing machines (like everything else in our disposable culture) have a major impact on the environment.

The industry-standard Bernina 1008 comes with quite a price tag, but also with the knowledge that, with proper maintenance, it can last decades. Most high-quality machines will more than pay for themselves in longevity and reliability. But this requires playing an active role in your machines' well-being. Regular oiling, cleaning, and otherwise maintaining the inner workings is a must for keeping your machines up to date.

I worked for a small theatre in Chicago that had invested in a sewing machine and serger for their costume area. This was a great expense for them at the time. Before I started my job, the serger had stopped working. It was a simple matter of the blade being too dull to cut cloth. This $200 machine needed a $5 part that could be replaced using a screwdriver. Yet, there it sat like an oversized paperweight.

Figure 12.7 Machines like the serger pictured require regular maintenance and cleaning to continue operating at peak efficiency. Photo by Jessica Pribble.

This isn't just an issue of finance; it is an issue of sustainability. Do we really need 30 cheap sewing machines in the landfill? And even if we wanted to fix them, to keep them running longer, many of them can't be fixed. They are made of flimsy materials that simply give out over time. They are not designed with removable or exchangeable parts. They are designed to discard and replace. Ironically, it is the expensive machines that you can get inside and repair. These workhorses are designed so that you can have a relationship with them. The virtues of understanding machinery aside, you want a machine worth maintaining.

Repairmen (or Women): The American Dream

Appliance-repair people are a dying breed in our disposable culture. Local sustainable businesses are closing down because we are not utilizing their services. Out with the old, in with the new. Yet caring for our machines, old or new, is at the heart of any sustainable practice. Learning to do your own maintenance is the least expensive option, but for those of us with no time or aptitude, trained professionals are often just a phone call away. If you have more than a couple of machines to service, the repairperson will typically come to you. Keeping machines in top working order not only prevents them from breaking, but can also keep them energy efficient. Local small businesses are the backbone of a community. Building relationships builds community. It is the definition of the American Dream.

Daily and Weekly Maintenance

Even for the mechanically disinclined, there are simple activities that can extend the life of machinery and cut down on energy expenditure. If your shop has multiple workers, be sure someone is trained to regularly oil and remove lint from the sewing machines. Covering the machines each night prevents dust from settling into the mechanisms. If you have a cluster of machines and lights, consider putting the group on a power strip so that you can turn off all the machines completely with a single switch. Train your staff to turn off their machines whenever they are not sitting at them. The incandescent light bulbs and standby power consumption will be dramatically reduced.

Shop Computers

The computer has become a central piece of costume-shop equipment. Everything from pattern-making software to Internet shopping means the shop computer is a constantly used tool. There are several things you can do to be sure the computer is as efficient as possible. While we want immediate access to the machine, we often also go several hours without using it. Set your screen saver options to turn the screen off after a short period of inactivity. Internet radio and any background programs will not be affected by the monitor. Make sure it is part of the daily routine to turn off the shop computers completely every night.

Washing Machines: Traditional vs. High-Efficiency

I've never met anyone who would like to return to the pre-washing machine era. We rarely, however, think about the price we are paying for the convenience. Washing machines, or washers for simplicity, consume energy and resources in a number of ways. They run on electricity, use water to wash and rinse, electricity to heat the water in the machines, energy to clean the water on its way to the machine and after it enters the waste stream. They wear down clothing, traditionally require detergents which can harm the environment, create noise pollution, and can be difficult to service which leads to thousands of models ending up in landfills.

No matter what kind of washer you use, you can save electricity by washing your clothing in cold water. Just heating water can consume up to 90% of the energy a machine uses. Most people do not notice improved cleanliness with the use of hot water. If sanitizing is a concern, add vinegar to the load. Allowing your clothes to presoak in cold water, which requires no effort or energy, allows the detergent time to penetrate and pre-treat clothing. Exactly how much electricity you will save will vary depending on the capacity of the machine, and whether the machine uses hot water from your hot water heater or heats the water itself.

There are two distinct styles of washing machines readily available on the commercial market. They are top-loading and front-loading. The traditional top-loading washer has a large drum that fills with water and uses a central agitator to force water and detergent through the clothing. Front-loading washers spin sideways and using a tumble action to allow gravity to push the water through the clothing. There has been a discernible shift toward front-loading washing machines in the market over the last ten years. It is easy to see why. Front-loading washing machines have many advantages for the average ecologically conscious consumer.

High Efficiency (HE) and Energy Star Washing Machines

Water Use: Traditional washers fill with water above the level of the clothing and mix the detergent and water through the clothing using an agitator. High Efficiency (HE) washers fill to a level well below the top of the clothing and mix the contents by rolling them into and out of the water. Instead of draining completely and filling again in order to rinse, HE washers spray clean water from above. This can result in a 70% reduction in water use per load.

The average traditional washer uses 40–45 gallons per load. If you average six loads a week, you can easily prevent over 5000 gallons of tap water from going down the drain each year. That is enough to overfill a 10'x16'x4' swimming pool. If that is not motivation enough, think about this: If your sewage fees, water treatment fees, and the cost of tap water average a combined $0.05/gallon you could save $250 per year on these utilities. Never mind that the machine requires less electricity to run and puts less stress on the water heater.

Detergent: Detergent is fully discussed in Chapter 11. However, it is important to note here that HE washers require less detergent because of their superior washing technology. This is, of course, good for the wallet and good for the earth.

Clothing Wear: One of the often untold advantages of HE washers is that the wash cycle, though more effective, is often less destructive to the garments. The central agitator in a traditional washer puts a great deal of stress on the fabric in the wash. Because front-loading washers do not have agitators, they are much less damaging to the clothing. This can dramatically increase the life of undershirts, socks, and other wardrobe consumables.

One caveat: Try to see any new style of washing machine at work. Top-loading Infusor washers are the new competition for HE front-loading machines. The Infusor uses less water; in fact so much less water that some models include the option for a second rinse on the machine dial. Poorly designed models also need an extra spin cycle, and the motion leaves wet clothing so twisted that it looks like macramé when pulled from the tub. While reducing the volume of water used is good, some do not fully rinse out the soap unless vinegar is added to the final rinse.

Price: While prices for your baseline top-loading washers have remained under $500, HE front-loading washers have dropped down to within a couple of hundred dollars of their competitors. With their increasing share of the market, we can expect prices to continue to become more competitive. The volume of laundry in a typical costume shop means a HE washer can pay back the difference in a year or less. Even if your laundry needs are irregular or sporadic, the HE model will pay for itself long before its life is up.

Those of you without a designated machine may consider taking your show laundry to a laundromat instead of using your old washer and dryer at home. Laundromats have large volume front-loading washers, fast dryers, and allow you to do multiple loads simultaneously. Many urban laundromats now offer Wi-Fi, allowing you to work while you wash. In the time it takes me to read and respond to my morning email, I can have the show laundry washed and dried.

Most new washers, both top- and front-loading, have multiple settings and sensors that allow you to get really specific about how your clothing is washed. In some ways, however, front-loading washers are less flexible than your traditional machines.

First, they lock when the cycle begins, preventing you from adding additional costume pieces to the load in progress. Likewise, pausing loads, removing clothing, or soaking clothing for times outside the customizable setting is impossible. While for most consumers, these are minor inconveniences, costumers often exploit these features for craft or dye purposes. It is often harder to see inside a front-loading washer and more ergonomically taxing to load them. If your job requires several loads of laundry a day, these inconveniences will add up quickly.

HE Top-Loading Washer: Recently, HE top-loading washers have been introduced to the marketplace combining the economic benefits and flexibility of top-loaders with the ecological and long-term financial benefits of the front-loading machine. As a disclaimer: I have never worked with one of these machines. It appears they may be the best of both worlds. They provide some of the important versatility missing from front-loading models while being comparably priced and offer the same ecological benefits as HE front-loaders.

Dryers

If there is a villain in our laundry story, it is the domestic tumble dryer. Americans use roughly 6% of their electricity drying their clothes. Not only do dryers suck up energy, they are inefficient in several other ways. They take air from indoors, air that has typically been heated or cooled to an ideal temperature and send it out the vent to the outside. Unconditioned air then comes into the building to replace it. Dryers can displace huge quantities of conditioned air like placing box fans in the windows pointed out. While some models have intake vents from the outside, they are much less common.

Traditional dryers have heat and time settings, but with few sensors to tell you if and when your clothes are dry. As frustrating as it is to open a completed dryer cycle to damp, unwearable clothing, it is equally wasteful to run a dryer for half again as long as needed. Extra time in the dryer wastes electricity, increases static cling, and wears out the fabric. Newer energy efficient dryers include sensors that determine when laundry is dry and stop automatically.

In order to save energy in drying, you should hang dry as much of your laundry as possible, ideally all of it. Assuming you have the time and space, this will translate to substantial energy savings. Since someone has to actually wear the clothes, there is a balance between saving energy and having costumes that feel like a washboard. Also wrinkles will fall out of certain fabrics in the dryer and eliminate the need for ironing or steaming. Balance is everything. You can also help by setting your machine to the shortest drying and lowest heat setting required to do the job. Cleaning the lint trap regularly will increase airflow and allow your clothing to dry faster. Make sure your dryer vent is unobstructed as this will prevent moist air from being reintroduced to your clothing, increasing the drying time.

High-Efficiency Dryers: The dryers that come as part of a HE washer/dryer set are not actually any more efficient than their predecessors. The technology has simply not advanced at the pace it has for washers. The HE label refers only to the washer. HE washers are able to rotate many hundred RPMs faster than traditional washers meaning they extrude a larger percentage of the water from clothing during the spin cycle. This has the benefit of shortening drying time and saving electricity; a trait which is often attributed to the dryer, not the washer. Many new dryers do have added sensors which allow you to customize how the dryer is used and assure that the dryer does not continue drying clothing which no longer requires it. New dryers may also have steam-heat features to release wrinkles and reduce the need for pressing.

Recycling Appliances

If you choose to replace your machines and appliances, make sure there is a responsible way to recycle the old machines. Most universities have an inventory department responsible for making sure the university receives the best possible remuneration for assets. State institutions may have very specific criteria for removing anything from inventory that was purchased with state funds. Outside of academia, there are commercial and domestic appliances recycling centers where you can send your old machines. Machines in working order can always be donated to a not-for-profit. Understand that your inefficient machinery will become someone else's inefficient machinery. This might help you reduce your carbon footprint, but that machine will continue its life elsewhere. The specifics of your machine will dictate if donation is an appropriate option for you.

Some areas have rebate programs to help pay you for your appliances. Many appliance-delivery companies will haul away your original machines. Make sure to ask how that company handles disposal.

Figure 12.8 M. Catherine McMillen, CWU Costume Shop Manager, applies make-up on BFA candidate in costuming, Ashley Baker, as part of a class. Photo by Jessica Pribble.

Cosmetics

The cosmetics we use in the theatre include stage make-up, street make-up, hair product, adhesives, eyelashes, latex, shampoo, conditioner, face wash, cold cream, antibiotic and antifungal creams, glitter, various lotions and powders. The list goes on. It is simply not possible to exhaustively cover each type of product and the many variations within. There are several universal guidelines that can be applied across the board to help you decide which of the many products available will best serve your goals as a producing organization and a sustainability enthusiast.

Cosmetics live at the crossroads of specific production requirements, individual actor needs, budgetary limitations, and sustainability goals. Finding a product to serve all these masters is not a small undertaking.

As the green movement continues to take shape, many cosmetics companies are coming out with complete lines of "eco-friendly" products. These might include products that are naturally derived, chemical-free, or contain certified organic ingredients. The USDA does not endorse beauty products, so there is no clear definition for what organic means on the cosmetic bottle. However, there are several agencies that give their seals of approval. The Environmental Working Group, for example, rates thousands of cosmetic products based on the potential risk posed by their ingredients. They have a searchable online database at www.ewg.org/skindeep.

To simplify, let's break down cosmetics into each product's constituent parts. Every product has ingredients, processing, delivery method, and packaging. Just as each can be rated for effectiveness, each of these criteria can be graded for sustainability. While each of the categories will apply to all products, the priority might be different depending on which product you are analyzing. As I explain each area, I will use the example of hairspray to help illustrate real-life considerations. Hairspray is an ideal product because it comes in a wide range of more and less sustainable options.

Ingredients

The ingredients in cosmetics can fall anywhere on the toxicity scale, can be naturally or synthetically derived, and can have other benefits and risks. Decoding the ingredient list of a typical tube of lipstick requires a degree in organic chemistry. That does not mean that every ingredient is bad. It can be difficult to recognize problematic ingredients. Many products are touting their percentage of naturally derived content. This can be the first clue as to whether a product is sustainable.

Look for products whose first few ingredients are understandable words. Many companies will translate the scientific terminology into understandable language, especially companies touting their environmental awareness. If a substantial percentage of the product is sustainably sourced, chances are the company will proclaim it. Because the practice of greenwashing has muddied the waters, be sure to fully research the products. One easy step is starting in the designated organic or "natural" section. Superstores like Target and Kroger have started organizing entire aisles especially for "green" cosmetics.

Check the company to see if they have a history of testing their products on animals. This information is not readily available and may require some research.

While there are few stringent regulations for what can be called organic, a certain amount of peer policing does happen. If a product states specifically that an ingredient is organic, chances are it is. Look for icons from voluntary certification organizations like NFS or ECOCERT described below.

Processing

Avoiding products and companies who use animal testing is another way to improve sustainability. The waste associated with raising animals in captivity, testing products on them, and disposing of their remains is astronomical. Aside from the

Organic Certification Agencies

United States Department of Agriculture: National Organic Program

While the USDA does not certify cosmetics, as such, it does allow cosmetics that use agricultural products certified by the agency to use the label if they meet all criteria. In order to use the logo on packaging, the USDA: NOP requires 95% organic content. The USDA does not allow synthetic preservatives or most chemical processing. It does not regulate the use of the word "organic" on cosmetics unless the cosmetic bears the agency's logo.

NSF International: The Public Health and Safety Company

The NSF American National Standard for personal care products containing organic ingredients (NSF/ANSI 305) allows the "contains organic ingredients" designation for products with organic content of 70% or more that comply with all other requirements of the standard. While still relatively stringent, the NSF/ANSI 305 label allows organic ingredients to undergo certain chemical processes—methods considered synthetic under the USDA National Organic Program.

EcoCert

The use of ingredients derived from renewable resources, manufactured by environmentally friendly processes. Ecocert therefore checks:

- Freedom from GMO, parabens, phenoxyethanol, nanoparticles, silicon, PEG, synthetic perfumes and dyes, animal-derived ingredients (unless naturally produced by them: milk, honey, etc.). The biodegradable or recyclable nature of packaging is reviewed.

A minimum threshold of natural ingredients from organic farming to be reached to obtain certification:

- For both labels, Ecocert Standard imposes that a minimum of 95% of the total ingredients come from natural origin.
- For the natural and organic cosmetic label: A minimum of 95% of all plant-based ingredients in the formula and a minimum of 10% of all ingredients by weight must come from organic farming.

For the natural cosmetic label: A minimum of 50% of all plant-based ingredients in the formula and a minimum of 5% of all ingredients by weight must come from organic farming.

Figure 12.9 Image courtesy of NSF International.

Figure 12.10 Image courtesy of Ecocert Groupe.

moral issues associated with ineffective testing and animal cruelty, the volume of waste is enough to warrant finding alternative ways to test products. Be aware that some companies label that their products are not tested on animals, but the individual ingredients may be. Others will use this selling point, but rely on the animal research some other company has already completed.

Delivery Method

How the product moves from the packaging to the person is the delivery method. Sometimes it is as simple as pouring; sometimes products require a pump or a brush. Does the product require disposable applicators each time it is used? A standard lipstick is delivered directly from the packaging. Lip gloss, on the other hand, often requires an applicator, either your finger or a brush. Some pump-action cosmetics add air as they are pumped through the applicator creating foam. This gives the appearance of more product when really it is just more air.

One popular delivery method for hairspray is aerosol; where the product is forced through a nozzle and dispersed in tiny droplets with the assistance of compressed gas. One of the major contributors to ozone layer depletion at the end of the twentieth century was the use of chlorofluorocarbons (CFCs) in aerosols and refrigerators. Luckily, 191 industrialized nations agreed to phase out CFCs more than 20 years ago. Though these ozone-depleting chemicals are banned, the chemicals used in their place are often VOCs and strong greenhouse gases. Not to mention, many of these chemicals are known carcinogens and exacerbate conditions like asthma and bronchitis. As time has passed, most hair-product companies have put out non-aerosolize products that have similar functionality. Because the technology in pump-action hairspray dispensers has improved, it is no longer necessary to depend on aerosol options. Typically the consumer receives more products in the plastic bottle than in the aerosol can.

Packaging

There are many other ways to improve the packaging and shipping issues associated with cosmetics. At CWU, we purchase our hairspray in gallon jugs from the beauty-supply store, and distribute it to actors in individual spray bottles. These individual bottles last several years and are easy to store and clean. Any unused product is returned to the jug at the end of the run, the spray bottles cleaned, and nothing goes to waste waiting for the next production.

If the product you are looking for does not lend itself to this kind of use, check to make sure you are buying the most appropriate size container. You want to make sure there are enough products that you are not buying it several times over, but also are sure that the container is not so large that either it is difficult to handle or half the product goes to waste before it can be used. I find smaller containers of liquid latex or spirit gum are preferable to large containers because the large containers dry out before we have used the majority of the product.

Working with What You Have

When switching to new cosmetics, it is not practical or affordable to throw everything out and start over. Replacing cosmetics should happen on an as-needed basis. It is important to allow time to test the product so that application adjustments can be made progressively. Plus, throwing out good product is no better for the environment than using what you have. Frequency of use is also an important factor. Replacing frequently used products will have more impact than those that are used less frequently. For example, I have not found a replacement for spirit gum that is not prohibitively expensive. The volume of spirit gum we use, however, is much smaller than the volume of hairspray so I have chosen to research and invest in sustainable hairspray products as a higher priority than spirit gum.

The theatre make-up and cosmetic industry has been developing theatre cosmetics for a century now. While some practices are obviously dated, there is value to the adage: *If it ain't broke, don't fix it.* Not every product will work in every situation. If you need to use a less sustainable option to get the effect you need, be sure the rest of your work can compensate. Every day, new products come out which are better for the earth. If a product doesn't exist for what you need, evaluate whether you really need it, and then use what you can.

Costume Storage: Taking Stock

"Taking stock" has come to mean so much more than counting inventory and checking boxes. We use the phrase to describe evaluating our place in the larger structure of the universe. We "take stock in" objects or attitudes we find valuable. A stock is the central structure of a plant or the base material of a soup; the animals we raise to feed each other and the pens we use to contain them. Taking stock is a natural step in any discussion of sustainability. Until you know what you have, how can you know what you need?

In the theatre, stock conjures up images of dusty cabinets or sweltering storage units. If you are lucky, it means quiet temperature-controlled rooms. For the unlucky, it means dusty garages, leaky attics, and long treks across campus or town. Sometimes, it is just plastic tubs in the hall closet. I've seen costume storage kept half an hour from the theatre in the back room of a factory, accessed while wearing hairnets and shoe covers. When faced with the unorganized chaos of poorly managed storage, the impulse to start from scratch is overwhelming and understandable. Time is always of the essence. It can be hard to justify a trip to stock if what you need is small or available online.

We need to rethink and reshape our costume storage to resemble, instead of a graveyard of past production, a larder. The place we find the ingredients to make our next meal. The main ingredient of each production may be new, but stock should contain the smaller pieces needed to round it out. You can think of suit coats and vests as rice and beans; hats and scarves as salt and pepper. Taking stock is a threefold process involving organization, preservation, and archiving.

Organization—Put Things Where You Look for Them

Your system of organization should reflect the style of work you do and the needs of your company. If you produce *A Christmas Carol* or *The Nutcracker* every fall, your storage system should reflect bringing these shows back from stock in their entirety. Yet even the most proscribed season will require reimagining for new bodies. I recommend keeping the unique show pieces together, but the more universal pieces go back into the larger stock. For example, our *Christmas Carol* area includes the ghosts, the children, Scrooge, and Marley. The remainder of the show, the majority, is reintegrated into the larger stock each year.

If you happen to be starting from scratch, or moving your storage, there are several things to take into consideration. How big is the space compared to the items being stored? Do you have a large collection of wedding dresses, furs, and other specialty items? How will you store hats, sweaters, purses, shoes, and other items that do not hang on a rack? Can you afford ample shelving and racks? Are you trying to use flimsy wire hangers from the dry cleaner for effective storage? Spending money for the appropriate choice will diminish damage and future replacement costs.

When you are setting up an empty room for storage, be sure to hang racks with ample space to move between rows. If you cannot hang an upper rack, make the lower rack high enough to store boxes or shoe racks under the clothing. While some of us have ample space and organization, most of us must exploit every nook and cranny.

Whenever possible, costume storage includes two sets of hanging racks at 5′ and 10′ from the floor. Be sure to include a taller area for hanging full-length dresses and cloaks without an under rack. The walls are covered with shelving large enough to hold 60-quart plastic tubs. If you are looking for a more sustainable storage options than plastic, I recommend second-hand steamer trunks and army surplus wooden munitions boxes. These are especially great for use on the floor under the racks. For items that will be stored at chest level or above, clear plastic tubs make it easy to see the contents, even if they have not been returned to the shelf with the label facing out. While we often have cardboard boxes at the ready, variations in moisture and temperature can quickly break down these boxes. They make easy work for mice and moths.

Most costume storage benefits from organizing similar kinds of items together instead of keeping entire ensembles or productions together. Unless tops and bottoms are made from the same material, breaking up costumes can help the future designer see, not how something was previously used, but what it might become. Obvious exceptions should be made for keeping suits together. Consistent organization can save you time, money, and frustration whether you are storing 50 years or two shows. If pants are divided by size then color, the same should be true of suits, shirts, and vests.

If you have a storage area which is separate from your work and fitting space, it is important to decide which pieces are worth keeping close at hand and which pieces live offsite. Undershirts, tights, socks, and accessories are best kept close by as you can pack a large quantity into a small area and will use them multiple

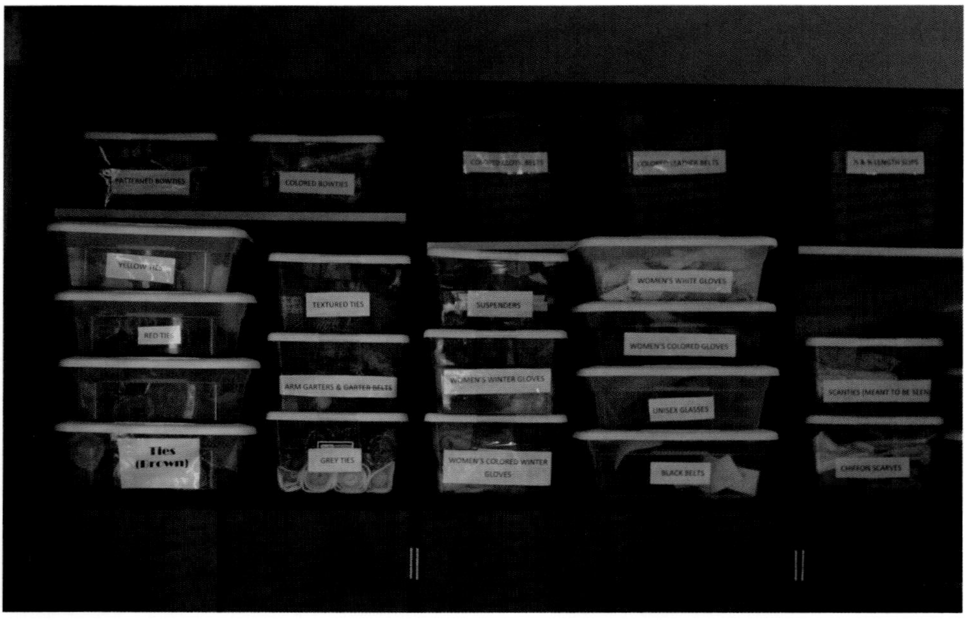

Figure 12.11 Small items can be stored in clear bins and labeled for easy access. Photo by Jessica Pribble.

times within a season. Shoes are often a good choice to keep onsite, especially character shoes and men's dress shoes as they can also make multiple appearances within a season. Performers may need to try on multiple pairs in the same size to find a shoe that truly fits, so storing onsite eliminates time and travel.

Any delicate or antique pieces should be stored flat in acid-free tissue paper in archival boxes. These pieces should be kept somewhere with consistent temperature and humidity because they are not typically stage worthy and are used mainly for research and inspiration. They should be readily accessible to designers and technicians for research.

For womenswear, I recommend organizing by historical period setting aside special sections for skirts (organized by length or color), fantasy pieces, and outerwear. Deciding where you will keep coordinated accessories such as small bags and matching collars can be made on a case-by-case basis.

For menswear, I organize by historical period only until 1920. After that, all garments are organized by style and size, formal wear, two-piece suits, three-piece suits, pants (by waist), shirts (by neck), and vests that are not part of a suit by style. This system favors a diverse, well-rounded production schedule with an emphasis on "real" clothes. Because our stock is limited, it is not necessary for us to divide things further. As your stock grows, you may find further delineations are helpful. Find a system that works with your organization's strengths.

Document the storage system digitally with a clear map and ample but simple descriptions. A single person is no longer responsible for searching and maintaining stock. Community volunteers, interns, or lab students are now empowered to do substantive work helping organize and retrieve costume pieces. There is no better way to create and maintain a sense of community than to let even the smallest cogs support the larger machine.

Preservation: Do Less Harm than Good

Moth holes, mildew, light fading, dry rot, crushed hats ... these are the stuff of costumers' nightmares. All can be prevented by choosing proper storage locations. Garage spaces and attics generously donated can be ideal for storing glassware and platforms, but when it comes to cloth: insulation, darkness, and moderate humidity are a must. There is nothing more sustainable than maintaining what we already have.

Cloth is both resilient and delicate. It is amazing what can be brought back to life with a steamer or a tumble in the dryer. Likewise, a crack in the window covering can ruin an entire rack of clothing. Once you have a storage facility free of mold and moths, it is important to look at how the pieces are maintained. It is impossible to avoid some of the side effects of keeping clothing in storage. Most, however, can be minimized by properly storing the pieces. The biggest culprit in storage disasters is trying to fit too many pieces in too small a space. Give each piece enough space on the rack that it can be removed and returned to the rack without great physical effort. I will start with menswear, because, let's be honest, most of us use that stock the most.

Archiving—Document What You Have For Yourself and the Community

A digital archive of your stock can be the first step to saving time and earning extra money. This is a place where technology can curb the tide of waste. Better than that, you may find yourself with a little extra cash on hand. Time is the obvious benefit of a digital archive. Less effort spent rummaging through what you have gives you more time for your other responsibilities. The photo morgue also allows quick and efficient rentals. Rentals provide you with extra operations budget and may open up your stock to the greater community of theatres who can share with each other. If we all knew and archived our stock, we could have the stock of a hundred theatres at our finger tips.

The larger your stock, the more important it is to document what you own. A photo morgue of pieces, either from production or on dress forms, is a fantastic final step to ensure that you have reclaimed control of costume storage. When going to stock is as simple as opening a file on your desktop, using what you have becomes both possible and desirable. Out-of-town designers can be sent pictures of pieces to incorporate into their design. Interns can be shown *exactly* what they are being sent to get. Send the picture to your phone

Best Storage Practices: Menswear

Pants: Pants should be hung from either the ankle or the waist on a clip hanger. The volume of the clip hanger itself often ensures that the garment has enough space on the rack. Storing pants folded over the hanger causes several problems. First, the crease lines at the knee can be difficult to remove after several years of hanging. If the item has acquired any light damage, it is concentrated in a strip across the center of the garment. It also takes up more room on the rack.

Vests: Most vests are light and thin enough to hang on simple metal hangers. I prefer to keep backless vests and sweater vests in tubs beneath the rack.

Shirts: We wear out and reuse our button-down shirts so frequently that it hardly makes sense to think of them in terms of long-term storage. Like vests, woven shirts should be hung on a rack with ample space on a basic hanger. This is an area of storage that is easy to overstuff. You will be hunting through it regularly, so make sure a good organizational system is in place. I separate short sleeve, long sleeve, and collarless into three sections. Organize them first by neck size then color. Store knit shirts like polos and Henleys in tubs.

Suits: Keeping suits together on a single hanger can increase the usability of your stock. I recommend using the hangers that are especially designed for this purpose. As the pants are protected from light damage by the suit coat, it is okay to hang the pants from the knee to conserve space. Whenever you have the vertical space, I recommend hanging them from the ankle.

Hats: Hats are one of the most annoying items to store properly. They need a great deal of space, yet the boxes they come in are so inefficient to store that they must be consolidated. Hats, especially those with a structure of buckram or straw, must be stored in their proper shape as the material will permanently take on any distortion.

Womenswear

Blouses: Women's blouses are versatile and can be stored hanging or folded. As a rule, I find it easier to find and use stock blouses if they are on hangers, but if hanging space is at a premium, tubs will do.

Skirts: Depending on the universality of the skirt I will either hang it with the period it was designed for or in a larger skirt section. Skirts are best stored hanging on a clip hanger. Clip hangers are worth what you pay for them. Invest in a set that can hold the weight of a full-length skirt and not wear out quickly. Even the strongest hanger will have trouble with an upholstery-weight pleated skirt. For these and other heavy skirts, stitch a loop of twill tape to the inside of each side seam where the waistband meets the body of the skirt. This loop should be long enough to come over the head of the hanger from each side and distribute the weight from the clips to the body of the hanger. If the loop is too long, the clips will still take the full weight of the skirt so be sure to measure based on your hangers.

Dresses: Dresses will make up a huge portion of women's stock. They tend to be less universal than menswear. It is important to keep as many women's dresses as you think can be reused. However, dresses tend to be the first pieces to be built for future productions. Heavy dresses should also have hanging loops to take the weight off the shoulder seams. Depending on the style of the dress, these loops can be attached either where the shoulder seam meets the armscye or where the armscye meets the side seam.

Shoes: Sprinkle shoes with baby power or baking soda to prevent fungus and bacteria from degrading the leather. While canvas shoes will survive simply being thrown in a box, it is easy to crowd them. It shouldn't take physical effort or meticulous organization to close the box. If it does, you have too many shoes in the container. Leather shoes are more likely to be damaged so should be stored in their original boxes if possible, or in hanging shoe holders. If you do store your shoes in plastic tubs I recommend placing a small box of baking soda in the bottom of each tub. The boxes designed for use in the refrigerator, with a large opening covered by thin fabric, are ideal.

Boots: Tall boots should be stored either standing or in their boxes with the calves padded out with brown paper or foam. Creases in the leather or plastic will become permanent if stored improperly.

Sweaters: Sweaters should be stored flat to prevent them from stretching out of shape. Sweaters are common targets of moths and there are several ways to avoid having your stock fall victim to them. Traditionally costumers have used mothballs, which have a strong odor and contain a known carcinogen. Instead, use a satchel of herbs including rosemary, thyme, and bay or a handful of cedar chips.

and it is easy to remember exactly what you are trying to match or contrast at the fabric store.

If organization seems overwhelming, archiving can seem insane. Photographing every piece in stock can take weeks or months. I recommend starting with things that require a lot of unpacking or freshening up. Or as I like to think of it, start from the top.

Once you have organized your hat collection and placed each uncrushed in a box, the last thing you want to do is unpack and repack to discover the contents. Place the hats on a head, snap a picture, and create a folder for each box on the computer. A digital rummage through stock takes five minutes, and the boxes remain on the shelf in pristine condition.

Wigs are another ideal starting point for very different reasons. Wigs will take the abuse of being crushed in boxes and thrown about. However, they are never stored looking anything like what they are. A wig in a bag will tell you little more than the color of the hair. A photo morgue tells you color, length, lace or hard front, bangs, and layers. In short, you will know everything you need to know with the click of a mouse.

If the main purpose of your digital archive is to expedite rentals, I recommend photographing your most unique or specific pieces. If you have a full design for *Beauty and the Beast* or *Peter Pan*, those pieces will require some effort to photograph properly but will be worth having. Period suits and dresses are great places to start as well. Everyone can find a pair of black slacks but unique or period pieces are helpful to designers. Be sure to limit rentals to items that will not disintegrate or be easily damaged. Establish the rental policy before you open up stock to examination. Having rules established in advance makes it easier to deflect unreasonable expectations. For example, make it clear all items must be cleaned before return so you do not add a huge dry cleaning bill to your annual operations budget.

Culling the Herd

It may seem counterintuitive but one of the most valuable and sustainable things you can do for your stock is limit what you keep. Storing junk only serves to hide the valuable pieces you have. You cannot and should not keep every garment that goes on stage. Whether it is because the item is light damaged, dry rotted, painted neon green, or faux blood-stained, not every garment has a real future. Be honest with yourself about what is worth keeping and what can be given away.

Stock should be useable. Simple, manageable, organized stock is the only stock worth having. Be honest about what you can truly care for. If you work full time with costuming as your avocation, do you really want to spend days working on cataloguing a room of stock? If you run a shop, teach a full load of classes, and design an entire season every year, maintaining a warehouse is more than should be on your plate. Strip down the unnecessary pieces. If you have no space, maybe you need more space. If you have space, maybe you need less stuff.

The neon-painted jacket and light damaged pants might be perfect as rehearsal pieces. Blood-stained garments sell like mad at Halloween sales. If you have too many everyday items in stock, donate some of the garments to second-hand stores. Our propensity to hoard seems sustainable, but one good pair of pants we can't find negates saving ten pairs we are likely never to use.

So what do you do with the cast-offs? If you work in public academia, you are probably aware of the particular hoops you have to jump through to get rid of your extra stuff. For everyone else, you can donate pieces to high-school or community-theatre groups, second-hand clothing stores or fabric-recycling programs. I highly recommend a Halloween sale when you have a selection of novelty and unusual pieces on hand.

A successful sustainability initiative in the auxiliary areas of the costume shop depends on being diligent in our choice of products and storage. These products and practices are directly related to worker safety and protection. Having a good stock of safe and sustainable products allows you to work efficiently and safely.

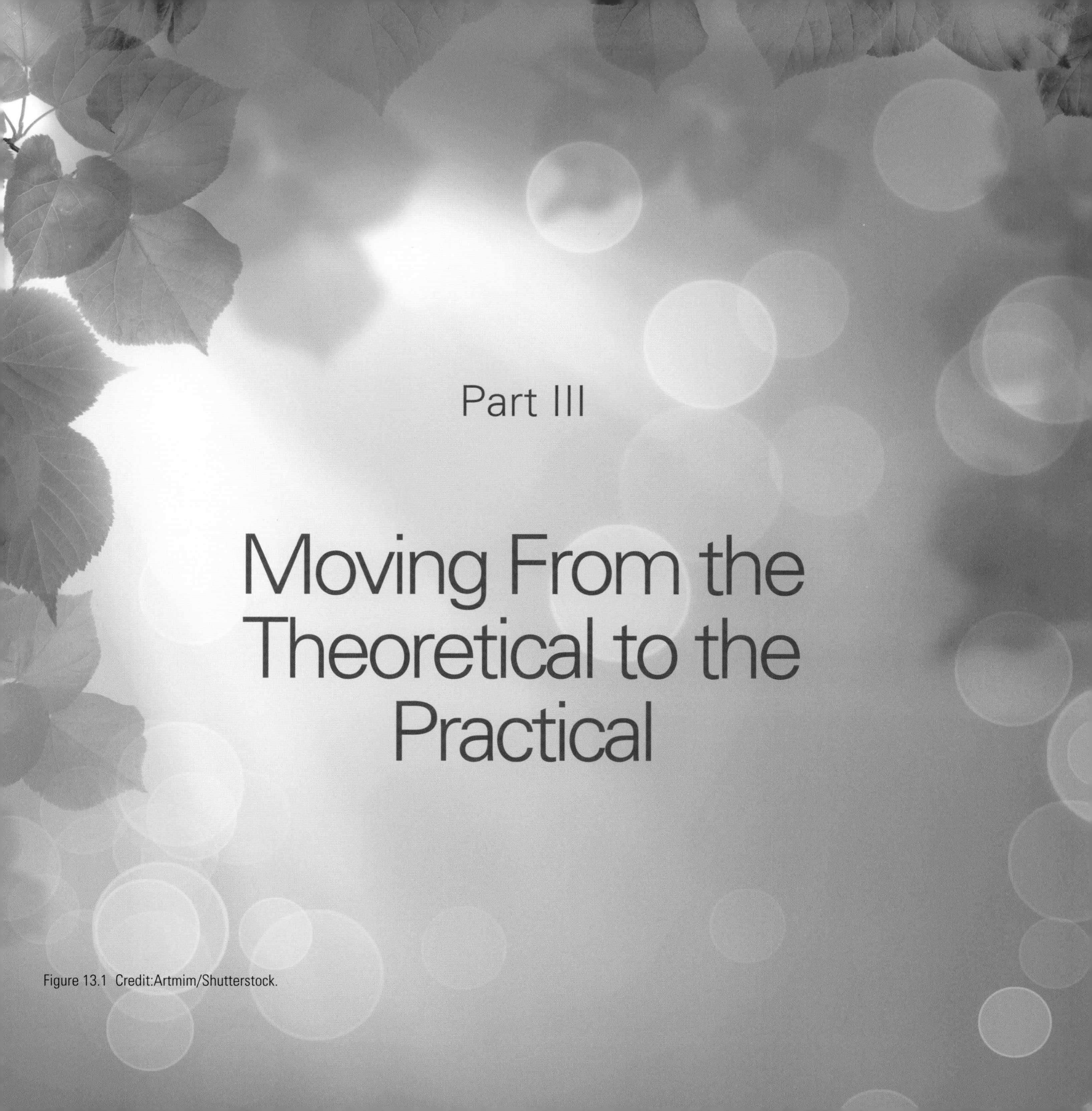

Part III

Moving From the Theoretical to the Practical

Figure 13.1 Credit:Artmim/Shutterstock.

It is Time to Put Plans into Action

It is time for a discussion about greening theatre production and design. However, brainstorming ideas and mapping out strategic plans is far different than actually putting principles into practice as part of a realized production. Greener choices have to serve the needs of the production without compromising the artistry of the show or exceeding the available resources.

The following three essays share the process and conclusions of a designer who balanced creativity and production obligations with greener production practices for at least one design element in a show. Each piece is written by the designer involved and captures her individual voice and style.

Chapter 13

Walking the Walk

Integrating Greener Practices into Realized Productions

How Green is My Valley: *The Tempest* at Central Washington University: Jessica Pribble on Green Costume Design

As so often happens, a single theme or idea presented itself in many disparate areas of my life simultaneously. In the spring of 2012, I began to grow my own vegetables for the first time. This constant engagement with the soil, even in my very modest patio garden, kept me thinking about how far things must travel to arrive in my kitchen. This was my second year living in rural Washington State and my frustration with traveling multiple mountain passes to find even a basic fabric store was beginning to come to a head. Distance, travel, gasoline, pesticides: These things were only loosely connected in my mind. It was also about this time I began speaking with Ellen Jones about sustainability in the theatre. The result of those conversations was my participation in the writing of this book.

As fate would have it, the College of Arts and Humanities at Central Washington University where I work as a lecturer and costume designer was adopting a theme for the following year, *How Green is My Valley: Land, Water, Wind, the Human Impact on the World, Sustainability, Our Relationship to the Earth*, neatly tying together all these different areas of my life. Much of my time and energy over the next year would be dedicated to exploring this motif.

The goals of the college theme are to promote interdepartmental programming and collaboration and emphasize the collaboration between academic and student life. The theme links activities and presentations across departments within the college. What would the theatre department be doing? As it happened, we were beginning design meetings for our fall production of William Shakespeare's *The Tempest*. I asked at an early meeting if anyone would be interested in exploring sustainable practices with the production to discover that the idea was already germinating in other areas. We were off to the races.

THE TEMPEST—PRODUCTION TEAM

Director: Keith Edie
Scenic Designer: Jerry Dougherty
Costume Designer: Jessica Pribble
Lighting Designer: Christina Barrigan
Wig Designer/Costume Shop Manager: M. Catherine McMillen
Asst. Wig Designer: Caitlin Cardinale
Asst. Costume Designers: Kelsey Sheppard, Shelbi Gilmond
Drapers: Megan Hawkins, Brandon Walker
Craft Artisan: Malana McKennett
Mask Artisan: M. Catherine McMillen
Wardrobe Supervisor: Shelbi Gilmond

The Goal of the Project

We, the production team, agreed to take on sustainability in whatever way served our individual processes. We agreed to improve our current practices without sacrificing safety or sanity. Everyone understood that our goal was not to come out of the production with a zero carbon footprint, but to make improvements within our cost and labor limitations.

Overall Production Goals: A 90-minute tour-de-force, fast-moving production of *The Tempest* that keeps the audience on the end of their seat. We wanted to play up the magic of the island and the humanity of the characters.

Educational theatre serves many masters. Before embarking on any production we have to consider the pedagogical implications of the project. How does the process inform the education of our students? Were we providing the necessary opportunities for students? Were we modeling the production process on a professional working environment? Promoting environmental stewardship is an excellent production goal, but how might it reduce or redefine the academic experience for our students? While we can take advantage of a very inexpensive workforce, we must also provide valuable educational experiences for those students.

In the costume shop, for example, we can usually rent or pull more and build less of the production, but we need opportunities for the students to work as first hands and drapers. CWU has a BFA theatre design and technology program with a large costume cohort. Logistically, this means we pattern and build some portion of each production. In addition to providing draping opportunities, we have an extensive wig-training program. The quarter we produced *The Tempest*, we needed opportunities for a student draper and a student assistant wig designer to prepare them for spring design positions.

With the needs of our students in mind, I chose to focus on sustainability in the implementation rather than the conceptualization of the show. This decision allowed me to focus on greening the execution of a design that was created while using my usual creative process. I made this decision partially because the costumes needed to be designed before casting, and partially because I wanted to insure that I was serving the world we created instead of the world of our stock.

Because the characters in *The Tempest* are so varied, it makes a good case study in sustainable costuming. The script has distinct groups of characters ranging from high to low class and from fully human to monsters to spirits. Each group of characters presents a different set of challenges stylistically and sustainably.

We decided on the following ten sustainability goals:

1. Limit purchasing of new pieces to those with a high probability of reuse.
2. When necessary to purchase material, buy biodegradable fabrics.
3. Use no aerosols.
4. Remove as many chemicals from the production as possible.
5. Ensure all chemicals used were organic and biodegradable instead of synthetic.
6. Attempt to use the back stock of fabric.
7. Employ rental options instead of purchasing when appropriate.
8. Support local small business and organic textile distributors if possible.
9. Use natural materials for craft and dye work.
10. Build clothing for reuse or simple deconstruction.

Our production broke down into the following character groups: The noblemen, essentially Alonso and his court; the sailors and passengers on the ship who would later double as island spirits; the clowns and band; Prospero, Miranda, and Ferdinand; the unnamed island spirits; and finally Ariel and Caliban.

The Production Concept

Because the show takes place on an island in the Mediterranean between Africa and Italy, we settled on Sicily for a location. The director was very interested in the human characters being modern and easy for the audience to relate to as the story unfolded. However, we also wanted to establish a time period when it was believable that the characters traveled by sailboat. We settled on the late 1940s. We agreed

Figure 13.2 Rendering of Ariel. Image courtesy of Jessica Pribble.

Figure 13.3 The Gentlemen of the Court: (SR-SL) Tom Fowler as Alonso, Blake Cranston as Sebastian, Henry Van Leishout as Antonio, and Brandon Walker as Gonzalo. Image courtesy of Jessica Pribble.

to steer away from the imperialist vs. indigenous encounter and focus instead on the encounter between the magical and the mundane.

Group One: The Noblemen (Six Characters)

Alonso's Court: The court carried the lion's share of the late 1940s period specificity on their shoulders. To that end, their costumes required period detail and needed to feel like real clothing. We accomplished this almost entirely through stock and rentals. In the end we purchased two men's dress shirts and a series of men's summer fedoras. We built a vest for Alonso using leftover stock fabric. All of the new pieces have a high potential for reuse. Sustainability grade 10/10 = A.

Group Two: The Sailors and Passengers (Eight Characters)

Our production included a lengthy preshow to establish life on the boat before the storm. The noblemen, clowns, and sailors are joined by several members of the marriage entourage. Though unnamed, these characters serve to establish time and place. After the storm the actors quick change into the island spirits. We pulled these costumes entirely from stock with the exception of a bag of new undershirts and two pair of 1940s women's pants. We pulled fabric from stock for one and purchased linen fabric for the other. We also purchased one pair of deck shoes for the ship's captain. Sustainability grade 9/10 = A-.

Group Three: The Clowns—a Skiffle Band (Six Characters)

Trinculo and Stephano the famous drunken clowns of *The Tempest* are, in our production, part of a skiffle band which has been commissioned to entertain the passengers during the voyage. They provide live music and comic relief throughout the production. We unified them with bandanas, Converse shoes, suspenders, boater hats, and striped blazers. We were able to pull these costumes entirely from stock except for one blazer (built from cotton fabric purchased for the production) and one pair of Converse. Converse always seem to be in high demand in our shop, so reusability is not a problem. Sustainability Grade 10/10 = A.

Figure 13.4 George Bellah III as Prospero, Janice Fix as Miranda, and James Clark as Ferdinand. Image courtesy of Jessica Pribble.

Group Four: The Islanders (Three Characters)

Prospero, Miranda, and Ferdinand. These characters, along with Ariel and Caliban, were the most traditionally designed characters in the production, in that they were fully rendered and then built from scratch by our shop. Prospero and Miranda's costumes were built from biodegradable materials including china silk, locally sourced leather, and linen from stock. Patterning and building Miranda and Prospero's clothing was an internship project for a student draper. We created handmade jewelry from shells, hemp, and fishing net. While we had hoped to use natural dyes for the ombre effect on Prospero and Miranda's clothing, we ran out of time to test the unknown processes.

Ferdinand's costume needed to transform slowly from the silhouette of a nobleman to that of the islanders. In order to support the organic textile industry, I decided it was important to invest in building an entire costume from organic material and found objects. We purchased organic linen online for his vest and pants, and a hemp dress shirt. I purchased buttons for his vest and pants made from coconut shell from a supplier in Seattle. We pulled a suit coat, tie, socks, shoes, undershirt, and suspenders from stock. We found a piece of decorative fishing net in stock to create a sash and used seashells to make his

Figure 13.5 James Clark as Ferdinand. Image courtesy of Jessica Pribble.

wedding jewelry. While the shirt and linen were expensive, I felt it was important to invest at least a small amount of the budget in sustainable textiles. Sustainability grade 9/10 = A-.

Group Five: The Island Spirits (Eight Characters)

The island spirits were a special case for us in the costume shop. While we knew that they were going to be part of the performance, how they were being used and what they might represent was developed in rehearsal. As often happens with magical and non-human characters, much of our time went into their costumes' intricate nontraditional construction while their role in the production continued to develop.

I adopted an organic design model for these characters. Each of the actors would have a human role in the preshow and those costumes were pulled from stock. After the first week of rehearsals, I had each of the actors in for fittings for their preshow costumes where they told me about the spirit characters they were developing. Each character was based around an element in nature and included a very specific way of moving. I pulled pieces from stock and built pieces from stock fabric. Each costume consisted of some kind of base costume, either a unitard or leotard, dance shoes, breastplate or corselet, additional costume pieces such as shirts and skirts, a mask and a headpiece. For the five female spirits wigs were also added.

Because of the physicality in their descriptions, I moved toward dance costumes as much as possible. In the end, we borrowed three unitards from the university dance department and three leotards from the actors. We built two breastplates out of a combination of Veriform, papier mâché, and hot glue; eight masks, five with attached headpieces, three with separate headpieces all made from papier mâché and purchased home decor pieces. We built or altered three belts from stock materials, used three existing corselets, and built one corselet.

Surprisingly, we purchased next to nothing for these characters. We needed one leotard, hot glue sticks, and home decor pieces for the headpieces. My goal was to use up some of our extensive back stock of small fabric pieces. Despite purchasing so little and using so much, we didn't even make a dent in the stock. Sustainability grade 9/10 = A-.

Group Six: Ariel and Caliban (Six Characters)

Up to this point, our sustainability goals in the costume shop were right on target. We only purchased items with a high probability of reuse and used stock pieces and back stock fabric to costume the majority of the production. Ariel and Caliban, however, are where our sustainability goals fell apart, or at the very least, hit some major logistical roadblocks.

Caliban: When I envisioned Caliban, I assumed the actor would be male. How wrong was I? We agreed as a design team that Caliban should not be sexual and should instead be vulgar and repulsive. Even so, Caliban, with his lust for Miranda and thirst for power, is a masculine character. Casting a female required playing up her masculine features and playing down her feminine features. What was designed as a unitard and breastplate became instead a sports bra, two unitards, a belly pad, and a hunchback. We built the actress a belly pad to fill in the narrowness of her waist and underbust, complete with hump on the back, from stock material and covered her in scaly patches made from a combination of stock fabric scraps and carpet grip. We pulled a wig and dance shoes from stock. We purchased the Wonderflex for her mask, the sports bra and unitards. The base unitard and bra will be valuable in stock, but everything else, including the shoes we pulled, has limited potential for future use. Sustainability grade 7/10 = C-.

Ariel: Five actors, one character. While I have long accepted the resources of time and money required to create duplicate costumes on stage, I had never fully appreciated the ecological ramifications. We created eight complete spirit costumes for the island spirits without derailing our sustainability goals but five Ariels was a challenge of a different order. One I do not believe we rose to in its entirety. At the beginning, I admit I had a certain amount of resistance and skepticism

Figure 13.6 Abigail Nathan as Caliban: An exercise in cross-gender casting. Photo by Jessica Pribble.

Figure 13.7 (SL-SR) Nikki Delmarter, Mara Hernandez, Kelly Pierre, Tara Nix, and Monica Domena as Ariel. Image courtesy of Jessica Pribble.

when the director asked to cast five women as Ariel. Duplicates can put a great deal of strain on any design budget. As so often happens, the show seemed to multiply in size and scale with each design meeting.

In the end, I admit I was a convert. How better to be in more than one place at a time? How better to do magic on stage? The five Ariels gave us a cinematic advantage that supported our goals of a fast-paced, spectacle-driven production. It did, however, spoil a perfectly admirable sustainability record.

When I decided to design the show first and implement in a sustainable way, I didn't factor in the difficulty of finding five of everything I needed, or the price of purchasing organic fabric on that scale. In hindsight, I would have shopped first and designed second. Not everything was a loss; I discovered recycled naturally dyed t-shirt yarn to braid into straps and waistbands. We made belts and gauntlets from locally sourced leather. In the end, however, the skirt fabric we could afford was mostly synthetic, the unitards we purchased were cut and painted in such a way I doubt they will ever be useful in stock, and we purchased five synthetic wigs which will have minimal reusability as they are jet black, hard front, and identical. Sustainability grade 5/10 = F.

While I find the above disheartening I chalk it up to a lesson learned. It appears I cannot have my cake and eat it too. Had I been asked to make one Ariel instead of five identical Ariels the same exact design could have been implemented in a much greener way. We would have used a wig from stock, a unitard from the dance department and I could have afforded to buy organic or at least biodegradable fabric. The mask could have been made from papier mâché instead of thermal plastic.

Wardrobe for the Show

Without the support of the costume shop even the most pedestrian sustainability goals are almost impossible to implement. As expected, some of the easiest and most effective changes were implemented outside the design area. As the production moved into dress rehearsals we adjusted our maintenance and wardrobe practices in the following ways:

Goal 1: Remove all possible aerosols from the production.

- We already use primarily pump-action refillable hairspray bottles. We maintained that policy and made sure the actors used the products we supplied.
- We made baking soda satchels to place inside the shoes each night to eliminate the need for Lysol.

Goal 2: Reduce the use of synthetic chemicals.

- The first weekend of the run we replaced our normal laundry detergent with Seventh Generation. The second weekend we made our own powder detergent from borax, bar soap, and laundry powder. There was no significant change in the cleanliness or scent of the laundry. The wardrobe mistress did mention that dissolving the detergent in hot water before adding it to the machine allowed us to wash the clothing with cold water.
- We replaced Febreze with a vodka, water, and eucalyptus oil spray. No noxious Febreze smell in the dressing rooms.
- We replaced dryer sheets with plastic dryer balls.
- We replaced our normal surface cleaners with naturally derived products. We could have gone further. However, by that point in the process we did not prioritize the training that would have been required.

Goal 3: Reduce energy use.

- We purchased new drying racks to decrease the use of the dryer.
- We reduced the use of mirror lights in the dressing room by assigning a wardrobe member to turn them off when not in use.

We learned a great deal by taking on sustainability in a very conscious way for this production. We invested in products like dryer balls, biodegradable detergent, and baking soda sachets that continue as our go-to products. We have eliminated the use of dryer sheets, Febreze, Lysol, traditional detergent, and aerosol hairspray. We researched vendors for organic fabric and hemp products. The most valuable lessons we learned were to consider the ramifications of uniforms and other matching sets on the greening of a design and to allow time to test and perfect the use of unfamiliar products. Sustainability is a journey and this production was a small but important step toward future advances.

Can We Light "Green" and Still Create Art? A Real Case Study at the University of Richmond: Assistant Professor Maja E. White with Summer Research Fellow Mark Ferguson on Sustainability in Lighting Design

Maja White began her academic career at the University of Richmond in the fall of 2009. This transition was her first experience in academia as a professor not a student.

After many years as a freelance designer along with a few years as a project manager for a lighting installation and rigging company, I realized I would finally be allowed the time and resources to explore new technology as it was becoming more prevalent in the entertainment industry. After my initial hire, I was fortunate enough to be given the opportunity to purchase some LED fixtures to light the cyclorama at the university. With this purchase I began to reinforce my ideas about how this newer technology would develop and was changing how I designed. I began to think about how this affected the visuals of what occurred on the stage.

In 2009 LED technology was new and expensive to purchase although the benefits to energy savings were undeniable, as had been seen in the architectural industry. All of a sudden the industry was hearing the terms "green" and "sustainable" lighting. As a designer for live performance, I was also concerned about how this was going to change the aesthetics which ultimately affect the art of design as we know it.

I had some firsthand experience as a lighting designer with using new technology and the occasional growing pains that come from adapting equipment from different venues for productions. The current buzz focused on how environmentally friendly lighting would save money and man hours, lower the carbon footprint of the venue, and allow for higher LEED classifications when remodeling facilities or planning new construction. Universities and colleges are concerned with all of these factors.

I wondered more about how new lighting technology was going to change my art; my aesthetic of what constitutes good lighting—not just the way the show looks, but the entire collaborative process and the audience perception of the finished production. Would they like what they saw or respond in the same way as to conventional lighting? The use of this LED technology has been integrated into the corporate and music industry. It is used less often in the realms of theater opera and dance, especially in regional and academic venues where the big budgets of the Broadway and grand opera and dance companies aren't available.

Planning the Study

I spent the following academic year researching this new technology at architectural and live entertainment conferences and trade shows. I spoke with vendors and manufacturers who enthusiastically demonstrated their products onsite and at the university. Learning about the science behind the technology and seeing numerous demonstrations in showrooms was valuable. Unfortunately, seeing a unit in isolation at a trade show could not address all of my questions.

The Research Process

I found that Lighting Design International (LDI), United States Institute of Theatre Technology (USITT) and Light Fair International were the most helpful trade shows for my research. Demonstrations at each of these narrowed down which equipment I wanted to experiment with in a venue during production. How could I really understand the intricacies of how this equipment would work for my purposes when I could only see one fixture at a time, often in comparison to another unit in a shoot-out to assess its features? How does that fixture work in a production where there are multiple instruments? I needed the opportunity to really use the technology in some sort of presentation to be able to compare it to the existing technology of conventional fixtures. No one on the trade show floors was really doing that kind of comparison.

I wanted to know: Does the audience notice a difference? Is there a drop off as things fade and is it noticeable? How does that impact the rhythm of the show?

I had a lot of technical information, but no real-time comparison that didn't come from a company's data sheet. With manufacturer's information there may be some sort of bias. Every company wants to make a sale and outline its product's performance in the best possible light.

The equipment in our black box was out of date and used energy inefficiently. Since there is a university wide focus on sustainability, considering the performing arts spaces for an upgrade to reduce the carbon footprint was logical. I wanted to bring this possibility to the attention of the administration.

Project Goal

My goal was to perform a case study that would show that using newer stage lighting technology met goals of safety, environmentally friendly power usage, cost efficiency and supported the arts as well.

The Case Study Plan Evolves

The only way to answer my questions was to create an experiment where I could actively assess both the quantitative and qualitative impact of using LED technology in a production.

A lighting designer can't start designing without a project to light. I needed a small, easily manageable space, a project, and an audience, as well as equipment to work with for an extended amount of time. Specific audience feedback and some scientific data would be available for comparison at the end of the run. As an artist, clearly I was concerned with the possible aesthetic changes; as a human being I was also concerned with the environmental and safety concerns with crew members, my students. As an educator, I was excited by the opportunity for my students to work with new LED technology and form their own ideas.

The Initial Planning Stages

The first step was to find an appropriate project. Having a real-time piece of material to work on was a key component. I wanted real feedback not only from the audience point of view but also from the talent. I thought about doing a lightshow without performers, but then the timing is all about me. I would not see this technology work in the collaborative process of theater, where both timing and the look can impact an audience's perception of the spoken dialogue and the actor's performance.

The UR Technical Director suggested I speak with a colleague, Dr. Patricia Herrera, about a possible collaboration. She was in the early stages of writing a new musical with Jose Joaquin Garcia called *Remnants*. We decided that this collaboration would be beneficial to both of us. It would give us a hard deadline to mount a small staged reading and the performances could be lit with LED fixtures one day and conventional fixtures the next. This musical for her was/is a work in progress. This project would give her team a forum in which to hear and see the work as it is being developed while at the same time giving me subject matter to light under performance conditions. The event would allow her to gain valuable feedback from the audience response regarding the concept of the written/musical part of her work. I could collect my audience data at the same time. After speaking with her co-creator we selected an opening date. The performances were set for May of 2011 and the data from surveys and measurements compiled afterwards.

She had writing and casting work to complete and I had the technology to deal with. We both realized that we needed some help. We had two major assets; an extremely supportive department and a university that allows students to work with faculty members as summer research fellows. This summer work was stage one of my research projects: *Can we light green and still create art?* My Summer Fellow undergraduate Mark Ferguson '12 and I presented information on this first stage of the project during the Association of Theatre in Higher Education (ATHE) conference in August 2011.

I had to find manufacturers or vendors willing to commit to the loan of equipment for an extended period of time. Ultimately I hope to buy a portion of the fixtures so they could be used in classes, but that subsequent purchase was never a stipulation of the manufacturers.

There was no rental budget for the project and I needed two weeks to complete the experiment. I was requesting the loan of multiple fixtures for two weeks. Typically manufacturers will loan one or two fixtures for about a week, so I was asking for a big favor.

I didn't anticipate some of the responses. Some manufacturers liked the idea of the project, but thought that this could potentially become a review of the fixture. They did not want to be involved if there was any possibility of a negative response. For others, it was a question of timing and how many demonstration models they would have on hand in the month of May for our use. Light Fair is held in May and some manufacturers were concerned about the possibility of shipping delays of equipment sent overseas for that trade show. A single fixture was not adequate for the experiment involved in this research project.

The university already owned several Altman Spectra Cycs and two American DJ P64 LED fixtures but those units were hardly enough to light this staged reading. Eventually two companies committed to the project. One offered to provide LED Pars and the other LED Profiles or Ellipsoidal Reflector Spotlight (ERS or leko) fixtures. I thought this combined inventory would provide adequate options for the experiment.

The process for analysis required lighting the two performances; one evening with "green" LED lighting and the next night with conventional theatrical lighting. Scientific data and subjective observations were collected to compare the two performances. The analysis and comparison of the power usage was easy. Using subjective responses to determine the impact of the lighting on aesthetic goals and artistic support of the performance resulted in little specific numeric data.

The Experiment Begins

As the date for the load-in neared, I tried to confirm the delivery of the loaned equipment. I had difficulty communicating with one of the companies, but moved forward with the design based on its previous promise. I decided to use a portion of the production budget to purchase three Strong LED Neeva profiles in case there was a problem with some of the loaned equipment. This proved to be a wise decision; I was notified the day before load-in that the loaner profile units would not be available. Altman Lighting, Inc., the other committed manufacturer, was extraordinarily generous. LED Spectra Pars arrived from multiple locations; some were even hand delivered by the regional Altman representative. This project would not have been possible without Altman Stage Lighting's support.

As in any other design situation, as the variables of available inventory changed, so did the approach to how we could light the staged reading. Equipment availability was not the only factor; as the show rehearsed discoveries by the performers required design choice changes as well. For most of this week I relied heavily on Mark and had additional help from Erin Brander, a performer in the reading, and Phil Hayes, the University of Richmond theatre department shop foreman.

Project Specifics

On May 6 and 7 the workshop production of *Remnants* was produced at the University of Richmond, in the Design Lab.

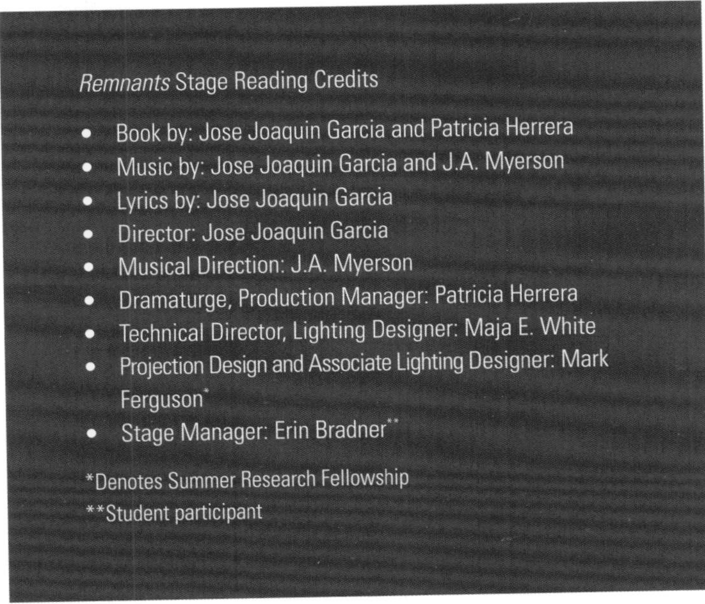

Remnants Stage Reading Credits

- Book by: Jose Joaquin Garcia and Patricia Herrera
- Music by: Jose Joaquin Garcia and J.A. Myerson
- Lyrics by: Jose Joaquin Garcia
- Director: Jose Joaquin Garcia
- Musical Direction: J.A. Myerson
- Dramaturge, Production Manager: Patricia Herrera
- Technical Director, Lighting Designer: Maja E. White
- Projection Design and Associate Lighting Designer: Mark Ferguson*
- Stage Manager: Erin Bradner**

*Denotes Summer Research Fellowship
**Student participant

The Technical Specifications

The unchanging parameters of the facility and both projects:

- 10′x20′ pipe grid suspended at 10′ off the ground.
- Lighting console: ETC Element.
- Houselights limited to the room fluorescents fixtures.
- Digital support programs used during the project: Vectorworks, Lightwright 5, Seachanger Color Bug.

Early on one additional and unexpected parameter became apparent. The actors needed to be able to see their scripts with both lighting scenarios since this was a staged reading. The main characters were masked so for some their eyesight was restricted.

I decided to keep a record of experimental processes, setbacks, and discoveries in journal style entries.

Daily Diary of the Project

Day 1

- Empty, clean and take space to four walls and an empty grid to prep for the project.
- Rehearsals begin with the director onsite and discussions of the performance space layout, concept and approach on how the lighting would reinforce the roles of each of the characters for the audience.
- Begin design process.

Day 2: Beginning of Equipment Arrival

- Spectra PARS from Altman Lighting begin to arrive.
- Evaluation of the space and initial design is required because the second manufacturer sends notification that they will not be able to make our deadline for this project.
- Plug and address all onsite equipment.
- Immediately we notice different makes and models of equipment have different color tones when powered to 100%. The Spectra Pars RGBA (red, green, blue, amber) color mixing appear much pinker than the Strong Neeva fixtures. The RGBW (red, green, blue, white) used by Strong have a significantly cooler look when all colors were at 100%. We also find that the Spectra PARS are visually significantly brighter than the Nevis. See Figure 13.8.

Designing with LED Technology

- Final design choices: Based on this visual inspection, I decide to use the Neevas to light the narrator, the stage manager, who is reading staging directions, and the musical director and then use three of the Altman Spectra PARS in white to provide front light for the three main characters. The other Altman PARS, and the stock American DJ LED P64 and Altman Spectra Cycs are assigned as

Figure 13.8 Examining the quality of light of the new equipment to determine the best allocation of those resources. Image courtesy of Maja White.

color toners to help establish mood and environment. They are placed in down and back lighting positions and used for cyclorama lighting.

Problem Solving

The Strong Neevas come with 26-degree lenses. Perfect for the stage, but too narrow a beam in the Design Lab where we were presenting the show. Examination suggests similarities with the ETC Source 4 barrel configuration and we swap out the 26-degree lenses for wider Source 4 lenses. Not a perfect physical match, but close enough to allow the unit to function. Clearly choosing focal length for a fixed focal length unit for the space where the fixtures are primarily used may impact the ability to use the fixture in other smaller or larger venues.

Our Neeva fixtures did not come with manuals and at the time, May 2011, we can not find a manual online to access. Using what we learned thus far from the profiling of other equipment, we try to use the generic RGBW profile on the ETC Element Control Console for operation. It doesn't work.

A phone call to Strong-Ballentyne tech support reveals that the Neevas actually need five control channels, not four. The fifth channel is for rate. A generic five-channel profile on the console works. However, the designated colors names on the lighting console are in a different order than the unit used so we have to keep track of that discrepancy.

Day 3

More equipment arrives and we finish cabling and addressing units for testing. Since some equipment is three-pin cables and some use five-pin DMX there are more minor issues to work out. The three-pin ADJ units have to be the last in the DMX daisy chain to accommodate the different pin configuration. We are waiting for the final five-pin fixtures to arrive, so spacing was left for those units.

First rehearsal in the space with lights begins. We planned to use the Light Lab white board for projections and a cyclorama like surface. I realize it was too reflective during this rehearsal and it is replaced with a muslin drop.

Day 4

I send a reminder to Facilities Management to schedule metering of the stage lighting and dimming system for the project. They planned to meter energy usage for the LED equipment and then move the meter to do the same analysis when conventional dimmers and fixtures are used for the production.

The Altman rep arrives to personally deliver the last of the Spectra PARS and to check out the experiment. When he realizes that we are short on fixtures from the second manufacturer, he loans us the Star PARS in his car in addition to the Spectra PARS that he has already provided. Remember the whole point of this exercise was a comparison of traditional versus LED technology, so having enough LED units is imperative to make it worthwhile.

After a quick design adjustment everything is finally hung, cabled, addressed, and patched. Each unit has been tested individually on the ground so we begin a test of the rig in place. The first light in the string works but as for everything else … nothing.

The troubleshooting begins: Cable is swapped out even though the DMX for this is new and the addressing checked. When this does not solve the problem, then a one-by-one bypass and load test begins. After eliminating the first fixture from the daisy chain, all the others work. The first Spectra PAR DMX input works, but the DMX output for the daisy chain is faulty.

These fixtures are hardwired so onsite repairs are not quick and tech rehearsal in the space was looming. We can not eliminate the unit or just move the unit with the bad DMX out to the end of the chain; the ADJs has to be last in the daisy chain due to their three-pin configuration.

My Associate Designer, Mark, suggests a plan. He knew that my intent was to use the lighting console second DMX universe for the "green" day lighting with the LED units and the first DMX universe for conventional fixtures the second day. He realizes it is possible to bypass the first compromised LED unit and run everything else as planned on the second universe. The compromised unit can be assigned to the first universe. He runs the cable, I repatch and we are good to go. Mark went back to his projection designs and I start to write cues. Mark and I sit in the room and looked at color integrity, fade curves, and all the behaviors of each type of LED fixture we are using.

Day 5

We do a color meter reading with the Seachanger Color Bug before the final dress rehearsal. This allows a more scientific color comparison than simply relying on our memory and visual interpretation. Our lighting lab space is successfully turned into a small performance space and it is almost time for the first show.

After the performance, the production team and cast have a discussion with the audience and remind the group about surveys that they would be receiving via email. The importance of this discussion and the surveys is to receive feedback not only about the script, but also about the lighting design using LED technology. Feedback about the lighting from audience members who see both performances was more relevant after the second performance since a comparison is possible. However, feedback from the LED-only performance was also interesting because it offers a baseline of an audience's response to the new technology. Did they notice moments that a lighting designer would characterize as different or even jarring?

Once the audience clears, everything is struck and the crew begins to hang the conventional fixtures. The new rig replaces the LED PAR units with conventionally lamped PARS. The LED Neeva profile units are replaced with ETC Source Fours ellipsoidal fixtures using the same barrels that had been subbed into Neevas in the "green" rig. Facilities Management personnel swap the electrical consumption meter to the dimmer pack power to allow comparison of the power loads of the two performances.

The hanging and cabling for this transition is faster than the hang and cable session for the LED units. There were fewer unknowns, so less problem solving is required. However the exact replication was going to prove to be difficult. If we hang as many PARs as we need to match the range of color options from the LED units, many more fixtures would be required and the lighting angles compromised. Scrollers could be added, but the fan noise will be overwhelming in the small space. The final solution is to double hang units for more color options. Those extra channels are patched and cued into the production.

All the cue timings and the Stage Manager's calls remain the same from the first performance. The color bug metering allows us to use Rosco gel to match the lighting cue color of the LEDs. Intensity levels of the Source Four ellipsoidals have to be changed in all cues because the incandescent lamps are significantly brighter than the Neevas. Four circuit MR16 strip lights replace the Sky Cycs. This needs to be done for two reasons: The conventional lighting requires RGBW color mixing and the Sky Cyc fixtures from the university inventory are large enough to physically block the projections. The MR16 strips are also lower wattage than the Sky Cycs and with only 12 dimmable circuits we need to be able to assign more fixtures per circuit for the cyc lighting if we use conventional higher wattage units.

Day 6

We complete one tech rehearsal in the morning and give the second performance later in the day. After the audience clears, we did a quick photo call and some Color Bug readings while the cast changed and took a break. Then we have a full company strike and party. The following weeks will be about returning equipment and processing the information we collected.

"Green" LED Lighting Day 1 Statistics

Loaned equipment from Altman Stage Lighting:

Three RGBA Spectra PARS, one SWW Spectra PAR, and three Star PARS

Stock Units Owned:

Two Altman Spectra CYCs—100 watts each
Two American DJ P64 LED pros—30 watts each
Three Strong Neevas—50 watts each

This lighting was run from a single 20-amp circuit and the maximum power draw was 1100 watts. This is less power than a 1.0 Cu. Ft 1100 microwave or most toasters. The approximate list price of the lighting equipment based on May 2011 Internet information was $17,540. Prices have dropped since then. The price of the lighting console and the DMX cable is not included. While this price may seem steep, consider the cost of installing dimmers, wiring, and circuitry and the issue of looking for multiple 20 amp circuits with portable conventional equipment.

Differences in Aesthetics and in Energy

This experiment was performed in May 2011. Since then technology has evolved with manufacturers' modifications and more new companies exploring this idea of environmentally friendly lighting.

Clearly we had some limitations within our space and because of equipment needs. As much as I am concerned with

Incandescent Lighting Day 2 Statistics

Stock Units:

- Three ETC source four lekos (ERS) 575w each
- 11 ETC source four pars 575w each
- One Altman par 64 1000w
- One 8′ Ministrip 4 circuit at 750w each—3000w total
- One 12 2.4 k dimmer pack.

The maximum power draw: 12,050 watts.

Approximate list cost based on Internet pricing in May 2011: $7342 *(does not include lamps or cost of color, cable, connectors or c-clamps).*

If I was not working with the parameter to replicate the design exactly on Day 2, I would have chosen to use the following equipment:

- Three ETC source four lekos (ERS) 575w each
- 24 ETC source four pars 575w each
- One 8′ Ministrip 4 circuit at 750w each- 3000w total
- Three 12 1.2 k dimmer pack.

Maximum power draw 18,525 watts.

Approximate list cost based on Internet pricing in May 2011: $17,801 *(does not include lamps or cost of color, cable, connectors or c- clamps).*

the aesthetics, they are somewhat subjective and can fall within an individual's prejudice of taste, generational, and personal sensibilities. The undeniable differences are in the hard data; color temperature, the instruments, and actual energy usage and that's just with the lighting equipment, not including the HVAC, fluorescents, console, or projection that were the considered constants for the purposes of this experiment. The HVAC was working harder on the conventional day but this experiment was focused on the lighting equipment used and the power supply for that equipment to work.

For our staged reading on Day 1 we used a single 120 volt outlet that never drew more than 12 amps. On Day 2 we used 12 2.4K dimmers on each leg which each drew 25–35 amps.

Even for our little controlled space that is a huge difference in power, especially when one considers that the conventional fixtures ran at a lower level than the LED fixtures to make the cues each day have the same intensity. The conventional day took 12 times as much power to replicate what we did on Day 1 and even then we ran out of enough power and control to fully recreate the look of the LED technology.

Below are actual readouts provided by our Facility's Management Department based on metered power usage.

There were some intensity adjustments between days, but the timing of the cues never changed. Why was this important? Without having to create a custom dimming curve in the board, I wanted to see how the fixture behaved when it came to color mixing, blackouts, and fades.

I knew from my own designing that when controlling conventional tungsten, arc, and LED fixtures on the same lighting console, they will fade at different rates. Even LED luminaires from the same manufacturer may have different fade rates. Also both the generic and manufacturer specific profiles provided in the console don't always behave as expected.

When a production mixes technologies, I notice the differences and am often bothered when something appears to pop. Was using a single specific technology, LED units that behave similarly, less jarring? Would I care as much, would the audience care or even notice? This is where the audience response is important. I wondered if audience expectations based on seeing previous productions would make them notice the difference in LED and incandescent lamp responses. Our audience included members of the theater and dance department and the music department, as well as staff from IT and the library, and friends and family of the cast and crew.

Some of the most interesting feedback we received was actually from the cast. For example, reading under primary blue LED light is significantly harder than a tungsten lamp gelled primary blue; the contrast between the white paper and the back ink made it difficult to see the printing. Dr. Herrera helped solve this by reprinting the updated version of the script on pale yellow paper.

The performers immediately noticed the heat of the conventional fixtures on Day 2. One of my favorite comments came from Erin Bradner, who was adjusting her chair, and when I asked her why she was wiggling about she simply stated, "*Today I can find my hotspot.*" (Something actors often are trained to look for to know they are in the brightest part of the light.) The LED fixtures didn't provide the same warmth as the brighter center point of a conventional stage lighting fixture.

The audience liked the vibrancy of the LED colors on Day 1. The LEDs helped give the pop of color which supported emotional shifts, but the LED front light seemed a bit cold on skin tones, even though warmer light was mixed in.

The theater folks and our IT person noticed the bump as the intensity of an LED fixture changed abruptly, but the rest of audience didn't seem to be bothered. One student did mention that the blackout seemed to happen faster on the LED day. This was accurate; because the LED does not have a glowing filament cooling after the cue is executed. This leads to LEDs always seeming faster on fades than the tungsten units. Luckily this is one of those places where the technology is only getting better and some companies have even created profiles to make the LED fixture behave more like tungsten fixtures.

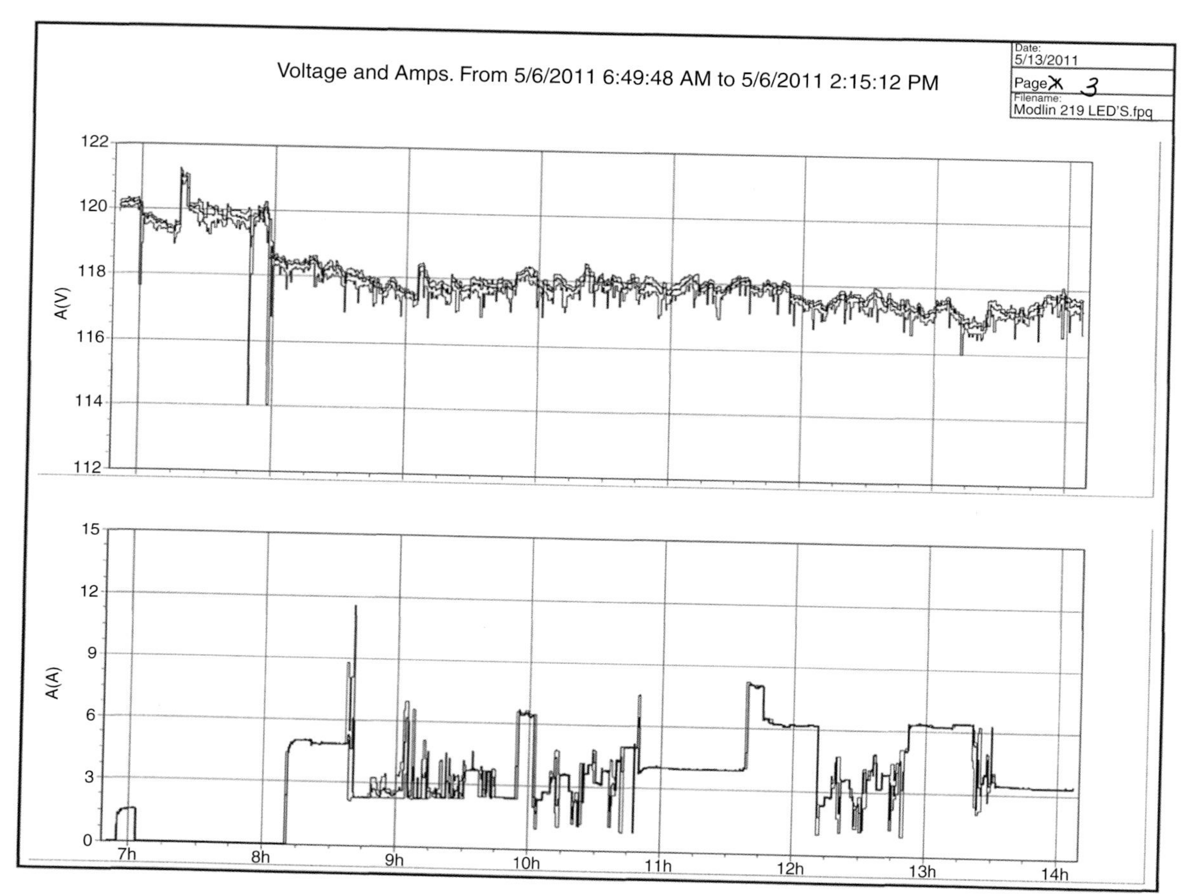

Figure 13.9 The LED power consumption is graphed. The top chart shows voltage and the bottom one shows amps. The LED rig never drew more than 12 amps. Image courtesy of Maja White.

As a designer, I personally like the warmth of the tungsten fixture, especially in front light, and preferred the LEDs for saturated color. This may change as the technology develops but this is the result of my experimental experience. For many universities or facilities looking to move to newer technology the selling point may be the safety and energy issues. The artists working with the light may have a different position based on aesthetics.

As you are looking at sustainability in stage lighting here are some other variables to consider:

- Traditional theatrical units have a lamp life of approximately 1,500 hours versus LED lamp life which is typically 20,000 to 50,000 hours. This means that if you ran your lights for eight hours per day 365 days a year it would take about five

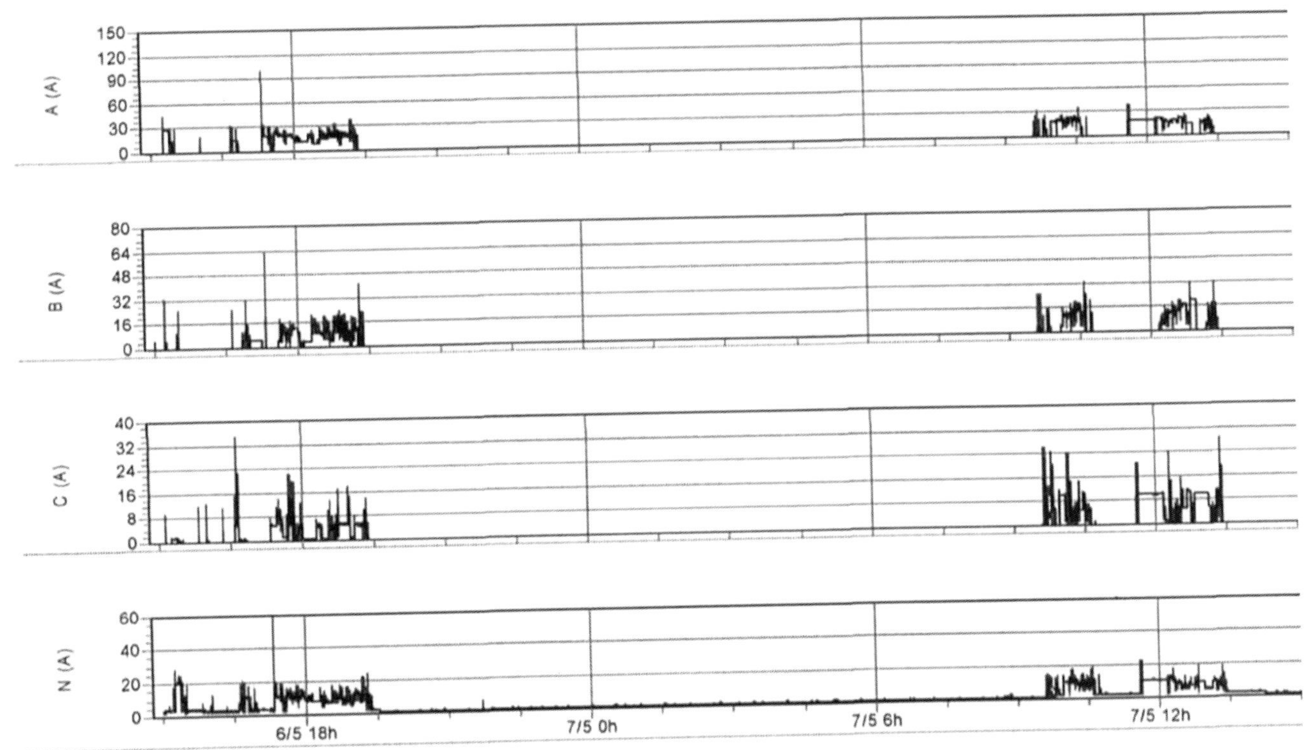

Figure 13.10 The graph of the conventional fixture rig shows amperage drawn by the three power legs. The fourth graph is the neutral. Significantly more amperage is drawn by the incandescent fixtures. Image courtesy of Maja White.

years before you would send the engine back to the manufacturer for replacement of the lighting array.

- LEDs can mix color so no gel is necessary, or if you need to use a silk or diffusion it is not going to burn through. There is a cost saving on color and potentially the man-hours to change it. Another added benefit is being able to change a whole system of color in a matter of seconds.
- Understand "Binning" when purchasing fixtures. When purchasing fixtures ideally you want them all to be from the same "bin," for those of you who understand the fabric world this is similar to wanting things from the same dye lot. If your fixtures come from different bins they will need to be adjusted to match each other. If you are purchasing a quantity of fixtures, ideally they should come from the same bin or at least be calibrated to match at the manufacturer.
- If you are renting LED units, factor in some time to balance your fixtures. Match each color across fixtures and then look at the white light. If your white light doesn't match from fixture to fixture, you can still uniformly match colors and then balance the white light in cues where there is an issue. If you match white on all the units, you will probably have to tweak each fixture to match all the other colors as you cue.

This experiment was my first in-depth look at working and having discussions about environmentally friendly lighting. It also allowed me to explore how I feel about the visual impact of LEDs as an artist. A simple demonstration of a fixture from a rep was never going to allow me to experiment with how they behaved in a production and I am very thankful for this being made possible. There was a great deal of interest at the 2011 Chicago Association of Theatre in Higher Education conference when Mark and I presented our initial findings from the case study. I hope other designers, technicians, and educators are inspired to do their own case studies to analyze the possibilities.

One of the things I pondered during the process of working with environmentally friendly lighting is the general use of terms "green" and "sustainable." Many of us throw out these terms as if they as synonymous and I do not feel we should. This experiment really made me define and defend how I want to use these terms for myself. I consider this technology in the field of lighting "green," in a similar way that I consider a hybrid car "green." As for the sustainability of this lighting technology, I am not sure there is enough information available yet. After all a brand new hybrid car is considered "green" but my former 1999 Subaru, now with family in Vermont, is definitely more sustainable.

Man of La Mancha: *Pushing the Green Envelope in Every Direction: Ellen E. Jones on Greening all the Design and Technical Elements*

I had been making piecemeal changes to green the production process at Bemidji State University for several months. I and my design and technical production students and staff decided to make the major spring production, *Man of La Mancha*, an experiment in green production and focus sustainable choices in every aspect possible. Making this kind of sweeping decision is always easier when the director, in this case Dr. Patrick Carriere, agrees to the experiment. This is an abridged treatment of the choices we made because some of the strategies have already been mentioned elsewhere in the book as part of other chapters.

Many of the systemic operational practices were already in place; for example, acquisition of the Energy Star HE washer and dryer for the costume shop, the addition of dust collection equipment in the scene shop, removal of fixtures with asbestos cords from the inventory and the caps disposed of by a Haz Mat specialist, and elimination of most chemicals and aerosols from the costume and paint shop. This process had actually begun months before the design and conceptualization process for *La Mancha*. The philosophy and process continued long after the strike. We now wanted to apply greener choices directly to a production to determine how it impacted the design aesthetic. We were also interested in feedback from the designers, technicians, cast, and the director to see if anyone felt that the production standards were compromised.

There were many discoveries along the way of obstacles and benefits we never realized would come to light. I also never anticipated the level of excitement my students would have for the goals of the project and the innovative ideas they would bring to the table. Although there was a part-time professional staff costume shop manager, every other support position was filled by student paraprofessionals or student employees. Without their support and conviction that this was a worthy endeavor, things would have continued as business as usual. In many ways, the student engagement was a reward by itself. Whenever I use "we" in this description, I am talking about those engaged students and myself.

Our first decision was to publicize the sustainability agenda for the show in every bit of preshow publicity and during the show's run with the program notes. We wanted to see if the audience would notice the differences and comment on them in talk backs. I also wanted to draw attention to our efforts in sustainability.

The Goal of the Project

We wanted to consider every design and execution choice for scenic, costume, and lighting design in light of the sustainability initiative. This meant reusing and recycling materials and elements whenever possible as well as choosing raw materials that were sustainably manufactured and/or fit into the Reduce, Reuse, Recycle model. An equal focus was on maintaining health and safety practices that protected workers and the environment.

Man of La Mancha Production Team

Director: Dr. Patrick Carrier
Musical Director: Ashley Bremseth
Scenic and Primary Costume Designer: Ellen E. Jones
Assistant Scenic Designer and Charge Artist: Candice Billups
Principal Males Costume Designer: Kirsten Wade
Lighting Designers: Ben Eng and Thomas Skime
Technical Director: Matthew Goinz
Assistant Technical Director: Warren Billups
Costume Shop Manager: Laurie Pommerening

One additional motive was somewhat self-serving. I wanted the audience to understand any change in house lights behavior if we were not able to eliminate the popcorn effect when the new LED lamps dimmed up during the show. Changing dimmer profiles had helped but there were still issues on the up fade. We finally discovered that preheating the channel, the way designers used to in order control the sounds of metal expanding in older ellipsoidals, solved that problem.

I served as the scenery and primary costume designer for the production. Student Kirsten Wade designed the costumes for the two principle characters, Cervantes and Sancho. Two of my undergraduate students, Ben Eng and Tom Skime, were co-lighting designers of the show. A live orchestra was onstage for the production and the student conductor was cast as one of the prisoners in the show. The cast had 20 members.

Lighting

When I arrived at Bemidji in fall 2008 the lighting inventory was comprised of equipment that was purchased for the grand opening of the building in 1969 and the assorted small lots purchased through the years by other faculty members. The majority of the ellipsoidals were Century-Strand units that were so old I could not find any frame of reference for the photometrics. I sent pictures out to friends and colleagues asking for help. Richard Pilbrow was finally able to identify the fixtures by their similarity to the ellipsoidals he had used to light the London production of *Blitz!* in 1962.

The most contemporary ellipsoidals was probably manufactured in the mid-1980s. There was a small collection of Source Four PARS as well. Reducing the carbon footprint of the stage lighting was a goal from the minute I saw the inventory. As I mentioned in Chapter 2, I quickly realized making a change in the house and lobby lights was even more important given the number of fixtures and the amount of time those lights burned. Fortunately the Bemidji State University Sustainability Officer, Erika Bailey-Johnson, and I were able to team up on a grant from the Minnesota Pollution Control Agency to make this dream a reality.

The lighting equipment arrived in time for use in MOLM. Ben and Tom were excited to put it into use for the inaugural production. The only LED choices made for new equipment were direct replacement lamps for the architectural lighting. I opted to keep the broader stage light inventory as conventional units in order to buy enough fixtures to upgrade the entire inventory. I was not interested in trying to integrate a few LED units with the antiquated fixtures and the thought of controlling them with an ETC Express made me woozy. For the record, I love the ETC Express/Expression line for conventional fixtures even though there are newer, jazzier consoles available. I just could not see making the integration of antiques and LEDs happen easily using that or any other console.

The new stage lights were much more efficient Source Four T-H fixtures. We replaced 69 old 1000 watt luminaires with new 750 watt units. We also went through all the fixtures from the old inventory that was still viable: Fresnels of various sizes made by different manufacturers, 14" scoops used as work lights, short throw Altman 360Qs (talk about a fixture that will stand the test of time), and traditional PAR Cans to relamp them at the lowest appropriate wattage. Because the theatre was part of a much larger multiuse building without an independent electric meter, we could not do a quantitative analysis of energy savings. However, simple subtraction revealed some of the energy savings. 17,250 potential watts were eliminated from the equation by making these upgrades in the lighting rig.

Some of the benefits in upgrading the lights I had not realized would be as evident as they were included:

- The old fixtures had to almost always run at 80% or higher for adequate visibility. The new units were so much brighter that a great deal more subtlety was possible in cueing. In hind sight, I realized I could have used 575 watt lamps instead of the 750 watt lamps to meet design goals.
- The nuances of additive color mixing are much more evident when the light source is a more neutral white that allows color media to function as designed. The better light quality also enabled the lighting designers, Tom and Ben, to transform the paint colors in the dungeon for the Cervantes book scenes more effectively than if they had been forced to use the older fixtures. In spite of having higher wattage lamps, the older units had a much lower, orangey color temperature.
- The new fixtures were much more responsive to changes in level with a smoother and more subtle fade in cue changes.
- High definition lenses and flat field units make a world of difference in the clarity of templates, allowing for a great deal more texture and subtlety in the use of patterns.

Scenery and Props

The shop staff and I had spent many long hours reorganizing building materials, including the scrap lumber and sheet good pieces. The props and furniture storage was also reorganized and culled to create easy access to items that were in good condition. We had committed to building a stock of platforms and flats that were easily reused and building larger specialty elements for deconstruction into reusable pieces. Air tackers and staples had been eliminated in favor of screws to limit damage of materials during strike.

Intellectually I knew these changes would make reuse easier. In reality it meant that very little had to be built from newly purchased materials for this show. The facilitation of the reuse of existing scenic elements made it much easier for me to make design decisions that incorporated existing pieces. For example, what had originally been 10′ tall screens in *Cabaret* became the dungeon doors for MOLM. The leftover pieces also served as screens in the Cervantes book "church" scene.

The scene design for the fall production of *Crucible* included three "wooden" beams that spanned the entire stage and terminated in a vertical piece of the same design to suggest hanging gallows. These pieces had been originally constructed so they came apart in 8′ segments for storage and could be easily reassembled. These became vertical beams in the dungeon setting for the MOLM set. Eventually their reuse became a kind of game—they went on to be repainted and serve as architectural sophits on the realistic interior sets of two other shows and to create a doorway to a mine on another.

Figure 13.11 Ensemble members Amanda Boring, Jesse Villarreal, Jon Heinen, Brianna Weber, Tessa Carter, and Eric Benson. Photo by Bob Smith, Image Photography, Bemidji, MN.

Storage of steps made with solid carriages had always been a problem. I wanted a staircase that curved into the dungeon space. We used the flat carriage design from Bill Raoul's *Stock Scenery Handbook Second Edition* shown in Appendix B. The steps were added to the inventory, creating a stock unit that could be used at any height and straight or with a curve. Using this construction technique also allowed for the use of scrap lumber instead of new full sheets of plywood. See an image of the steps with their cardboard facing in Chapter 7.

We experimented with cardboard as a construction material. Part of the reason we decided to try this was because we had just received 4000 pounds of freight in the form of new audience risers for the black box, all packed in large pieces of cardboard. You have to have large spans of undamaged corrugated for cardboard to be a reasonable construction choice. In spite of having the material on hand, I still would not have experimented with it for scenery if I had not been excited by the new Rosco FR product line that included a formula for paper products. We actually did burn tests on the cardboard after it was treated, not because I did not trust the product's quality, but to make sure our cardboard and application process allowed the FR solution to serve its purpose. (There is an advantage to have a trained fireman working in your scene shop.)

Because the MOLM set included tall levels with openings on the front to allow cast members to scurry away in the dungeon there was a whole lot of upstage real estate to hide with facings. We used the cardboard for decorative facings and even more of it for black upstage facings. My students calculated the cardboard facings eliminated the need for 12 sheets of board material for those masking facings. Those facings went into stock for use in future shows after strike.

In spite of our best efforts, we were unable to use cardboard to cover flats. It did not maintain its structural integrity when used in a full 4'x8' sheet on a flat or a sweep. We were able to make vertical framed cut outs as long as they were no more than 2'-6" wide. As an experiment, I designed larger, irregularly shaped scenic elements using framed corrugated. The shop used corrugated to cover large sweeps and full flats, but the painting technique to get the desired effect was too wet to create a finished paint face that was stage worthy.

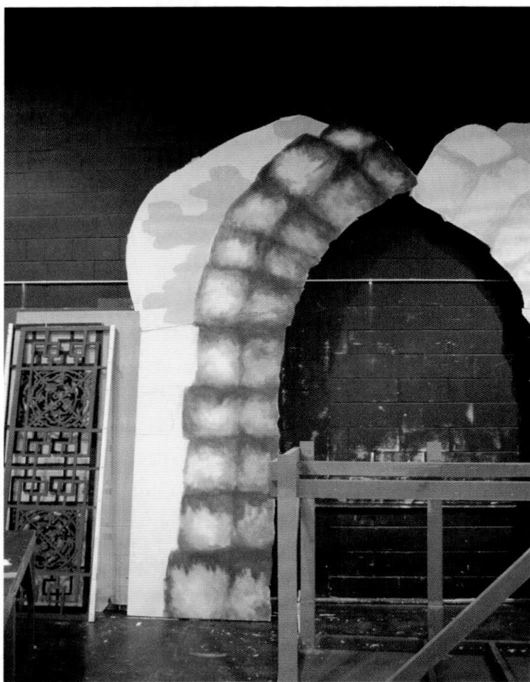

Figure 13.12 This wing masking piece in progress is made of framed cardboard. Photo by EEJ.

If there had been more time for experimentation we might have resolved the issue of the flats; certainly George L. Petitt has been able to create beautiful vertical units with cardboard.

The corrugated cardboard did work well for curved surfaces. There was concern that the actors might accidentally kick cardboard facings on vertical surfaces and leave holes in the surface. As a test, different coatings including Rosco Flexcoat and Crystal Gel were applied to some of the facing surfaces before painting. Others were painted without any coating. I wanted to see if the coatings added durability to the cardboard.

It turned out that all three surfaces held up well in a show with a lot of physical action and stage combat. The experiment was successful and for the first time I was sold on the possibility of using framed cardboard for scenery.

Every prop in the show, except Cervantes' trunk, was an example of reuse of existing items. Tables and benches that had been constructed for earlier shows integrated perfectly into the dungeon set. The transformation of prisoners into horses for Sancho and Cervantes is an important part of the show. The director and I agreed early on we did not want to see

Figure 13.13 The well under construction. Photo by EEJ.

Figure 13.14 The well as used during the production. Ensemble members: K.D. Howells, Miranda Vega, Tessa Carter, and Fawn Belgarde. (SR-SL) Photo by Bob Smith, Image Photography, Bemidji, MN.

a horse costume that looked like it belonged at a costume party be pulled out of Cervantes' trunk. We had also decided that every prop used in the stories had to be onstage from the beginning of the show.

Carol Cooley, the costumer at Saint Cloud State University, was already loaning me armor for the guards. She also had some horse heads from a production of *Equus* that she was willing to give me. The two heads were used as bases and retrimmed for the horse heads. The bodies were put together from small casted platforms, wooden handles, and sawhorses that were part of the prison clutter on stage.

Costumes

Given the scope of the first piece on costuming I won't spend too much time on the MOLM costume process. A few of the choices we made from the outset were that no material which required dry cleaning would be purchased for the show and that all distressing would be done with natural products. We had already eliminated chemical detergents and any aerosols from the costume and make-up area.

Many of the costumes were pulled from stock, an easy task when the bulk of the cast is supposed to be in a dungeon as prisoners of the Spanish Inquisition. For costumes that would be additionally distressed, we made a conscious effort to find the most bedraggled pieces of that line and cut in stock so that pieces in good shape would not be damaged for the show. The costume shop supervisor, Laurie Pommerening, and her student staff had spent considerable time reorganizing and culling the existing stock the previous semester. That organizational work made pulling costumes that fit the designs an easy task.

Figure 13.15 Jeremiah Liend as Cervantes and Fawn Belgarde as his faithful steed. Photo courtesy of Bob Smith, Image Photography, Bemidji MN.

Everyone involved in the production areas and the cast and crew were proud of the number of green choices we were able to make in executing the designs for the show. The audience and the creative team did not feel like the artistic vision or production values were compromised. It also made us realize how much impact good organization and planning had on being able to make greener choices in production. The experiment was successful and we went on to implement many of the techniques in future productions. I was also able to integrate a number of the practices on freelance designs with professional companies as well.

All three of these realized productions included successes in greening theatre production. Each also included experiments that did not yield the expected results. In each case, we all said that had we had more time we might have been able to resolve the issue that thwarted the attempted strategy.

Perhaps the most valuable tip to offer based on these experiences is to add some time to the production period if at all possible when integrating new ideas and new techniques into the production process. The other important note is that while each project made enormous strides in sustainable production practices, no one felt that creativity or artist quality was compromised by the green strategies. By trying new ideas and sharing the results we can all help improve sustainability in theatre design and production.

In Conclusion

There may be some surprise at seeing so much safety information integrated into a book about greener theatre production. My work in trying to create a more sustainable design and production model initially grew out of my interest in safety. The intersection of the two fields is obvious once you try to integrate both into your design and production work.

Even the Environmental Protection Agency defines itself with the following statement: "*The mission of EPA is to protect human health and the environment.*"

It also lists its first purpose as ensuring "*that all Americans are protected from significant risks to human health and the environment where they live, learn and work*" (http://www.epa.gov/aboutepa/whatwedo.html).

One final reminder: nothing in this book should be taken as a substitute for advice from a licensed or otherwise certified and trained professional with expertise in the area addressed, especially in the areas of health and safety. Please seek out expert advice when needed.

Remember too that there is variation in laws designed to protect the environment and ecosystems and the health and safety of the public. Determine the municipal, state, and/or federal statutes and standards in place in your region that may impact any aspect of your theatre's operations and your own responsibilities.

Any equipment or materials suggested or pictured in the book are products that we, the collective contributors, are familiar with and have found to be effective. We may or may not use that product exclusively or we may use a range of similar products. It is not meant to be an advertisement or endorsement for any manufacturer or vendor, nor is the failure to mention any manufacturer, business, or product intended as a negative evaluation of the quality of their products or expertise in the industry.

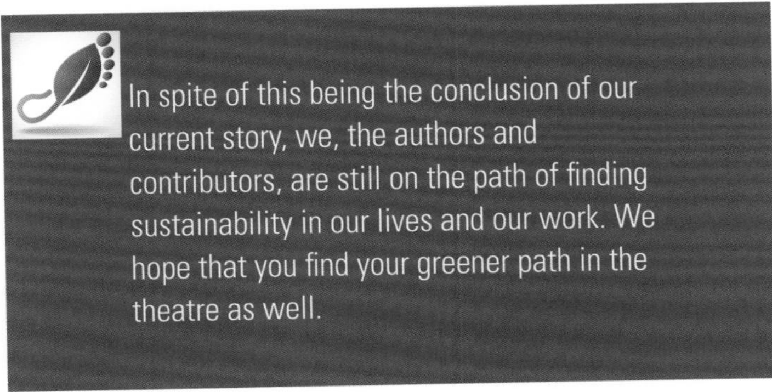

In spite of this being the conclusion of our current story, we, the authors and contributors, are still on the path of finding sustainability in our lives and our work. We hope that you find your greener path in the theatre as well.

Dariush M/Shutterstock

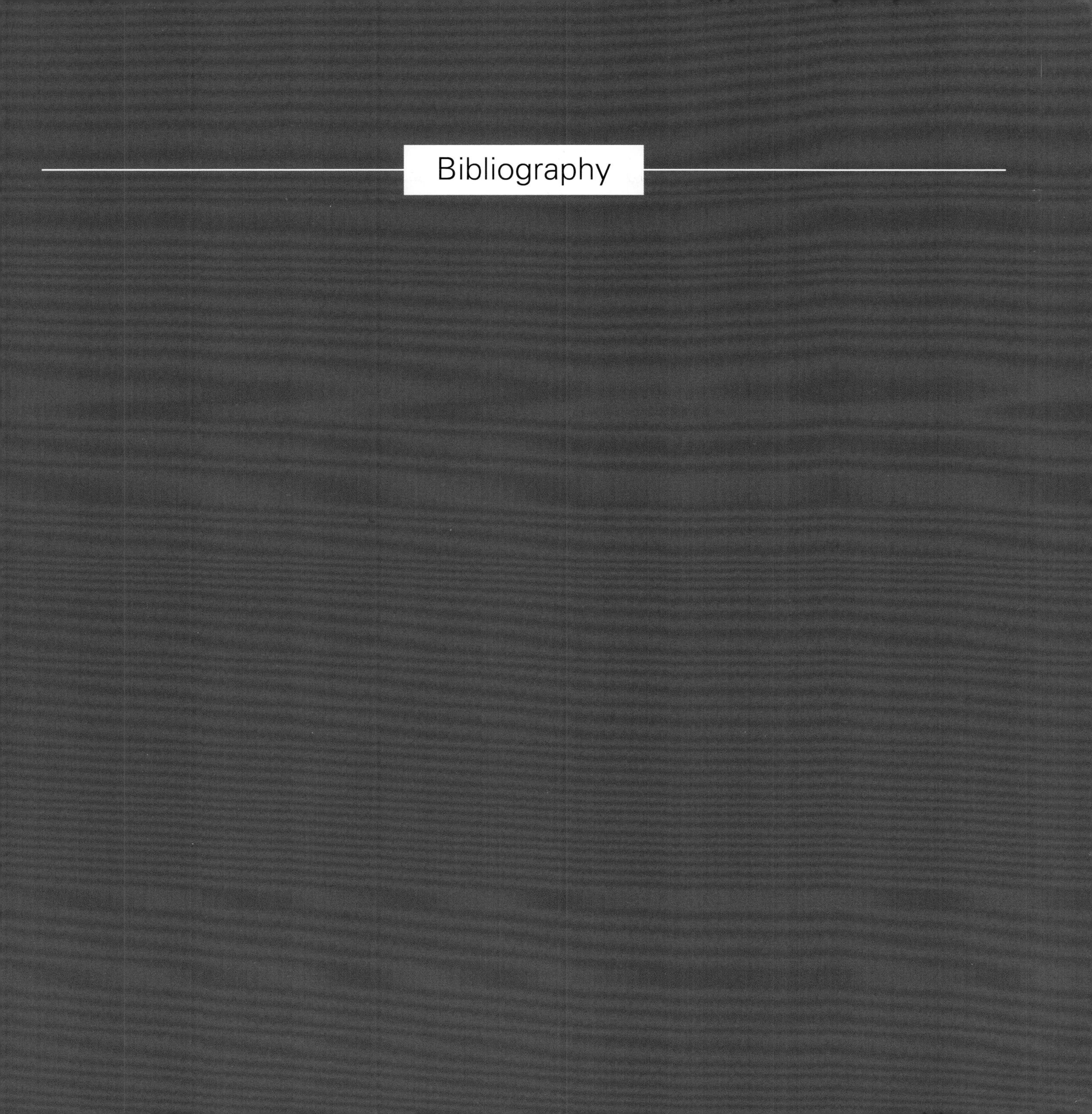

Bibliography

American Tree Farm System (ATFS). http://www.treefarmsystem.org/. Accessed February 2013.

Altman Lighting. http://www.altmanltg.com/.

"An Update on Formaldehyde,." U.S. Consumer Product Safety Administration, 1997.

BlueGreen Alliance Foundation and Purdue Technical Assistance Program. "Dumpster Dive: Materials Use & Solid Waste Management": Purdue Research Foundation: Gary: 2010. Class Taken November 2012.

——. "Green Chemistry: Managing Chemical Use & Hazardous Waste": Purdue Research Foundation: Gary: 2010. Class Taken November 2012.

——. "Energy Management: Efficient Energy Use": Purdue Research Foundation: Gary: 2010. Class Taken October 2012.

Bowyer, Jim. "Agricultural Residues: An Exciting Bio-Based Raw Material for the Global Panels Industry," *Forest Products Journal*, 55.1, 2001.

Bradfield, Johyn. "CARB: A Challenge and an Opportunity for Composite Panels" (Presented at the International Wood Composite Symposium), April 2008.

Broadway Green Alliance. http://www.broadwaygreen.com/what-were-doing/. Accessed September 2013.

Burgess, Rebecca. *Harvesting Color: How to Find Plants and Make Natural Dyes*. Muskogee, OK: Artisan, 2011.

Burke, Sarah. *Sustainable Living Explained*. Kindle Edition: Amazon Digital Services, 2012.

Center for Sustainable Practice in the Arts (CSPA). http://www.sustainablepractice.org/. Accessed November 2012

"Composite Wood Products: Green by Nature. Composite Panel Association, www.pbmdf.com.

"Design and Fabrication of Plywood Stress-Skin Panels." Engineered Wood Association, Plywood Design Specification, Supplement 3, August 1990, Tacoma, Washington.

EasyCurve, Upsonite. http://niagarafiberboard.com/upsonite.htm. Accessed February 2013.

Environmental Protection Agency (EPA). http://www.epa.gov/.

ETC Lighting. http://www.etcconnect.com/. Accessed February 2013

Forestry Stewardship Council (FSC). https://us.fsc.org/. Accessed January 2013

Garrett, Ian. "Theatre Production's Carbon Footprint," in *Readings in Performance and Ecology*. Editors Wendy Arons and Theresa J. May. New York: Palgrave Macmillan, 2012, p. 201.

Global Stewards. http://globalstewards.org/. Accessed September 2012

Granum, R.M., and Eustis, O.B. "Hardboard (Masonite), What is it?" www.panel.com/uploads/whatisitcda0.pdf.

"Green is a Number featuring Richard Cadena and James Bedell." CSL Webinar, Creative Stage Lighting's Blog. http://blog.creativestagelighting.com/2012/05/csl-webinar-green-is-a-number-2/. Accessed February 2013.

The Green Theatre Choices Toolkit. Available from Mo'olelo Performing Arts Company. http://moolelo.net/green/. Accessed June 2012.

Greenguard Certification. http://www.greenguard.org/en/index.aspx. Accessed March 2013.

Holden, Alys E., and Sammler, Bronislaw J. *Structural Design for the Stage*. Boston: Focal Press, 1999.

"Homasote Company History." www.homasote.com, February 2013.

"Homasote: Sensible. Sound. Solutions." www.homasote.com, February 2013.

Julie's Bicycle IG Tools. http://www.juliesbicycle.com/resources/ig-tools/faqs. Accessed December 2012.

Lauan. http://bct.eco.umass.edu/publications/by-title/wood-underlayments-for-resilient-flooring/. Accessed July 2009.

Leavell, Chuck. *Forever Green: The History and Hope of the American Forest*. Atlanta: Longstreet, 2001.

"Low-VOC Paints: Preferable, Affordable, Available". National Resource Defense Council (NRDC). http://www.nrdc.org/thisgreenlife/0905.asp. Accessed February 2013.

McCann, Michael. *Health Hazards Manual For Artists*, Sixth Edition Guilford, CT: The Lyons Press, 2008.

McDonough, William, and Braungart, William. *Cradle to Cradle: Remaking the Way We Make Things* Kindle Edition: North Point Press, 2010.

Massey, Robert. *Formulas for Painters*. New York: Watson-Guthill Publications, 1979.

Melton, Paula. "Georgia Outlaws Leeds in Latest 'Wood Wars' Battle." http://www.buildinggreen.com/auth/article.cfm/2012/8/20/Georgia-Outlaws-LEED-in-Latest-Wood-Wars-Battle/. Accessed February 13, 2013.

Miller, Justin A, "The Labor of Greening Love's Labour's Lost," in *Readings in Performance and Ecology*, Editors Wendy Arons and Theresa J. May. New York: Palgrave Macmillan, 2012, p. 191.

MSDS Online: EH&S Compliance Made Simple. http://www.msdsonline.com/blog/2012/08/from-msds-to-sds/. Accessed July 2012

National Fire Protection Association. NFPA 101 Life Safety Code, 2009.

Nims, Debra K. *Basics of Industrial Hygiene*. New York: John Wiley and Sons, Inc., 1999.

Occupational Health and Safety Administration (OSHA). http://www.osha.gov/. Accessed February 2012

"OSB Design Manual: Construction Sheathing and Design Rated Oriented Stand Board," Structural Board Association (DM-801) 2004, Ontario, Canada.

OSHA. 29CFR 1910 OSHA General Industry Regulations. Mancomm Publications, 2009.

Paints and Coatings Resource Center (PCRC). http://www.paintcenter.org/newcalc.cfm. Accessed February 2013.

"Paints, Coatings Formulated for Sustainability." http://www.greenmanufacturer.net/product/materials/paints-coatings-formulated-for-sustainability. Accessed January 2013.

Patriot Timber Products. http://www.patriottimber.com/revolutionply.htm. Accessed March 2013.

Pecktal, Lynn. *Designing and Painting for the Theatre*. New York: Holt, Rinehart and Winston, 1975.

Philips Lighting University. http://www.lighting.philips.com/main/connect/Lighting_University/online-courses.wpd. Accessed February 2013.

"Pigments Through the Ages-Prehistory." Web Exhibits. http://www.webexhibits.org/pigments/intro/early.html. Accessed January 2013.

Plutonium Paint. http://www.plutoniumpaint.com. Accessed February 2013.

"Plywood (lauan, meranti, serai)." Rain Forest Relief. http://www.rainforestrelief.org/What_to_Avoid_and_Alternatives/Rainforest_Wood/What_to_Avoid_What_to_Choose/By_Product/Plywood.html. Accessed March 2013.

Raoul, Bill. *Stock Scenery Handbook*, Second Edition. Louisville, KY: Broadway Press, 1999.

Rosco Laboratories. http://www.rosco.com/us/index.cfm. Accessed August 2012

Rossol, Monona. *Pick Your Poison: How Our Mad Dash to Chemical Utopia is Making Lab Rats of Us All*. Hoboken, NJ: John Wiley & Sons, 2011.

——. *The Health & Safety Guide for Film, TV & Theatre*. New York: Allworth Press, 2000.

——. *Stage Fright: Health & Safety in the Theatre*. New York: Allworth Press, 1991.

Theatre Artisan Green Skills. http://www.yorku.ca/tags/Theatre_Artisan_Green_Skills/Home.html. Accessed January 2013.

Weinert, Jonathan. *LED Lighting Explained*. Burlington, MA: Philips, 2012.

Appendices

Appendix A

Checklists

Figure A.1 alexmillos/Shutterstock.

Appendix A includes five different checklists. Checklists offer guidance when beginning the sustainability process. However, their use alone will not allow you to achieve a long-term sustainability plan. The Forest View Checklist will take you through your production facility as you complete a broad overview survey of the current green status. It will help you identify specific problems in different areas that will require further examination in order to develop goals and strategies.

The Tree View Checklists cover three specific production areas; the scene and prop shop, the light shop, and the costume shop and dressing rooms. It is designed to be used both for an initial baseline audit and later evaluation audits once green strategies are in place.

These four checklists may be copied or scanned and modified as long as you keep the header and footer intact.

The last checklist was created by Terry Gips. It is based on the Natural Step Framework system and philosophy and covers areas more broadly. He has graciously given permission for it to be included in the book. You may copy it and use it freely with full attribution. Please do not modify or alter it.

Sustainability CheckList for Initial Assessment

The Forest View

Everywhere

- ☐ Garbage: Where are the garbage and recycle bins? Can someone easily determine which containers are for specific kinds of recycling?
- ☐ What is in the garbage cans and dumpster on a daily basis and after strike?
- ☐ Are computers and printers on power strips so they can be turned off?
- ☐ Are the lights on when you walk into empty rooms?
- ☐ What kind of light bulbs are in the task lighting fixtures and room lights?
- ☐ Is the bulletin board covered with old paper announcements?
- ☐ Are there stacks of old programs and posters in the office, lobby, and front of house?
- ☐ Are storage spaces full of really old items that will never be used again? Can you see what is in the storage space easily and find what you are looking for at any given time?
- ☐ If any room is very hot, determine what kinds of lamps are in use or if the thermostat is blocked.
- ☐ Are areas of refuge or emergency exits blocked?
- ☐ Are faucets leaking or toilets running constantly?

In the Shops

- ☐ Are the MSDS (or SDS) books complete, in order, and easily accessible?
- ☐ Do your students, employees, and volunteers know how to use the MSDS books?
- ☐ Is the space covered with sawdust or dirt?
- ☐ Are flats and platforms stock sizes?
- ☐ Are emergency exits or electrical panels blocked by garbage, scenic elements, tools, or materials?
- ☐ What kinds of paints, coatings and solvents are in storage?
- ☐ Is the paint organized to facilitate easy storage and efficient clean up?
- ☐ Are there aerosols that use propellants and any products that require chemical solvents?
- ☐ Are cleaning and laundry supplies chemical based? (Remember organic products can still contain hazardous materials)
- ☐ Is inventory neatly stored and accessible?

Sustainability CheckList to Monitor Progress

The Scene and Prop Shops

The Tree View

- ☐ Count the unused copies – is there a way to limit the number of copies of drawings and paperwork generated for each show?
- ☐ MSDS (or SDS) books are labeled and in place.
- ☐ Lumber and other building materials are separated and labeled for easy use.
- ☐ Scrap bin for useable lumber and sheet goods is constructed.
- ☐ Metal and Glass Recycle Bins are in place and labeled.
- ☐ Potentially toxic adhesives replaced with safer glues.
- ☐ Hardware and fasteners are in separate and well labeled bins for use and recycle.
- ☐ Screws in appropriate sizes stocked to replace staples. (Facilitates deconstruction.)
- ☐ Stock culled of irregular sized or damaged units.
- ☐ Storage for platforms has been created.
- ☐ Storage for flats has been created.
- ☐ Stock units including flats, platforms, and soft goods have been inventoried.
- ☐ Full line of FR products purchased and stored to facilitate use of all materials.
- ☐ Paper towels replaced with reusable rags.
- ☐ Spray paints have been removed according to hazardous materials disposal policy.
- ☐ Hand sprayer purchased to replace spray paints with H_2O based paints.
- ☐ Brush and roller cleaning system built or adopted.
- ☐ Products requiring chemical solvents removed.
- ☐ Chemical solvents and cleaners eliminated.
- ☐ Bulletin Board replaced with announcement center than can be erased and modified.
- ☐ Dust collection systems installed.
- ☐ Prop storage has been culled.
- ☐ Prop storage has been organized and labeled.
- ☐ Any needed Personal Protection Devices are maintained and stored for easy use.
- ☐ General Housekeeping Policies provide a clean and safe workplace environment.

Sustainability Check List to Monitor Progress

The Light Shop

The Tree View

- ☐ Any pyro requiring a license to use has been disposed of according to Hazardous Material disposal regulations.
- ☐ Mineral Oil based fogs and hazes eliminated.
- ☐ Lamps are organized and labeled with correct fixture designation.
- ☐ Bottle of rubbing alcohol available to wash touched quartz lamps.
- ☐ Higher wattages lamps have been replaced with appropriate lower wattages.
- ☐ CFL or LED lamps in stock for replacement in task lighting units.
- ☐ Cut gel folder system is organized for easy reuse.
- ☐ Gobo stock is organized and labeled.
- ☐ Chart of gel frame size and correct lamp for fixture is posted to eliminate waste.
- ☐ Any units with asbestos cords are removed from service according to Hazards Material disposal regulations.
- ☐ Older inefficient units (radial lamp placement) are removed from service.
- ☐ Fixture lenses are washed using water, rags, and white cotton gloves.
- ☐ Reflectors of fixtures are blown out with air.
- ☐ Efficient full spectrum light sources are hung for use as work lights and rehearsal lights.
- ☐ Dimmer rack Command Module upgraded to digital control for greater efficiency.
- ☐ Paperwork copies are limited to needs based printings.
- ☐ Medium screw based reflector flood lamps phased out with direct replacement dimmable LED lamps.
- ☐ Energy audit arranged and completed with local public utility provider.
- ☐ Grants applications made to facilitate reducing carbon footprint.
- ☐ Any cables, twofers, plugs that do not meet current standards are removed from service.

Sustainability CheckList to Monitor Progress

The Costume Shop and Dressing Rooms

The Tree View

- ☐ MSDS Book is complete and accessible.
- ☐ Chlorine Bleach is phased out and replaced with oxygen based products.
- ☐ Inventory cataloged in a way that facilitates reuse of existing stock.
- ☐ Chemical detergents are phased out and replaced with Soap Nuts or comparable soaps.
- ☐ Fragranced fabric softeners eliminated and replaced with Baking Soda or Vinegar.
- ☐ Dryer venting inspected and repaired for greater efficiency and better air quality.
- ☐ Drying racks added to limit dryer use.
- ☐ Dryer steam setting used to limit washing costumes.
- ☐ Propellant based spray paint, hair coloring and hair spray phased out.
- ☐ Chemical Dyes replaced with natural dye products where possible.
- ☐ Stock culled to provide correct clearance for sprinklers and emergency exits.
- ☐ Old stock repurposed into rags for cleaning in the other shops.
- ☐ Bulletin Board replaced with announcement center that can be erased and modified.
- ☐ Commitment to reduce use of costumes and fabrics that require dry cleaning is in place.
- ☐ Washable dress shields and undershirts used to limit washing and ironing.
- ☐ Inefficient steamers replaced.
- ☐ The steam iron put on a switch or timer during the day.
- ☐ Reusable fabric accessory bags and character markers for costume racks added.
- ☐ Make up mirror lights replaced with lower wattage LED lamps if possible.
- ☐ Make up and beauty products evaluated using the Skin Deep web site to ascertain harmful ingredients. (www.ewg.org/skindeep/)
- ☐ Make up mirror bulbs placed in a box for the actor at each station so only those in use are lit.
- ☐ Scrap muslin and fabric recycling bins in place.
- ☐ Stock organized and labeled for reuse.
- ☐ Sewing machines, sergers, and irons are cleaned and properly maintained.

Natural Step Framework – Workplace Action Checklist

Four Principles for Sustainability	Now	Commit	3 mos
1. Limit What We Take from the Earth: Find Substitutes for Mined Metals/Minerals & Burning Fossil Fuels			
Turn off lights & computers, "Smart" power strips, occupancy sensors, maintain HVAC			
Energy Star electronics, servers, appliances & lighting (T-8s, LEDs, CFLs) & recycle			
Decrease heating in winter (68° day, 58° night), insulate, energy audit, zone heating			
Reduce cooling in summer (72° day, 88° night), use window film, sun shading & fans			
Day lighting, vending energy misers, renewable energy, purchase green energy & offset			
Encourage telecommuting, biking (provide storage & showers), public transit & carpool			
Energy-efficient vehicles, tune-ups, properly inflated tires, eco-driving, ground shipping			
Natural landscaping & shading, battery electric lawn mower, avoid leaf blowers			
Recycle cans/bottles, batteries, fluorescents, cell phones, computers & electronics			
Green procurement: Recycled content office furniture, products & building materials			
Rechargeable batteries (& recycle), soy inks & non-lead cables, zero-emissions			
LEED and sustainable building & remodeling with deconstruction & flexible design			
Other			
2. Avoid Toxic Substances We Make – Find Substitutes for Hazardous Pesticides, Plastics & Chemicals			
Natural, non-chlorine cleaning products, avoid anti-bacterial soaps & air fresheners			
Recycle plastics, filtered water (not bottles), purchase post-consumer recycled products			
Avoid plastics with reusable mugs & foodservice ware (or bio-based, compostable)			
Cater organic, local food in buffet style; use natural pest control and lawn care			
Reuse shipping containers and peanuts (use bio-based) & eliminate Styrofoam & PVC			
Replace hazardous chemicals, properly handle hazardous waste, recycle solvents			
Low-VOC paints, non-plastic laminates, formaldehyde-free furniture, green carpeting			
Other			

tgips@sustainabilityassociates.com
www.sustainabilityassociates.com
9000 W. 28th St., St. Louis Park, MN 55426 612-374-4765

Four Principles for Sustainability	Now	Commit	3 mos
3. Care for What We Do to the Earth – Protect Biodiversity, Eco-systems and Natural Resources			
Reduce paper use: 2-sided copies, electronic records/communication, junk mail removal			
100% post-consumer, chlorine-free recycled paper (copying, cards, towels, tissues, TP)			
Reuse wood and use non-Old Growth, certified, sustainably-harvested wood products			
Compost waste food and organic materials			
Reduce water use: efficient faucets/toilets, low flush urinals, HVAC condensate, grey water use			
Protect and enhance wildlife habitat, use permeable paving, water gardens & green roof			
Location selection to minimize sprawl (brown fields instead of green fields)			
Provide plant-based foods and avoid endangered, industrial sea food			
Develop tree planting program to address CO_2 footprint, use green hotels			
Other			
4. Meet Fundamental Human Needs – Encourage Health, Well-being, Social Justice & Community			
Smile, treat everyone with respect, create shared vision and aligned teams			
Safe, healthy, and ergonomically-sound workplace and products (compliant cell phones)			
Affirmative action, open communication, fair pay/benefits			
Wellness programs, flex hours and policies encouraging healthy, balanced lifestyles			
Seek stakeholder & community input, participate in community activities & groups			
Work to create a just society; donate time, money & resources to help the disadvantaged			
Participate in socially responsible pension funds			
Purchase Fair Trade products and support local living economy			
Regularly measure progress in meeting fundamental needs, annual sustainability report			
Support sustainable public policies and participate in triple bottom line programs (GRI)			
Other			

tgips@sustainabilityassociates.com
www.sustainabilityassociates.com
9000 W. 28th St., St. Louis Park, MN 55426 612-374-4765

Appendix B

Construction Details

In Chapter 7 some specific construction techniques were mentioned that offer opportunities for greening production when creating stock elements.

Triscuits

The first was the use of Triscuit or stress-skinned platforming instead of traditional 1x or 2x framed units. The stress-skinned platform creates a strong building block for decks that is easily stored when it is appropriately constructed. The Triscuit panel was developed at Yale School of Drama and shared with the industry in *Yale Tech Brief No.1249*, written by Don Harvey, Yale Repertory Theatre, in April 1993.

The first three drawings are enlargements of the images related to Triscuits included in Chapter 7. Although Paul Brunner is not the developer of the Triscuit design, he has created these three informational drawings in AutoCAD to illustrate the principals involved.

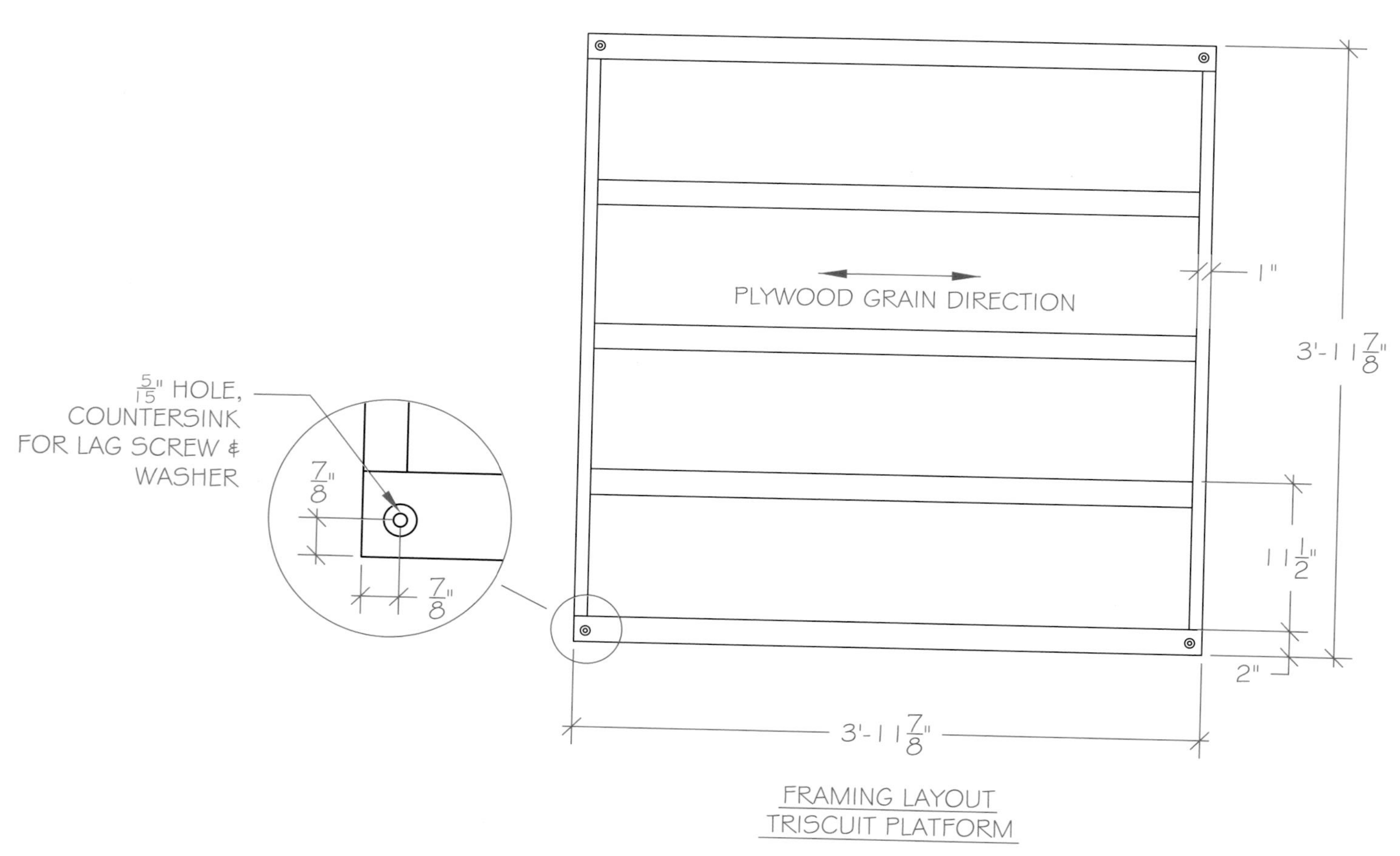

Figure B.1 Framing layout of a Triscuit platform. Drawing by Paul Brunner.

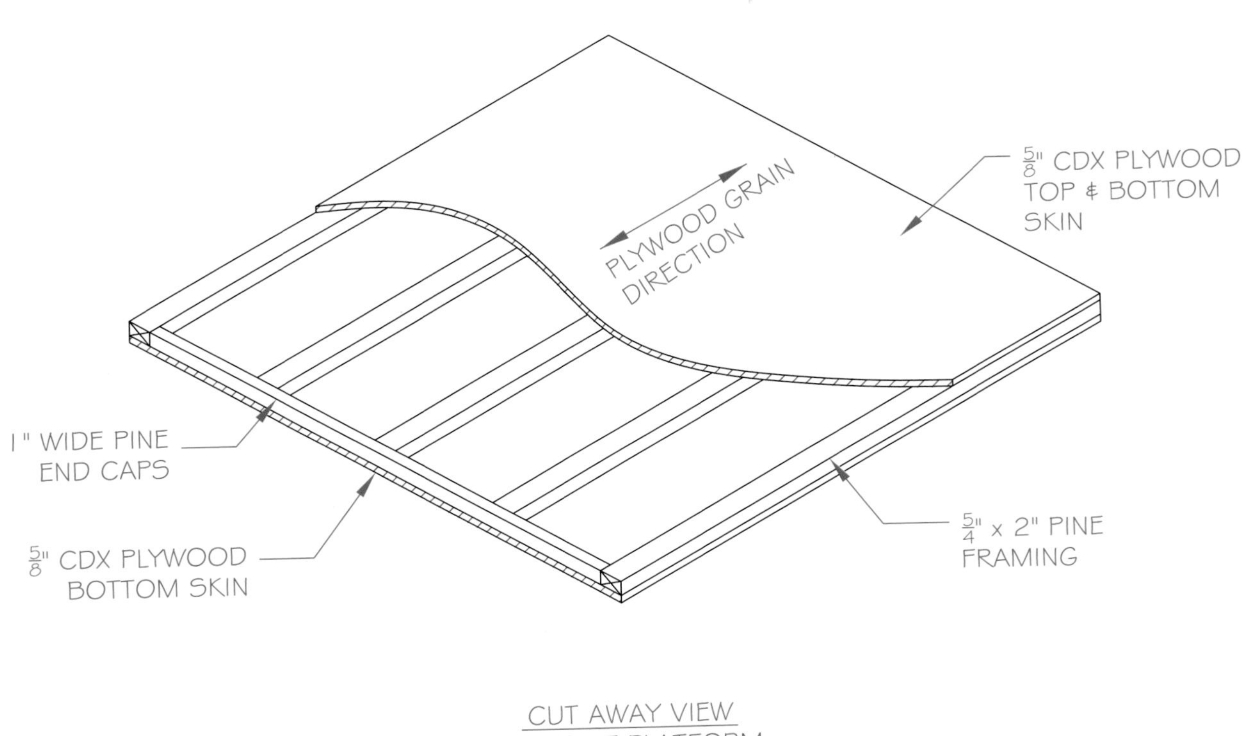

Figure B.2 Cut away view of a Triscuit platform. Drawing by Paul Brunner.

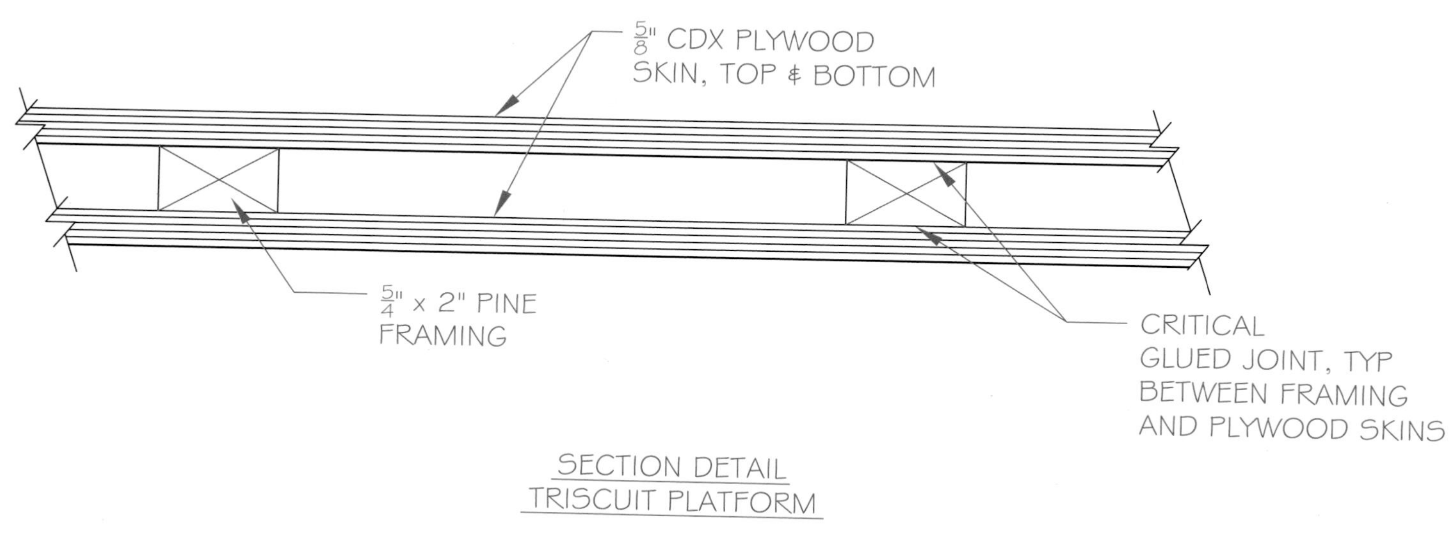

Figure B.3 Section detail of a Triscuit platform. Drawing by Paul Brunner.

The second construction technique illustrated in Figures B.4 – B.6 is the construction of a flat frame carriage step units developed by Bill Raoul. It allows for deconstruction and reuse of the components to build step units of varying heights and that are straight or curved runs. The drawings illustrating this technique are included courtesy of Broadway Press. They are from Bill Raoul's book, *The Stock Scenery Handbook*, published by Broadway Press in 1999. These plates were all hand drafted by Raoul for the publication and Broadway Press has provided digital files of the drawings for reprint in this book.

The final drawing is also from Raoul's *Stock Scenery Handbook*. It offers an illustration of the use of engineered wood products like plywood for traditional platform framing in place of dressed lumber.

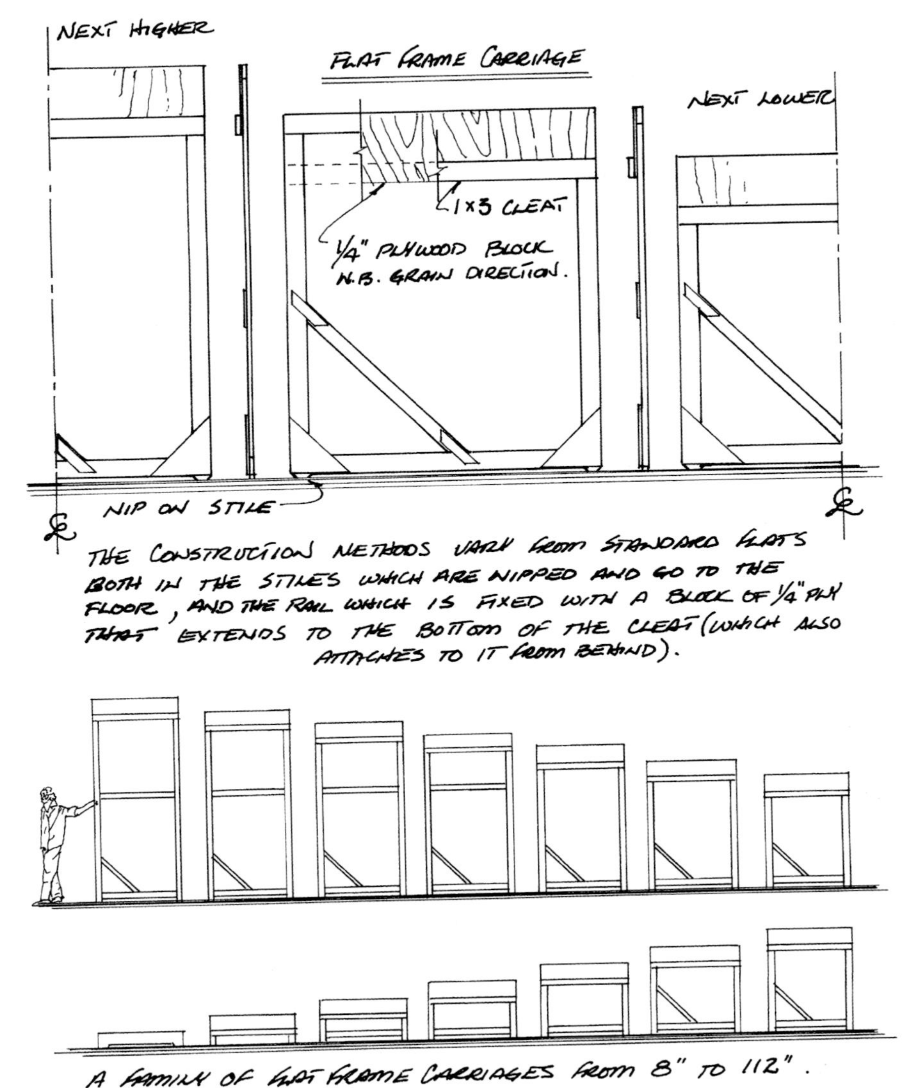
NEXT HIGHER
FLAT FRAME CARRIAGE
NEXT LOWER
1x3 CLEAT
1/4" PLYWOOD BLOCK
N.B. GRAIN DIRECTION.
NIP ON STILE
THE CONSTRUCTION METHODS VARY FROM STANDARD FLATS BOTH IN THE STILES WHICH ARE NIPPED AND GO TO THE FLOOR, AND THE RAIL WHICH IS FIXED WITH A BLOCK OF 1/4" PLY THAT EXTENDS TO THE BOTTOM OF THE CLEAT (WHICH ALSO ATTACHES TO IT FROM BEHIND).
A FAMILY OF FLAT FRAME CARRIAGES FROM 8" TO 112".

Figure B.4 Flat frame carriages-1 DWG. V-17—the construction technique. Raoul, Bill. *Stock Scenery Handbook*, Louisville: Broadway Press, 1999. p. 210.

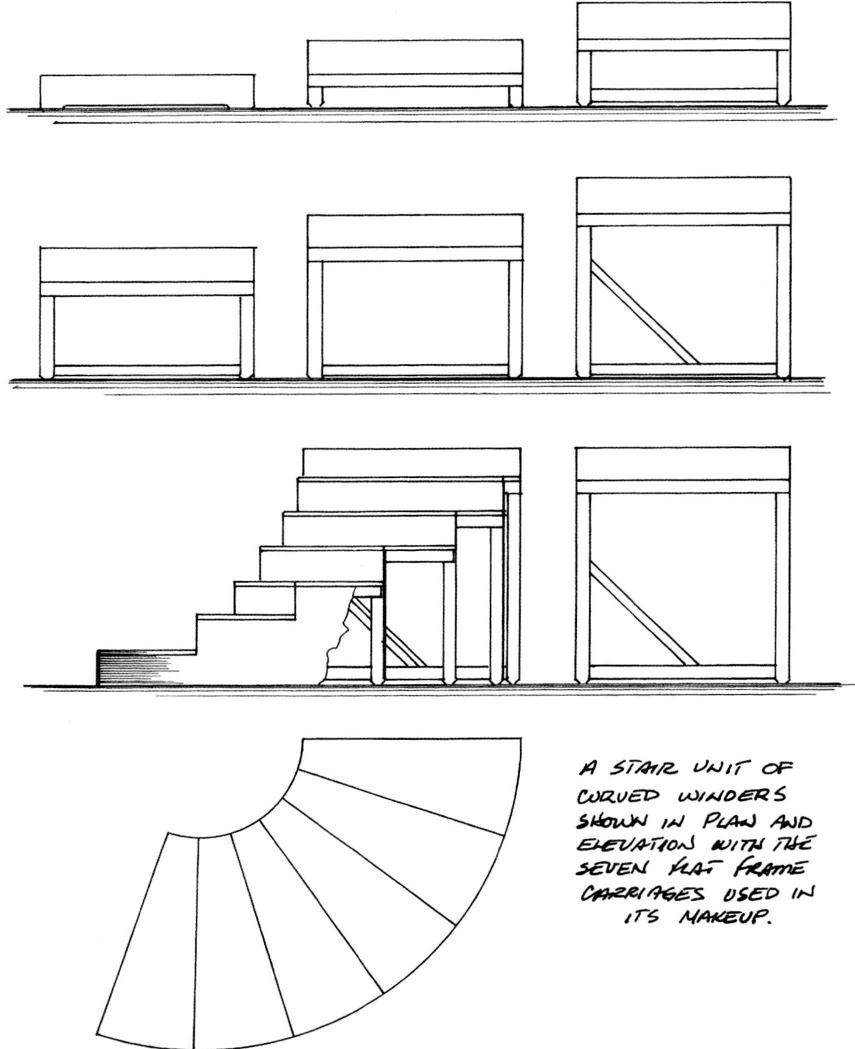
A STAIR UNIT OF
CURVED WINDERS
SHOWN IN PLAN AND
ELEVATION WITH THE
SEVEN FLAT FRAME
CARRIAGES USED IN
ITS MAKEUP.

Figure B.5 Flat frame carriages-2 DWG. V-18—curved winders shown in plan view and elevation. Raoul, Bill. *Stock Scenery Handbook*, Louisville: Broadway Press, 1999. p. 211.

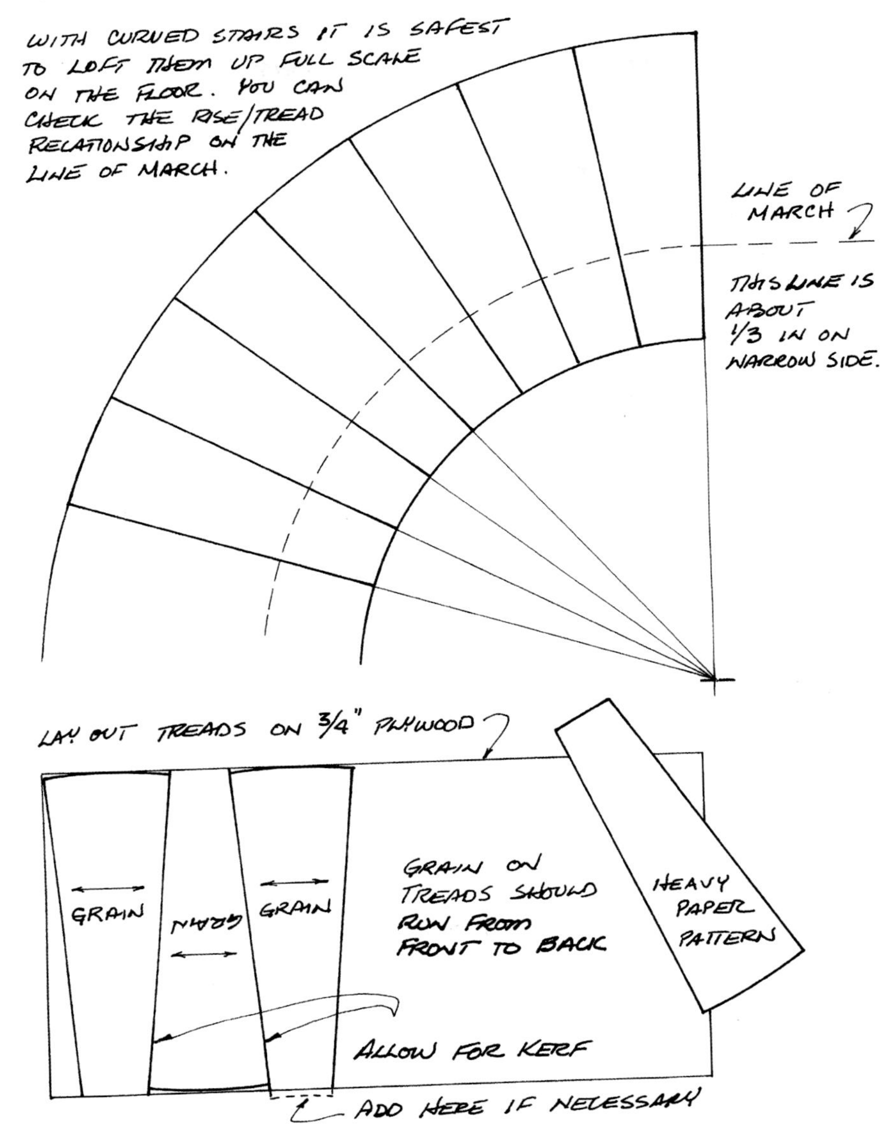
WITH CURVED STAIRS IT IS SAFEST TO LOFT THEM UP FULL SCALE ON THE FLOOR. YOU CAN CHECK THE RISE/TREAD RELATIONSHIP ON THE LINE OF MARCH.
LINE OF MARCH
THIS LINE IS ABOUT 1/3 IN ON NARROW SIDE.
LAY OUT TREADS ON 3/4" PLYWOOD
GRAIN
GRAIN
GRAIN
GRAIN ON TREADS SHOULD RUN FROM FRONT TO BACK
HEAVY PAPER PATTERN
ALLOW FOR KERF
ADD HERE IF NECESSARY

Figure B.6 Lofting up curved winders DWG. V-19—technique to lay out the treads for curved winders. Raoul, Bill. *Stock Scenery Handbook*, Louisville: Broadway Press, 1999. p. 212.

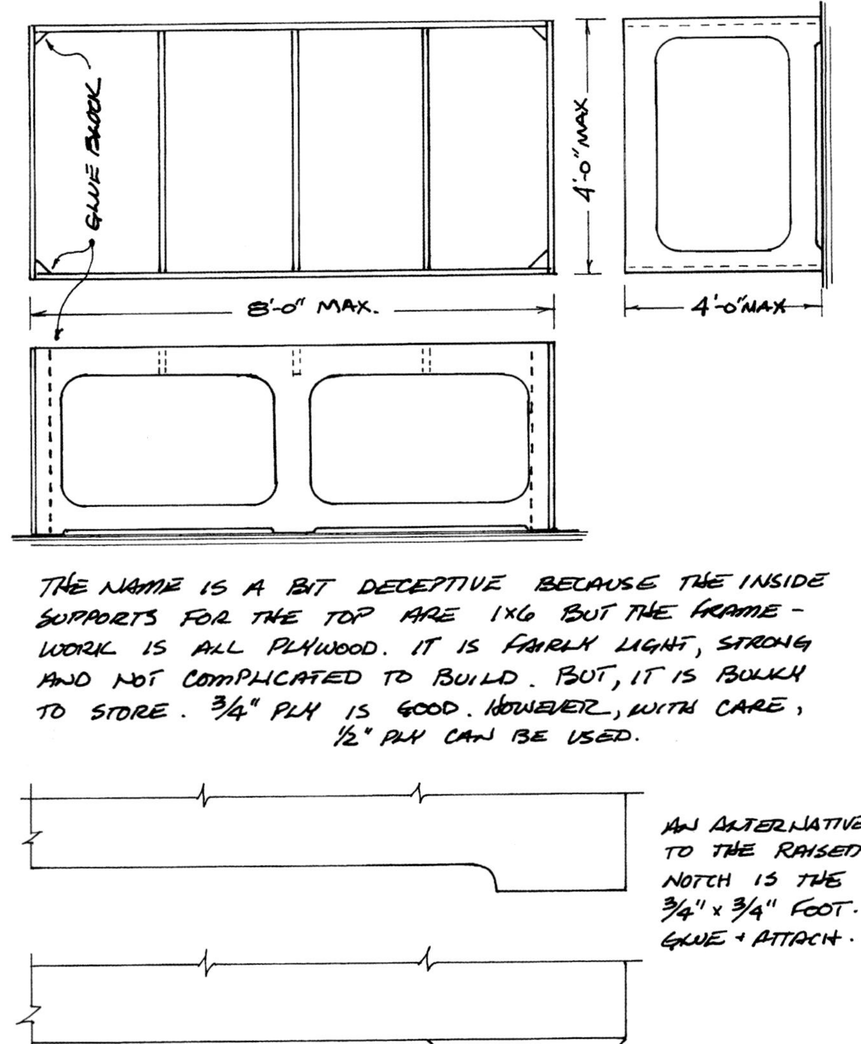

GLUE BLOCK
4'-0" MAX
8'-0" MAX.
4'-0" MAX
THE NAME IS A BIT DECEPTIVE BECAUSE THE INSIDE SUPPORTS FOR THE TOP ARE 1x6 BUT THE FRAME-WORK IS ALL PLYWOOD. IT IS FAIRLY LIGHT, STRONG AND NOT COMPLICATED TO BUILD. BUT, IT IS BULKY TO STORE. 3/4" PLY IS GOOD. HOWEVER, WITH CARE, 1/2" PLY CAN BE USED.
AN ALTERNATIVE TO THE RAISED NOTCH IS THE 3/4" x 3/4" FOOT. GLUE + ATTACH.

Figure B.7 The all-plywood platform DWG. IV-6 Replacing dressed lumber with plywood for the exterior framing of a traditional platform. Raoul, Bill. *Stock Scenery Handbook*, (Louisville: Broadway Press, 1999.) p. 142.

Index